THE

SAXONS IN ENGLAND.

A HISTORY OF

THE ENGLISH COMMONWEALTH

TILL THE PERIOD OF

THE NORMAN CONQUEST.

BY

JOHN MITCHELL KEMBLE, M.A., F.C.P.S.,

MEMBER OF THE ROYAL ACADEMY OF SCIENCES AT MUNICH, AND OF THE ROYAL
ACADEMY OF SCIENCES AT BERLIN,
FELLOW OF THE ROYAL SOCIETY OF HISTORY IN STOCKHOLM, AND OF THE
ROYAL SOCIETY OF HISTORY IN COPENHAGEN,
ETC. ETC. ETC.

" Nobilis et strenua, iuxtaque dotem naturae sagacissima gens Saxonum, ab antiquis etiam
scriptoribus memorata."

A NEW EDITION, REVISED BY

WALTER DE GRAY BIRCH, F.R.S.L.,

Senior Assistant of the Department of Manuscripts in the British Museum, Honorary
Librarian of the Royal Society of Literature, Honorary Secretary of the
British Archæological Association, etc.

VOLUME II.

AMS PRESS
NEW YORK

Reprinted from the edition of 1876, London

First AMS EDITION published 1971

Manufactured in the United States of America

International Standard Book Number:
Complete set   0-404-03647-3
Volume 2   0-404-03649-X

Library of Congress Catalog Number: 72-151600

AMS PRESS INC.
NEW YORK, N.Y.   10003

CONTENTS.

VOL. II.

BOOK II.

THE PRINCIPLES AND PROGRESS OF THE CHANGE IN ENGLAND.

THE

SAXONS IN ENGLAND.

BOOK II.

THE PRINCIPLES AND PROGRESS OF THE CHANGE IN ENGLAND.

CHAPTER I.

GROWTH OF THE KINGLY POWER.

THE object of the First Book was generally to give a clear view of the principles upon which the original settlement of the Anglosaxons was founded. But as our earliest fortunes are involved in an obscurity caused by the almost total absence of contemporary records, and as the principles themselves are not historically developed in all their integrity, at least in this country, many conclusions could only be arrived at through a system of induction, by comparing the known facts of Teutonic history in other lands, or at earlier periods, by tracing the remnants of old institutions in their influence upon society in an altered, and perhaps somewhat deteriorated, condition, and lastly by general reasoning derived from the nature of society itself. This

Second Book is however devoted to the historical development of those principles, in periods whereof we possess more sufficient record, and to an investigation of the form in which, after a long series of compromises, our institutions slowly and gradually unfolded themselves, till the close of the Anglosaxon monarchy. The two points upon which this part of the subject more particularly turns, are, the introduction of Christianity, and the progressive consolidation and extension of the kingly power; and round these two points the chapters of this Book will naturally group themselves. It is fortunate for us that the large amount of historical materials which we possess, enables us to follow the various social changes in considerable detail, and renders it possible to let the Anglosaxons tell their own story to a much greater extent than in the first Book.

In the course of years, continual wars had removed a multitude of petty kings or chieftains from the scene; a consolidation of countries had taken place; actual sovereignty, grounded on the law of force, on possession, or on federal compacts, had raised a few of the old dynasts above the rank of their fellows; the other nobles, and families of royal lineage, had for the most part submitted to the law of the comitatus, swelling the ranks, adorning the court, and increasing the power of princes who had risen upon their degradation; and at the commencement of the seventh century, England presented the extraordinary spectacle of at least eight independent kingdoms, of greater or less power and influence, and, as we may reasonably believe, very various degrees of civil and moral cultivation. In the extreme south-eastern corner of the island was the Kentish confederation, comprising in all probability the present counties of Kent, Essex, Middlesex, Surrey, and Sussex, whose numerous kings acknowledged the supremacy of Æðelberht, the son of Eormanríc, a prince of the house of Æscings, originally perhaps a Sussex family, but who claimed their royal descent from Wóden, through Hengist, the first traditional king of Kent. Under this head three of the eight named kingdoms were thus united; but successful warlike enterprise or the praise of superior wisdom had extended the political influence of the Æscing even to the southern bank of the Humber. Next to Sussex, along the southern coast, and as far westward as the border of the Welsh in Dorsetshire or Devon, lay the kingdom of the Westsaxons or Gewissas, which stretched northward to the Thames and westward to the Severn, and probably extended along the latter river over at least a part of Gloucestershire: this kingdom, or rather confederation, comprised all or part of the following counties; Hampshire with the Isle of Wight, a tributary sovereignty; Dorsetshire, perhaps a part of Devonshire, Wiltshire, Berkshire, a portion of Oxfordshire, Buckinghamshire, and Middlesex, up to the Chiltern Hills. Eastanglia occupied the extreme east of the island, stretching to the north and west up to the Wash and the marshes of Lincoln and Cambridgeshire, and comprehending, together with its marches, Norfolk and Suffolk, and part at least of Cambridge, Hunting-

don, Bedfordshire and Hertfordshire. Mercia with
its dependent sovereignties occupied nearly all the
remaining portion of England east of the Severn
and south of the Humber, including a portion of
Herefordshire, and probably also of Salop, beyond
the western bank of the former river : while two
small kingdoms, often united into one, but when
separate, called Deira and Bernicia, filled the remaining space from the Humber to the Pictish
border, which may be represented by a line running irregularly north-east from Dumbarton to Inverkeithing [1]. In the extreme west the remains of
the Keltic populations who had disdained to place

---

[1] There is not much positive evidence on this subject : but perhaps
the following considerations may appear of weight. The distinctive
names of Water in the two principal Keltic languages of these islands,
appear to be *Aber* and *Inver* : the former occurs frequently in Wales,
the latter never : on the other hand, Aber rarely, if ever, occurs in
Ireland, while Inver does. If we now take a good map of England
and Wales and Scotland, we shall find the following data.
In Wales :
Aber-avon, lat. 51° 36′ N., long. 3° 47′ W.
Abergavenny, lat. 51° 49′ N., long. 3° 2′.
Abergwilli, lat. 51° 52′ N., long. 4° 17′ W.
Aberystwith, lat. 52° 25′ N., long. 4° 4′ W.
Aberfraw, lat. 53° 12′ N., long. 4° 28′ W.
Abergele, lat. 53° 20′ N., long. 3° 38′ W.
In Scotland :
Aberlady, lat. 56° 0′ N., long. 2° 52′ W.
Aberdour, lat. 56° 3′ N., long. 3° 17′ W.
Aberfoil, lat. 56° 20′ N., long. 4° 21′ W.
Abernethy, lat. 56° 19′ N., long. 3° 18′ W.
Aberbrothic (Arbroath), lat. 56° 33′ N., long. 2° 35′ W.
Aberfeldy, lat. 56° 37′ N., long. 3° 51′ W.
Abergeldie, lat. 57° 3′ N., long. 3° 6′ W.
Aberchalder, lat. 57° 6′ N., long. 4° 46′ W.
Aberdeen, lat. 57° 8′ N., long. 2° 5′ W.
Aberchirdir, lat. 57° 34′ N., long. 2° 37′ W.
Aberdour, lat. 57° 40′ N., long. 2° 11′ W.   [In

themselves under the yoke of the Saxons, still maintained a dangerous and often threatening independence : and Cornwall and Devon, North and South Wales, Cheshire, Lancashire, Cumberland, perhaps even part of Northumberland, still formed important fortresses, garrisoned by this hardy and unsubjugated race. Beyond the Picts, throughout the north of Scotland, and in the neighbouring island of Ireland, were the Scots, a Keltic race, but not so nearly allied as the Cornish, Cymric and Pictish tribes.

It is probable enough that the princes who presided over these several aggregations of communities, had their traditional or family alliances and friendships, as well as their enmities, political and

In Scotland :
 Inverkeithing, lat. 56° 2' N., long. 3° 23' W.
 Inverary, lat. 56° 15' N., long. 5° 4' W.
 Inverarity, lat. 56° 36' N., long. 2° 54' W.
 Inverbervie, lat. 56° 52' N., long. 2° 21' W.
 Invergeldie, lat. 57° 1' N., long. 3° 12' W.
 Invernahavon, lat. 57° 1' N., long. 4° 9' W.
 Invergelder, lat. 57° 2' N., long. 3° 15' W.
 Invermoriston, lat. 57° 12' N., long. 4° 40' W.
 Inverness, lat. 57° 28' N., long. 4° 13' W.
 Invernetty, lat. 57° 29' N., long. 1° 48' W.
 Invercaslie, lat. 57° 58' N., long. 4° 36' W.
 Inver, lat. 58° 9' N., long. 5° 10' W.

The line of separation then between the Welsh or Pictish, and the Scotch or Irish Kelts, if measured by the occurrence of these names, would run obliquely from S.W. to N.E., straight up Loch Fyne, following nearly the boundary between Perthshire and Argyle, trending to the N.E. along the present boundary between Perth and Inverness Aberdeen and Inverness, Banff and Elgin, till about the mouth of the river Spey. The boundary between the Picts and English may have been much less settled, but it probably ran from Dumbarton, along the upper edge of Renfrewshire, Lanark and Linlithgow till about Abercorn, that is along the line of the Clyde to the Frith of Forth.

personal, and that some description of public law may consequently have grown up among them, by which their national intercourse was regulated. But we cannot suppose this to have been either very comprehensive or well defined. Least of all can we find any proof that there was a community of action among them, of a systematic and permanent character. A national priesthood, and a central service in which all alike participated, had any such existed, might have formed a point of union for all the races; but there is no record of this, and, I think, but little probability of its having been found at any time. If we consider the various sources from which the separate populations were derived, and the very different periods at which they became masters of their several seats; their constant hostility and the differences of language[1] and law; above all the distance of their settlements, severed by deep and gloomy forests, rude hills, unforded streams, or noxious and pestilential morasses, we can hardly imagine any concert among them for the establishment of a common worship; it is even doubtful—so meagre are our notices of the national heathendom—whether the same gods were revered all over England; although the descent of all the reigning families from Wóden would seem to speak for his worship at least having been universal. Again, there is reason to doubt that the priesthood occupied here quite so commanding a position as they may have enjoyed upon

[1] In the very early periods the Saxon inhabitants of different parts of England would probably have found it difficult to understand one another.

the continent, partly because the carelessness or hatred of the British Christians refused to attempt the conversion of their adversaries[1], and thus afforded no opportunity for a reaction or combined effort at resistance on the part of the Pagans; and partly because we cannot look for any very deep rooted religious convictions in the breast of the wandering, military adventurer, removed from the time-hallowed sites of ancient, local worship, and strongly tempted to "trow upon himself," in preference to gods whose powers and attributes he had little leisure to contemplate. The words of Coifi, a Northumbrian high-priest, to Eádwini, do at any rate imply a feeling on his part, that his position was not so brilliant and advantageous as he thought himself entitled to expect; and the very expressions he uses, implying a very considerable degree of subordination to the king of one principality[2], are hardly consistent with the hypothesis of a national hierarchy, which must have assumed a position scarcely inferior to that of the sovereigns them-

[1] Beda, Hist. Eccl. i. 22. "Qui, inter alia inenarrabilium scelerum facta, quae historicus eorum Gildas flebili sermone describit et hoc addebant, ut nunquam genti Saxonum sive Anglorum secum Brittaniam incolenti verbum fidei praedicando committerent."

[2] "Tu vide, rex, quale sit hoc quod nobis modo praedicatur: ego autem tibi verissime quod certum didici, profiteor, quia nihil omnino virtutis habet, nihil utilitatis, religio illa quam hucusque tenuimus; nullus enim tuorum studiosius quam ego culturae deorum nostrorum se subdidit, et nihilominus multi sunt qui ampliora a te beneficia quam ego, et maiores accipiunt dignitates, magisque prosperantur in omnibus quae agenda vel adquirenda disponunt. Si autem dii aliquid ualerent me potius iuvare vellent, qui illis impensius servire curavi." Beda, H. E. ii. 13. That Coifi is a genuine Northumbrian name, and not that of a Keltic druid, is shown in a paper on Anglosaxon surnames, read before the Archæological Institute at Winchester by the author in 1845

selves. Finally, I cannot believe that, had such an organization and such a body existed, there would be no trace of the opposition it must have offered to the introduction of the new creed: some record there must have been of a triumph so signal as that of Christianity under such circumstances; and the good believers who lavish miracles upon most inadequate occasions, must have given us some well-authenticated cases by which the sanctity of the monk was demonstrated to the confusion of the pagan. The silence of the Christian historian is an eloquent evidence of the insignificant power of the heathen priesthood.

Much less can we admit that there was any central political authority, recognized, systematic and regulated, by which the several kingdoms were combined into a corporate body. There is indeed a theory, respectable for its antiquity, and reproduced by modern ingenuity, according to which this important fact is assumed, and we are not only taught that the several kingdoms formed a confederation, at whose head, by election or otherwise, one of the princes was placed with imperial power, but that this institution was derived by direct imitation from the custom of the Roman empire: we further learn that the title of this high functionary was Bretwalda, or Emperor of Britain, and that he possessed the imperial decorations of the Roman state[1]. When this discovery was first made I know not, but the most detailed account that I have seen

[1] Palgrave, Anglos. Commonw. i. 562 *seq.* The Roman part of the theory is very well exploded by Lappenberg, who nevertheless gives far too much credence to the rest.

may be given from the, in many respects, excellent
and neglected work of Rapin.   He tells us [1] :—

" The Saxons, Jutes, and Angles, that conquered
the best part of Britain, looking upon themselves
as one and the same people [2], as they had been in
Germany, established a form of government, as like
as possible to what they had lived under in their
own country.   They formed their Wittena-Gemot,
or assembly of wise men, to settle the common
affairs of the seven kingdoms, and conferred the
command of their armies upon one chosen out of
the seven kings, to whom, for that reason no
doubt, some have given the title of Monarch, on
pretence of his having the precedence and some
superiority over the rest.   But to me that dignity
seems rather to have been like that of Stadtholder
of the United Provinces of the Low Countries.
There was however some difference between the
Saxon government in Britain and that in Germany.
For instance, in Germany the governor of each
province entirely depended on the General Assem
bly, where the supreme power was lodged ; whereas
in Britain, each king was sovereign in his own dominions.   But notwithstanding this, all the kingdoms together were, in some respects, considered
as the same state, and every one submitted to the
resolutions of the General Assembly of the Seven
Kingdoms, to which he gave his consent by him-

---

[1] Vol. i. p. 42 of Tindal's translation.
[2] This seems very doubtful, at least until lapse of years, commerce,
and familiar intercourse had broken down the barriers between different races.

self or representative . . . A free election, and sometimes force, gave the Heptarchy a chief or monarch,
whose authority was more or less, according to their
strength[1]. For though the person invested with
this office had no right to an unlimited authority,
there was scarce one of these monarchs but what
aspired to an absolute power."

This description has at least the advantage of
detail and of consistency, even though it should unfortunately lack that of truth; but most of those
who in more modern times have adopted the hypothesis, refrain from giving us any explanation of
the fact it assumes: they tell us indeed the title,
and profess to name those who successively bore
it, but they are totally silent as to the powers of
this great public officer, as to the mode of his appointment, the manner in which he exerted his authority, or the object for which such authority was
found necessary. I must frankly confess that I am
unable to find any evidence whatever in favour of
this view, which appears to me totally inconsistent
with everything which we know of the state and
principles of society at the early period with which
we have to deal. In point of fact, everything depends upon the way in which we construe a passage of Beda, together with one in the Saxon
Chronicle, borrowed from him, and the meaning
which history and philology justify us in giving to

---

[1] In the second edition of Tindal's Rapin there is a print representing the Kings of the Heptarchy in council. The president, Monarch
or Bretwalda, is very amusingly made larger and more ferocious than
the rest, to express his superior dignity!

the words made use of by both authors.   As the question is of some importance, it may as well be disposed of at once, although only two so-called Bretwaldas are recorded previous to the seventh century.

Modern ingenuity, having hastily acquiesced in the existence of this authority, has naturally been somewhat at a loss to account for it; yet this is obviously the most important part of the problem: accordingly Mr. Sharon Turner looks upon the Bretwalda as a kind of war-king, a temporary military leader: he says[1],—

"The disaster of Ceawlin gave safety to Kent. Ethelbert preserved his authority in that kingdom, and at length proceeded to that insulary predominance among the Anglosaxon kings, which they called the Bretwalda, or the ruler of Britain. Whether this was a mere title assumed by Hengist, and afterwards by Ella, and continued by the most successful Anglosaxon prince of his day, or conceded in any national council of all the Anglosaxons, or ambitiously assumed by the Saxon king that most felt and pressed his temporary power,— whether it was an imitation of the British unbennaeth, or a continuation of the Saxon custom of electing a war-cyning, cannot now be ascertained."

To this he adds in a note :—

" The proper force of this word Bretwalda cannot imply conquest, because Ella the First is not said to have conquered Hengist or Cerdic; nor did the

[1] Hist. Angl. Sax. bk. iii. ch. 5, vol. i. p. 319.

other Bretwaldas conquer the other Saxon kingdoms."

Again he returns to the charge : in the eighth chapter of the same book, he says[1] :—

" Perhaps the conjecture on this dignity which would come nearest the truth, would be, that it was the Walda or ruler of the Saxon kingdoms against the Britons, while the latter maintained the struggle for the possession of the country,—a species of Agamemnon against the general enemy, not a title of dignity or power against each other. If so, it would be but the war-king of the Saxons in Britain, against its native chiefs."

Lappenberg, adopting this last view, refines upon it in detail: he believes the Bretwalda to have been the elected generalissimo of the Saxons against the Welsh or other Keltic races, and that as the tide of conquest rolled onwards, the dignity shifted to the shoulders of that prince whose position made him the best guardian of the frontiers. But this will scarcely account to us for the Bretwaldadom of Ælle in Sussex, Æðelberht in Kent, or Rædwald in Eastanglia; yet these are three especially named. Besides we have a right to require some evidence that there ever was a common action of the Saxons against the Britons, and that they really were in the habit of appointing war-kings in England, two points on which there exists not a tittle of proof. Indeed it seems clear to me that a piece of vicious philology lurks at the bottom of

<hr />

Hist. Angl. Sax. i. 378.

this whole theory, and that it rests entirely upon the supposition that *Bret*walda means Ruler of the *Britons*, which is entirely erroneous. Yet one would think that on this point there ought to have been no doubt for even a moment, and that it hardly required for its refutation the philological demonstration which will be given. Let us ask by whom was the name used or applied? By the Saxons: but surely the Saxons could never mean to designate themselves by the name *Bret*, Britain; nor on the other hand could a general against the Britons be properly called their *wealda* or king, the relation expressed by the word *wealda* being that of sovereignty over subjects, not opposition to enemies.

Moreover, if this British theory were at all sound, how could we account for the title being so rarely given to the kings of Wessex, and never to those of Mercia, both of whom were nevertheless in continual hostile contact with the Welsh, and of whom the former at least exercised sovereign rights over a numerous Welsh population dispersed throughout their dominions? Again, why should it have been given to successive kings of Northumberland, whose contact with the British aborigines, even as Picts, was not of any long continuance or great moment[1]? Above all, why should it not have been given to Æðelfrið, who as Beda tells us was the most severe scourge the Kelts had ever met with[2]?

---

[1] I am not aware of the Picts, Peohtas, having ever been numbered among the Bretwealhas.

[2] Hist. Eccl. i. 34. "Nemo enim in tribunis, nemo in regibus plures eorum terras, exterminatis vel subiugatis indigenis, aut tributarias genti Anglorum, aut habitabiles fecit."

But there are other serious difficulties arising from the nature of the military force which, on any one of the suppositions we are considering, must have been placed at this war-king's disposal: is it, for example, conceivable, that people whose military duty did not extend beyond the defence of their own frontiers, and who even then could only be brought into the field under the conduct of their own shire-officers, would have marched away from home, under a foreign king, to form part of a mixed army? still more, that the comites of various princes, whose bond and duty were of the most strictly personal character, could have been mustered under the banner of a stranger[1]? Yet all this must be assumed to have been usual and easy, if we admit the received opinions as to the Bretwalda. We should also be entitled to ask how it happened that Wulfhere, Æðelbald, Offa, Cénwulf, the preeminently military kings of the Mercians, should have refrained from the use of a title so properly belonging to their preponderating power in England, and so useful in giving a legal and privileged authority to the measures of permanent aggrandizement which their resources enabled them to take?

Another supposition, that this dignity was in

---

[1] Nearly the only instance recorded of a mixed army, is that of Penda at Winwedfeld; but it does not appear that this consisted of anything more than the Comitatus of various chieftains personally dependent upon, or in alliance with, himself. We do·not learn that Oswiu's victory gave him any rights over the freemen in Eastanglia, which could hardly have been wanting had the Eastanglian *hereban* or *fyrd* served under Penda.

some way connected with the ecclesiastical establishment, the foundation of new bishoprics [1] or the
presidency of the national synods, seems equally
untenable ; for in the first place there were Bretwaldas before the introduction of Christianity; and
the intervention of particular princes in the foundation of sees, without the limits of their own dominions, may be explained without having recourse
to any such hypothesis ; again, the Church never
agreed to any unity till the close of the seventh
century under Theodore of Tarsus ; and lastly the
presidency of the synods, which were generally
held in Mercia[2], was almost exclusively in the
hands of the Mercian princes, till the Danes put
an end to their kingdom, and yet those princes
never bore the title at all.   In point of fact, there
was no such special title or special office, and the
whole theory is constructed upon an insufficient
and untenable basis.

It will be readily admitted that the fancies of the
Norman chroniclers may at once be passed over
unnoticed ;   they are worth no more than the still
later doctrines of Rapin and others, and rest upon
nothing but their explanation of passages which
we are equally at liberty to examine and test for
ourselves : I mean the passages already alluded to
from Beda and the Saxon Chronicle.   Let us see

---

[1] Lappenberg seems to connect these ideas together.

[2] The synods were mostly held at Cealchýð or at Clofeshoas. The
first of these places is doubtful : all that can be said with certainty, is,
that it was not Challock in Kent, as Ingram supposes : the Saxon
name of that place was Cealfloca.   I entertain little doubt that Clofeshoas was in the county of Gloucester and hundred of Westminster.

then what Beda says upon this subject. He speaks thus of Æðelberht[1] :—

"In the year of our Lord's incarnation six hundred and sixteen, which is the twenty-first from that wherein Augustine and his comrades were despatched to preach unto the race of the Angles, Æðelberht, the king of the men of Kent, after a temporal reign which he had held most gloriously for six and fifty years, entered the eternal joys of the heavenly kingdom : who was indeed but the third among the kings of the Angle race who ruled over all the southern provinces, which are separated from those of the north by the river Humber and its contiguous boundaries ; but the first of all who ascended to the kingdom of heaven. For the first of all who obtained this empire was Ælli, king of the Southsaxons : the second was Caelin, king of the Westsaxons, who in their tongue was called Ceaulin : the third, as I have said, was Æðilberht, king of the men of Kent : the fourth was Redwald, king of the Eastanglians, who even during the life of Æðilberht, obtained predominance for his nation : the fifth, Aeduini, king of the race of Northumbrians, that is, the race which inhabits the northern district of the river Humber, presided with greater power over all the populations which dwell in Britain, Britons and Angles alike, save only the men of Kent ; he also subdued to the empire of the Angles, the Mevanian isles, which lie between Ireland and Britain : the sixth Oswald, him-

[1] Hist. Eccl. ii. 5.

self that most Christian king of the Northumbrians, had rule with the same boundaries: the seventh Osuiu, his brother, having for some time governed his kingdom within nearly the same boundaries, for the most part subdued or reduced to a tributary condition the nations also of the Picts and Scots, who occupy the northern ends of Britain."

Certainly, it must be admitted that the exception of the Men of Kent, in the case of Eádwini, is a serious blow to the Bretwalda theory. I have used the word *predominance*, to express the *ducatus* or *leadership*, of Beda, and it is clear that such a leadership is what he means to convey. But in all the cases which he has cited, it is equally clear from every part of his book, that the fact was a merely accidental one, fully explained by the peculiar circumstances in every instance: it is invariably connected with conquest, and preponderant military power: a successful battle either against Kelt or Saxon, by removing a dangerous neighbour or dissolving a threatening confederacy, placed greater means at the disposal of any one prince than could be turned against him by any other or combination of others; and he naturally assumed a right to dictate to them, *iure belli*, in all transactions where he chose to consider his own interests concerned. But all the facts in every case show that there was no concert, no regular dignity, and no regular means of obtaining it; that it was a mere fluctuating superiority, such as we may find in Owhyhee, Tahiti, or New Zealand, due to success in war, and lost in turn by defeat. On the

rout of Ceawlin, the second Bretwalda, by the
Welsh, we learn that he was expelled from the
throne, and succeeded by Ceólwulf, who spent many
years in struggles against Angles, Welsh, Scots and
Picts[1] : according to Turner's and Lappenberg's
theory, he was the very man to have been made
Bretwalda; but we do not find this to have been
the case, or that the dignity returned to the inter-
vening Sussex ; but Æðelberht of Kent, whose ambition had years before led him to measure his
force against Ceawlin's, stepped into the vacant
monarchy. The truth is that Æðelberht, who had
husbanded his resources, and was of all the Saxon
kings the least exposed to danger from the Keltic
populations, was enabled to impose his authority
upon his brother kings, and to make his own terms :
and in a similar way, at a later period, it is clear
that Rædwald of Eastanglia was enabled to deprive
him of it. I therefore again conclude that this so-
called Bretwaldadom was a mere accidental predominance ; there is no peculiar function, duty or
privilege anywhere mentioned as appertaining to
it; and when Beda describes Eádwini of Northumberland proceeding with the Roman *tufa* or banner before him, as an ensign of dignity, he does so
in terms which show that it was not, as Palgrave
seems to imagine, an ensign of imperial authority
used by all Bretwaldas, but a peculiar and remarkable affectation of that particular prince. Before
I leave this word *ducatus*, I may call attention to

---

[1] Chron. Sax. an. 591, 597.

the fact that Ecgberht, whom the Saxon Chronicle
adds to the list given by Beda, has left some charters in which he also uses it[1], and that they are
the only charters in which it does occur. From
these it appears that he dated his reign ten years
earlier than his *ducatus*, that is, that he was *rex* in
802, but not *dux* till 812. Now it is especially observable that in 812 he had not yet commenced
that career of successful aggression against the
other Saxon kingdoms, which justified the Chronicler in numbering him among those whom Camden
and Rapin call the Monarchs, and Palgrave the Emperors of Britain. He did not attack Mercia and
subdue Kent till 825 : in the same year he formed
his alliance with Eastanglia: only in 829 did he
ruin the power of Mercia, and receive the submission of the Northumbrians. But in the year 812
he did move an army against the Welsh, and remained for several months engaged in military operations within their frontier : there is every reason
then to think that the *ducatus* of Ecgberht is only
a record of those conquests over his British neighbours, which enabled him to turn his hand with
such complete success against his Anglosaxon
rivals; and thus that it has no reference to the expression used by Beda to express the factitious preponderance of one king over another. Let us now
inquire to what the passage in the Saxon Chronicle
amounts, which has put so many of our historians

---

[1] Cod. Dipl. Nos. 1038, 1039, 1041.

upon a wrong track, by supplying them with the suspicious name Bretwalda. Speaking of Ecgberht the Chronicler says[1], "And the same year king Ecgberht overran the kingdom of the Mercians, and all that was south of the Humber; and he was the eighth king who was Bretwalda." And then, after naming the seven mentioned by Beda, and totally omitting all notice of the Mercian kings, he concludes,—"the eighth was Ecgberht, king of the Westsaxons."

Now it is somewhat remarkable that of six manuscripts in which this passage occurs, one only reads Bretwalda: of the remaining five, four have Bryten-walda or -wealda, and one Breten-anweald, which is precisely synonymous with Brytenwealda. All the rules of orderly criticism would therefore compel us to look upon this as the right reading, and we are confirmed in so doing by finding that Æðelstán in one of his charters[2] calls himself also "Brytenwealda ealles ðyses ealondes,"—ruler or monarch of all this island. Now the true meaning of this word, which is compounded of *wealda*, a ruler, and the adjective *bryten*, is totally unconnected with Bret or Bretwealh, the name of the British aborigines, the resemblance to which is merely accidental: *bryten* is derived from *breótan*, to distribute, to divide, to break into small portions,

---

[1] Chron. Sax. an. 827.
[2] Cod. Dipl. No. 1110. "Ongolsaxna cyning ꝛ brytænwalda ealles ðyses iglandæs;" and, in the corresponding Latin, "Rex et rector totius huius Britanniae insulae." an. 34.

to disperse: it is a common prefix to words denoting wide or general dispersion[1], and when coupled with *wealda* means no more than an extensive, powerful king, a king whose power is widely extended. We must therefore give up the most attractive and seducing part of all this theory, the name, which rests upon nothing but the passage in one manuscript of the Chronicle,—and that, far from equal to the rest in antiquity or correctness of language: and as for anything beyond the name, I again repeat that we are indebted for it to nothing but the ingenuity of modern scholars, deceived by what they fancied the name itself; that there is not the slightest evidence of a king exercising a central authority, and very little at any time, of a combined action among the Saxons; and that it is quite as improbable that any Saxon king should ever have had a federal army to command, as it is certainly false that there ever was a general Witena gemót for him to preside over. I must therefore in conclusion declare my disbelief as well in a college of kings, as in an officer, elected or otherwise appointed, whom they considered as their head. The development of all the Anglosaxon kingdoms was of far too independent and fortuitous a character for us to assume any general concert among them, especially as that independence is

---

[1] The following words compounded with *Bryten* will explain my meaning to the Saxon scholar: *Bryten-cyning* (exactly equivalent to *bryten-wealda*), a powerful king. Cod. Exon. p. 331. *Bryten-grund,* the wide expense of earth. Ibid. p. 22. *Bryten-rice,* a spacious realm. Ibid. p. 192. *Bryten-wong,* the spacious plain of earth. Ibid. p. 24. The adjective is used in the same sense, but uncompounded, thus: *breotone bold,* a spacious dwelling. Cædm. p. 308.

manifested upon those points particularly, where a
central and combined action would have been most
certain to show itself [1].

But although I cannot admit the growth of an
imperial power in any such way, I still believe the
royal authority to have been greatly consolidated,

---

[1] I allude more particularly to the introduction of Christianity, the
enactment of laws, the establishment of dioceses, and military measures against the Britons. In two late publications, Mr. Hallam has
bestowed his attention upon the same subject, and with much the same
result. His acute and well-balanced mind seems to have been struck
by the historical difficulties which lie in the way of the Bretwalda
theory, though he does not attach so much force as I think we ought,
to its total inconsistency with the general social state of Anglosaxon
England in the sixth and seventh centuries, or as seems justly due to
the philological argument. He cites from Adamnan a passage in these
words : "(Oswald) totius Britanniae imperator ordinatus a deo." But
these words only prove at the utmost that Adamnan attributed a certain power to Oswald, connected in fact with conquest, and implying
anything but consent, election or appointment, by his fellow-kings.
And Mr. Hallam himself inclines to the belief that the title may have
been one given to Oswald by his own subjects, rather than the assertion of a fact that he truly ruled over all Britain. He conceives that the
three Northumbrian kings, having been victorious in war and paramount
over the minor kingdoms, were really designated, at least among their
own subjects, by the name Bretwalda, or ruler of Britain, and "totius
Britanniae imperator,"—an assumption of pompous titles characteristic
of the vaunting tone which continued to increase down to the Conquest.
(Supplemental Notes to the View of the Middle Ages, p. 199 *seq.*) This
however is hardly consistent with Beda and the Chronicle. The only
passage in its favour is that of Adamnan, and this is confined to one
prince. Adamnan however was a Kelt, and on this account I should
be cautious respecting any language he used. Again, I am not prepared
to admit the probability of a territorial title, at a time when kings were
kings of the people, not of the land. But most of all do I demur to the
reading Bretwalda itself, which rests upon the authority neither of coins
nor inscriptions, and is supported only by one passage of a very bad
manuscript; while it is refuted by five much better copies of the same
work, and a charter : I therefore do not scruple to say that there is no
authority for the word. In all but this I concur with Mr. Hallam,
whose opinion is a most welcome support to my own.

and thereby extended, before the close of the sixth century. It is impossible, for a very long period, to look upon the Anglosaxon kingdoms otherwise than as camps, planted upon an enemy's territory, and not seldom in a state of mutual hostility. All had either originated in, or had at some period fallen into, a state of military organization, in which the leaders are permitted to assume powers very inconsistent with the steady advance of popular liberty; and in the progress of their history, events were continually recurring which favoured the permanent establishment and consolidation of those powers. Upon all their western and northern frontiers lay ever-watchful and dangerous Keltic populations, the co-operation of whose more inland brethren was always to be dreaded, and whose attacks were periodically renewed till very long after the preponderance of one crown over the rest was secured,—attacks only too often favoured by the civil wars and internal struggles of the Germanic conquerors. Upon all the eastern coasts hovered swarms of daring adventurers, ready to put in practice upon the Saxons themselves the frightful lesson of piracy which these had given the Roman world in the third and fourth centuries, and ever welcomed by the Keltic inhabitants as the ministers of their own vengeance. The constant state of military preparation which was thus rendered necessary could have no other result than that of giving a vast preponderance to the warlike over the peaceful institutions; of raising the practised and well-armed comites to a station yearly more and more important; of leading to the multiplication of fortresses, with their royal castellans and stationary garrisons; nay—by constantly placing the freemen under martial law, and inuring them to the urgencies of military command—of finally breaking down the innate feeling and guarantees of freedom, and even of materially ruining the cultivator, all whose energy and all whose time were not too much, if a comfortable subsistence was to be wrung from the soil he owned. It is also necessary to bear in mind the power derived from forcible possession of lands from which the public enemy had been expelled, and which, we may readily believe, turned to the advantage, mostly if not exclusively, of the king and his nobles. No wonder then if at a very early period the Mark-organization, which contained within itself the seeds of its own decay, had begun to give way, and that a systematic *commendation*, as it was called, to the adjacent lords was beginning to take its place. To the operation of these natural causes we must refer the indisputable predominance established by a few superior kings before the end of the sixth century, not only over the numerous dynastic families which still remained scattered over the face of the country, but also over the free holders in the gá or scýr.

To these however was added one of still greater moment. The introduction of Christianity in a settled form, which finally embraced the whole Saxon portion of the island, dates from the commencement of the seventh century. Though not unknown to the various British tribes, who had long been in communication with their fellow-believers of Gaul and, according to some authorities[1], of Rome, it had made but little progress among the German tribes, although a tendency to give it at least a tolerant hearing had for some time been making way among them[2]. But in 595 Pope Gregory the Great determined upon giving effect to his scheme of a missionary expedition to Britain, which he had long revolved, had at one time determined to undertake in person, and had relinquished only as far as his own journey was concerned, in consequence of the opposition manifested by the inhabitants of Rome to his quitting the city. Having finally matured his plan, he selected a competent number of monks and ecclesiastics, and despatched them under the guidance of Augustine, with directions to found an episcopal church among the heathen Saxons. The progress and success of this missionary effort must not be treated of here ; suffice it to say that, one by one, the Teutonic kingdoms of the island accepted the new faith, and that

[1] See Schrödl, Erste Jahrhund. der Angl. Kirche, 1840, p. 2, notes. If the assertion of Prosper Tyro is to be trusted, that Celestine sent Germanus into Britain as his vicar, *vice sua*, the relation must have been an intimate one. See also Nennius, Hist. cap. 54. Neander however declares against the dependence of the British church upon Rome, and derives it from Asia Minor. Alg. Geschichte der Christ. Relig. u. Kirche, vol. i. pt. 1. p. 121. The question has been treated in late times as one of bitter controversy.

[2] This may be inferred from Gregory's letters to Theódríc and Theódbert and to Brunichildis. "Atque ideo pervenit ad nos Anglorum gentem ad fidem Christianam, Deo miserante, desideranter velle converti, sed sacerdotes e vicino negligere," etc. ; again : " Indicamus ad nos pervenisse Anglorum gentem, Deo annuente, velle fieri Christianam ; sed sacerdotes, qui in vicino sunt, pastoralem erga eos sollicitudinem non habere." Bed. Op. Minora, ii. 234, 235.

before the close of the first century from the arrival
of Augustine, the whole of German England was
united into one church, under a Metropolitan, who
accidentally was also a missionary from Rome[1].

Strange would it have been had the maxims of
law or rules of policy which these men brought
with them, been different from those which prevailed in the place from which they came. Roman
feelings, Roman views and modes of judging, the
traditions of the empire and the city, the legislation
of the emperors and the popes,—these were their
sources both of opinion and action. The predominance of the kings must have appeared to them
natural and salutary; the subordination of all men
to their appointed rulers was even one of the doctrines of Christianity itself, as taught by the great
apostle of the gentiles, and recommended by the
example of the Saviour. But the consolidation and
advancement of the royal authority, if they could
only form a secure alliance with it, could not but
favour their great object of spreading the Gospel
among populations otherwise dispersed and inaccessible : hence it seems probable that all their
efforts would be directed to the end which circumstances already favoured, and that the whole spiritual and temporal influence of the clergy would
be thrown into the scale of monarchy. Moreover
the clergy supplied a new point of approach between our own and foreign courts : to say nothing
of Rome, communication with which soon became

---

[1] Theodore of Tarsus.

close and frequent, very shortly after their establishment here, we find an increased and increasing intercourse between our kings and those of Gaul; and this again offered an opportunity of becoming familiar wtth the views and opinions which had flowed, as it were, from the imperial city into the richest and happiest of her provinces. The strict Teutonic law of wergyld, they perhaps could not prevail to change, and to the last, the king, like every other man, continued to have his price; but the power of the clergy is manifest even in the very first article of Æðelberht's law, and to it we in all probability owe the ultimate affixing of the penalty of death to the crime of high-treason,—a marvellous departure from the ancient rule. Taking all the facts of the case into account, we cannot but believe that the introduction of Christianity, which not only taught the necessity of obedience to lawful authority, but accustomed men to a more central and combined exercise of authority through the very spectacle of the episcopal system itself, tended in no slight degree to perpetuate the new order which was gradually undermining and superseding the old Mark-organization, and thus finally brought England into the royal circle of European families [1].

The chapters of the present Book will be devoted to an investigation of the institutions proper to this altered condition, to the officers by whom the

---

[1] Æðelberht of Kent married a Frankish princess, so did Æðelwulf of Wessex. Offa of Mercia was engaged in negotiations for a nuptial alliance with the house of Charlemagne, and several Anglosaxon ladies of royal blood found husbands among the sovereign families of the Continent.

government of the country was conducted, from the seventh to the eleventh centuries, and to the general social relations which thus arose. If in the course of our investigation it should appear that a gradually diminishing share of freedom remained to the people, yet must we bear in mind that the old organization was one which could not keep pace with the progress of human society, and that it was becoming daily less suited to the ends for which it first existed; that in this, as in all great changes, a compromise necessarily took place, and mutual sacrifices were required ; after all, that we finally retained a great amount of rational and orderly liberty, full of the seeds of future development, and gained many of the advantages of Roman cultivation, without paying too high a price for them, in the loss of our nationality.

CHAPTER II.

THE REGALIA, OR RIGHTS OF ROYALTY.

IN the strict theory of the Anglosaxon constitution the King was only one of the people [1], dependent upon their election for his royalty, and upon their support for its maintenance. But he was nevertheless the noblest of the people, and at the head of the state, as long as his reign was felt to be for the general good, the keystone and completion of the social arch. Accordingly he was invested with various dignities and privileges, enabling him to exercise public functions necessary to the weal of the whole state, and to fill such a position in society as belonged to its chief magistrate. Although his life, like that of every other man, was assessed at a fixed price,—the price of an æðeling or person of royal blood,—it was further guarded by an equal amount, to be levied under the name of *cynebót*, the price of his royalty; and the true character of these distinctions is clear from the fact of the

---

[1] The names by which the King is commonly known among most of the Germanic nations are indicative of his position. From þeód, the people, he is called þeóden: from his high birth (cyne nobilis, and cyn genus, i.e. generosus a genere), he is called Cyning: from Dryht, the troop of comites or household retainers, he is Dryhten: and as head of the first household in the land, he is emphatically Hláford: his consort is seó Hlǽfdige, the Lady. His poetical and mythical names need not be investigated on this occasion.

first sum belonging to the family, the second to the people[1].

His personal rights, or royalties, consisted in the possession of large domains which went with the crown[2], a sort of τέμενος, which were his own property only while he reigned, and totally distinct from such private estates as he might purchase for himself; in short his Woods and Forests, which the Crown held under the guarantee and supervision of the Witena gemót. Also, in the right to receive *naturalia*, or voluntary contributions in kind from the free men, which gradually became depraved into compulsory payments. Of these the earliest mention is by Tacitus[3], who tells us that it was the custom, voluntarily and according to the power of the people, to present their princes with cattle and corn, which was not only a mark of honour but a substantial means of support; and the annals of

---

[1] Be Wergyldum, Norðleóda laga, § 1. Myrcna laga, § 1. Thorpe, i. 186, 190 : "Se wer gebira∂ magum ꝥ seó cynebót ∂ám leódum."

[2] Æðelred about 980, gives the following reasons for a grant made by him to Abingdon. During the lifetime of Eádgar, this prince had given to the monastery certain estates belonging to the appanage of the princes of the blood, "*terras ad regios pertinentes filios*:" these, on Eádgar's death and Eádweard's accession, the Witena gemót very properly claimed and obtained, handing them over to Æðelred, then prince royal: "quae statim terrae iuxta decretum et praeceptionem cunctorum optimatum de praefato sancto coenobio violenter abstractae, *meaeque ditioni, hisdem praecipientibus, sunt subactae*: quam rem si iuste aut iniuste fecerint, ipsi sciant." All the crown lands thus fell to Æðelred, he having no children at his brother Eádweard's death : "et *regalium* simul, et *ad regios filios pertinentium terrarum* suscepi dominium." Having now scruples of conscience about interfering with his father's charitable intentions, he gave the monastery an equivalent out of his own private property,—"*ex mea propria haereditate*." Cod. Dipl. No. 1312.   [3] Germ. xv.

the Frankish kings abound with instances of these
presentations, which generally took place at the
great meetings of the people, or Campus Madius[1].
His further privileges consisted in the right to receive a portion of the fines payable for various
offences, and the confiscation of offenders' estates
and chattels; in various distinctions of dress, dwelling, and the like; above all, in the maintenance
of a standing army of comrades, called at a late
period Húscarlas or household troops. It was for
him to call together the Witena gemót or great
council of the realm, whenever occasion demanded,
and to lay before them propositions touching the
general welfare of the state; in concurrence also
with them, to extend or amend the existing legislation. At the same time I do not find that he
possessed the power of dismissing these counsellors
when he thought he had had enough of their advice, or of preventing them from meeting without
his special summons: in which two rights, when

---

[1] See Domesday, *passim.* Cnut commanded to put an end to these
compulsory demands: no man was to be compelled to give his reeves
anything towards the king's feormfultum, against his will, under a
heavy penalty, but the king was to be provided for out of the royal
property. Cnut, § 70. Thorpe, i. 412. If Phillips is right in supposing the Fóster of Ini's law (§ 70. Thorpe, i. 146) to be this burthen,
heavy charges lay upon the land in the eighth century. Angels. Recht.
p. 87. But I doubt the application in this particular case. See also,
Anon. Vita Hludov. Imp. § 7; Pertz, ii. 610, 611; Annal. Laurish.
753; Ann. Bertin. 837; Pertz, i. 116, 430, and Hincmar. Inst. Carol.
ibid. ii. 214. *Aids* and *benevolences* have acquired a notoriety in English history which will not be forgotten while England survives: but
the prerogative lawyers had ancient prescription to back them. On
the whole subject see Grimm, Rechtsalt. p. 245. Eichhorn, § 171.
vol. i. p. 730 *seq.*

injudiciously exercised, the historian finds the key to the downfall of so many monarchies. As general conservator of the public peace, both against foreign and domestic disturbers, the king could call out the *fyrd*, an armed levy or militia of the freemen, proclaim his peace upon the high-roads, and exact the cumulative fines by which the breach of it was punished. He was also the proper guardian of the coinage; and, in some respects, the fountain of justice, seeing that he might be resorted to, if justice could not be obtained elsewhere. We may also look upon him as, at least to a certain degree, the fountain of honour, since he could promote his comrades, thanes or ministers to higher rank, or to posts of dignity and power. All these various rights and privileges he possessed and exercised, by and with the advice, consent and licence of his Witena gemót or Parliament. It is desirable to consider the various details connected with this subject, in succession, and to illustrate them by examples from Anglosaxon authorities.

Although under a Christian dispensation the king could no longer be considered as appertaining to a family exclusively divine, yet the old national tradition still aided in securing to him the highest personal position in the commonwealth. He had a wergyld indeed, but it far exceeded that of any other class: nor was it in this alone that his paramount dignity was recognized, but in the comparative amount of the fines levied for offences against himself, his dependents or his property. And as the principle of all Teutonic law is, that the

amount of *bót* or compensation shall vary directly
with the dignity of the party leased, the high tariff
appointed for royalty is evidence that the king
really stood at the summit of the social order, and
was the first in rank and honour, whatever he may
have been in power. This is equally apparent in
the earliest law, that of Æðelberht, as in Eádweard
the Confessor's, the latest. Thus, if he called his
Leóde, *fideles* or thanes, to him, and they were in-
jured on the way, a compensation double the ordinary amount could be exacted, and in addition a
fine of fifty shillings to the king[1]. And so likewise,
if he honoured a subject by drinking at his house,
all offences, then and there committed, were punishable by a double fine[2]. Theft from him bore a
ninefold, from a ceorl or freeman only a threefold,
compensation[3]. His mundbyrd or protection was
valued at fifty shillings; that of an eorl and ceorl
at twelve and six respectively[4]: this applied to the
cases where a man slew another in the king's tún,
the eorl's tún, or the ceorl's edor[5]; and to the dishonour of his maiden-serf, which involved a fine of
fifty shillings, while the eorl's female cupbearer was
protected only to the amount of twelve, the ceorl's
to that of six shillings[6]. His messenger or armour-
er, if by chance they were guilty of manslaughter,
could only be sued for a mitigated wergyld, by

---

[1] Æðelb. i. § 2. This enactment has been supposed to be the foundation of one of those privileges of Parliament, which we have seen solemnly discussed on a late occasion.

[2] Æðelb. i. § 3.   [3] Ibid. § 4, 9.
[4] Ibid. § 8, 15.   [5] Ibid. § 5, 13.
[6] Ibid. § 10, 14, 16.

which they, though probably unfree, were placed
upon a footing of equality with the freeman[1]. His
word, like that of a bishop, was to be incontrovertible, that is, no oath could be tendered to rebut
it[2]. He that fought in the king's hall, if taken in
the act, was liable to the punishment of death, or
such doom as the king should decree[3]: the king's
burhbryce, or violence done to his dwelling, was
valued at 120 shillings, an archbishop's at 90, a
bishop's or ealdorman's at 60, a twelfhynde man's
at 30, a syxhynde's at 15, but a ceorl's or freeman's only at 5; and these sums were to be dou-
bled if the militia was on foot[4]. His borhbryce, or
breach of surety, and his mundbyrd or protection
were raised by Ælfred to five pounds, while the
archbishop's was valued at three, the bishop's or
ealdorman's at two pounds[5]. He could give sanctuary to offenders for nine days[6], and peculiar privileges of the same kind were extended to those
monasteries which were subject to his farm or *pastus*[7]. His geneát or comrade, if of the noble class,
could swear for sixty hides of land[8]. His horse-
wealh, the Briton employed in his stables, was
placed on an equal footing with the freeman, at a

---

[1] Æðelb. § 7, 21.

[2] Wihtr. § 16. The position and privileges of the clergy at this very
early period, and especially in Kent, were very exalted. Æðelberht
places the king only on the footing of a priest, in respect to his stolen
property. Æðelb. § 1. But this grave error was remedied as society became better consolidated, although to the very last the clergy were left
in possession of far too much secular power.

[3] Ini, § 6. Ælf. § 7.   [4] Ini, § 45. Ælfr. § 40.
[5] Ælfr. § 3. Cnut, ii. § 59.   [6] Æðelst. iii. § 6; iv. § 4; v. § 4.
[7] Ælfr. § 2.   [8] Ini, § 19.

wergyld of 200 shillings[1]; and even his godson had a particular protection[2]. Lastly, high-treason, by compassing the king's death, harbouring of exiles, or of the king's rebellious dependents, was made liable to the punishment of death[3].

The political position of the king, at the head of the state, was secured by an oath of allegiance taken to him, by all subjects of the age of twelve years[4],

[1] Ini, § 33.   [2] Ibid. § 76.

[3] Ælf. § 4.   Cnut, ii. § 58.

[4] "Imprimis ut omnes iurent in nomine Domini, pro quo sanctum illud sanctum est, fidelitatem Eádmundo regi, sicut homo debet esse fidelis domino suo, sine omni controversia et seditione, in manifesto, in occulto, in amando quod amabit, nolendo quod nolet." Eádm. iii. § 1. Thorpe, i. 252. "And it is our will, that every man above twelve years of age, make oath that he will neither be a thief, nor cognizant of theft." Cnut, ii. § 21. Thorpe, i. 388. "Omnis enim duodecim annos habens et ultra, in alicuius frithborgo esse debet et in decenna; sacramentumque regi et hæredibus suis faccre fidelitatis, et quod nec latro erit, nec latrocinio consentiet." Fleta, lib. i. cap. 27. § 4. This was the basis upon which the associations of freemen among the Anglosaxons entered into their alliances, offensive and defensive, with their kings. Charlemagne caused an oath to be taken to himself as emperor, by all his subjects above twelve years old. Dönniges, p. 3. The Hyldáð or oath of fealty is given in the Anc. Laws, i. 178. The dependent engages to love all the lord loves, and shun all that he shuns: these are the technical terms throughout Europe. The king himself took a corresponding oath to his people. We still have the words of that which was administered by Dúnstán to Æðelred at Kingston.

"Ðis gewrit is gewriten, stæf be stæfe, be ðám gewrite ðe Dúnstán arcebisceop sealde úrum hláforde æt Cingestúne á on dæg ðá hine man hálgode tó cinge, and forbeád him ælc wedd tó syllanne bútan ðysan wedde, ðe he úp on Cristes weofod léde, swá se bisceop him dihte. 'On ðære hálgan Þrynnesse naman, Ic þreo þing beháte cristenum folce and me underþeóddum:

"This writing is copied, letter for letter, from the writing which archbishop Dunstán delivered to our lord at Kingston on the very day when he was consecrated king, and he forbad him to give any other pledge but this pledge, which he laid upon Christ's altar, as the bishop instructed him. 'In the name of the Holy Trinity, three things do I promise to this Chris-

D 2

the legal period of majority among the Germans,
for public purposes.   In this capacity he appointed

án ærest, ðæt ic Godes cyrice and eall cristen folc mínra gewealda sóðe sibbe healde : óðer is, ðæt ic reáflác and ealle unrihte þing eallum hádum forbeóde : þridde, ðæt ic beháte and bebeóde on eallum dómum riht and mildheortnisse, ðæt ús eallum ærfæst and mildheort God þurh ðæt his écean mittse forgife, se lifað and rixað.'"
—Reliq. Ant. ii. 194.

tian people, my subjects : first, that I will hold God's church and all the Chistian people of my realm in true peace : second, that I will forbid all rapine and injustice to men of all conditions : third, that I promise and enjoin justice and mercy in all judgements, whereby the just and merciful God may give us all his eternal favour, who liveth and reigneth !' "

It is worth while to compare with this the coronation oath of king Eirek Magnusson, of Norway, which we learn from the following valuable document of July 25th, 1280.

" Pateat universis tam clericis quam laicis per regnum Norwegie constitutis presens scriptum visuris vel audituris quod anno domini m⁰. ·cc⁰. lxxx⁰. in festo sancti Suithuni Bergio in ecclesia cathedrali magnificus princeps et nobilis dominus . Eiricus dei gracia rex Norwegie illustris filius domini Magni quondam regis coram reverendo patre et venerabili domino Johanne secundo divina miseracione . Nidrosiensi archiepiscopo qui eum coronando in regem coronam capiti eius imposuit . ipsiusque suffraganeis et multis clericis et laicis qui presentes fuerant . tactis ewangeliis iuramentum prestitit in hunc modum . Profiteor et promitto coram deo et sanctis eius a modo pacem et iusticiam ecclesie dei . populoque mihi subiecto observare . pontificibus et clero . prout teneor . condignum honorem exhibere . secundum discrecionem mihi a deo datam . atque ea que a regibus ecclesiis collata ac reddita sunt . sicut compositum est inter ecclesiam et regnum . inviolabiliter conservare . malasque leges et consuetudines perversas precipue contra ecclesiasticam libertatem facientes abolere et bonas condere prout de concilio fidelium nostrorum melius invenire poterimus . þat jatta ek gudi ok hans helgum mannum . at ek skal vardvæita frid ok rettyndi hæilagre kirkiu ok þui folki sem ek er overðugr ivir skipaðr . Byscopum ok lærdom mannum skal ek væita vidrkvæmelega soemd efter þui sem ek er skyldugr . ok gud giæfr mer skynsemd til . ok þa luti halda obrigðilega . sem af konunggum ero kirkiunni gefner . ok aftr fegner sua sem samþykt er millum kirkiunnar ok rikissens . Rong log ok illar siðueniur einkanlega þær . sem mote ero hæilagrar kirkiu frælsi af taka ok betr skipa eftir þui sem framazt faam ver raad til at varom tryggastu mannum . Cum igitur ante coronacionem dicti regis dubitacio fuerit . de regis iuramento . volens predictus pater ne huiusmodi dubitacio rediviva

the ealdormen in the shires, the geréfan in the various districts or towns, summoned his witan and

foret in posterum precavere . utile quippe etenim est eam rem cognitam esse que ignorata vel dubia possit occasionem litigii ministrare . iuramentum seu professionem factam a domino rege . ad perpetuam memoriam . presentibus literis duxit inserendam . et ad pleniorem rei evidenciam sigillum suum apposuit una cum sigillis venerabilium patrum . domini Andree Osloensis . Jorundi Holensis . Erlendi Ferensis . Arnonis Skalotensis . Arnonis Stawangrensis . Nerue Bergensis . Thorfinni Hamarensis suffraganeorum Nidrosiensis ecclesie . Actum viii. Kal. Augusti loco et anno supradictis."—Diplomatarium Norwegicum, No. 69. p. 62.

It is very uncertain at what time the custom of coronation, and *unction*, by the hands of the clergy, commenced. The usurpation which Pipin ventured and Pope Zachary lent himself to, which Charlemagne repeated and Pope Leo confirmed, may have acted as a valuable precedent, especially as the power of the King was sufficient to justify the claim of the Pope. Thirty years later (A.D. 787), the English bishops put forward the somewhat bold claim to be, with the *seniores* populi, electors of the king: "Duodecimo sermone sanximus; Ut in ordinatione regum nullus permittat pravorum praevalere assensum ; sed legitime reges a sacerdotibus et senioribus populi eligantur, et non de adulterio vel incoestu procreati; quia sicut nostris temporibus ad sacerdotium, secundum Canones, adulter pervenire non potest, sic nec Christus domini esse valet, et rex totius regni, et haeres patriae, qui ex legitimo non fuerit connubio generatus." Conc. Calcuth. Legat. Spelm. p. 296. No doubt from their position in the Witena gemót, and the authority which they derived from their birth as well as station, they always played an important part in the elections of kings, but not quite so leading a part in the eighth century as they here attempt to claim. The Diplomatarium Norwegicum supplies an interesting illustration of the above-cited canon, in a dispensation issued by Pope Innocent IV. (A.D. 1246) to Haakon Haakonson, from the disqualification of illegitimate birth: "Cum itaque clare memorie Haquinus, Norwegie rex pater tuus, te, prout accepimus, solutus susceperit de soluta, nos tuam celsitudinem speciali benevolentia prosequentes, ut huiusmodi non obstante defectu ad regalis solii dignitatem. et omnes actus legitimos admittaris, nec non quod heredes tui legitimi tibi in dominio et honore succedant, fratrum nostrorum communicato consilio, tecum auctoritate apostolica dispensamus." No. 38, p. 30. This was not however considered a valid ground of objection among the Anglosaxons, if the personal qualities of the prince were such as to recommend him. From the words used by William of Malmesbury we might infer that as late as the time of Æðelstán, the functions of the bishops at the coronation were

named the members of their body[1]. In this capacity he was empowered to inflict fines upon the
public officers, and even private individuals, for
such neglect of duty as endangered the public interests : these fines were paid under the title of the
king's oferhýrnes, literally his *disobedience:* thus,
if a man when summoned refuse to attend the gemót; if a geréfa refuse to do justice, when called
upon, or to put the law in execution against offenders[2], and in other similar cases where the whole
framework of society requires the existence of a
central support, having power to hold its scattered
elements together, and in their places.

The maintenance of the public peace is the first
duty of the king, and he is accordingly empowered
to levy fines for all illegal breaches of it, by offences against life, property or honour[3] : in very
grave cases of continued guilt, he is even entrusted

confined to anathematizing those who would not be obedient subjects,
but that the nobles performed the actual coronation : he cites the following lines from an earlier author, and one apparently contemporaneous
with Æðelstán himself :—

> " Tunc iuvenis nomen regni clamatur in omen,
> Ut fausto patrias titulo moderetur habenas :
> Conveniunt proceres et componunt diadema,
> Pontifices pariter dant infidis anathema."
>
> De Gest. ii. § 133.

That Harold crowned himself is an old story ; but it is very certain
that whatever he did, was done with the full consent of the Witena
gemót.

[1] See hereafter the several chapters Ealdorman, Geréfa and Witena
gemót.

[2] The principal cases will be found in the following passages of the
Laws : Eádw. § 1. Æðelst. i. § 20, 22, 26; iii. § 7; iv. § 1, 7; v. § 11.
Eádm. iii. § 2, 6, 7.   Eádg. i. § 4 ; ii. § 7, etc.

[3] Hloðh. § 9, 11, 12, 13, 14. Ælf. § 37. Æðelst. i. § 1 ; iii. § 4 ; v. § 5.

with the right of banishing and outlawing offenders, whose wealth and family connexions seem to
place them beyond the reach of ordinary jurisdictions[1]. Where the course of private war is to be
settled by the legal compensations, it is the king's
peace which is established between the contending
parties, the relatives and advocates of the slayer
and the slain[2]. And in accordance with these
principles, we find the kings's peace peculiarly proclaimed upon the great roads which are the high-
ways of commerce and means of internal communication, and the navigable streams by which cities
and towns are supplied with the necessary food for
their inhabitants[3]. And hence also he was allowed
to proclaim his peace over all the land at certain
times and seasons; as, for eight days at his coronation, and the same space of time at Christmas,
Easter and Whitsuntide. He might also, either by
his hand or writ, give the privileges of his peace to
estates which would otherwise not have possessed
it, and thus place them upon the same footing of
protection as his own private residences[4]. The great
divisions of the country, that is the shires, could only

[1] Æðelst. iii. § 3; iv. § 1.
[2] Eád. Guð. § 13. Eádm. ii. § 1, 6, 7.
[3] Eád. Conf. § 12. Cross roads and small streams are not in the
king's peace, but that of the county.
[4] This peace was called the King's Handsell, "cyninges handsealde
griðð." The extent to which his peace extended around his dwelling,
that is, within the verge of the court, has been noticed in the fourth
chapter of the First Book. The right subsisted throughout the Middle
Ages and yet subsists, though differently motived and measured. The
king's handsealde grið was by Æðelred's law made bótless, that is,
had no settled compensation. Æðelr. iii. § 1.

be determined by the central power : it is therefore
provided that these shall be in the especial right
of the king: " Divisiones scirarum regis proprie
cum iudicio quatuor chiminorum regalium sunt[1]."
And to the end of maintaining peace, it appears
to me that the king must also have been the authority to whom, at least in theory, it was left
to settle the boundaries even of private estate ;
which on the conversion of folcland into bócland,
he did, generally by his officers, but sometimes in
person[2].

But the great machinery for keeping peace between man and man, is the establishment of courts
of justice, and a system by which each man can
have law, by the consent and with the co-operation
of his neighbours, without finding it necessary to
arm in his own defence.   It has been shown in the
First Book, that such means did exist in the Mark
and Gá courts ; and that for nearly all the purposes
of society, it is sufficient and advisable that justice
should be done within the limits and by the autho-

[1] Eádw. Conf. § 13.

[2] " Æðelingawudu, Colmanora and Geátescumbe belong to these
twenty hides, which I myself, now rode, now rowed, and widely divided
off, for myself, my predecessors, and those that shall come after me, for
an eternal separation, before God and the world." Eádred. an. 955. Cod.
Dipl. No. 1171. " Now I greet well my relative Mygod of Walling-
ford, and command thee in my stead [on mínre stede] to ride round
the land to the saint's hand." Eádw. Conf., Cod. Dipl. No. 862. The
force of the word berídan is very difficult to convey in words, but still
perfectly obvious. Another difficulty arises from the word stede, which
is properly masculine, but here given as a feminine. I think it impossible that it should mean stéde, a mare (i. e. on my mare), and prefer
the supposition either that stede had changed its gender, or that the
copy of the charter is an incorrect one.

rity of the freemen. A centralized system however
brings modifications with it, even into the administration of justice. If, as I believe, the original
king was a judge, who superinduced the warlike
upon his peaceful functions, we can easily see how,
with the growth of the monarchy, the judicial authority of the king should become extended. I
cannot doubt that, in the historical times of the
Anglosaxons, the king was the fountain of justice;
by which expression I certainly do not mean that
every suit must be commenced in one of the superior courts, or by an original writ, issuing out of
the royal chancery [1], but that the king was looked
upon as the authority by whom the judges were
supported and upheld, who was to be appealed to,
if no justice could be got elsewhere, and who had
the power to punish malversation in its administration by his officers.

We may leave the tale of Ælfred's hanging the
unjust judges to the same veracious chapter of
history as records his invention of trial by jury:
but it is obvious, from the words of his biographer,
that he assumed some right to direct them in the
exercise of their functions. He there appears
not to have waited until complaints were made of
their maladministration; but to have adopted the
Frankish and Roman custom of dispatching *Missi*
or royal commissioners into the provinces subject
to his rule, in order to keep a proper check upon the

[1] There are cases nevertheless which seem to favour the supposition
that a similar power was ultimately lodged in the king and, at least
occasionally, exercised.

proceedings of the public officers of justice. Asser says,—and I record his words with the highest respect and admiration of Ælfred's real and great deserts,—that " he investigated with great sagacity the judgments given throughout almost all his region, which had been delivered when he was not present, as to what had been their character, whether they were just, or unjust. And if he detected any injustice in such judgments, he, either in person, or by people in his confidence, mildly enquired why the judges had given such unjust decisions, whether through ignorance, or through malversation of another kind, as fear, or favour, or hope of gain. And then, if the judges admitted that they had so decided, because they knew no better in the premises, he would gently and moderately correct their ignorance and folly, and say: ' I marvel at your insolence, who, by God's gift and mine, have taken upon yourselves the ministry and rank of wise men, but have neglected the study and labour of wisdom. Now it is my command that ye either give up at once the administration of those secular powers which ye enjoy, or pay a much more devoted attention to the studies of wisdom.' "

A certain pedantry is obvious enough in all this story, which, taken literally, under the circumstances of the time, is merely childish. Still, as Asser, though he may not entirely represent the facts of this period[1] in their true Germanic sense,

---

[1] I may here say once for all, that I see no reason to doubt the authenticity of Asser's Annals, or to attribute them to any other period than the one at which they were professedly composed.

does very likely represent some of the king's private wishes and opinions, this, among other passages, may serve to show why, in spite of his great merits, Ælfred once in his life had not a man to trust to in his realm. Let us look at the matter a little more closely. In the many kingdoms and districts which by conquest or inheritance came under the Westsaxon rule, various customary laws had prevailed[1]. It is very natural that judgments given in accordance with these customs should often appear inconsistent and discordant to a body of men collected from different parts of the realm. Asser is therefore very probably in the right, when he says: " The nobles and non-nobles alike were frequently at variance in the meetings of the comites and praepositi, [that is, in the Witena gemóts,] so that scarcely any one would admit the decisions of the comites and praepositi [that is, in the shire, hundred and burhmót] to be correct." But it is also probable that he misstates or overstates the extent of the royal power, when he continues: " But Ælfred, who for his own part knew that some injustice arose thereby, was not very willing to meddle with the decision of this judge or that; although he was compelled thereunto both by force of law and by stipulation[2]."

For in fact the king was the authority to be resorted to in the last instance; not because he could

---

[1] Ælfred himself mentions the Kentish, Mercian and Westsaxon laws. The Danes had another. Peculiarities of the Northangle and Southangle laws are also noticed.

[2] By the contract entered into with his people: but when? when they first elected him? or when they restored him to his throne?

introduce a system of jurisprudence founded upon
Roman Decretals or Alaric's Breviary,—which his
favourite advisers would probably have liked much
better than his ealdormen, præfects and people,—
but because he could lend the aid of the state to
enforce the judgments of the several courts, or
even compel the courts to give judgment, by reason of the central power which he wielded as king.
As long however as the courts themselves were
willing to decide causes brought before them, which
the people assembled in the gemóts did, under the
presidency and direction of the customary officers,
the king had no right to interfere : and even to
appeal to the king until justice had been actually
denied in the proper quarter was an offence under
the Saxon law, punishable by fine[1]. In short, under
that law, the people were themselves the judges,
and helped the geréfa to find the judgment, be the
court what it might be. The king's authority could
give no more than power to execute the sentence.
It is remarkable enough that while Asser speaks
of the instruction and correction which Ælfred administered to his judges, he does not even insinuate
that their decisions were reversed,—a fact perfectly

---

[1] " And let him that applies to the king before he has prayed for
justice as often as it behoveth him [that is, made the legal number of
formal applications to the shiremoot, etc.] pay the same fine as the
other should had he denied him justice." Æðelst. i. 1. § 3. Thorpe,
i. 200. Eádgar, ii. § 2. Thorpe, i. 266. "And let no one apply to the
king, unless he cannot get justice within his hundred : but let the hun-
dred-gemót be duly applied to, according to right, under penalty of the
wíte, or fine." Cnut, ii. § 17. Thorpe, i. 384 seq. Similarly Will. Conq.
i. § 43. Thorpe, i. 485. It is impossible to believe that Ælfred possessed a right which later and much more powerful kings did not.

intelligible when we bear in mind that these decisions were not those of judges in our sense of the
word, and as the Mirror plainly understood them,
but of the people in their own courts, finding the
judgment according to customary law. It would
have been a very different case had the courts been
the king's courts; and in those where the class
called king's thanes stood to right either before the
king himself, or the king's geréfa, it is possible that
Ælfred may have interfered. This he had full right
to do, inasmuch as these thanes were exclusively
his own sócmen, and must take such law as he
chose to give them[1]. Indeed the words of Asser
seem reconcileable with the general state of the law
in Ælfred's time only on the supposition that he
refers to these royal courts or þeningmanna gemót;
for the king could never have been expected to be
present at every shire- or hundred-mót, and yet
Asser says he diligently investigated such judgments as were given when he was not present, almost all over his region. This only becomes probable when confined to the administration of justice
in the several counties in his own royal courts, and
by his own royal reeves, in whose method of proceeding he was at liberty to introduce much more
extensive alterations at pleasure, than he could
have done in the customary law of the shires or
other districts.

If however justice was entirely denied in the
shire or hundred, then, *iure imperii*, the king had

---

[1] "And let no one have sócn over a king's thane save the king himself." Æðelr. iii. § 11. Thorpe, i. 296.

the power of interfering: and as it seems clear that
such a case could only arise from the influence of
some great officer being exerted to prevent the due
course of law, it follows that the only remedy would
lie in the king's power to repress him; either by
removing him from his office, if one derived from
the crown, or *iure belli*, putting him down as a nui-
sance to the realm[1].

In the later times of the Anglosaxon monarchy,
a more immediate interference of the king in the
administration of justice is discernible. It consists
in what might be called the commendation of suits
to the notice of the proper courts: and this, which
was done by means of a writ or *insigel*, probably at
first took place only in the .case where a sócman of
the king was impleaded in the shiremoot touching
property subject to its jurisdiction, in fact where
one party was a free landowner, the other in the
king's service or sócn; where of course the first
would not stand to right in the royal courts, but
before his peers in the shire or hundred[2]. There is

---

[1] If the ealdorman connive at theft, or at the escape of a thief, he is
to forfeit his office. Ini, § 36. Thorpe, i. 124. If a geréfa do so, he
shall forfeit all he hath. Æðelst. i. § 3. If he will not put the law in
execution, he shall lose his office. Æðelst. i. 26; v. § 11. Eádg. ii. § 3.
Thorpe, i. 200, 212, 240, 266.

[2] There is an instance where the parties to a suit were similiarly cir-
cumstanced. The matter was brought into the king's þeningmanna
gemót in London, and there decided in favour of the plaintiff, a bishop.
But the defendant was not satisfied, and carried the cause to the shire,
who at once claimed jurisdiction and exercised it too, coming to a decision diametrically opposite to that of the þeningmen or *ministri regii*.
It seems to have been a dirty business on the part of the bishop of
Rochester, and the freemen of Kent so treated it, in defiance of the
King's Court. Cod. Dipl. No. 1258. The document is so important,

no mention in the laws of the Insigel or Breve [1],
but the charters give some evidence of what has

that it appears desirable to give it at full length. " Thus were the
lands at Bromley and Fawkham adjudged to king Eádgár in London,
through the charters of Snodland, which the priests stole from the
bishop of Rochester and secretly sold for money to Ælfric the son of
Æscwyn : and the same Æscwyn, Ælfric's mother, had previously
granted them thither. Now when the bishop found the books were
stolen he made earnest demand for them. Meanwhile Ælfric died, and
he (the bishop) afterwards sued the widow so long that in the king's
thanes-court the stolen books of Snodland were adjudged to him, and
damages for the theft, thereto ; that was in London, and there were
present Eádgár the king, archbishop Dúnstán, bishop Æðelwold, bishop Ælfstán and the other Ælfstán, Ælfhere the ealdorman and many
of the king's witan : then they adjudged the books to the bishop for
his cathedral : so all the widow's property stood in the king's hand.
Then would Wulfstán the geréfa seize the property to the king's hand,
both Bromley and Fawkham ; but the widow sought the holy place and
the bishop, and surrendered to the king the charter of Bromley and
Fawkham : and the bishop bought the charters and the land of the
king at Godshill, for fifty mancuses of gold, and a hundred and thirty
pounds, through intercession and interest : afterwards the bishop permitted the widow the usufruct of the land. During this time the king
died ; and then Bryhtríc the widow's relative began, and compelled her,
so that they took violent possession of the land [brúcon ðára landa on
reáfláce]. And they sought Eádwine the ealdorman, who was God's
adversary, and the folk, and compelled the bishop to restore the books
on peril of all his property : he was not allowed to enjoy his rights in
any one of the three things which had been given him in pledge by all
the *leódscipe*, neither his plea, his succession, nor his ownership. This
is the witness of the purchase : Eádgár the king, Dunstan the archbishop, Oswald the archbishop, bishop Æðelwold, bishop Æðelgar,
bishop Æscwig, bishop Ælfstán, the other bishop Ælfstán, bishop Si-
deman, Ælfðryð the king's mother, Osgar the abbot, Ælfhere the ealdorman, Wulfstan of Delham, Ælfric of Epsom, and the leading people
[dúguð folces] of West Kent, where the land and lathe lie." Here I
take it the þeningmen or *servientes regis* and the leódscipe (leudes) are
identical and opposed to the *Folc* who under "God's adversary" Eádwine
made the bishop disgorge his plunder. We see who they were ; Dun-

[1] Excepting a very indefinite expression in the Law of Henry the
First, § 13.

been averred. In a very important record of the
time of Æðelræd (990–995) these words occur[1]:—
"This writing showeth how Wynflæd led her
witness at Wulfamere before King Æðelræd; now
that was Sigeríc the archbishop, and Ordbyrht the
bishop, and Ælfríc the ealdorman, and Ælfðryð the
king's mother: and they all bore witness that Ælfríc gave Wynflæd the land at Hacceburnan, and
at Brádan-felda in exchange for the land at Dec-
cet. Then at once the king sent by the archbishop
and them that bore witness with him, to Leófwine,
and informed him of this. But he would consent
to nothing, but that the matter should be brought
before the shiremoot. And this was done. Then

stan and various bishops, ealdorman Ælfhere and several of the king's
witan. This is the only instance I have been able to discover of anything approaching to a *curia regis* apart from the great Witena gemót.
There are, no doubt, several cases where the king appears to have been
applied to in the first instance, by one of the parties; but in all of them
trial subsequently was had before the shiremoot. It is natural that
agreements should have been made by consent, before the king as ar-
bitrator, and these were probably frequent among his intimate councd-
lors, friends and relatives : but they were not trials, nor did they settle
the litigation as a judgement of the courts would have done. Such ar-
bitrements were also made by the ealdorman, who like the king received
presents for his good offices. The advantage gained was this; both
parties were satisfied, without the danger of trying the suit, which entailed very heavy penalties on the loser, amounting sometimes to total
forfeiture. The disadvantage was that there was no *ge-endodu spræc*
or finished plea, and consequently the award was sometimes violated,
when either party thought this could be done with impunity.

[1] Cod. Dipl. No. 693. Cwichelmeshlǽw, now Cuckamsley or Cuck-
amslow Hills, in Berkshire ; these run east and west and probably cut
off the north-western portion of the county, forming the watershed
from which the Ock and Lambourn descend on opposite sides. The
exact spot of the gemót was probably near a mound which is now
called Scutchamfly Barrow, and which is very plainly marked in the
Ordnance Map, nearly due north of West Ilsey.

the king sent by Ælfhere the abbot, his *insigel* to
the gemót at Cwichelmeshlǽw, and greeted all the
Witan who were there assembled,—that is, Æðelsige
the bishop, and Æscwig the bishop, and Ælfríc the
abbot, and all the shire, and bade them arbitrate
between Leófwine and Wynflæd, as to them should
seem most just[1]."

There can be no mistake about the fact; but it
does not amount to a proof that the cause could
not have been settled without this formality: both
parties to it were of the highest rank; but if the
king's arbitration were refused, the title to the land
at Bradfield could legally be tried only in the county
of Berkshire in which it lay. Something similar
may have been intended by the notice which occurs
in the record of another shiregemót (held about
1038 at Ægelnóðes stán in Herefordshire) where it
is said that Tófig Prúda came thither *on the king's
errand*[2].

PARDON.—When judgment was pronounced,
it appears that in certain cases, at least, the king
possessed the power to stay execution and pardon
the offender,—an exertion of the royal prerogative
which one feels pleasure in thus referring to so

---

[1] The lands are Bradfield, Hagborne and Datchet, in Berks and
Bucks. Wulfamere I am unable to identify. At all events, had the
matter been cognizable in a superior court of the king's, Leófwine
could not have carried his point of having it brought to trial before
the shiremoot in Berkshire, which he clearly did against the king's
wish.

[2] Cod. Dipl. No. 641.

ancient a period. The necessary evidence is supplied in many passages of the Laws[1].

ESCHEAT AND FORFEITURE. — As the
royal power became consolidated, and the great
struggle between centralization and local independence assumed the new form of offences against the
state, the nature of punishments became somewhat
changed. The old pecuniary fines were found insufficient to repress disorder, and forfeiture to the
king was resorted to, as a measure of increased
severity. The laws proclaim this in the case of
various breaches of the public peace: in treason
Ælfred's witan decreed not only the punishment of
death, but also confiscation of all the possessions[2]:
in addition to the capital penalty which was incurred by fighting in the king's house, forfeiture
of all the chattels was decreed by Ini[3]. If a lord
maintained and abetted a notorious thief, he was to
forfeit all he had[4]. And if he neglected the fines
provided, and would break the public peace either
by thieving or supporting thieves, it was provided
that the public authorities should ride to him, that
is make war upon him, and despoil him of all he

---

[1] "If a man fight or draw weapon in the king's hall and be taken in
the act, he shall lie at the king's mercy, to slay or pardon him." Ælf.
§ 7.   Ini, § 6.   Thorpe, i. 66, 106.   "The ealdorman who connives at
theft shall forfeit his office, unless the king pardon him.   Ini, § 36.
Thorpe, i. 124. See also Æðelst. v. 1. § 4, 5, Eádm. § 6. Eádg. ii. § 7
Æðelr. iii. § 16; vii. § 9. Thorpe, i. 230, 250, 268, 298, 330.
[2] Ælf. § 4. Thorpe, i. 62.   [3] Ini, § 6. Thorpe, i. 106.
[4] Æðelst. i. § 3. Thorpe, i. 200.

had, whereof half was to go to the king, half to the persons who took part in the expedition[1]. But the charters supply numerous instances of forfeiture in consequence of crime, where the bóclands as well as the chattels are seized into the king's hand; though in the case of folcland it is possible that the king could not claim the forfeiture without a positive grant of the witan. About 900, Helmstán having been guilty of theft, Eánwulf, the king's geréfa at Tisbury seized all his chattels to the king's hand[2]: he held only lǽnland, and that could not be forfeited by him; but the words made use of show, that had it been his own bócland, it would not have escaped. We have an instance of a thane forfeiting lands to the king for adultery[3], although he only held them on lease from the bishop of Winchester; and in like manner, a lady was deprived of her estate for incontinence[4]. In 966 the bishop of Rochester having obtained judgment and damages against a lady, for forcible entry upon his lands (reáflác), the sheriff of Kent seized her manors of

---

[1] Æðelst. i. § 20. Thorpe, i. 210; see also § 26. Thorpe, i. 214. Æðelst. iii. § 3. Thorpe, i. 218; iv. § 1; v. § 1, 5. Eádm. ii. § 1, 6. Eádg. Hund. § 2, 3. Eádg. i. § 4. Æðelr. v. § 28, 29; vi. § 35, 37: vii. § 9; ix. § 42. Cnut, ii. § 13, 58, 67, 78, 84. Thorpe, i. 220, 228, 230, 248, 250, 258, 264, 310, 312, 324, 330, 350, 382, 408, 410, 420, 422.

[2] Cod. Dipl. No. 328. "Eánwulf the reeve....took all he owned at Tisbury....and the chattels were adjudged to the king, because he was the king's man: and Ordláf took to his own land, because it was his lǽn that he sat upon: that he could not forfeit.

[3] Cod. Dipl. Nos. 601, 1090.

[4] Cod. Dipl. No. 1295. "Quae portio terrae cuiusdam foeminae fornicaria praevaricatione mihimet vulgari subacta est traditione." Æðelred, an. 1002.

Fawkham and Bromley ; all her possessions being
forfeited to the king[1] : lastly in various instances
of theft, treason, and maintenance of ill-doers, we
learn that their lands were forfeited to the king[2].

[1] Cod. Dipl. No. 1258. "Đá stód ðáre wydewan áre on ðæs cynges
handa : ðá wolde Wulfstán se geréfa niman ða áre tó ðæs cynges handa,
Brómleáh ┑ Fealcnahám."
[2] Cod. Dipl. Nos. 579, 1112. " Quo mortuo praedicta mulier Ælfgyfu alio copulata est marito, Wulfgat vocabulo ; qui ambo crimine
pessimo iuste ab omni incusati sunt populo, causa suae machinationis
propriae, de qua modo non est dicendum per singula, propter quam vero
machinationem quae iniuste adquisierunt iuste perdiderunt." Cod.
Dipl. No. 1305. The exile of Wulfgeat is mentioned by the Chronicle
and Florence, an. 1006. Again, " Nam quidam minister Wulfget vulgari relatu nomine praefatam terram aliquando possederat, sed quia
inimicis regis se in insidiis socium applicavit, et in facinore inficiendo
etiam legis satisfactio ei defecit,ideo haereditatis suberam penitus amisit,
et ex ea praedictus episcopus praescriptam villulam, me concedente,
suscepit." Cod. Dipl. No. 1310. " Has terrarum portiones Ælfríc cognomento Puer a quadam vidua Eádfléd appellata violenter abstraxit,ac
deinde cum in ducatu suo contra me et contra omnem gentem meam reus
existeret, et hae quas praenominavi portiones et universae quas possederat
terrarum possessiones meae subactae sunt ditioni, quando ad synodale
conciliabulum ad Cyrneceastre universi optimates mei simul in unum
convenerunt, et eundem Ælfricum maiestatis reum de hac patria
profugum expulerunt, et universa ab illo possessa michi iure pos-
sidenda omnes unanimo consensu decreverunt." Cod. Dipl. No.
1312. "Emit quoque praedictus vir Æðelmarus a me, cum triginta
libris, duodecim mansiones de villulis quas matrona quaedam nomine
Leóflæ'd suis perdidit ineptiis et amisit." Cod. Dipl. No. 714. " Hoc
denique rus cuiusdam possessoris Leofricus onomate quondam et etiam
nostris diebus paternae haereditatis iure fuerat, sed ipse impie vivendo,
hoc est rebellando meis militibus in mea expeditione, ac rapinis insuetis
et adulteriis multisque aliis nefariis sceleribus semetipsum condempnavit
simul et possessiones." Cod. Dipl. No. 1307. "Erat autem eadem villa
cuidam matronae, nomine Æðelflæde, derelicta a viro suo, obeunte illo,
quae etiam habebat germanum quendam, vocabulo Leófsinum, quem de
satrapis nomine tuli, ad celsioris apicem dignitatis dignum duxi promo-
vere, ducem constituendo, scilicet, eum, unde humiliari magis debuerat,
sicut dicitur, 'Principem te constituerunt, noli extolli,' et caetera. Sed
ipse hoc oblitus, cernens se iñ culmine maioris status sub rogatu famu-
lari sibi pestilentes spiritus promisit, superbiae scilicet et audaciae.

In a case of intestacy, where there were no legal heirs, the king was allowed to enter upon the lands of Burghard, probably because he had been a royal geréfa[1]. And in the ninth century, Wulfhere, an ealdorman, having deserted his duchy, his country and his lord, without license, his lands were adjudged as forfeit to the king[2]. It would seem however that the mere neglect to cultivate or inhabit the land involved its confiscation to the king's hand[3], which may have been confined to folcland.

FINES.—It is hardly necessary to enter into any

quibus nichilominus ipse se dedidit in tantum, ut floccipenderet quin offensione multimoda me multoties graviter offenderet; nam praefectum meum Æficum, quem primatem inter primates meos taxavi, non cunctatus in propria domo eius eo inscio perimere, quod nefarium et peregrinum opus est apud christianos et gentiles. Peracto itaque scelere ab eo, inii consilium cum sapientibus regni mei petens, ut quid fieri placuisset de illo decernerent; placuitque in commune nobis eum exulare et extorrem a nobis fieri cum complicibus suis: statuimus etiam inviolatum foedus inter nos, quod qui praesumpsisset infringere, exhaereditari se sciret omnibus habitis, hoc est, ut nemo nostrum aliquid humanitatis vel commoditatis ei sumministraret. Hanc optionis electionem posthabitam nichili habuit soror eius Æðelflæd omnia quae possibilitatis eius erant, et utilitatis fratris omnibus exercitiis studuit explere, et hac de causa aliarumque quamplurimarum exhaeredem se fecit omnibus." Cod. Dipl. No. 719.

The murder of Æfic is mentioned in the Chronicle, an. 1002, where he is called heáhgeréfa.

[1] Cod. Dipl. No. 1035. But not if he had legal heirs. See Cnut, ii. § 71. Thorpe, i. 412. In this case the king could claim only the Heriot, a custom retained even by the Normans. "Item si liber homo intestatus decesserit, et subito, dominus suus nihil se intromittet de bonis suis, nisi tantum de hoc quod ad ipsum pertinuerit, scilicet quod habeat suum Heriettum." Fleta, ii. cap. 57, § 10.

[2] Cod. Dipl. No. 1078.

[3] Hist. Eliens. i. 1. "Sicque postea per destitutionem, regiae sorti, sive fisco, idem locus additus est." See also vol. i. p. 302, note 2.

great detail respecting the fines which were imposed for various offences against the state, and which were levied by the public officers to the king's use. The laws abound with examples: it may in general be concluded that the proceeds were nearly absorbed by the cost of collection, and that little remained to the king when the portions of the ealdorman and geréfa had been deducted. But still these fines require a particular notice, because they are especially enumerated by Cnut among the rights of his crown. He says:—"These are the rights which the king enjoys over all men in Wessex: that is, Mundbryce, and Hámsócne, Foresteal, Flýmena fyrmð, and Fyrdwíte, unless he will more amply honour any one, and concede to him this worship[1]." In Mercia, he declares himself entitled to the same rights[2], and also by the Danish law, that is in Northumberland and Eastanglia,—with the addition of Fihtwíte, and the fine for harbouring persons out of the Frið or public peace[3]. These evidently belong to him in his character of conservator of that peace: Mundbryce is breach of his own protection: Hámsócn is an aggravated assault upon a private dwelling: Foresteal here, the maintenance of criminals and interference to prevent the course of justice: Flýmena fyrmð, the comforting and supporting of outlaws or fugitives: Fyrdwíte, the penalty for neglecting to attend, or for deserting, the armed levy when

[1] Cnut, ii. § 12. Thorpe, i. 382. [2] Cnut, ii § 14. Thorpe, i. 384.
[3] Cnut, ii. § 15. Thorpe, i. 384.

duly proclaimed : Fihtwíte is the penalty. for making private war. These regalia he could grant to a subject if such were his pleasure. But they are far from exhausting the catalogue of his rights : he possessed many others, which were either honourable or profitable, and were by him alienated in favour of his lay or clerical favourites.

TREASURE TROVE.—The first of these is Treasure-trove, which was, in all probability, of considerable importance and value : it is designated in Anglosaxon charters by the words "ealle hordas búfan eorðan and binnan eorðan," and frequently occurs in the grants to monastic houses. In very early and heathen periods various causes combined to render the burial of treasure common. It was a point of honour to carry as much wealth with one from this world to the next as possible ; and it was a recognized duty of the comites and household of a chief to sacrifice at his funeral, whatever valuable chattels they might have gained in his service. We may infer from Beówulf[1] that a portion at least of the treasure he gained by his fatal combat with the firedrake was to accompany him in the tomb. Some of it was to be burnt with his body, but some, according to the practice of the pagan North, to be buried in the mound raised over his ashes[2].

Hí on beorg dydon	They put into the mound
beág ꝥ beorht siglu,	rings and bright gems,
. . . .	. . . .
forléton eorla gestreón	they let earth hold

[1] Beow. l. 6016 *seq.* : compare l. 5583 *seq.*　　　[2] Ibid. l. 6320.

eorðan healdan,	the gains of noble men,
gold on greóte,	gold in the dust,
ðǽr hit nú gen lífað	where it doth yet remain
eldum swá unnýt	useless to men
swá hit ǽror wæs.	even as before it was[1].

When we consider the truly extraordinary number of mounds or *heathen burial-places* which are mentioned in the boundaries of Saxon charters, we cannot doubt that large quantities of the precious metals were thus committed to the earth. To this superstitious cause others of a more practical nature were added. In all countries where from want of commerce and convenient internal communication, or from general insecurity, there is no profitable investment for capital, hoarding is largely resorted to by those who may chance to become possessed of articles of value : we need go no further than Ireland or France for an example, where one of the most striking signs of the prevalent barbarism, is the concealment of specie and plate, often underground[2]. And in cases of sudden invasion, especially by enemies who had not the habit of sparing religious houses, the earth may have been resorted to as the safest depository of treasure

[1] See the account of the burial of Haraldr Hilditavn in the Fornald. Savg. i. 387. " Ok áðr enn havgrinn væri aptr lokinn, þá biðr Hríngr Konúngr til gánga allt stórmenni ok alla Kappa, ok við voru staddir, at kasta í havginn stórum hríngum ok góðum vápnum, til sæmdr Haraldi Konúngi Hilditavn ; ok eptir þat var aptr byrgði havgrinn vandliga." Brynhildr caused the jewels which her father Buðli had given her, to be burnt with herself and Sigurðr. Sigurd. evid. iii. 65.

[2] In Ireland this is so common as to have caused the existence of what we may call a professional class of treasure-seekers, whose idle, gambling pursuit is in admirable harmony with the Keltic hatred for honest, steady labour.

which it was impossible to transport[1]. William of
Malmesbury attributes to the fears of the Britons
the accumulations which he says were frequently
discovered in his own day[2], and there can be little
doubt that this even among the Saxons tended to
increase the quantity of gold and silver withdrawn
from general use. It may have been partly the conviction of the mischief resulting to society from
this habit,—by which gold was made "eldum swá
unnýt swá hit æror wæs,"—that caused the very
frequent and strong expression of blame which we
find in Anglosaxon works applied to those who
bury treasure, and apparently also to treasure-
hunters. It may be that it was thought impious
to violate even the heathen sanctuary of the dead ;
at all events, the popular belief was encouraged
that buried treasure was guarded by spells, watched
by dragons[3], and loaded with a curse which would
cleave for ever to the discoverer : hidden gold is in

---

[1] To this cause may be attributed the hoards discovered within a few
years at Cuerdale, Hexham, and other places on the borders ; and some
perhaps of the numerous *finds* at Wisby and in Gothland.

[2] "Partim sepultis thesauris, quorum plerique in hac aetate defodiuntur, Romam ad petendas suppetias ire intendunt." Gest. Reg. i. § 3.
It is well worth the consideration of our antiquarians who have devoted
pains and money to the opening of barrows, how far the notorious
searches which have been made for treasure in these repositories, by
successive generations of Saxons, Danes and Normans, may have interfered with the *original* disposition of sepulchral mounds, cairns and
cromlechs. The legend of Gúðlác supplies a Saxon instance of the
highest antiquity. "Wæs ð ér on ðám ealande sum hláw mycel ofer
eorðan geworht, ðone ylcan men iúgeara for feos wilnunga gedulfon
and brǽcon : ðá was ðǽr on óðre sídan ðæs hláwes gedolfen swylíc
mycel wæterseáð wǽre." Cap. 4. Godw. Ed. p. 26.

[3] Beów. l. 6100. In the North it is difficult to find a hoard without
a dragon, or a dragon without a hoard.

fact always represented as *heathen* gold, which, we may readily suppose, could only be purified from its mischievous qualities by passing through the hands of the universal purifiers in such cases, the clergy. Strictly however the king was the proper owner of all treasure-trove, and where the lord of a manor obtained the right to appropriate it to himself, it could only be by grant from the representative of the whole state[1]. Probably the sovereigns were not quite so superstitious as the bulk of their subjects, and certainly they were much better able to defend their own rights than the simple landowners in the rural districts. Still in a very great number of cases they granted away their privilege; probably finding it easier and more profitable to give it up to those who would have used it, without a grant, than to undergo the trouble of detecting and punishing them for taking it unpermitted into their own hands.

PASTUS or CONVIVIUM, *Cyninges feorm.*— One of the royal duties was to make, in person or by deputy, periodical journeys through the country, progresses, in the course of which the king visited different districts, proclaimed his peace, confirmed

---

[1] Concealment of treasure-trove is a grave offence, inasmuch as it immediately touches the person and dignity of the king: "De inventoribus thesauri occultati inventi, haec quidem graviora sunt et maiora, eo quod personam regis tangunt principaliter. Sunt etiam crimina aliquantulum minora......sicut haec; de homicidiis causalibus et voluntariis," *seq.* Fleta, lib. 1. cap. 20. § 1, 2, 3 *seq.*, where this offence is assimilated to high-treason, and classed above all offences against individuals, including murder, rape, arson and burglary.

the rights and privileges of the freemen or free communities, and heard complaints against the officers of the executive, if such had arisen during the exercise of their functions. This, which on its first occurrence immediately after his election was known in Germany by the name of the *Einritt ins land*, or *Landbereisung*[1], was probably connected with the principle of the king's being the proper guardian of the boundaries : and in the period when the people had lost the power of electing their king at a general meeting, it may have served the purpose of giving them an opportunity of becoming acquainted with the person of their ruler. It is difficult to say when the system of progresses entirely ceased ; but there can be no doubt that it subsisted in one form or another till a very late period in England. Under the Anglosaxon law it was by no means a matter of amusement or caprice, but of positive duty, on the part of the king ; and Royalty *in eyre* was a necessary condition of a state of society which would have rejected as a ludicrous tyranny the pretension of any one city to be the central deposit of all the powers and machinery of government. The kings of the Merwingian race in France, who probably retained something of an old priestly character, made these circuits in the celebrated chariot drawn by oxen, which later and ill-informed writers have imagined was a sign of their degradation, instead of their dignity[2]. Of this particular part of the ceremony no trace re-

---

[1] For a full account of this see Grimm, Rechtsalt. p. 237.
[2] See Grimm, Rechtsalt. p. 262.

mains in England, and it is probable that as occasion served, the king either rode on horseback, circumnavigated, or was towed or rowed along the navigable rivers[1]. On these occasions particularly, he had a right to claim harbour and refection for himself and a certain number of his suite in various places, principally religious houses. These claims, which answer in many respects to the *procuratio* of the ecclesiastical law, were gradually extended so as to include the royal commissioners or *Missi*, and in many cases became a fixed charge upon the lands, whether the king actually visited them or not[2].

[1] I have little doubt that, when Beda speaks of the pomp with which Eádwini of Northumberland was accustomed to ride, he refers to this ceremony. Hist. Eccl. ii. 16. The well-known tales of Eádgár, rowed by six kings on the Dee, and Cnut at Ely, will at once occur to the reader : but has it never occurred to him to ask what Eádgár could possibly be doing at the one place, or Cnut at the other? See Will. Malm. Gest. Reg. ii. § 148. The same author tells us of Eádgár: " Omni aestate, emensa statim Paschali festivitate, naves per omnia littora coadunari praecipiebat; ad occidentalem insulae partem cum orientali classe, et illa remensa cum occidentali ad borealem, inde cum boreali ad orientalem remigare consuetus ; pius scilicet explorator, ne quid piratae turbarent. Hyeme et vere, per omnes provincias equitando, iudicia potentiorum exquirebat, violati iuris severus ultor ; in hoc iustitiae, in illo fortitudini studens ; in utroque reipublicae utilitatibus consulens." Gest. Reg. ii. § 156. Flor. Wig. an. 975. "Cum *more assueto* rex Cnuto regni fines peragrarat." Hist. Rames. Eccl. (Gale, iii. 441.)

[2] Cod. Dipl. No. 143. "Necnon et trium annorum ad se pertinentes pastiones, id est sex convivia, libenter concedendo largitus est." Probably they were in arrear, and Offa excused them : but they could not have been in arrear unless they were payable any under circumstances ; that is, whether the king visited the monastery or not. I take this to be a standing tax, known under the name of Cyninges feorm, the king's farm : it was probably commuted for money, and after a time rendered certain as to amount. In 814 Cénwulf released the Bishop of Worcester from a *pastus* of twelve men which he was bound to find at his different monasteries, and the exemption was worth an estate of thirteen hides. Cod. Dipl. No. 203.

Very many of the charters granted to monasteries record the exemption from them, purchased at a heavy price by prelates, from his avarice or piety[1]. And as the king himself gradually ceased to undertake these distant and fatiguing expeditions, and entrusted to his special messengers the task of seeing and hearing for him, so they in time established a claim to harbourage and reception in the same places. This was extended to all public officers going on the king's affairs, called Angelcynnes men, Fæsting men, Ræde fasting, and the like: to all messengers dispatched on the public service from one kingdom to another, while there were several kingdoms; and very probably to those who carried communications from the ealdormen to the king, when one rule comprehended all the several districts. And not only for those who travelled on important affairs of state, and who were very often persons of high birth and distinguished station, but even for certain servants of the royal household were these claims enforced. The huntsmen, stable-keepers and falconers of the court could demand bed and board in the monasteries, where they were often unwelcome guests enough: and this royal right, no doubt frequently used by the ealdorman or sheriff as an engine of oppression, was also bought off at very high prices.

PALFREYS.—Somewhat allied to this was the

---

[1] See Vol. I. p. 294, *seq.* Examples may be found in almost every other page of the Codex Diplomaticus. See also Hist. Rames. Eccl. 85.

king's right to claim the service of horses or palfreys, for the carriage of effects from one royal vill to another, or for the furtherance of his messengers or the public servants[1]. This, which in Hungary still subsists under the name of Vorspann, was a heavy burthen, as it tended to withdraw horses from agricultural labour, at the moment when they were most wanted; and it is to be feared that they were, on this pretext, only too often taken from the harvesting of the bishop or abbot and his tenants, to secure that of the ealdorman. This therefore is frequently compounded for, at a dear rate, under the expression of freedom a parafrithis or paraveredis[2].

---

[1] "Faciebant servitium regis cum equis vel per aquam usque ad Blidbeream, Reddinges, Sudtone, Besentone : et hoc facientibus dabat praepositus mercedem non de censu regis, sed de suo." Domesd. Berks. Many of these burthens are summed up in a charter of liberties granted by Eádweard of Wessex at Taunton, to Winchester: "Erat namque antea in illo supradicto monasterio pastus unius noctis regi, et octo canum, et unius caniculari pastus, et pastus novem noctium accipitrariis regis, et quidquid rex vellet inde ducere. usque ad Curig vel Willettun [Curry and Wilton in Somerset] cum plaustris et equis, et si advenae de aliis regionibus advenirent, debebant ducatum habere ad aliam regalem villam quae proxima fuisset in illorum via." Cod. Dipl. No. 1084. The Vorspann in Hungary, which is a right to a peasant's horses on the production of an order from the county authorities, is generally a convenience to himself as well as the traveller, who does not object to pay for much better accommodation than he could obtain from the ordinary posting establishment. But it is nevertheless a remnant of barbarism which we may now hope to see vanish, together with every other obstacle o free communication, under the management of that most patriotic and enlightened gentleman Count Stephen Szechenji.

[2] On the complaint of the clergy of the diocese of Cremona, the emperor Lothaire decided that they were not bound to supply waggons and horses for his service. Böhm. Reg. Karol. No. 544.

VIGILIA. — Another right which the king
claimed was that of having proper watch set over
him when he came into a district. This, called
Vigilia and Custodia in the Latin authorities, is
the Heáfodweard, or *Headward* of the Saxons. It
extended also to the guard kept for him on his
hunting excursions[1]; and coupled with it was his
claim to the assistance of a certain number of men
in the hunt itself, either as beaters or managers of
the nets in which deer were taken[2].

Sǽweard or coast-guard was also a royal right,
performed by the tenants of those landowners whose
estates lay contiguous to the sea. The miserable
condition to which England was frequently reduced,
by the systematic incursions of Scandinavian invaders, rendered this a very important duty, even
in spite of the efforts of successive kings who early
comprehended the destinies of this nation, and
entrusted her defence to maritime armaments. It
seems probable that various ports on the coast
of Kent and Norfolk may have been particularly
charged with this burthen, and that the *butsecarlas*
or shipmasters were held bound to supply craft on
emergencies, or even for a regular system of

---

[1] "Homines de his terris custodiebant regem apud Cantuariam vel
apud Sandwic per tres dies, si rex illuc venisset." Domesd. Kent.
"Quando rex iácebat in hac civitate, servabant eum vigilantes duodecim homines de melioribus civitatis. Et cum ibi venationem exerceret,
similiter custodiebant eum cum armis meliores burgenses cabalos habentes." Domesd. Shropsh. "Isti debent vigilare in curia domini,
cum praesens fuerit." Chartul. Evesh. f. 24.

[2] "Qui monitus ad stabilitionem venationis non ibat quinquaginta
solidos regi emendabat." Domesd. Berks.

patrolling. In this may have lain the foundation of the privileges enjoyed by the Cinque Ports, and similar coast towns, even before the Norman conquest.

ÆDIFICATIO.—It was further a royal right to claim the aid even of the freemen towards building and fencing the residence or fortress of the king: a certain amount of personal labour was thus demanded of them, in analogy with the *trinoda necessitas* from which no estate could possibly be relieved. This kind of *corvée* was no doubt performed by tenants whom the landowners settled on their estates, but really was due from the landowners themselves, except where their estates of bócland had been expressly freed from the royal burthens. Where the royal vill was also a district fortification, not even this general exception relieved the bóclands; fortifications being especially reserved in every charter, as well as building and repair of bridges.

WRECK.—Doubts have been started upon the subject of wreck, which do not appear well founded: it is true that circumstances of suspicion attach to the documents upon which the arguments pro and con were based in the time of Selden; but we are now in possession of further evidence, of a nature to remove all difficulty. I have no hesitation in including Wreck, both jetsam and flotsam, among the Regalia, which were granted not only to ecclesiastical corporations, but even to private land-

owners. The History of Ramsey[1] states that Eádweard the Confessor, whereby he might show a profitable love to the place, bestowed upon it Ring-
stede[2] with the adjacent liberty, and all that the
sea cast up, which is called *Wreck*. We have yet
the charter by which this grant is supposed to
have been made[3], and it is very explicit upon the
subject. After conveying lands and other possessions in Huntingdonshire, he proceeds to give several places, tenements or rents, on the coast of Norfolk and the Wash, at Wells, and Branchester, etc.
In the last-named place, he adds, " cum omni
maris proiectu, quod nos anglicè shipwrec appellamus." He further adds, " de meo iure quod mihi
soli competebat, absque ullius reclamatione vel contradictione ista addidi : inprimis Ringested, cum
omnibus ad se pertinentibus, et cum omni maris
eiectu, quod shipwrec appellamus," etc. Now, although the authenticity of this charter, in its present form may be open to question, this fact does
not of itself justify us in at once concluding against
the privilege claimed under it. On the other hand
the recognized right of the king throughout the
Norman times, and the total absence of any opposition to its exercise, are *primâ facie* evidence of its
having resided in the crown before the Conquest[4].

[1] Hist. Rams. 106.

[2] There are two places of this name on the coast of the Wash near
Burnham Market in Norfolk. The one intended is most probably
Ringstead St. Andrew's.   [3] Cod. Dipl. No. 809.

[4] See Bracton, ii. 5. § 7. Westm. i. cap. 4. Stat. Praerog. Reg.
cap. 11. Also 17. Edw. II. cap. 11. Rot. Chart. 20. Hen. III. m. 3.
and 14. Edw. III. m. 6. Pat. 42. Hen. III. m. 1. dorso. See also
Sir W. Stamford, Expos. King's Prerog. fol 37, b.

Naufragium and Algarum maris are distinctly stated to be rights of the crown, in the laws of Henry the First[1], and we can give examples from other Saxon charters whose genuineness is beyond dispute. The Saxon Chronicle under the date 1029 records a grant made by Cnut to Christchurch, Canterbury, of the haven of Sandwich. The passage is defective, but enough of it remains to prove that it refers to an original document, of which very early copies are still in our possession[2]. In this he says:—

" Concedo eidem aecclesiae ad victum monachorum portum de Sanduuíc et omnes exitus eiusdem aquae, ab utraque parte fluminis cuiuscumque terra sit, a Pipernæsse usque ad Mearcesfleóte, ita ut natante nave in flumine, cum plenum fuerit, quam longius de navi potest securis parvula quam Angli vocant *Tapereax* super terram proici, ministri aecclesiae Christi rectitudines accipiant, ... Si quid autem in magno mari extra portum, quantum mare plus se retraxerit, et adhuc statura unius hominis tenentis lignum quod Angli nominant *spreot*, et tendentis ante se quantum potest, monachorum est. Quicquid etiam ex hac parte medietatis maris inventum et delatum ad Sanduuíc fuerit, sive sit vestimentum, sive rete, arma, ferrum, aurum, argentum, medietas monachorum erit, alia pars remanebit inventoribus."

These words are quite wide enough to carry *wreck*, although this be not distinctly stated by name. But Eádweard the Confessor furnishes us

[1] Leg. Hen. I. 10. § 1. Ducange reads *laganum* for *algarum*.
[2] Cod. Dipl. No. 737, where it is printed both in Latin and Saxon.

with still further evidence. In a writ addressed by him to Ælfwold bishop of Sherborne, earl Harold, and Ælfred the sheriff of Dorsetshire, he says[1] : "Eádweard the king greets well Bishop Ælfwold, earl Harold, Ælfred the sheriff and all my thanes in Dorsetshire : and I tell you that Urk my hús-carl is to have his strand, over against his own land, freely and well throughout, up from sea, and out on sea, and whatsoever may be driven to his strand, by my full command."

In this, as in many other cases, the principle seems to be, that that which has no ostensible owner is the property of the state, or of the king as its representative; and hence, in the later construction of the law of *wreck*, it was necessary that an absolute abandonment should have taken place, before wreck could be claimed. If there were *life* on board, even a dog, cat, or lower animal, there could legally be no wreck, and this provision of the law has very often led to the perpetration of the most savage murders, as a precaution lest any living creature, by reaching the strand, should defeat the avarice of its barbarous owners. From the little evidence we can now recover, of the Saxon practice, this limitation does not appear to have existed.

MINT.—The coinage has always in every country been numbered among the regalia, and this land appears to make no exception. Although the

---

[1] Cod. Dipl. No. 871.

Witena gemót, in conjunction with the king, exercise a general superintendence over this most important branch of the public affairs, still certain details remain which belong to the king exclusively. The number of moneyers generally in the various localities, the necessity of having one standard over all the realm, the penalties for unfaithful discharge of the moneyer's duty, or for fraudulently imitating the money of the state, and similar enactments, might be determined by the great council of the realm; but the coin bore the image and superscription of the king, he received a description of *seigneuriage* upon delivery of the dies, and he changed the coin when it seemed to require renovation or improvement. Thus we learn that Eádgár called in the old, and issued a new coinage, in the year 975, because it had become so clipped as to fall far short of the standard weight [1]: and in the Domesday record, the dues payable to the king on each change of die are noticed [2]. It seems clear that this royal right had been assumed by private individuals, or granted to them, like other royalties, previous to the time of Æ𝜕elræd: that prince enacted not only that there

---

[1] Matt. Westm. an. 975.

[2] "Ibi erant duo monetarii ; quisque eorum reddebat regi unam marcam argenti, et viginti solidos, quando moneta vertebatur." Domesd. Dorset. "Septem monetarii erant ibi ; unus ex his erat monetarius episcopi. Quando moneta vertebatur, dabat quisque eorum octodecim solidos pro cuneis recipiendis, et ex eo die quo redibant usque ad unum mensem, dabat quisque eorum regi viginti solidos, et similiter habebat episcopus de suo monetario. In civitate Wirecestre habuit rex Edwardus hanc consuetudinem. Quando moneta vertebatur, quisque monetarius dabat xx solidos ad Londoniam, pro cuneis monetae accipiendis." Domesd. Worcester. See also Domesd. Hereford.

should be no moneyers beside the kings, but also that their number should be altogether diminished[1]; by which we may suppose that it was his intention to do away with the mints which the bishops had before possessed legally[2] in various towns, and which from the passages cited out of Domesday book, evidently continued to subsist, in spite of the provisions of the Council of Wantage. But if the coins themselves are to be trusted, we may conclude that on some occasions this right had been granted by the crown to others than the clergy. One piece still bears the name and head of Cyne-ðryð, probably Offa's queen[3]; and another with the impress of Hereberht, was probably coined by a Kentish duke. Both these cases, which are in themselves doubtful, are a hundred years earlier than Æðelræd's law, above quoted.

MINES.—Mines and minerals are also among the regalia of a German king, and were so in England. The cases which principally come under our observation in the charters are salt-works and lead-mines; but in a document of the year 689, which however is not totally free from suspicion, Osuuini of Kent grants to Rochester a ploughland at Lyminge in Kent, in which he says there is a mine

[1] Æðelr. iii. § 8; iv. § 9. Thorpe, i. 296, 303.
[2] Æðelst. i. § 14. Thorpe, i. 206.
[3] Or perhaps his relative, the abbess of Bedford, for it is difficult to conceive how during coverture, the queen could have coined, and proof is wanting that she was ever regent of his kingdom.

of iron [1]. In 716, Æðelbald of Mercia granted certain salt-works near the river Salwarpe at Lootwíc in Worcestershire, in exchange however for others to the north of the river [2]. In the same year he granted a híd of land in Saltwych, *vico emptorio salis*, to Evesham [3]. In 732, Æðelberht of Kent gave abbot Dun a quarter of a ploughland at Lyminge, where there were salt-works, that is evaporating pans [4], and added to it a grant of a hundred loads of wood per annum, necessary to the operation. In 738 Eádberht of Kent includes salt-works in a grant to Rochester [5], and similarly in 812, 814, Coenuulf, in grants to Canterbury [6]. In 833 Ecgberht gave salt-works in Kent, and a hundred and twenty loads of wood from the weald of Andred, to support the fires [7]. Three years later Wigláf of Mercia confirmed the liberties of Hanbury in Worcestershire, with all its possessions, including salt-wells and lead-works [8]. In 863, Æðel-

---

[1] Cod. Dipl. No. 30. So likewise I imagine the ísengráfas (eisengruben) of Cod. Dipl. No. 1118 to be iron-mines.

[2] Cod. Dipl. No. 67. "Aliquam agelli partem in qua sal confici solet .... ad construendos tres casulos et sex caminos.... sex alios.... caminos in duobus casulis, in quibus similiter sal conficitur, vicarios accipiens."

[3] Cod. Dipl. No. 68.

[4] Cod Dipl. No. 77. "Quarta pars aratri....sali coquendo accommoda....Et insuper addidi huic donationi....in omni anno centum plaustra onusta de lignis ad coquendum sal."

[5] Cod. Dipl. No. 85.   [6] Cod. Dipl. Nos. 199, 201.

[7] Cod. Dipl. No. 234. "Et in eodem loco sali coquenda iuxta Limenae, et in silva ubi dicitur Andred, centum viginti plaustra ad coquendum sal."

[8] Cod. Dipl. No. 237. "Cum putheis salis et fornacibus plumbis."

berht granted salt-works in Kent to Æðelred, with
four waggons going for six weeks into the royal
forest [1].   In 938, Æðelstán gave to Taunton three
híds of land, and salt-pans [2].

The king in all these cases had possessed a right
to levy certain dues at the pans or the pit's mouth,
upon the waggons as they stood, and upon the load
being placed in them : these dues were respectively
called the wænscilling and seámpending, literally
wainshilling and *loadpenny*, and were entirely independent of the rent which might be reserved by
the landlord for the use of the ground, whether he
were the king or a private person.   And immunity
from these dues might also be granted by the crown,
and was so granted.   In 884, Æðelred, duke of
Mercia, who acted as a viceroy in that new portion
of Ælfred's kingdom, and exercised therein all the
royal rights as fully as any king did in his own
territories, gave Æðelwulf five híds at Humble-
ton, and licence to have six salt-pans, free from all
the dues of king, duke or public officer, but still
reserving the rights of the landlord [3].   But the

----

[1] Cod. Dipl. No. 288.   "Unamque salis coquinariam, hoc est án
sealternsteall, and ðer cota to, in illa loco ubi nominatur Herewíc, et
quatuor carris transductionem in silba regis sex ebdomades a die Pentecosten hubi alteri homines silbam cedunt, hoc est in regis commu-
nione."

[2] Cod. Dipl. Nos. 374. (cf. 1002).   "Et tres [mansas] in loco qui Cearn
nuncupatur ad coquendam salis copiam."   In 854, Æðelwulf mentions
salinaria in a grant to the same place.   Cod. Dipl. No. 1051.

[3] Cod. Dipl. No. 1066.   "Ego Æðelred, divina largiente gratia
principatu et dominio gentis Merciorum subfultus, donatione trado
Æðelwulfo terram quinque manentium in loco qui dicitur Hy-
meltun . . . . . salisque cóctionibus, id est, sex vascula possint praepa-

same prince, about the same period, when confer-
ring various royalties upon the cathedral of Worcester, retained the king's dues at the pans in Saltwíc [1].

The peculiar qualities of salt, which make it a
necessary of life to man, have always given a special
character to the springs and soils which contain
it. The pagan Germans considered the salt-springs
holy, and waged wars of extermination for their
possession [2]; and it is not improbable that they may
generally have belonged to the exclusive property
of the priesthood. If so, we can readily understand
how, upon the introduction of Christianity, they
would naturally pass into the hands of the king:
and this seems to throw light upon the origin of
this royalty, which Eichhorn himself looks upon
as difficult of explanation [3]. Many of the royal
rights were unquestionably inherited from the pagan priesthood.

rari salva libertate, sine aliquo tributo dominatoris gentis praedictae,
sive ducum, iudicumve et praesidum, id est statione sive inonera-
tione plaustrorum, nisi solo illi qui huic praedictae terrae Hymeltune
dominus existat......ut haec traditio, sive in terra praedicta, sive in
vico salis, absque omni censu atque tributo perpetualiter libera permaneat."
    [1] Cod. Dipl. No. 1075. "Bútan ðæt se wægnscilling and se seám-
pending gonge tó ðæs cyninges handa, swá he ealning dyde æt Saltwíc:"
except that the wainshilling and loadpenny ("statio et inoneratio
plaustrorum") shall go to the king's hand, as they always did, at
Saltwíc.
    [2] Tacit. Ann. xiii. 57. "Eadem aestate inter Hermunduros Cattosque
certatum magno praelio, dum flumen gignendo sale fecundum et con-
terminum vi trahunt, super libidinem cuncta armis agendi religione
insita, eos maxime locos propinquare coelo, precesque mortalium a deis
nusquam propius audiri."
    [3] Deut. Staatsr. ii. 426. § 297.

MARKET.—The grant of a market, with power to levy tolls and exercise the police therein, was also a royalty, in the period of the consolidated monarchy; and to this head may be added the right to keep a private beam or steelyard, *trutina* or *tróne*, yard-measure, and bushel. Of these the charters supply examples. The last-named rights were purchased in 857 by bishop Alhhun of Worcester, from Burgred, who, as king of Mercia, disposed of them to him, with a small plot of land in London. The price paid was sixty shillings, or a pound, to Ceólmund, the owner of the land, a like sum to the king, and an annual rent of twelve shillings to the latter[1]. Thirty-two years later, Ælfred and Æ∂elred of Mercia gave another small plot in the same city to Werfri∂, also bishop of Worcester. He was to have a steelyard, and a measure, both for buying and selling, or for his own private use. And if any of his people dealt in the street or on the bank where the sales took place, the king was to have his toll: but if the bargain was struck within the bishop's *curtis*, he was to have the toll[2].

In 904 Eádweard gave a market in Taunton to the bishop of Winchester, with the toll therefrom

---

[1] Cod. Dipl. No. 280. "Habeat intus liberaliter modium et pondera et mensura[m], sicut in porto mos est ad fruendum."

[2] Cod. Dipl. No. 316. " Et intro urnam et trutinam ad mensurandum in emendo sive vendendo ad usum, sive ad necessitatem propriam et liberam omnimodis habeat. . . . Si autem foris vel in strata publica seu in ripa emptorali quislibet suorum mercaverit, iuxta quod rectum sit, thelonium ad manum regis subeat: quod si intus in curte praedicta quislibet emerit vel vendiderit, thelonium debitum ad manum episcopi supramemorati reddatur."

arising, by the name of " ᚦæs túnes cýping "[1]: and
a few years earlier Æðelred of Mercia granted half
the market-dues and fines at Worcester to the
bishop of that city[2]. The Frankish emperors possessed and exercised the same right[3]. The strict
law of the Anglosaxons, which treated all strangers
with harshness, was unfavourable to the chapmen
or pedlars, who in thinly-peopled countries are
relied upon to bring markets home to every one's
door: and it must be admitted that, where internal
communication is yet imperfect, stringent measures
are necessary to guard against the disposal of goods
improperly obtained. The details of these measures
belong to another part of this work, but it is necessary to call attention here to the endeavour on
the part of the authorities, to confine all bargaining
as much as possible to towns and walled places[4]:
the small tolls payable on these occasions to the
proper officers were a reasonable sacrifice for the
sake of a certificate of fair dealing, and the assured warranty of what the Saxon law calls *unlying*
witnesses. The king, as general conservator of
the peace, had this royalty, and, as we have seen,
granted it in various towns to those who would

[1] Cod. Dipl. No. 1084. "Praedictae etiam villae mercimonium,
quod anglicè ᚦæs túnes cýping appellatur, censusque omnus civilis
sanctae dei aecclesiae in Wintonia civitate, sine retractionis obstaculo
cum omnibus commodis aeternaliter deserviat."

[2] Cod. Dipl. No. 1075.

[3] See Böhmer, Regest. Karol. Nos. 439, 628, 700, 2065, 2078.

[4] Eádw. § 1. Æðelst. i. § 10, 12, 13; iii. § 2; v. § 10. Eádm. i.
§ 5. Eádg. Sup. § 6. Æðelb. i. § 3. Cnut, ii. § 24. Eádw. Conf.
§ 38. Wil. Conq. i. § 45; iii. § 10, 11.

be able and willing to perform the duties which it
implied.

TOLL.—Closely connected with this are tolls,
which, here as well as in Germany, the king claimed in harbours, and upon transport by roads and
by navigable streams[1], and which he either remitted
altogether in favour of certain favoured persons or
empowered them to take ; thus, in the first instance,
creating for them a commercial monopoly of the
greatest value, by enabling them to enter the market on terms of advantage. As early as the eighth
century we find Æðelbald of Mercia granting to a
monastery in Thanet, exemption from toll throughout his kingdom for one ship of burthen[2], remitting
to Milræd, bishop of Worcester, the dues upon two
ships, payable in the port of London[3], and to the
bishop of Rochester the toll of one ship, whether
his own or another's, in the same port[4]. And the

---

[1] See Böhmer, Regest. Karol. Nos. 7, 14, 28, 31, 67, 71, 83, 89, 97,
111, 163, 206, 217, 220, 227, 231, 240, 252, 260, 272, 283, 288, 304,
308, 398, 415, 461, 463, 559, 561, 564, 566, 586, 592, 593, 605, 652,
693, 739, 787, 837, 885, 1528, 2067, 2073. These charters contain
full particulars relative to the levy, release and grant of tolls in the
Frankish empire.

[2] Cod. Dipl. No. 84. "Navis onustae transvectionis censum qui a
theloneariis nostris tributaria exactione impetitur, perdonans attribuo ;
ut ubique in regno nostro libera de omni regali fiscu et tributo maneat."

[3] Cod. Dipl. No. 95. "Ða forgeofende ic him álýfde alle nédbade
twégra sceopa ða ðe ðǽr ábædde beoð fram ðám nédbaderum in Lun-
dentúnes hýðe ; ond næfre ic né míne lastweardas né ða nédbaderas
geþristlæcen ðæt heó hit onwenden oððe ðon wiðgǽn." See similar
exemptions in Cod. Dipl. Nos. 97, 98, 112.

[4] Cod. Dipl. No. 78. "Indico me dedisse. . . . unius navis, sive illa
propria ipsius, sive cuiuslibet alterius hominis sit, incessum, id est
vectigal, mihi et antecessoribus meis iure regio in portu Lundoniae

grant to St. Mild☥ry☥ in Thanet was confirmed for himself, and increased by Eádberht of Kent in 761, and extended to London, Fordwíc and Seorre [1]; and if the actual ship to which this privilege was attached should become unseaworthy through age, or perish by shipwreck, a new one was to receive the same favour.

A common privilege in charters of liberties is Tol, but this probably refers rather to a right of taking it upon sales within the jurisdiction, than properly to dues levied on transport. Such however are occasionally mentioned as matter of grant. Eádmund Irensída, conveying lands which had belonged to Sigefer☥ (whose widow he had married), includes toll upon water-carriage among his rights [2]. Cnut gave the harbour and tolls of Sandwich to Christchurch Canterbury [3], together with a ferry. This right, under Harald Haranfót, was attempted to be interfered with by the abbot of St. Augustine's, who even at last went so far as to dig a canal in order to divert the channel of trade; but the monks of Christchurch nevertheless succeeded in

usque hactenus conpetentem." And this was confirmed a century later by Berhtwulf of Mercia.

[1] Cod. Dipl. No. 106. After mentioning one ship, relieved from toll in London, he continues: "Alterius vero.... omne tributum atque vectigal concedimus, quod etiam a thelonariis nostris iuste impetitur publicis in locis, qui appellantur Forduuíc et Seorre."

[2] Cod. Dipl. No. 726. "Ita habeant sicut Siuerthus habuit in vita, in longitudine et in latitudine, in magnis et in modicis rebus, campis, pascuis, pratis, silvis, theloneum aquarum, piscationem in paludibus."

[3] Cod. Dipl. No. 737. "Eorum est navicula et transfretatio portus, et theloneum omnium navium, cuiuscunque sit et undecumque veniat, quae ad praedictum portum et ad Sanduuíc venerint."

retaining their property [1]. These examples, although
not very numerous, are sufficient to show that the

[1] Cod. Dipl. No. 758. The story is altogether so good, and so well
told, that it may be given here entire.

" This writing witnesseth how Harold the king caused Sandwich to
be ridden about to his own hand : and he kept it for himself well nigh
a twelvemonth, and at any rate fully two herring-seasons, all against
God's will, and against the Saints' who lie at Christchurch, as it turned
out ill enough for him afterwards. And during this time there went
Ælfstán the abbot of St. Augustine's, and got, with his lying flatteries
and his gold and silver, all secretly from Steorra who was the king's
redesman, a right to the third penny of the toll at Sandwich. Now when
archbishop Eádsige and all the brotherhood at Christchurch learnt this,
they took counsel together, that they should send Ælfgár, the monk of
Christchurch, to king Harold. Now the king lay at Oxford very ill,
so that his life was despaired of; and there were with him Lýfing, bishop of Devonshire, and Tancred the monk. Then came the messenger
from Christchurch to the bishop ; and he forth at once to the king,
and with him Ælfgár the monk, Osweard of Harrietsham, and Tancred ; and they told the king that he had deeply sinned against Christ,
in ever daring to take back anything from Christchurch which his predecessors had given : and then they told him about Sandwich, how it
had been ridden about to his hand. There lay the king and turned
quite black in the face at their tale, and swore by God Almighty and
all his saints to boot, that it never was either his rede or his deed, that
Sandwich should be taken from Christchurch. So it was plain enough
that it was other peoples' and not king Harold's contrivance : and to
say the truth, Ælfstán the abbot's counsel was with the men who
counselled it out of Christchurch. Then king Harold sent Ælfgár the
monk back to archbishop Eádsige and all the monks at Christchurch,
and gave them God's greeting and his own, and commanded that they
should have Sandwich, into Christchurch, as fully and wholly as they
had ever had it in any king's day, both in rent, in stream, on strand,
in fines, and in everything which any king had ever most fully possessed before them. Now when abbot Ælfstán heard of this, he came
to archbishop Eádsige and begged his support with the brotherhood,
about the third penny : and away they both went to all the brotherhood and begged the Convent that abbot Ælfstán might be allowed the
third penny of the toll, and he to give the Convent ten pounds. But
they refused it altogether throughout, and said it was no use asking :
and withal archbishop Eádsige backed him much more than he did
the Convent. And when he could not get on in this way, he asked
leave to make a wharf over against Mildðrýð's acre, opposite the

Anglosaxon kings fully possessed the right of levying and granting toll, as well as exemption from
its payment; and they are sufficiently confirmed by
Domesday and the laws of the kings themselves [1].

FOREST.—It may be doubted whether the right
of Forest was at any time carried among the Saxons
to the extent which made it so hateful a means of
oppression under the Norman kings; but there can
be no question that it was one of the royalties. In
every part of Germany the *bannum Forestae* or *Forst-*

ferry (?) to keep, but all the Convent decidedly refused this : and archbishop Eádsige left it all to their own decision.   Then abbot Ælfstán
set to, with a great help, and let dig a great canal at Hyppeles fleót,
hoping that craft would lie there, just as they did at Sandwich : however he got no good by it; for he laboureth in vain who laboureth against
Christ's will.   So the abbot left it in this state, and the Convent took
to their own, in God's witness, and Saint Mary's, and all the Saints'
who rest at Christchurch and Saint Augustine's.   This is all true, believe it who will : abbot Ælfstán never got the third penny at Sandwich in any other way.   God's blessing be with us all now and for ever
more ! Amen."
   [1] The following is the tariff of tolls levied at Billingsgate. Æðelr. iv.
§ 2.   " De telonio dando ad Bylingesgate. Ad Billingesgate, si adve-
nisset una navicula, unus obolus telonei dabatur : si maior et haberet
siglas, unus denarius. Si adveniat ceól vel hulcus, et ibi iaceat, quatuor
denarios ad teloneum.   De navi plena lignorum, unum lignum ad teloneum.   In ebdomada panum telonium tribus diebus, die dominica, et
die Martis et die Jovis.   Qui ad pontem venisset cum uno bato, ubi
piscis inesset, ipse mango unum obolum dabat in telonium, et de una
maiori nave, unum denarium.   Homines de Rotomago, qui veniebant
cum vino vel craspice, dabant rectitudinem sex solidorum de magna
navi, et vicesimum frustum de ipso craspice.   Flandrenses et Ponteien-
ses et Normannia et Francia, monstrabant res suas et extolneabant.
Hogge et Leodium et Nivella, qui per terras ibant, ostensionem dabant
et teloneum.   Et homines Imperatoris, qui veniebant in navibus suis,
bonarum legum digni tenebantur, sicut et nos.   Praeter discarcatam
lanum et dissutum unctum et tres porcos vivos licebat eis emere in
naves suas ; et non licebat eis aliquod foreceápum facere burhmannis ;

bann was so[1], and even to this day is as much an
object of popular dislike in some districts as it ever
was among our forefathers. In countries which depend much upon the immediate produce of the soil
for support, hunting is not a mere amusement to
be purchased or rented by the rich as a luxury, but
a very necessary means of increasing the supply of
food ; and where coal-mines have not been worked,
the forest alone or the turf-heap can furnish the
means of securing warmth, as indispensable a necessary of life as bread or flesh : we have seen moreover that it was essential to the comfort of a Saxon
family to possess a right of masting cattle in the
neighbouring woods.

In the original division of the lands large tracts
of forest may have fallen to the king's share, which
he could dispose of as his private property. Much
of the folcland also may have been covered with
wood, and here and there may have lain sacred
groves not included within the limits of any community[2]. It is not unreasonable to suppose that
all these were gradually brought under the immediate influence and authority of the king; and that
when once the royal power had so far advanced as
to reduce the scír-geréfa to the condition of a crown

et dare telonium suum, et in sancto Natali Domini duos grisengos pan-
nos, et unum brunum, et decem libras piperis, et cirotecas quinque hominum, et duos caballinos tonellos aceto plenos, et totidem in Pascha :
de dosseris cum gallinis, una gallina telonei, et de uno dossero cum
ovis, quinque ova telonei, si veniant ad mercatum. Smeremangestre,
quae mangonant in caseo et butiro, quatuordecim diebus ante Natale
Domini, unum denarium, et septem diebus post Natale, unum alium."

[1] Eichhorn, Deut. Staatsr. i. 813, § 199.

[2] " Lucos et nemora consecrant." Tac. Germ. ix.

officer, the shire-marks or forests would also become subject to the royal *ban*[1]. That very considerable forest rights still continued to subsist in
the hands of the free men, in their communities,
may be admitted, and is evidence of the firm foundation for popular liberty which the old Mark-
organization laid.   But even in these, the possession was not left totally undisturbed, and the public
officers, the king, ealdorman and geréfa appear to
have gradually made various usurpations valid.

Over his private forests the king naturally exercised all the rights of absolute ownership; and as
his *ban* ultimately implies this, at least in theory,
it becomes difficult to distinguish those which he
dealt with as *dominus fundi*, from those in which he
acted *iure regali.* That he reserved the vert and
venison in some of them, and *preserved* with a
strictness worthy of more enlightened ages, is clear
from the severe provisions of Cnut's Constitu-
tiones de Foresta[2]. According to this important
document, the forest law was as follows.   In every
county there were to be four thanes, whose business it was, under the title of Head-foresters, *primarii forestae*, to hold plea of all offences touching the
forest, and having the *ban* or power of punishing
for such offences.   Under them were sixteen lesser
thanes, but gentlemen, whose business it was to

---

[1] As early as 825 we find questions of pasture contested by the
swángeréfa as an officer of the ealdorman. Cod. Dipl. No. 219.   The
scírholt mentioned in this document would seem to have been the
shire-forest or public wood of the county; hence probably a royal ban-
forest, subject to the royal officer, the ealdorman.

[2] See these in Thorpe, i. 426.

look after the vert and venison; and these had nothing to do with the process in the forest court. To each of the sixteen were assigned two yeomen, who were to keep watch at night over the vert and venison, and do the necessary menial services: but they were freemen, and even employment in the forest gave freedom. All the expenses of these officers were defrayed by the king, and he further supplied the outfit of the several classes: to the head-foresters, yearly, two horses, one saddled, a sword, five lances, a spear, a shield and two hundred shillings of silver: to the second class, one horse, one lance, one shield and sixty shillings: to the yeomen, a lance, a cross-bow and fifteen shillings. All these persons were quit and free of all summonses, county-courts, and military dues: but the two secondary classes owed suit and surface to the court of the *primarii* (Swánmót), which held plea and gave judgment in their suits: in those of the *primarii* themselves, the king was sole judge. The court of the Forest was to be held four times a year, and was empowered to administer the triple ordeal, and generally to exercise such a jurisdiction as belonged only to the higher and royal courts. The persons of the head-foresters were guarded by severe penalties; violence offered to them was punished in a free man with loss of liberty, in a serf with loss of the hand; and a second offence entailed the penalty of death.

The offences against the forest-law were various and of very different degrees: the *ferae forestae* were not nearly so sacred as the *ferae regales*, and

as for the *vert*, it was of so little regard that the
law hardly contemplated it, always excepting the
breaking the king's chace.   To hunt a beast of the
forest (*fera forestae*), either voluntarily or inten-
tionally, till it panted, was punished in a free man
by a fine of ten shillings: in one of a lower grade [1],
by a fine of twenty: in a serf, by a flogging.   But
if it were a royal beast (*fera regalis*) which the
English call a stag, the punishments were to be
respectively, one and two years servitude, and for
the serf, outlawry.   If they killed it, the free man
was to lose *scutum libertatis* [2], the next man his liberty, and the serf his life.   Bishops, abbots and
barons were not to be vexed with prosecutions for
hunting, except they killed stags: in that case they
were liable to such penalty as the king willed.   Besides the beasts of the forest, the roebuck, hare and
rabbit were protected by fines.   Wolves and foxes
were neither beasts of the forest nor chace, and
might be killed with impunity, but not within the
bounds of the forest, as that would be a breaking
of the chace; nor was the boar considered a beast
of venery.   No one was to cut brushwood without
permission of the *primarius*, under a penalty; and
he that felled a tree which supplied food for the
beasts, was to pay a fine of twenty shillings over
and above that for breaking the chace.   Every
free man might have his own vert and venison on
his own lands, but without a chace; and no man

---

[1] *Illiberalis;* perhaps a freedman, or a free man not a landowner.
The distinctions here are *liber, illiberalis, servus.*

[2] This must denote *gentry,* something more than mere freedom.

of the middle class (*mediocris*) was to keep grey-hounds. A gentleman (*liberalis*[1]) might, but he must first have the knee-sinew cut in presence of the head-forester, if he lived within ten miles of the forest: if his dogs came within that distance, he was to be fined a shilling a mile: if the dog entered the precincts of the forest, his master was to pay ten shillings. Other kinds of dogs, not considered dangerous, might be kept without mutilation; but if they became mad and by the negligence of their masters went wandering about, heavy fines were incurred. If found within the bounds of the forest, the fine was two hundred shillings: if such a rabid dog bit a beast of the forest, the fine rose to twelve hundred: but if a royal beast was bitten, the crime was of the deepest dye.

Such is the forest legislation of Cnut, and its severity is of itself evidence how much the power of the king had become extended at the commencement of the eleventh century. It is clear that he deals with all forests as having certain paramount rights therein, and it seems probable that this organization was intended to be established all over England. Still it is observable that he gives certain rights of hunting to all his nobles, reserving only the stags to himself, and that he allows every freeman to hunt upon his own property, so that he does not interfere with the royal chaces[2]. We may

---

[1] The *mediocris* is defined as twȳhynde, the *liberalis* as twelfhynde. § 33, 34.

[2] This regulation was very likely forced upon him by his Witan, inasmuch as it is also recorded in his laws, § 81. " Every one shall be

however infer that at an earlier period the matter was not regarded so strictly. A passage has been already cited[1] where Ælfred implies that a dependent living upon lænland could support himself by hunting and fishing, till he got bócland of his own. The bishops possessed the right in their forests— whether *proprio iure* or by royal grant, I will not venture to decide—as early as the ninth century[2], and still retained it in the tenth[3]. And while the communities were yet free it is absurd to suppose that they allowed any one to interfere with this pursuit, so attractive to every Teuton, so healthy, so calculated to practise his eye and limbs for the sterner duties of warfare, and so useful to recruit a larder not over well stored with various or delicate viands.

However this may have been with the game, it is certain that the most important privileges were those of masting swine, and cutting timber or brushwood in the forests[4]. Grants to this effect are

entitled to his hunting both in wood and field, upon his own property. And let every one forego my hunting : take notice where I will have it untrespassed upon, on penalty of the full wíte."

[1] See Vol. I. p. 312.

[2] Cod. Dipl. No. 1086. Bishop Denewulf gave Ælfred forty hides at Alresford, loaded with various conditions : among them, that his men should be ready " ge tó ripe ge tó hunt[n]oðe," that is at the bishop's harvest and hunting.

[3] Cod. Dipl. No. 1287. Oswald bishop of Worcester, stating the terms on which he let the lands of his see, includes among them the services of his tenants at his hunting : " Sed et venationis sepem domini episcopi [clearly *a park*] ultronei ad aedificandum repperiantur, suaque, quandocumque domino episcopo libuerit, venabula destinent venatum."

[4] The importance of pannage or masting was such as to cause the introduction of a clause guarding it, in the Charta de Foresta, — a document considered by our forefathers as hardly less important than Magna

common, and it is plain that a considerable quantity
of woods were in the hands of corporations, and
even of private individuals, as well as of the Crown.
How they came into private hands is not clear;
some perhaps by bargain and sale, some by inheritance, some by grant, some no doubt by usurpation. The most powerful markman may at last
have contrived to appropriate to himself the ownership of what woodland remained, though he was
still compelled to permit the hereditary axe to ring
in the forest[1]; and all experience shows that both
here and in Germany monasteries were often
founded in the bosom of woods, granted for religious purposes, out of what perhaps had once endowed an earlier religion, and which supplied at
once building materials, fuel and support for cattle[2]. But even in these, it seems that the king,
the duke and the geréfa interfered, claiming a right
to pasture certain numbers of their own swine
or cattle in them, and to give this privilege to
others.

In 845, Æðelwulf gave pasture to Badonoð for
his cattle with the king's beasts, apparently in the

Charta itself: see § 9. Domesday usually notes the amount of pannage in an estate, and Fleta (Bk. ii. cap. 80) thinks it necessary to devote a chapter to the subject.

[1] The Oldsaxons in Westphalia called a distinguished class of persons Erfexe, or Hereditary axes, from their right to hew wood in the
Mark. Möser (Osnab. i. 19) gives an erroneous derivation for this name,
but Grimm corrects him: Deut. Rechtsalt. 504.

[2] " Dunhelmum veniens, locum quidem natura munitum, sed non
facile habitabilem invenit, quoniam densissima eum silva totum occu-
pabat," etc. Transl. Sci. Cuðb. Bed. Hist. vol. ii. p. 302. The earliest grants of land on which these establishments were placed, usually
state the land to be *silva* or *silvatica*.

pastures of the town of Canterbury[1]. In 855, the
same king gave his thane Dun a tenement in Rochester, together with two waggon-loads of wood
from the king's forest, and common in the marsh[2].
In 839 he licensed for Dudda two waggons to the
common wood, probably Blean[3]; in 772, Offa
granted lands to Abbot Æðelnoð, and added a perpetual right of pasture and masting in the royal
wood, together with licence for one goat to go with
the royal flock in the forest of Sænling[4]. Numerous other examples are supplied by the charters,
which may be classed under the following heads:
first, royal forests, as Sænling, Blean, Andred and
the like, called *silvae regales*, and in which the king
granted timber, common of mast and pasture or
estovers: secondly, forest appertaining to cities
and communities (ceasterwara-weald, burhwara-
weald, *silva communis*), in which the king granted
commons: thirdly, small woods, appurtenant to
and part of estates, but not named, and the enjoyment of which is conveyed in the general terms of
the grant, as *terram cum communibus utilitatibus,
pascuis, pratis, silvis, piscariis*, etc. : lastly, private
forests or commons of forest specially named as

[1] Cod. Dipl. No. 259.
[2] Cod. Dipl. No. 276. "Et decem carros cum silvo (*sic*) honestos in
monte regis, et communionem marisci quae ad illam villam antiquitus
cum recto pertinebat."
[3] Cod. Dipl. No. 241. "Duobusque carris dabo licentiam silfam ad illas
secundum antiquam consuetudinem et constituidem (*sic*) in aestate per-
ferendam in commune silfa quod nos saxonicae in geménnisse dicimus."
[4] Cod. Dipl. No. 119. "Et ad pascendum porcos et pecora, et iu-
menta in silva regali aeternaliter perdono ; et unius caprae licentiam in
silva quae vocatur Saenling ubi meae vadunt."

appurtenant to particular estates, or given by favour of the king to the tenant of those estates.
To all these heads ample references will be found
in the note below[1]. His right to deal at pleasure
with the *silvae regales* requires no particular notice,
but the grants of pasture and timber in the forests
of cities and communities[2] can only be explained
by the assumption of a paramount royalty in the
Crown. And that this was exercised in the private
forests of monasteries, also appears from exemptions sometimes purchased by them. In 706,
Æ∂elweard of the Hwiccas consented to confine his
right of pasture to one herd of swine, and that only
in years when mast was abundant, in the forests
belonging to Evesham; and he released them from
all claims of princes and officers, except this one
of his own[3]. Similarly, with regard to timber,
Ecgberht in 835 gave an immunity to Abingdon,
against the claim of king or prince, to take large
or small wood for his buildings from the forests of

[1] Royal forests in which common of pasture, or timber is given by
the king. Cod. Dipl. Nos. 77, 107, 108, 201, 207, 234, 239, etc. Civic
and common forests in which the king makes similar grants. Cod. Dipl.
Nos. 96, 160, 179, 190, 198, 216, 219, etc. Private forests, conveyed
in general terms of the grant. Cod. Dipl. Nos. 16, 17, 27, 32, 35, 36,
80, 83, 85, etc. Private forests particularly defined as appurtenant.
Cod. Dipl. Nos. 80, 89, 138, 152, 161, 165, 187, 214, etc.

[2] Cod. Dipl. Nos. 47, 86, 96, etc.

[3] Cod. Dipl. No. 56. " Excepto eo, ut si quando in insula eidem ruri
pertinente proventus copiosior glandis acciderit, uni solummodo gregi
porcorum saginae pastus regi concederetur; et praeter hoc nulli, neque
principi, neque praefecto, neque tiranno alicui, pascua constituantur."
This right of the king's was called *Fearnleswe:* " Et illam terram. . . .
liberabo a pascua porcorum regis quod nominamus Fearnleswe." Cod.
Dipl. No. 277.

the monastery[1]. This right of the king to timber
for public purposes was maintained and claimed till
the time of the rebellion, and was a fertile source
of malversation and extortion[2].

STRANGER.—To the king belonged also the
protection of all strangers within his realm, and the
consequent claim to a portion of their wergyld, and
their property in case of death, a *droit d'aubaine.*
This was a natural deduction from the principles
of a period and a state of society in which every.
man's security was founded upon association either
with relatives or guildsmen: and as no one could
have these in a foreign mark,—the associations
being themselves in intimate connection with the
territory,—it is obvious that the public authorities
alone could exercise any functions in behalf of the
solitary chapman. As general conservator of the
peace, these necessarily fell to the king; but the
duties and advantages which he thus assumed became in turn matter of grant, and were conferred
by him upon other public persons or corporations.
The laws declare the king, earl and bishop to be

[1] Cod. Dipl. No. 236. "Silva quoque omnis quae illi aecclesiae et
suburbanis eius suppetit, in omnibus causis sit libera, et non secetur
ibi ad regis vel principis aedificia aliqua pars materiae grossi vel gra-
cilis, sed ab omnibus defensa et libera maneat." Compare Böhm. Reg.
Karol. Nos. 387, 1157, 1598.

[2] From a speech of Lord Bacon's against the abuses of purveyors, it
appears that those who were to purvey timber for the king, even as late
as the reign of James the First, used to extort money by the threat of
felling ornamental trees in the avenues or grounds of mansion-houses.
Barrington, Anc. Stat. p. 7, note.

the relatives and guardians of the stranger[1]; and the charters show that the consequent gains were alienated by him at his pleasure. In 835, Ecgberht gave the inheritance of Gauls and Britons, and half their wergyld, to the monastery at Abingdon[2]. Among these strangers, the Jews were especially mentioned. Anglosaxon history has not indeed recorded any of those abominable outrages upon this long-suffering people which fill the annals of our own and other countries during the middle ages; but there can be no doubt that a false and fanatical view of religion, if not their way of life and their accumulations, must have ever marked them out for persecution. Eichhorn has justly characterized the feeling which prevailed respecting them in all parts of Europe[3], and has remarked to the honour of the Popes that they were the first

---

[1] "If any one wrong an ecclesiastic or a foreigner, in anything touching either his property or his life, then shall the king, or the earl there in the land [*i. e.* among the Danes] or the bishop of the people be unto him as a kinsman and protector: and let compensation be strictly made, according to the deed, both to Christ and the king; or let the king among the people severely avenge the deed." Eádw. Guð. § 12. Thorpe, i. 174. See also Ranks. § 8. Æðelr. ix. § 33. Cnut, ii. § 40. Hen. I. x. § 3; lxxv. § 7.

[2] Cod. Dipl. No. 236. "Similiter de haereditate peregrinorum, id est Gallorum et Brittonum et horum similium, aecclesiae reddatur. Praetium quoque sanguinis peregrinorum, id est *wergyld*, dimidiam partem rex teneat, dimidiam aecclesiae antedictae reddant."

[3] Deut. Staatsr. i. 422, § 297. He cites an instruction of Margrave Albrecht of Brandenburg an. 1462, which contains this Christian-like provision:—"When a Roman emperor and king is crowned, he has a right to take all they possess throughout his realm, yea and their lives also, and to slay them, until only a little number of them be left, to serve as a memorial." Kings and populations, without being heads of the holy Roman empire, assumed a similar right only too often.

to preach toleration and command the attempt at conversion. But the utility of the Jewish industry especially in thinly peopled countries, and their importance as gatherers of capital, were ever engaged in a struggle against bigotry; hence the Jews could generally obtain a qualified protection against all but sudden outbreaks of popular fury. As these latter had mostly other deep-seated causes, the ruling classes may sometimes have seen without regret the popular indignation vent itself in a direction which did not immediately endanger themselves: but as a general rule, the Jews enjoyed protection, and were made to pay dearly for it. Both parties were gainers by the arrangement. Among the Saxons this could not be otherwise, for it was impossible for a Jew to be in a hundred or tithing as a freeman; and he would probably have had but little security in the household and following of an ordinary noble. The readiest and most effective plan was to place him, wherever he might be, especially under the king's mundbyrd. Accordingly the law of Eádweard the Confessor declares the king to be protector of all Jews[1], and this right descended to his Norman successors. Similarly as the clergy relinquished their mægsceaft or bond of kin, on entering into orders, the king became their natural mundbora[2].

---

[1] Eádw. Conf. § 25. "Sciendum est quod omnes Judaei, ubicunque regno sint, sub tutela et defensione regis ligie debent esse. Neque aliquis eorum potest subdere se alicui diviti sine licentia regis; quia ipsi Judaei et omnia sua regis sunt. Quod si aliquis detinuerit illos vel pecuniam eorum, rex requirat tanquam suum proprium, si vult et potest."

[2] Cnut, ii. § 40. Thorpe, i. 400.

BRIDGE.—It is probable that no one could
build a bridge without the royal licence, though I
am not aware of any instance in the Saxon times:
but I infer this from grants of the Frankish emperors and kings to that effect [1]. It is possible that
this may have depended upon the circumstance
that toll would be taken by the owner of such a
bridge; but we may believe that other reasons concurred with this, and that the bridge originally had
something of a holy character, and stood in near
relation to the priesthood [2].

CASTLE.—In like manner we may doubt whether the kings did not gradually draw into their
own hands the right to have fortified houses or
castles, which we find them possessing in the Norman times, and which they extended to their
adherents and favourites by special licence. In

---

[1] Böhm. Reg. Karol. Nos. 88, 680, 1931.

[2] It has already been noticed as remarkable that Pontifex, the bridge-
builder, should be the name for the priestly class. There are many su-
perstitions connected with bridges, and the spirit of the bridge even to
this day, in Germany, demands his victims as inexorably as the spirit
of the river. Deut. Mythol. p. 563. The passage in Schol. Ælii Aristid.
which speaks, according to a modern emendation, of Palladia in connection with bridges, is hopelessly corrupt. But Servius, Æneid, ii. 661,
says the Athenian Pallas was called γεφυρῖτις (not γεφυρίστης as the
copies have), and this is confirmed by the Interp. Virgil. published by
Mai, where from her position on a bridge the goddess is called γεφυρῖτις 'Αθηνᾶ. Pherecydes (No. 101) and Phylarchus (No. 79) both appear to refer to this, if indeed the proposed readings can be admitted.
See Fragm. Hist. Græc. pp. 95, 356. There was in very early times a
gens of γεφυραῖοι at Athens, but I do not know if they had any priestly
functions. They had the worship of Δημήτηρ Ἀχαια, and were Cad-
mæans who had immigrated into Attica; from among them sprung
Harmodius and Aristogeiton.

mediæval history, the fortification of their houses
by the inhabitants of a city is the very first result
of the establishment of a Communa, commûne or
free municipality ; and the destruction of such fortifications the first care of the victorious count,
bishop or king upon his triumph over the *outre-
cuidance* of the burghers[1]. The clearest instance of

---

[1] Thierry, Lettres sur l'Hist. de France, p. 272. "Ainsi élevés de la
triste condition de sujets taillables d'une abbaye au rang d'alliés poli-
tiques d'un des plus puissants seigneurs, les habitans de Vézelay cher-
chèrent à s'entourer des signes extérieurs qui annonçaient ce change-
ment d'état. Ils élevèrent autour de leurs maisons, chacun selon sa ri-
chesse, des murailles crénelées, ce qui était alors la marque de la garantie du privilége de liberté. L'un des plus considérables parmi eux,
nommé Simon, jeta les fondements d'une grosse tour carrée, comme
celle dont les restes se voient à Toulouse, à Arles, et dans plusieurs
villes d'Italie. Ces tours, auxquelles la tradition joint encore le nom
de leur premier possesseur, donnent une grande idée de l'importance
individuelle des riches bourgeois du moyen âge, importance bien autre
que la petite considération dont ils jouirent plus tard sous le régime
monarchique. Cet appareil seigneurial n'était pas, dans les grandes
villes de commune, le privilége exclusif d'un petit nombre d'hommes,
seuls puissants au milieu d'une multitude pauvre : Avignon, au commencement du treizième siècle, ne comptait pas moins de trois cents
maisons garnies de tours."
This last fact rests upon the authority of Matthew Paris. On the
defeat of the Commune, the order was given to raze their fortifications.
The king himself, Louis le Jeune (A.D. 1155), distinctly decreed in the
sentence which he pronounced against them, that within a given time
the towers, walls and enclosures with which they had fortified their
houses should be demolished. But the burghers had no such intention ; "ces signes de liberté leur étaient plus chers que leur argent ;"
and they continued to resist even after the Pope himself had written to
the king of France to demand the execution of the decree. At length
however the Abbot of Vézelay took the matter into his own hands. "Il
fit venir, des domaines de son église, une troupe nombreuse de jeunes
paysans serfs, qu'il arma aussi bien qu'il put, et auxquels il donna pour
commandants les plus déterminés de ses moines. Cette troupe marcha
droit à la maison de Simon, et ne trouvant aucune résistance, se mit à
démolir la tour et les murailles crénelées, tandisque le maître de la
maison, calme et fier comme un Romain du temps de la république,

the royal licence to a subject is a grant of Æðelræd and Æðelflæd to the bishop of Worcester,
about 880, which recites that they built a burh or
fortress for him, in his city, probably to defend his
cathedral in those stormy days of Danish ravage[1].
In very early times there may have been fortresses
belonging to private persons; this may be inferred
from names of places such as Sulmonnes burh,
Sulman's castle; and under the later Anglosaxon
kings, various great nobles may have obtained the
privilege of fortifying their own residences, as for
example we read of Pentecost's castle and Rod-
berht's castle under Eádweard the Confessor[2], an
example very likely to have been followed by the
powerful chieftains of Godwine's, Sigeweard's and
Leófríc's families; but the cases were probably few.
Of course fortresses built and garrisoned by the
king for the public defence are quite another matter: these were imperial, and to their construction,
maintenance and repair, every estate throughout
the land, whether of folcland or bócland, was in-

était assis au coin du feu avec sa femme et ses enfants. Ce succès, ob-
tenu sans combat, décida la victoire en faveur de la puissance seigneu-
riale, et ceux d'entre les bourgeois qui avaient des maisons fortifiées
donnèrent à l'abbé des otages, pour garantie de la destruction de tous
leur ouvrages de défense. ' Alors,' dit le narrateur ecclésiastique, 'toute
querelle fut terminée, et l'Abbaye de Vézelay recouvra le libre exercice
de son droit de juridiction sur ses vassaux rebelles.'" Ibid. pp. 291,
292.

[1] Cod. Dipl. No. 1075.

[2] Chron. Sax. 1052. "Ðá geáxode Rotberd arcebisceop ꝺ ða Fren-
cisce ðæt, genamon heora hors ꝺ gewendon, sume west tó Pentecostes
castele, sume norð tó Rodberhtes castele." However these were fo-
reigners, a culpable complaisance towards whom is a grievous stain
upon Eádweard's otherwise amiable, though weak, character.

evitably bound, not even excepting the demesne lands of the king himself or of the ecclesiastical corporations.

ROADS and CANALS.—There is no very clear evidence respecting roads and canals, licence to make which was a subject of grant by the Frankish emperors[1]. But except as regarded the great roads which were especially the king's, and the cross roads, which were the county's, it is probable that there was no interference on the part of the state. Every landowner must have had the privilege of making private paths, large or small at his pleasure, by which access could be given to different parts of his own property. We do occasionally find roads mentioned by the name of the owners, and a common service of the settlers on an estate was the liability to assist in making a new road to the farm or mansion[2]. In an instance already cited we have seen an abbot of St. Augustine's digging a canal with the object of diverting traffic from the haven of Sandwich. It may unhesitatingly be asserted that he claimed this right under his general power as a landlord, and not by any special grant for the purpose: this is evident from the whole tenour of the narrative.

PORTS.—Ports and Havens were, however, essentially royalties, and, as we have seen, could be granted to religious houses. They were naturally in

[1] Böhm. Reg. Karol. Nos. 248, 316.
[2] Rect. Sing. Pers. Thorpe, i. 432.

the king's hand, for this reason : in the early times
of which we treat, the stranger is looked upon as an
enemy, and every one who does not belong to the
association for the maintenance of peace, is *primâ
facie* out of the peace altogether.   This applies to
sailors, as well as travelling chapmen who wander
from mark to mark or county to county; and it applied with peculiar force to England after her coasts
became exposed to repeated invasions from the
North.   Still as England could not subsist without
foreign commerce, and early became alive to that
great principle of her existence, a system of what
we may call navigation laws was established.   The
bottoms of friendly powers were of course received
upon terms of reciprocal favour, but even strange
ships had the privilege of safety if they made certain harbours, designated for that purpose.   At the
treaty of Andover, in 994, Æðelræd and his witan
agreed, that every merchant-ship that voluntarily
came into port should be in the peace; and even
if it were driven into port (whether by force or by
stress of weather is not specified), and there were a
friðburh, asylum, or building in the peace, in which
the men took refuge, they and their ship and cargo
should enjoy the peace[1].   It is hardly to be doubted
that the king had the power of declaring what ports
should be gefriðod or in the peace; and as this privilege would necessarily draw many advantages to
any harbour that possessed it, we can reasonably
conclude that it was made a source of profit, both

---

[1] Æ elr. ii. § 2.   Thorpe, i. 284.

by the king and those to whom he might think fit to grant it.

WARDSHIP and MARRIAGE.—Wardship and Marriage appear to have been royalties; we must however believe them to have been confined to the children and widows of the thanes or comites, and to be a deduction from the principles of the Comitatus itself.

In the secular law of Cnut there is a series of provisions, extending from the 70th to the 75th clause, which can only be looked upon in the light of alleviations, and which in the 70th clause the king himself declares so to be. From the nature of the relief thus afforded, we may infer that the royal officers had exercised their powers in a manner oppressive to the subject. Accordingly the king and his witan proceed to regulate the voluntary nature of the *feormfultum,* the legal amount of heriot, the descent of property in the case of intestacy, and the kings's guardianship of the same; they protect the widow and heirs against vexatious suits, by providing that they shall not be sued, if the lord and father had remained undisturbed, and lastly they regulate what appear to me to be the rights of wardship and marriage.

" And let every widow remain for a twelvemonth without a husband; then let her do her pleasure. But if within the year she choose a husband, let her forfeit the *morgengyfu* and all the property she had through her first husband, and let her nearest kin take the land and property she had before.

And let the husband be liable in his *wer* to the king, or to whomsoever he may have granted it. And even if she have been taken by force, let her forfeit her possessions, unless she be willing to go home again from the man, and never become his again. . . . . . And let no one compel either woman or maiden to him whom she herself mislikes, nor for money sell her, unless the suitor will give something of his own good will[1]."

This of itself does not imply the royal right of marriage; but it becomes much more significant, when we learn that estates had been given to influential nobles, for their intercession with the king, on behalf of profitable alliances: then, the circumstances, combined together, seem to imply that Cnut desired to reform the miserable condition in which he found England, in the hope, no doubt, by such reform to consolidate his own power. The evidence of what may almost be called purchasing a marriage—though not in the truly gross and vulgar sense of such purchases among those whom writers of romances represent as the *chivalrous* Normans,—is supplied by the monk of Ramsey: the instance dates from the middle of the tenth century. In mentioning an estate of five hides at Burwell, the chronicler adds: "This is the estate which—as we find in the very ancient English charters referring to it—a certain man named Eádwine, the son of Othulf, had in old times granted to archbishop Oda, as a reward for his pains and trouble in bringing king Eádred to consent, that

[1] Cnut, ii. § 74, 75.

Eádwine might have leave to marry the daughter of a certain Ulf, whom he desired[1]." This Ulf does not, I believe, occur among the signitaries to any of the charters, unless the name represent some one of the many Wulfgárs or Wulfláf's of the time: but still we must suppose him to have been a person of consideration, since a large estate was given for his daughter's marriage. In the absence of all details we cannot form any clear decision as to the royal right in this respect, though the balance of probability seems to me to incline to the view that the king had some right of wardship and marriage over the children and widows of his own thanes or sócmen. This seems to lie in the very nature of their relative position. With the widow or child of a free man, it is of course not to be imagined that the king could interfere; but in the time of Eádred there were probably not many free men whose wealth rendered interference worth the trouble.

HEREGEATWE. HERIOT.—The general nature of Heriot has been explained in the First Book: it was there shown that it arose from the theory of the *comes* having been originally armed by the king, to whom upon his death the arms reverted: and in imitation of this, Best-head or Melius catallum, distinguished in our law as Heriot-custom, was shown to have arisen. But whatever may have been its origin or early amount,—and its earliest amount

---

[1] " Pro mercede solicitudinis et laboris, quo regem Ædredum ad consensum inflexerat, ut ei liceret filiam cuiusdam viri Ulfi, quam concupiverat, maritali sibi foedere copulare." Hist. Rames. cap. 23.

was no doubt unsettled, depending upon the will of the chief who might take all or some of his thanes' chattels at his pleasure,—in process of time it became assessed at a fixed amount, according to the rank of the person from whose estate it was paid. The law of Cnut[1] which determined this amount was probably only a re-enactment, or confirmation of an older custom, and appears to have been introduced to put an end to disputes upon the subject; it declares as follows:—

" Let the heriots be as fits the degree. An earl's as belongs to an earl's rank, viz. eight horses, four saddled, four unsaddled, four helmets, four coats-of-mail, eight spears, eight shields, four swords and two hundred mancuses of gold. From a king's thane, of those who are nearest to him, four horses, two saddled, two unsaddled; two swords, four spears, four shields, a helmet, a coat-of-mail and fifty mancuses of gold. From a medial thane, a horse equipped, and his arms; or his healsfang in Wessex, and in Mercia and Eastanglia two pounds. Among the Danes, the heriot of a king's thane who has his sócn[2] is four pounds: if he stand in nearer relation to the king, two horses, one equipped, a sword, two spears, two shields and fifty mancuses of gold. And from a thane of the lower order, two pounds."

The following are examples of heriots paid both before and after the time of Cnut.

The estate of Ðeódræd bishop of London and

---

[1] Cnut, ii. § 72. Thorpe, i. 414.   [2] A baronial court.

H 2

Elmham, about 940, paid, four horses the best he had, two swords the best he had, four shields, four spears, two hundred marks of red gold, two silver cups, and his lands at Anceswyrð, Illingtún and Earmingtún[1].

In 946-956, the estate of Æðelwald the ealdorman paid four horses, four spears, four swords, four shields, two rings each worth one hundred and twenty mancuses, two rings each worth eighty mancuses (in all four hundred mancuses) and two silver vessels[2].

About 958, Ælfgár gave the king two swords with belts, three steeds, three shields, three spears, and two rings each worth fifty mancuses of gold[3].

. The heriot of Beorhtríc, about 962, was, four horses, two equipped, two swords and belts, a ring worth eighty mancuses of gold, a sword of the same value, two falcons, and all his stag-hounds[4].

The great duke Ælfheáh of Hampshire, 965-971, gave to Eádgár, who had married his cousin Ælf-ðrýð, duke Ordgár's daughter, the following property: it is hard to say how much of it was heriot: six horses with their trappings, six swords, six spears, six shields, one sword worth eighty mancuses of gold, one dish of three pounds, one cup of three pounds, three hundred mancuses of gold, one hundred and twenty hides of land at Wyrð, and his estates at Cóchám, Dæchám, Ceóleswyrð, Incge neshám, Æglesbyrig and Wendofra[5].

---

[1] Cod. Dipl. No. 957.
[2] Ibid. No. 1173.
[3] Ibid. No. 1223.
[4] Ibid. No. 492.
[5] Ibid. No. 593.

Æðelríc, in 997, paid two horses, one sword
and belt, two shields, two spears, and sixty marks
of gold[1].

Archbishop Ælfríc, 996–1006, devised to the
king, as his heriot, sixty helmets, sixty coats-of-
mail, and his best ship with all her tackle and
stores[2].

Ælfhelm paid four horses, two equipped, four
shields, four spears, two swords, and one hundred
mancuses of gold[3].

Wulfsige paid two horses, one helmet, one coat-
of-mail, one sword, one spear twined with gold[4].

The majority of these cases belong to periods
previous to Cnut's accession, but they seem to
imply an assessment very similar to his own. And
in this view of the case, where the payment had
become a settled amount due from persons of a particular rank, it became possible for women to be
charged with it, which we accordingly find. In 1046
Wulfgýð commences her will by desiring that her
right heriot may be paid to the king[5]: Æðelgyfu in 945 gave the king thirty mancuses of gold,
two horses and all her dogs[6]: Ælflæd left him by
will her lands at Lamburnan, Ceólsige and Read-
ingan, four rings worth two hundred mancuses of
gold, four palls, four cups, four drinking-horns and
four horses[7]: and lastly queen Ælfgyfu in 1012

---

[1] Cod. Dipl. No. 699. This is very nearly the exact heriot. Æðelríc,
who was no friend to the king, probably meant to give him no doit
more than he could legally claim.

[2] Cod. Dipl. No. 716.   [3] Ibid. No. 967.
[4] Ibid. No. 979.   [5] Ibid. No. 782.
[6] Ibid. No. 410.   [7] Ibid. No. 685.

left the king, six horses, six shields, six spears, one cup, two rings worth one hundred and twenty mancuses each, and various lands[1]. Taken in connection with the case of Wulfḡȳð, these bequests appear very like heriots. The heriots mentioned in Domesday agree with the details given above, and serve to show that the right had undergoṇe no material alteration till the time of the Confessor[2]. That the Best-head or Melius catallum was paid to the king by his unfree tenants, as well as to other lords, is probable, but we have no instance of it[3]. By the law of Cnut, the widow was to have a reasonable time for payment of the heriot, and it was altogether remitted to the family of him who fell

---

[1] Cod. Dipl. No. 721.

[2] Domesd. Berks. "Tanius vel miles regis dominicus moriens pro relevamento dimittebat regi omnia arma sua, et equum unum cum sella, unum sine sella. Quod si essent ei canes vel accipitres, praesentabantur regi, ut si vellet, acciperet."

[3] Fleta, ii. cap. 57, § 1, 2. "Imprimis autem debet quilibet qui testaverit dominum suum de meliori re quam habuerit recognoscere, et postea aecclesiam de alia meliori, et in quibusdam locis habet aecclesia melius animal de consuetudine, in quibusdam secundum vel tertium melius, et in quibusdam nihil: et ideo observanda est consuetudo loci." § 2. "Item de morte uxoris alicuius viri, dum vir superstes fuerit, de toto grege communi secundum melius averium, quasi de parte sua: sed hoc non nisi de permissione et gratia viri." This Melius catallum, Bestehaupt or Best-head was in fact a servile due: but in this sense it was an alleviation; for strictly speaking the lord could take the whole inheritance of his unfree tenant. In 1252 Margaret Countess of Flanders gave this alleviation to the serfs of the crown: "Tous les serfs demeurant en Flandre, sous la justice propre de la comtesse, furent affranchis de servitude en 1252, à charge de payer par homme trois deniers, et par femme un denier annuellement; et le droit qu'elle avait à la moitié des meubles en catteux des serfs morts, fut reduit au meilleur cattel, [melius catallum] autre que maison ou bête de somme." Warnkönig. Hist. Fland. i. 259. On this subject generally see Nelson, Lex Maneriorum, p. 154,

bravely fighting in the field before the presence of his lord.

It appears from what has been said in this chapter that the kings were provided very sufficiently with the means of maintaining their dignity: the benefactions which they were enabled to make out of the folcland relieved their private estates from the burthen of supporting the thanes, clerical and lay, who flocked to their service. Still there must have been a constant drain upon their possessions; and many of the regalia became lost to the crown by successive alienations. It is true that they were generally purchased at a high price, but in this case the king who sold them was the only gainer: he secured considerable sums for himself, but he impoverished all his successors to a much greater amount. The loans for which we occasionally find him indebted to his prelates, show how completely at times the crown had been pillaged, as well as who were the principal sharers in the plunder. The attempt to draw in lands and privileges which had once been alienated, was questionable in policy and harsh to the innocent holders; but it does not always seem to have been viewed impartially even by those least concerned; we may however now express our conviction that in many cases the alienations themselves had been made improperly and without sufficient authority; and, that if it was hard upon an abbot or bishop to lose what his predecessor had gained, it was very hard upon a king to be without what *his* predecessor had unjustly and often illegally squandered.

CHAPTER III.

THE KING'S COURT AND HOUSEHOLD.

THE Anglosaxon Court appears to have been modelled upon the same plan as that of the Frankish Emperors: our documents do not however permit us to judge whether this was the case before a sufficient intercourse had taken place to render a positive imitation probable.

It is not at all unlikely that, from the very first establishment of the Comitatus, the possession of those household offices was coveted, which brought the holder into closer personal connection with the prince: and more or less of dependence could be of little moment with those who had erected into a system the voluntary sacrifice of the holiest of all possessions, their freedom of action. Hence we can readily account for the assumption by men nobly born of offices about the royal person, which were at first directly and immediately menial [1]. Nor, as the opportunities of personal aggrandisement through favouritism or affection were multiplied, does it seem strange to us that these offices should assume a character of dignity and real power, which,

---

[1] Speaking of the Pincerna regis Æðelstani, one of the great officers of the Household, in the early part of the tenth century, William of Malmesbury says, "Itaque cum forte die solenni vinum propinaret," etc. Gest. Reg. § ii. 139.

however little in consonance with their original intention, yet made them objects of ambition with the wealthy and the noble. We do not any longer wonder at the struggles of dukes and barons for the offices of royal cupbearer at a coronation, or Steward or Chamberlain of the Household, because time and the attribution of judicial or administrative functions have given those offices a distinction which at the outset they did not possess : and we see without surprise the electors of Germany personally serving at his table the member of their body whom they had invested with imperial rank ; and, when they fixed the throne hereditarily in him, providing for the succession in their own families of Butlers, Stewards, Marshals or Chancellors of the empire.

As the progress of society drew larger and larger numbers of men into the circle of princely influence, and, by withdrawing them from the jurisdiction of the free courts, rendered a systematic establishment of the Lord's court more necessary, the officers who were charged with the superintendence of the various royal vassals, rose immeasurably in the social scale. Thus the Major Domus or Mayor of the palace, at first only a steward, who had to regulate the affairs of the Household, gradually assumed the management of those of the kingdom, and ended by placing on his own head the crown which he had filched from his master's. So was it with the rest.

The four great officers of the Court and Household in the oldest German kingdoms are the

Chamberlain, the Marshal, the Steward and the Butler.

The names by which the Chamberlain was designated are Hrægel þegn, literally thane or servant of the wardrobe, Cubicularius, Camerarius, Búrþegn, perhaps sometimes Dispensator, and Thesaurarius or Hordere. It is difficult to ascertain his exact duties in the Anglosaxon Court, but they probably differed little from those of the corresponding officer among other German populations, and there is reason to compare those of the Frankish Cubicularius with the functions of the Comites sacrarum largitionum and rerum privatarum of the Roman emperors. Hence we may presume that he had the general management of the royal property, as well as the immediate regulation of the household [1]. In this capacity he may have been the recognized chief of the cyninges túngeréfan or king's bailiffs, on the several estates; for we find no traces of any districtual or missatic authority to whom these officers could account. At the same time it appears that this officer was not what we now call the Lord Great Chamberlain, but rather the Lord Chamberlain of the Household, and that more than one officer of the same rank existed at the same time [2].

---

[1] Eichhorn, i. 197. § 25, b. Eichhorn argues the first from a passage in Greg. Turon. vii. 24. The latter portion of the Chamberlain's duties is defined by Hincmar of Rheims, § 22. " De honestate vero palatii, seu specialiter ornamento regali, necnon et de donis annuis militum, absque cibo et potu, vel equis, ad Reginam praecipue, et sub ipsa ad Camerarium pertinebat: et sollicitudo erat, ut tempore congruo semper futura prospicerent, ne quid, dum opus esset, defuisset. De donis vero diversarum legationum ad Camerarium aspiciebat."

[2] "Cubicularios regis duos." Will. Malm., ii. § 180.

Hence we can hardly suppose that the dignity of the
office was comparable to that of the Lord Chamberlain at present, with the great and various powers
and duties which are now committed to that distinguished member of the Court.   Among the nobles
who held this office I find the following named :—

Ælfríc thesaurarius,   under Ælfred, 892 [1].
Æðelsige camerarius,   ... Eádgár, 963 [2].
Leófríc hræglþegn,   ... Æðelred, 1006 [3].
Eádríc dispensator regis, ... Hardacnut, 1040 [4].
Hugelinus camerarius,   ... Eádweard, 1044 [5].
.... cubicularius   ... Eádweard, 1060 [6].
.... stiweard,   ... Eádweard [7].
.... búrþegn   ... Eádweard [8].

The Marshal (among the Franks Marescalcus, and
Comes stabuli) was properly speaking the Master
of the Horse, and had charge of everything connected with the royal equipments, in that department.   But as he gradually became the head of
the active and disposable military force of the palace, he must be looked upon rather as the general
of the Household troops.   It was thus that the
high military dignity of Constable, or Grand Marshal, by degrees developed itself.   This office was
held by nobles of the highest rank, and frequently
by several at once,—a sufficient explanation of a
fact which otherwise would appear strange, viz.
that we never find the royal power endangered by

[1] Cod. Dipl. No. 320.
[2] Ibid. No. 1246.
[3] Ibid. No. 715.
[4] Flor. Wig. an. 1040.
[5] Cod. Dipl. Nos. 771, 810.
[6] Ibid. No. 809.
[7] Ibid. No. 899, very doubtful.
[8] Ibid. No. 904.

that of this influential minister. The Anglosaxon titles are Steallere and Horsþegn, Stabulator and Strator regis. We have no evidence of the existence of the office before the close of the ninth century, and it might therefore be imagined that it was introduced into England after the establishment of the family of Ecgberht had familiarized our countrymen with the Frankish court and its customs, did we not find it as an essential institution in all German courts, of all periods. Among the Anglosaxon Marshals the following names occur:—

Ecgwulf strator regis : cyninges horsþegn, an. 897 [1].

Đored steallere, about 1020 [2].

E'sgár steallere, 1044–1066 [3].

Robert filius Wimarc steallere [4].

Ælfstán steallere [5].

Eádgár steallere, 1060–1066 [6].

Raulf steallere, 1053–1066 [7].

Bondig steallere, 1060–1066 [8].

. . . . . stabulator [9].

Eádnóð steallere [10].

Lýfing steallere [11].

Ælfred regis strator, 1052 [12].

Osgod Clapa steallere, 1047 [13].

The Steward, usually called Dapifer or Discifer regis, answered to the Seneschal of the Franks (the

[1] Flor. Wig. an. 897. Chron. Saxon. *eod. an.*
[2] Cod. Dipl. No. 1328.   [3] Ibid. Nos. 771, 828, 855, 864.
[4] Ibid. Nos. 771, 822, 828, 859, 871, 904, 956, 1338.
[5] Ibid. No. 773.   [6] Ibid. No. 809.
[7] Ibid. Nos. 822, 956, 1338.   [8] Ibid. No. 822.
[9] Ibid. No. 945.   [10] Ibid. No. 845.
[11] Ibid. Nos. 956, 1338.   [12] Flor. Wig. an. 1052.
[13] Chron. Sax. an. 1047.

Truchsess of the German empire); his especial business was to superintend all that appertained to the service of the royal table, under which we must probably include the arrangements for the general support of the household, both at the ordinary and temporary residences of the king. His Anglosaxon name was Discþegn, or thane of the table; and I find the following nobles recorded as holding this office:—

Eata dux et regis discifer, under Offa, 785 [1].
Wulfgár discifer,   ...   Eádwig, 959 [2].
Æðelmǽr discþegn,   ...   Æðelred, 1006 [3].
Raulf dapifer, ⎱
Ésgar dapifer, ⎰   ...   Eádweard, 1060 [4].
Atsur regis dapifer, ⎱
Yfing regis dapifer, ⎰   ...   Eádweard, 1062 [5].

In the year 946 Florence tells us of a dapifer regis, whom he does not name. The queen and princes of the blood had also a similar officer for the management of their households. In 1060 we read of Godwine, reginae dapifer [6], and Æðelred's son Æðelstán had a Discþegn named Ælfmǽr [7]. High as this office was, we yet cannot expect to find in it that overwhelming power wielded in later times by the Seneschal or Dapifer Angliae,—a power which might easily have converted the Grandmesnils and De Montforts into the Ebroins or Pepins of a newly established dynasty, and after their fall was

[1] Cod. Dipl. No. 149.   [2] Ibid. No. 1224.
[3] Ibid. No. 715.   [4] Ibid. No. 808.
[5] Ibid. No. 813.   [6] Ibid. No. 813.
[7] Ibid. No. 722.

wisely retained in the royal family by our kings.
We have now, as is well known, only a Lord High
Steward, or Major domus, on particular occasions,
for which he is especially created: but the Lord
Steward of the Household is an officer of great
power and high dignity in the Court of our kings.
A Major domus regiae occurs, as far as I know, but
once in our Ante-Norman history, and may there
probably denote only the dapifer or seneschal: he
is mentioned by Florence, an. 1040, as " Stir, major
domus . . . . . magnae dignitatis vir "; but we hear
nothing more of him, or of any such influence as the
corresponding high officer exercised in the Frankish
court.   The title Regiae procurator aulae, borne by
the great Esgár, whom we have also seen among
the Marshals, may very likely only refer to his
office of dapifer[1], which, from the list given above,
it will be evident that he held.

The last great officer is the Pincerna, in Germany
the Schenk or Buticularius,—the Butler.   What his
particular duties were, beyond his personal service at the royal board, and no doubt his general
superintendence of the royal cellars, we cannot
now discover ; but the office was one of the highest dignity, and was held by nobles of the loftiest
birth and greatest consideration.   O'slác, a direct
descendant from the royal Jutish blood of Stuff and
Wihtgár, was the pincerna of king Æðelwulf ; and
by this prince's daughter, " femina nobilis ingenio,
nobilis et genere,"—his first wife O'sburh,—Æðel-

---

[1] Cod. Dipl. No. 813.

wulf became the father of Ælfred [1]. The Anglo-saxon name of this officer may have been Byrele, or Scenca, but I am not aware of its occurrence. The following are among the Pincernae mentioned.

> Dudda pincernus, about 780 [2].
> Sigewulf pincerna, 892 [3].
> Æðelsige pincerna, 959 [4].
> Wulfgár pincerna, 1000 [5].
> Wigod regis pincerna, 1062 [6].

The queen, as she had a dapifer, had also a pincerna: in 1062, Herdingus is reported to have held that office [7].

There can be no doubt that these offices were entirely Palatine or domestic, that is that they were household dignities, and did not appertain to the general administration. Only when the spirit and feeling of the comitatus had completely prevailed over the older free organization, did they rise into an importance which, throughout the course of mediæval history, we find continually on the increase. They were the grades in the comitatus of which Tacitus himself speaks, which depended upon the good pleasure of the prince: and with the power of the prince their power and dignity varied. The functionaries who held them were the heads of different departments to which belonged all the vassals, *leudes* or *fideles* of the king: and as by degrees the freemen perished away, and every

---

[1] Asser, an. 849.
[2] Cod. Dipl. No. 148.
[3] Ibid. No. 320.
[4] Ibid. No. 1224.
[5] Ibid. No. 1294.
[6] Ibid. No. 813.
[7] Ibid. No. 813.

one gladly rushed to throw himself into a state of thaneship, the trusted and familiar friends of the prince became the most powerful agents of his administration : till the feudal system having seized on everything, converted these court-functions also into hereditary fiefs, and rendered their holders often powerful enough to make head against the authority of the crown itself. As long as a vestige of the free constitution remained, we hear but little of the court offices: what they became upon its downfall is known to every reader of history. It seems to me improbable that Godwine, or Harald, or Leófríc or Sigeward should ever have filled them : these men were ealdormen or dukes, geréfan, civil and military administrators; but not officers of the royal household, powerful and dignified as these might be. It is probable that the first and most important of their duties was the administration of justice to the king's sócmen in their various departments; from which in later times were clearly derived the extensive powers and attributions of the several royal courts: but as the intimate friends and cherished counsellors of the king, they must have possessed an influence whose natural tendency was to complete that great change in the social state, which causes of a more general nature,—increasing population, commerce and the disturbance of foreign and civil discord,—were hurrying relentlessly onward.

In various situations of trust and authority, either by the side of these officers, or subordinated to them, we find a number of other persons under different titles. Among these are the clergymen who acted as clerks or notaries in the imperial chancery. The Frankish court numbered among its members a functionary of the highest rank, and always a clergyman, from the very necessity of the case, who went by the name of Apocrisiarius, Archicapellanus, Capellanus [1], or at an earlier period, of Referendarius [2] ; at a later again, of Archicancellarius, because he had a subordinate officer or deputy commonly called the Cancellarius. He was the head of those whose business it was to prepare writs and other legal instruments, and who went by the general names of Notarii or Tabelliones [3]. In a state which admitted of what are now called Personal laws, that is, where each man might be judged, not according to the law of the place in which he was settled, but that of his parents, that under which he was born,—where Frank, Burgundian, Alaman and Roman might claim each to be tried and judged by Frankish, Burgundian, Alamanic or Roman law respectively, whatever might be the prevalent character of the territory in which he was domiciled,—such an officer was indispensable. The administration of the customary, unwritten

---

[1] Hincmar. § 32.

[2] " Qui referendarius ideo est dictus, quod ad eum universae publicae deferentur conscriptiones, ipseque eas annulo regis, sive sigillo ab eo sibi commisso muniret seu primaret." Aimo. Gest. Franc. iv. 41. Eichhorn, i. 194, note f. § 25, b.

[3] " Apocrisiario sociebatur summus cancellarius, qui a secretis olim appellabatur, erantque illi subiecti prudentes et intelligentes ac fideles viri, qui praecepta regia absque immoderata cupiditatis venalitate scriberent, et secreta illius fideliter custodirent." Hincmar. § 16. Eichhorn, loc. cit.

law of the Teutonic tribes might have been left to
Teutonic officers ; but what was to be done when
a Provincial claimed the application to his case
of the maxims and provisions of Roman jurisprudence ? What was to be done when a collision of
principles and a conflict of laws took place, and
must be provided for ? A clergyman, whose own
nation, whatever it might be, merged in the Roman
per clericalem honorem [1], must necessarily become a
principal officer of a state which numbered both
Romans and clergymen among its subjects ; and
hence the Apocrisiarius had a seat in the Carolingian parliament [2], as well as in the Council of the
Household, and ultimately became the principal minister for the affairs of the clergy [3]. But no such
necessity existed in England, where there was no
system of conflicting laws, and where the use of
professional notaries was unknown [4], and I therefore
see no *à priori* probability of there having been any
such officer as the Referendarius or Apocrisiarius
in our courts. Nor till the reign of Eádweard the
Confessor is there the slightest historical evidence
in favour of such an office [5] : under this prince
however, whose predilection for Norman customs is

[1] " Landulfus et Petrus clericus germani, ... qui professi sumus ex
natione nostra legem vivere Langobardorum, sed ego Petrus clericus
per clericalem honorem lege videor vivere Romana." Lupi. p. 223, cited
by Savigny, Röm. Recht. i. 120.

[2] Hincmar. § 16, 19, 21. Döninges, Deut. Staatsr. p. 24 *seq.*

[3] Eichhorn, § 25, b. i. 195.

[4] " Quoniam tabellionum usus in regno Angliae non habetur." Mat.
Paris, Hen. III.

[5] In Cod. Dipl. Nos. 3, 4, an Angemundus referendarius is mentioned, but these two charters are glaring forgeries.

notorious, it is not improbable that some change may have taken place in this respect, and that a gradual approximation to the continental usage may have been found. The occurrence therefore of a Cancellarius, Sigillarius and Notarius among his household does not appear matter of great surprise, and may be admitted as genuine, if we are only careful not to confound the first officer with that great functionary whom we now call the Lord High Chancellor of the realm. We are told that, among his innovations, Eádweard attempted to introduce the use of seals ; the uniform tenor of his writs certainly renders it not improbable that he had also notaries or professional clerks, and I can therefore admit the probability of his having appointed some faithful chaplain to act as his chancellor, that is, to keep his seal,—though not yet used for public instruments,—and to manage the royal notarial establishment. There are many persons named as royal chaplains ; some, whose successive appointments to bishoprics appeared to our simple forefathers to encroach too much upon the proper and canonical mode of election. Among them are the following :—

Eádsige capellanus,   1038 [1].

Stigandus capellanus,   1044 [2].

Heremannus capellanus, 1045 [3].

Wulfwig cancellarius, Eádweard, 1045 [4].

Reginboldus sigillarius, ... [5].

---

[1] Flor. Wig. an. 1038, Abp. Canterbury.
[2] Ibid. an. 1044, Abp. Canterbury.
[3] Ibid. an. 1045, Bp. Ramsbury.   [4] Cod. Dipl. No. 779.
[5] Cod. Dipl. No. 810.

Reginboldus cancellarius, Eádweard, 1045[1].

Ælfgeat notarius,	...	... [2].
Petrus capellanus,	...	... [3].
Baldwinus capellanus,	...	... [4].
Osbernus capellanus,	...	... [5].
Rodbertus capellanus,	...	... [6].
Heca capellanus,	1047 [7].	
Ulf capellanus,	1049 [8].	
Cynesige capellanus,	1051 [9].	
Wilhelmus capellanus,	1051 [10].	
Godmannus capellanus,	1053 [11].	
Gisa capellanus,	1060 [12].	

Eádweard's queen Eádgyfu and her brother Harald had also their chaplains; Walther, afterwards bishop of Hereford[13], and Leófgár who preceded him in the same see [14], and who, being probably of the same mind as his noble and warlike lord, was no sooner a bishop than " he forsook his chrism and rood, his spiritual weapons, and took to his spear and sword," and so going to the field against Griffin the Welsh king, was slain, and many of his priests with him. The establishment of chaplains in the royal household is, of course, of the highest antiquity; it is probable that they were preceded there

---

[1] Cod. Dipl. Nos. 813, 824, 825, 891.
[2] Ibid. No. 825.
[4] Ibid. No. 813.
[6] Ibid. No. 825, Abp. Canterbury.
[7] Flor. Wig. an. 1047, Bp. Selsey.
[8] Ibid. an. 1049, Bp. Leicester.
[10] Ibid. an. 1051, Bp. London.
[12] Ibid. an. 1060, Bp. Wells.
[14] Ibid. an. 1056, Chron. 1056.

[3] Ibid. Nos. 813, 825.
[5] Ibid. No. 825.

[9] Ibid. an. 1051, Abp. York.
[11] Ibid. an. 1053.
[13] Ibid. an. 1060.

by Pagan priests, and formed a necessary part of the royal comitatus in all ages [1].

Among the royal officers was also the Pedissequus or as he is sometimes called Pedessessor, whose functions I cannot nearer define, unless he were a king's messenger. The following instances occur:— Æðelheáh pedessessor, who appears to have been a duke [2] : Bola pedisecus [3] : Ælfred pedisecus [4]. Eástmund pedisecus [5]. In Beówulf, Hunferð the orator is said to *sit* at the king's *feet*, " ðe æt fótum sæt freán scyldinga." (l. 994.)

In the year 1040, Hardacnut's *carnifex* or executioner is described as a person of great dignity [6]. Other titles are also enumerated, some of which appear to denote offices in the royal household : thus we find Radulfus aulicus [7], Bundinus palatinus [8], Deórmód cellerarius [9], Wiferð claviger [10], Leófsige signifer [11], Ælfwine sticcere [12], Æðelríc bigenga [13]. It is uncertain whether the following are to be considered as regular members of the court, or whether their presence was merely accidental, on a particular occasion : Brihtríc and Ælfgár, consiliarii [14], Ælfwig [15] and Cyneweard [16] praepositi, Godricus tri-

---

[1] " Desiderante rege [Alchfrið] ut vir tantae eruditionis ac religionis sibi specialiter individuo comitatu sacerdos esset et doctor." Beda, H. E. ii. 19.   [2] Cod. Dipl. Nos. 196, 199, 207.
[3] Ibid. No. 220.   [4] Ibid. No. 227.   [5] Ibid. No. 281.
[6] " Ælfricum Eboracensem archiepiscopum, Godwinum comitem, Stir majorem domus, Thrond suum carnificem, et alios magnae dignitatis viros, Lundoniam misit." Flor. Wig. an. 1040.

[7] Cod. Dipl. No. 813.	[8] Ibid. No. 813.
[9] Ibid. No. 320.	[10] Ibid. No. 346.
[11] Ibid. No. 346.	[12] Ibid. No. 799.
[13] Ibid. No. 745.	[14] Ibid. No. 811.
[15] Ibid. Nos. 792, 793, 800.	[16] Ibid. Nos. 792, 800.

bunus [1], Aldred theloniarius [2]. Nor is it absolutely demonstrable that those who claimed consanguinity with the king formed part of his household, although they probably made their connexion valid as a recommendation to royal favour. "The king's poor cousin [3]" seems at all events to have taken care that his light should shine before men, as we learn from the signatures, Ælfhere ex parentela regis [4], Leófwine propinquus regis [5], Hesburnus regis consanguineus [6], Rodbertus regis consanguineus [7], and similar entries.

But no such doubt applies to the household troops, or immediate body-guard of the king. These are commonly called Húscarlas, by the Anglosaxon writers, and continued to exist under that name after the Norman conquest. Lappenberg has very justly looked upon them as a kind of military gild, or association, of which the king was the master [8]. I doubt whether they were organized as a separate force before the time of Cnut; but it is certain that under that prince and his Danish successors they attained a definite and settled position. It is probable that this resulted from the circumstances under which he obtained the crown of England, and that the institution was not known to his Saxon predecessors: as an invader, not at all secure of his

[1] Cod. Dipl. No. 945.   [2] Ibid. No. 218.
[3] Shaksp. Hen. IV. Pt. ii. sc. 2.   [4] Cod. Dipl. No. 436.
[5] Ibid. No. 436.   [6] Ibid. No. 813.
[7] Ibid. No. 813.
[8] Thorpe's Lappenberg, ii. 202, and his references to Suen Aggonis, Hist. Legum Castrens. Regis Canuti Magni, c. iv. ap. Langebek, iii. 146; ii. 454, note *d*. Palgrave, ii. p. ccclxxxi. Ellis, Introd. Domesd. i. 91; ii. 151 *seq*.

tenure, and surrounded by nobles whose previous conduct offered but slight guarantee of their fidelity, it became absolutely necessary to his safety to organize his own peculiar force in such a way as to secure the readiest service if occasion demanded it. This was the object of the Witherlags Ret, by which the privileges and duties of the Húscarlas were settled. Of this law Lappenberg observes:—" With greater probability may be reckoned among the earlier labours of Cnut, the composition of the Witherlags Ret, a court- or gild-law, framed for his standing army, as well as for the body-guards of his jarls. As the greater part of his army remained in England, the Witherlags Ret was there first established, and as the introduction of strict discipline among such a military community must precede all other ameliorations in the condition of the country, the mention of this law in its history ought not to be omitted [1]. The immediate military

---

[1] This observation requires to be taken with some caution. The Witherlags Ret was a private and bye-law, not a public law, and had little to do with the public law, except in as far as it connected the conquering force by closer bonds, and secured their energetic action as a body, upon emergency. It was devised to keep the household troops together, not to apply in any way to their public relation towards the Saxons. Its influence was therefore only such as derived mediately from the fact of its maintaining the king at the head of a select *prætorian* cohort,—important occasionally, but always accidental. There is no evidence that the great men of England, the Godwines, or Leófrics, were ever Húscarlas, or that the leaders of this force were ever Ealdormen or Geréfan. In fact it was the king's " Army-club," and had neither constitutional place nor recognized power. The Húscarlas were probably very like what the Mousquetaires and Gardes-de-corps were in France before the first Revolution, and what the Lifeguards, Leib-regimente, Guardia Real, and so on, have been in other states of Europe ; nor altogether unlike the Garde Impériale of Napoleon.

attendants of a conqueror always exercise vast influence, and these originally Danish soldiers (thinga-
menn, thingamanna lith, by the English called
Húscarlas) have at a later period, both as body-
guards of the king and of the great vassals, acted
no unimportant part in the country. They were
armed with axes, halberds and swords inlaid with
gold, and in purpose, descent and equipment cor-
responded to the Warangian guard (Wæringer), in
which the throne of the Byzantine emperors found
its best security. In Cnut's time the number of
these mercenaries was not very great,— being by
some reckoned at three thousand, by others at six
thousand [1] — but they were gathered under his
banner from various nations, and consequently required the stricter discipline. Even a valiant Wend-
ish prince, Gottschalk, the son of Udo, stayed long
with Cnut in England, and gained the hand of a
daughter of the royal house [2]. Cnut himself appears rather as a sort of grand-master of this military gild, than as its commander, and it is said that,
having in his anger slain one of the brotherhood
in England, he submitted himself to its judgment
in their assembly (stefn) and paid a ninefold compensation [3]. The degrading epithet of ' nithing '

[1] Three thousand men, all disciplined, all well-armed, all united by
the certainty that the struggle must be for life or death, formed a force
morally, if not physically and numerically, superior to any that could
be brought against them on a sudden. Such a body were amply secure
in a state which could only set on foot a clumsy and reluctant militia.
They were, in fact, nearly the only professional soldiers,—and as yet
there had been no Rocroy, Sempach or Morgarten.

[2] Adam Bremen. ii. 48, 59 ; iii. 21.

[3] Suen Aggon. i. cap. 10.

applied to an expelled member of the gild, is an Anglosaxon word, which at a later period occurs in a way to render it extremely probable that the gild-law of the royal house-carls was in existence after the Norman conquest[1]."

The details of this law are of the most stringent description, regulating even the minutest points of social intercourse. Its extreme punishment was expulsion; but expulsion was nearly equivalent to death, situated as the Húscarlas were expected to be, among a hostile population. And though the offending brother had his election, whether he would retire from the gild by sea or land, yet the circumstances which attended his ejection were not those of mercy or alleviation. To the seashore, the whole body of his ancient comrades were to accompany him; then launching him in a boat, with oars or sails, they were to commit him to his fortune: henceforth he was not only a stranger but an enemy, an outlaw: if stress of weather or other accident brought him back to the shore, he might be fallen upon and slain without remorse or retribution. Or if he chose to retire by land, he was to be led to the nearest wood, and there to be watched till his form was lost in the darkness of the thickets: three successive shouts were then to be raised, to warn him of the direction in which

---

[1] Sax. Chron. 1049. Will. Malm. lib. iv. de Willelmo Secundo, an. 1088 (Hardy's ed. ii. 489). But Lappenberg's conclusion is not justified by the premises, for Niðing, which Mat. Paris declares to have been so especially an Anglosaxon word as to be untranslatable, was probably in use as a term of supreme contempt, long before the establishment of the Húscarlas in England and long after their disbanding.

his gild-brothers lay in wait. If then, through the devious error of the forest he returned into their presence, his life was forfeit. To insult, injure or dishonour a brother was an offence punished with the utmost severity; and if three of the Húscarlas concurred in accusing one of the body, there was neither denial nor exculpation allowed; the penalty followed inevitably. Such severe regulations as these fully explain their object; and it seems to have been successfully attained, for we are told that, at least during the life of Cnut, the penalties were never once incurred or enforced[1].

From the collocation of names among the witnesses to a very important charter of 1052–1054, we may infer that the Stealleras or Marshals were the commanding officers of the Húscarlas[2]. We cannot doubt that they did really exercise an important personal influence in England, although they filled no recognized position under the law: it is probable that they were reckoned as thanes or ministers, as far as their wergyld and heriot were concerned; but we have no evidence of this, and I

[1] Except in his own case, where they were incurred, but not enforced. The story (found in great detail in Saxo-Grammaticus, book x.) seems exaggerated; but nevertheless it is easy to see that the strict application of the law to the king would have caused the destruction of the whole system. As they could not do without Cnut, and had no law whereby to judge him, save the one whose application in his case was impossible, they suffered him to assess his own penalty. He paid nine times the wergyld of the brother he had slain.

[2] Cod. Dipl. No. 956. After the testimonies of the king, queen, archbishops, bishops, earls, and abbots, we have, "And on Esgáres stealres, and on Raulfes stealres, and on Lifinges stealres, and on ealra ðæs kynges húscarlan." Then follow the subscriptions of chaplains and others.

should not dispute the assertion that from first to last they had a law of their own,—a personal right, —that they were not generally or originally land-owners, and that their institution was a modified revival of the system of the Comitatus in its strictest form. But upon these points we cannot decide. It is very rarely that we find the Húscarlas acting as witnesses to charters, which perhaps may lead to the inference that they were not members of the Witena gemót[1] : but in 1041 we are told that Hardacnut sent two of his Húscarlas, Feader and Turstan, to collect an unpopular tax, and that a sedition was raised against them in Worcester, which was not suppressed till the force of several counties, under the most celebrated leaders of the day, was brought against the city[2].

In a charter of the Confessor, we find the word Húscarl translated by "praefectus palatinus[3],"—a title which scarcely seems applicable to all the members of a body numbering six, or even three, thousand men: but, however this may be, we must not confound these *praefecti palatini* with the other, earlier *praefecti* who occur in Anglosaxon history[4]: these are clearly only geréfan or reeves, and have nothing to do with the especial body of household troops.

It remains only to add that, in imitation of the

---

[1] But Wulfnoð a húscarl is mentioned, Cod. Dipl. No. 845, and Urk, a húscarl in No. 871, both as grantees. So again þurstán húscarl, a holder of land in Middlesex. Cod. Dipl. No. 843.

[2] Flor. Wig. an. 1041.

[3] Cod. Dipl. No. 843.

[4] Cod. Dipl. Nos. 746, 751, 762, 767.

king, the great nobles surrounded themselves with a body-guard of Húscarlas [1], who probably stood in the same relation to their lord, as he did to the king: in short the institution is only a revival of the Comitatus, described in the First Book, and must have gone through a similar course of development. Nay, the details which have reached us of the later establishment may possibly throw light upon the earlier, and serve to explain some of the peculiarities which strike us in the account of Tacitus. This difference indeed there is, that in the later form the king and the comites unite in a definite bond, with respective, stipulated rights; in the earlier form, the comites attach themselves to the king, without stipulation or reserve, although no doubt under the protection of a customary and recognized, although unwritten, law.

[1] Florence of Worcester, speaking of the revolt of the Northumbrians against their duke Tostig, in 1065, says: " Eodem die primitus illius Danicos húscarlas Amundum et Ravensueartum, de fuga retractos, extra civitatis muros, ac die sequente plus quam cc. viros ex curialibus illius in boreali parte Humbrae fluminis peremerunt." an. 1065. One manuscript of the Saxon Chronicle thus relates these events : "And sona æfter ðison gegaderedon ða þegenas hi ealle on Eoforwícscyre ˀ on Norðhymbralande togædere, ˀ geútlagedan heora eorl Tosti, ˀ ofslógon his híredmenn ealle ðe hig mihten tócumen. But another says : " Tostiges eorles húskarlas ðar ofslógon, ealle ða ðe hig geáxian mihton." Hírédmen are *familiares,* those who live in the house, or form part of the house or family; and this seems the original and strict definition of the húscarl.

CHAPTER IV.

THE EALDORMAN OR DUKE.

It is of much less importance to a people, what its constitution is, than what is its administration; nothing can be easier than to make what are called charters, and it is a rhetorical commonplace to talk of resting under a constitution, the growth of ages: but no nation rests, or ever did rest, under the one or the other. The source of a nation's comfort,— of its success in realizing the great principle of the mutual guarantee of peace, lies in the administration of what is called its constitution, in the skill with which it has devised its machinery of government, in the balance of power which it represents in the election of its instruments. We shall therefore pass now to the members of the Anglosaxon administration.

The dignity next in importance to the royal, is that of the Ealdorman or Duke.

The proper Anglosaxon name for this officer, as ruler and leader of an army, is Heretoga, in Oldgerman Herizohho, and in modern German, Herzog,—a word compounded of *Here* an army, and *toga* a leader[1]. It is in this sense only that Tacitus appears to understand the word Dux, when he tells

---

[1] In this sense the Sax. Chron. translates the word *duces* applied by Beda to Hengest and Hors, by *heretogan*: an. 448.

us that dukes (i. e. generals) are chosen for their valour, in contradistinction to kings, who are recommended by their birth. But inasmuch as the ducal functions in the Anglosaxon polity were by no means confined to service in the field, the peculiar title of Heretoga is very rarely met with, being for the most part replaced by Ealdorman or Aldorman, which denotes civil as well as military preeminence. The word Heretoga accordingly is nowhere found in the Saxon Chronicle, or in the Laws, except in one late passage interpolated into the collection called the Laws of Eádweard the Confessor, and to the best of my remembrance it is found but once in the Charters[1]. From a very extensive and careful comparison between the titles used in different documents, it appears that Latin writers of various periods, as Beda, the several compilers of Annals, and the writers of charters, have used the words Dux, Princeps and Comes, in a very arbitrary manner to denote the holders of one and the same office. It is indeed just possible that the grant of peculiar and additional privileges may have been supposed to make a distinction between the duke and the prince, as the charters appear to show something like a system of promotion at least among the Mercian nobility, the same person being found to sign for some time as dux, and afterwards as princeps. In consequence of this confusion, it is necessary to proceed with very great caution the moment we leave contemporaneous history, and

---

[1] It occurs however in the document called "Institutes of Polity:" Thorpe, ii. 319: but these can hardly be considered authority for a strict *legal* use of words.

become dependent upon the expressions of annalists long subsequent to the events described : for strictly and legally speaking, the words count, duke and prince express very different ranks and functions.

The pure Anglosaxon authorities however are incapable of making any such blunder or falling into any such confusion : where Simeon of Durham, Florence of Worcester, Æðelweard, Henry of Huntingdon, nay even Beda himself, use Consul, Princeps, Dux and Comes, the Saxon Chronicle and the charters composed in Saxon have invariably Ealdorman. A few instances, down to the time of Cnut, when a new organization, and with it a new title, was adopted, will make this clear [1].

[1] Beorht ealdorman. Chron. an. 684.   Dux. Beda, iv. 26. Flor. 684.

....	.... 699.	
Æðelhun	.... 750.	Dux. Æðelw. ii. Flor. 750. Consul. H. Hunt. iv.
Beorhtfríð	.... 710.	Præfectus. Flor. 710.
Cumbra	.... 755.	Dux. Æðelw. ii. 17. Flor. 755. Consul. H. Hunt. iv.
O'srìc...........	.... 755.	Dux. Æðelw. ii. 17. Flor. 784.
Beorn	.... 780.	Patricius. Sim. D. 780. Consul et justiciarius. H. Hunt. iv.
Æðelheard	.... 794.	
Wor	.... 800.	
Æðelmund	.... 800.	Dux. Flor. 800. Consul. H. Hunt. iv.
Weohstán........	.... 800.	Dux. Flor. 800. Consul. H. Hunt. iv.
Heábyrht	.... 805.	Comes. Flor. 805.
Eádbyrht	.... 819.	
Burghard	.... 822.	Dux. Flor. 822.
Muca...........	.... 822.	Dux. Flor. 822.
Wulfheard	.... 823.	Dux. Flor. 823. Consul. H. Hunt. iv.
Ealdormen	.... 825.	Duces. Flor. 825.
Dudda	.... 833.	
O'smód	.... 833.	

The word *ealdor* or *aldor* in Anglosaxon denotes
princely dignity without any definition of function
whatever.   In Beówulf it is used as a synonym for
cyning, þeóden and other words applied to royal
personages.   Like many other titles of rank in the
various Teutonic tongues, it is derived from an adjective implying age, though practically this idea
does not by any means survive in it, any more than
it does in the word Senior, the origin of the feudal

Wulfheard	Chron. an. 837.	Dux. Flor. 837.
Æðelhelm	....	837. Dux. Flor. 837.
Herebyrht	.....	838. Dux. Flor. 838.
Eánwulf	.....	845. Dux. Flor. 845.
O'sríc	....	845. Dux. Flor. 845.
Ceorl	....	851. Comes. Flor. 851.
Ealhhere	....	851, 853. Comes. Flor. 851, 853.
Æðelheard	....	852.
Hunberht........	....	852. Comes. Flor. 852.
Huda	....	853. Comes. Flor. 853.
O'sríc	....	860. Comes. Flor. 860.
Æðelwulf........	....	860, 871. Comes. Flor. 860, 871.
Æðelred	....	886. Comes. Flor. 886. Dux. Flor. 894.
Æðelhelm	....	886, 894, 898. Dux. Flor. 894.
Beocca..........	....	888. Dux. Flor. 889.
Æðelwold	....	888. Dux. Flor. 889.
Æðelred	....	894. Dux. Flor. 894.
Æðelnóð........	....	894. Dux. Flor. 894.
Ceólwulf........	....	897. Dux. Flor. 897.
Beorhtwulf	....	897. Dux. Flor. 897.
Wulfred	....	897.
Æðelred	....	901.
Æðelwulf	....	903. Dux. Flor. 903.
Sigewulf	....	905. Dux. Flor. 905.
Sigehelm	....	905. Comes. Flor. 905.
Æðelred	....	912. Dominus et subregulus. Flor. 912.
Ælfgár..........	....	946.
Ordgár..........	....	965. Dux. Flor. 964.
Ælfhere	....	980, 983. Dux. Flor. 979.
Æðelmǽr........	....	982. Dux. Flor. 982.

term Seigneur[1]; and similarly the words "ða yldestan witan," literally the eldest councillors, are used to express merely the most dignified[2].

If we compare the position and powers of the ealdorman with those of the duke on the continent, we shall find several points of difference which deserve notice. In the imperial constitution of the German states, as it was modified and settled by Charlemagne, the duke was a superior officer to the comes, count or graf, and a duchy for the most part comprehended several counties, over which the duke exercised an immediate jurisdiction[3]. Occasionally no doubt there were counties

Eádwine........Chron. an. 982. Dux. Flor. 982.
Ælfríc..........   .... 983, 985, 992, 993.   Dux. Flor. 983.
Birhtnóð........ .... 991. Dux. Flor. 991.
Æðelwine .... 992. Dux. Flor. 992.
Æðelweard .... 994. Dux. Flor. 994.
Leófsige .... 1002. Dux. Flor. 1002.
Ælfhelm .... 1006. Dux. Flor. 1006.
Eádríc.......... .... 1007, 1009, 1012, 1015, 1016. Dux. Flor. in an.
Æðelmær ealdorman .... 1013. Comes. Flor. 1013.
Ælfríc .... 1016. Dux. Flor. 1016.
Godwine .... 1016. Dux. Flor. 1016.
Æðelwine .... 1016. Dux. Flor. 1016.

The same thing is observable in the charters: thus O'swulf Aldormon, Cod. Dipl. No. 226, but "Dux et princeps Orientalis Canciae," No. 256. Again the nobleman who in the body of the charter No. 219 is called Eádwulf ealdorman, signs himself among the witnesses, Eádwulf Dux.

[1] The Roman *Senatus,* the Greek γερουσία, the ecclesiastical πρεσβύτεροι are all examples of a like usage.

[2] Chron. Sax. an. 978.

[3] I refer generally here to the doctrines of Eichhorn, Staats- und Rechtsgesch. i. 460. etc.; and to the works of the great German authors who have treated this subject and others connected with it, more especially to Dönniges, Deutsches Staatsrecht, p. 96 *seq.*

without duchies, and duchies without counties, that is where the duke and count were the same person: sometimes the dukes were hereditary dynasts, representing sovereign families which had become subject to the empire of the Franks, and who continued to govern' as imperial officers the populations which either by conquest or alliance had become incorporated with it; such were the dukes in Bavaria and Swabia. In other cases they were generals, exercising supreme military power over extensive districts committed to their charge, and mediately entrusted with the defence and government of the Markgraviats or border-counties which were established for the security of the frontiers. The variable, and very frequently exceptional, position of these nobles or ministerials, while it renders it difficult to give an accurate description of their powers which shall be applicable to all cases, often accounts for the events by which we are led to recognize modern kingdoms in the ancient duchies, and to trace the derived and mediate authority down to its establishment as independent royalty.

But this state of things which was possible in an empire comprising a vast extent of lands held by tribes of different descent, language, and laws, and often hostile to one another, was not to be expected in a country like England. Neither were the districts here sufficiently large, nor in general was the national feeling in those districts sufficiently strong, to produce similar results. Strictly speaking, during what has been loosely termed the Heptarchy, the various kingdoms or rather principal kingdoms bore a much greater resemblance to the Frankish duchies, and the small subordinate principalities to the counties; and could we admit the existence of a central authority or Bretwaldadom, we should find a considerable resemblance between the two forms: but this is in fact impossible: the kings, such as they were, continued to enjoy all the royal rights in their limited districts; and the dukes remained merely ministerial officers, of great dignity indeed, but with well-defined and not very extensive powers. The rebellion of a duke in English seems nearly as rare as it is frequent in German history. We may therefore conclude that the Anglosaxon Ealdorman in reality represented the Graf or Count of the Germans, before the powers of the latter had been seriously abridged by the imperial constitution of the Carlovings, by the growing authority of the duke, the Missus or royal messenger and the bishop. And this will tend to explain the comparatively subordinate position of the geréfa, who answers, in little more than name, to the Graphio or Graf.

In the Anglosaxon laws we find many provisions respecting the powers and dignity of the ealdorman, which it will be necessary to examine in detail. It is highly probable that different races and kingdoms adopted a somewhat different course with respect to them,—a course rendered inevitable by the connection of the ealdorman with territorial government. The laws of the Kentish kings do not make any mention of such an officer: the ceorl, eorl and king are the only free classes whose

K 2

proportionable value they notice; and if there were
ealdormen at all, they were comprised in the great
caste of eorls or nobles by birth, even as Æ𝔡elberht's
law uses *eorlcund*, that is of earl's rank, as a synonym for *betst*, that is the best or highest rank[1]. In
the law of Eádríc and Hló𝔡here, though various
judicial proceedings are referred to, we hear nothing of the ealdorman : suit is to be prosecuted at
the king's hall[2], before the stermelda[3], or the wícgeréfa[4], but no other officer is mentioned; probably because at this period, the little kingdoms into
which Kent itself was divided, supplied ample machinery for doing justice, without the establishment
of ealdormen for that or any other purpose. The
law of Wihtræd has no provision of the sort, and
it is remarkable that in the proem to his dooms,
which a king always declares to be made with the
counsel, consent and license of his nobles, the word
eádigan, the wealthy or powerful, twice occurs[5],
but not the word *ealdormen*. I therefore think it
probable that Kent had no such officers at the commencement of the eighth century[6].

[1] "Mund 𝔡ǽre betstan widuwan eorlcundre, fiftig scillinga gebéte."
For the mund of a widow of the highest class, that is of earl's degree,
be the bót fifty shillings. Æ𝔡elb. § 75. Thorpe, i. 20.

[2] Eád. Hló𝔡. § 5. Thorpe, i. 28.

[3] Eád. Hló𝔡. § 7, 16. Thorpe, i. 30, 34.

[4] Eád. Hló𝔡. § 16. Thorpe, i. 34.   [5] Leg. Wiht. Thorpe, i. 36.

[6] I do not think the expression of the Sax. Chron. an. 568 can be
considered to contradict this. The ealdormen recorded there are
merely princes in a general sense : as are Cerdíc and Cyneríc named
an. 495, just as the same Chronicle an. 465 mentions twelve Welsh
ealdormen. So also in 653, Peada the king of the Southangles is called
aldorman. The Kentish charters in which we find Hamgisilus, *dux*,
and Graphio, *comes*, are impudent forgeries. Cod. Dipl. Nos. 2, 3, 4.

In general Beda uses the words *tribunus* or *prae-fectus* to express the authority of a royal officer either in the field or the city: with him *comes* represents the old and proper sense of the king's comrade, as we find it in Tacitus, and *dux* is applied in the Roman sense to the leader or captain of a *corps d'armée*. But it is possible that in one passage he may have had something more in view, where he states that after the death of Peada, that is in 661, the dukes of the Mercians, Immin, Eaba and Eádberht rebelled against Osuuiu of Northumberland and raised Wulfhere to his father's throne[1]; and he goes on to say that, having expelled the princes, — " principibus eiectis," — whom the foreign king had imposed upon them, they recovered both their boundaries and their liberty. It is every way probable both that the Mercian dukes and Northumbrian princes mentioned in this passage were fiscal and administrative, not merely military officers[2]. Not much later than this we find dukes in Wessex[3] and Sussex[4]; and from this period we can follow the dukes with little intermission till the close of the genuine Anglosaxon rule with Eádmund Irensída.

From the time of Ini of Wessex we have the means of tracing the institution with some certainty; and we may thus commence our enquiry

---

[1] Beda, H. E. iii. 24.

[2] The forged foundation charter of Peterborough mentions the following ealdormen: Immin, Eádberht, Herefriŏ, Wilberht, Abon.— Chron. Sax. 657. Cod. Dipl. No. 986.

[3] Cod. Dipl. Nos. 31, 54, 987, etc.

[4] Ibid. No. 994. Beda, H. E. iv. 13.

with the first years of the eighth century, nearly one hundred years before Charlemagne modified and recast the German empire. At first the ealdormen are few in number, but increase as the circuit of the kingdom extends; we can thus follow them in connection with the political advance of the several countries, till we find at one time no less than three dukes at once in Kent, and sixteen in Mercia. This number attended a witena gemót held by Coenwulf in the year 814.

The reason of this was, that the ealdorman was inseparable from a shire or gá : the territorial and political divisions went together, and as conquest increased or defeat diminished the number of shires comprised in a kingdom, we find a corresponding increase or diminution in ·the number of dukes attendant upon the king. Ælfred decides that if a man wish to leave one lord and seek another, (hláfordsócn, a right possessed by all freemen,) he is to do so with the witness of the ealdorman whom he before followed in his shire, that is, whose court and military muster he had been bound to attend [1] : and Ini declares that the ealdorman who shall be privy to the escape of a thief shall forfeit his shire, unless he can obtain the king's pardon [2]. The proportionably great severity of this punishment arises, and most justly so, from the circumstance of the ealdorman being the principal judicial officer in the county, as the Graf was among the

---

[1] Leg. Ælfr. § 37. Thorpe, i. 86.

[2] "Gif he ealdormon síe, þolie his scíre, búton him cyning árian wille." Leg. Ini, § 36. Thorpe, i. 124.

Franks. The fiftieth law of Ini provides for the case where a man compounds for offences committed by any of his household, where suit has been either made before the king himself or the king's ealdorman[1]. He was commanded to hold a shiremoot or general county-court twice in the year, where in company of the bishop he was to superintend the administration of civil, criminal and ecclesiastical law: Eádgár enacts[2],—" Twice in the year be a shiremoot held ; and let both the bishop of the shire and the ealdorman be present, and there expound both the law of God, and of the world : " which enactment is repeated in nearly the same words by Cnut[3]. And this is consistent with a regulation of Ælfred, by which a heavy fine is inflicted upon him who shall break the public peace by fighting or even drawing his weapon in the Folcmoot before the king's ealdorman[4]. In the year 780 we learn from the Saxon Chronicle that the high-reeves or noble geréfan of Northumberland burned Beorn the ealdorman to death at Seletún[5] : but Henry of Huntingdon records the same fact with more detail : he says[6],—" The year after this the princes and chief officers of Northumberland burned

---

[1] Thorpe, i. 134.   [2] Eádgár, ii. § 5. Thorpe, i. 268.

[3] Cnut, Sec. § 18. Thorpe, i. 386. And so in the Frankish law the graff or count was to hold his court together with the bishop. Dönniges, p. 29.

[4] Ælfr. § 38. Thorpe, i. 86.   [5] Chron. Sax. an. 780.

[6] Hen. Hunt. book iv. " Anno autem hunc sequente principes et praepositi Nordhumbre quendam consulem et justiciarium suum, quia rigidior aequo extiterat, combusserunt." This seems like a judicial execution, not a mere act of popular vengeance. Simeon however says " Osbald et Æðelheard duces, congregato exercitu, Bearn patricium

to death a certain *consul* and justiciary of theirs, because he was more severe than was right: " from which it would appear not only that this ealdorman had been guilty of cruelty and oppression in the exercise of his judicial functions, but, from the hint of Simeon, also that the king acquiesced in his punishment. We have occasional records in the Saxon charters which show that the shiremoot for judicial purposes was presided over by the ealdorman of the shire. In 825 there was an interesting trial touching the rights of pasture belonging to Worcester cathedral, which the public officers had encroached upon : it was arranged in a synod held at Clofeshoo, that the bishop should give security to the ealdorman and witan of the county, to make good his claim on oath, which was done within a month at Worcester, in the presence of Háma the woodreeve, who attended on behalf of Eádwulf the ealdorman[1]. Another very important document records a trial which took place about 1038 in Herefordshire : the shiremoot sat at Ægelnóðes stán, and was held by Æðelstán the bishop, and Ranig the ealdorman in the presence of the county thanes[2]. Another but undated record of a shiremoot held at Worcester again presents us with the presidency of an ealdorman, Leófwine[3].

It is thus clear that the ealdorman really stood

Elfuualdi regis in Seletune succenderunt ix Kal. Jan.," which can hardly be anything but what is referred to in the entry of the preceding year, where Simeon says of Ælfwald, "Erat enim rex pius et iustus, ut sequens demonstrabit articulus." Sim. Gest. Reg. an. 779, 780.

[1] Cod. Dipl. No. 219.   [2] Ibid. No. 755.
[3] Ibid. No. 898.

at the head of the justice of the county, and for this purpose there can be no doubt that he possessed full power of holding plea, and proceeding to execution both in civil and criminal cases. The scírmen, scírgeréfan or sheriffs were his officers, and acted by his authority, a point to which I shall return hereafter. That the executive as well as the judicial authority resided in the ealdorman and his officers seems to me unquestionable: Ælfred directs that no private feud shall be permitted, except in certain grave cases, but that if a man beleaguers his foe in his own house, he shall summon him to surrender his weapons and stand to trial. If the complainant be not powerful enough to enforce this, he is to apply to the ealdorman (a mode of expression which implies the presence of one in every shire), and on his refusal to assist, resort may be had to the king[1]. For this there was also good reason: the ealdorman in the shire, like the Frankish graf, was the military leader of the *hereban*, posse comitatus or levy *en masse* of the freemen, and as such could command their services to repel invasion or to exercise the functions of the higher police: as a noble of the first rank he had armed retainers, thanes or comites of his own; but his most important functions were as leader of the armed force of the shire. Throughout the Saxon times we read of ealdormen at the head of particular counties, doing service in the field: thus in 800 we hear of a battle between the Mercian ealdorman

---

[1] Leg. Ælfr. § 42. Thorpe, i. 90.

Æðelmund with the Hwiccas, and the Westsaxon
Weoxstán with the men of Wiltshire[1]: in 837,
Æðelhelm led the men of Dorset against the Danes[2]:
in 845 Eánwulf with the men of Somerset, and Osríc with the men of Dorset, obtained a bloody victory over the same adversaries[3]: in 853 a similar
fortune attended Ealhhere with the men of Kent,
and Huda with them of Surrey, the latter of whom
had marched from their own county into Thanet,
in pursuit of the enemy[4]. In 860, Osríc with his
men of Hampshire, and ealdorman Æðelwulf with
the power of Berkshire, gave the Danes an overthrow in the neighbourhood of Winchester[5]; in
905 the men of Kent with Sigewulf and Sigehelm
their ealdormen were defeated on the banks of the
Ouse[6]: lastly in 1016, we find Eádríc the ealdorman deserting Eádmund Irensída in battle with the
Magesætan or people of Herefordshire[7],—a treason
which ultimately led to the division of England
between Eádmund and Cnut, and later to the monarchy of the latter. Everywhere the ealdorman
is identified with the military force of his shire or
county, as we have already seen that he was with
the administration of justice.

The internal regulation of the shire, as well as
its political relation to the whole kingdom, were

[1] Chron. Sax. an. 800.   [2] Ibid. an. 837.
[3] Ibid. an. 845.   [4] Ibid. an. 853.
[5] Ibid. an. 860.   [6] Ibid. an. 905.
[7] Ibid. an. 1016. Other instances of ealdormen as military leaders,
but without reference to particular localities, may be found in the
Chron. Sax. under the years, 684, 699, 710, 823, 825, 838, 851, 871,
894, 992, 993, 1003, etc., and in all the annalists.

under the immediate guidance and supervision of the ealdorman: the scírgeréfa or sheriff was little more than his deputy: it is not to be doubted that the cyninges geréfan, wícgeréfan and túngeréfan were under his superintendence and command, and it would almost appear as if he possessed the right to appoint as well as control these officers: at all events we find some of them intended by the expression "ðæs ealdormonnes gingran," literally the ealdorman's subordinate officers; Ælfred having affixed a severe punishment to the offence of breaking the peace of the folcmoot, in the ealdorman's presence, continues: " If anything of this sort happen before a king's ealdorman's subordinate officer, or a king's priest, let the fine be thirty shillings[1]."

In the year 995 certain brothers, apparently persons of some consideration, having been involved in an accusation of theft, a tumultuary affray took place, in which, amongst others, they were slain: the king's wícgeréfan in Oxford and Buckingham permitted their bodies to be laid in consecrated ground: but the ealdorman of the district, on being apprised of the facts, attempted to reverse the judgment of the wic-reeves[2]. It would therefore appear that these officers were subordinated to his authority. The analogy which we everywhere trace between the ealdorman and the graf, induces the conclusion that the former was the head fiscal officer of the shire; and that, in this as in all other cases, the scírgeréfa was his officer and accounted to him.

[1] Leg. Ælfr. § 38. Thorpe, i. 86.	[2] Cod. Dipl. No. 1289.

The means by which his dignity was supported were, strictly speaking, supplied by the state: they consisted in the first place of lands within his district[1], which appear to have passed with the office, and consequently to have been inalienable by any particular holder: but he also derived a considerable income from the fines and other moneys levied to the king's use, his share of which probably amounted to one-third[2]. But as it invariably happened that the ealdorman was appointed from among the class of higher nobles, it is certain that he always possessed large landed estates of his own[3], either by inheritance or royal grant: moreover it is probable that among a people in that stage of society in

[1] I cannot otherwise account for the mention of "ðæs ealdormonnes lond, ðæs ealdormonnes mearc, gemǽro," etc. which so often occur. The boundaries of charters not being accidental and fluctuating, but permanent, it follows that "the alderman's mark" was so also.

[2] "Dovere reddebat 18 libras, de quibus denariis habebat rex Edwardus duas partes et comes Goduinus tertiam." Domesd. Chenth. Whether all the estates of folcland were charged with payments to the duke is uncertain, but yet this is probable. The monastery lands appear to have been so; for in 848 Hunberht, ealdorman, prince or duke of the Tonsetan, released the monastery of Bredon from all payments heretofore due from that monastery to himself, or generally to the princes of that district. Cod. Dipl. No. 261. Again in 836, Wigláf of Mercia granted to the monastery at Hanbury perfect freedom and exemption from all demands, known and unknown, save the three inevitable burthens: the ealdormen Sigered and Mucel, whose rights were thus diminished, were indemnified, the first with a purse of six hundred shillings in gold, the second with three hundred acres at Croglea. Cod. Dipl. No. 237.

[3] The highest rank, that is the ealdorman's, appears to have implied the absolute possession of land to the amount of 40 hides, or 1200 acres. See Hist. Eliens. ii. 40: "Sed quoniam ille 40 hidarum terrae dominium minime obtineret, licet nobilis esset, inter proceres tunc nominari non potuit," etc. The charters show what large estates were devised by many of these ealdormen.

which we find the Saxons, voluntary offerings to
no small amount would find their way into the
spence or treasury of so powerful an officer : no
one ever approaches a Pacha without a present.
One form of such gratuities we can trace in the
charters ; I mean the grant of estates either for
lives or perpetuity, made by the clergy in consideration of support and protection ; thus in 855, we
find that Ealhhun, bishop of Worcester, and his
chapter gave eleven hides of land to duke Æðelwulf
and Wulfðryð, his duchess, for their lives, on condition that he would be a good and true friend
to the monastery, and protector of its liberties[1].
Fifty years later, in 904, Werfrið and the same
chapter granted to duke Æðelred, his duchess and
their daughter, a vill in Worcester and about 132
acres of arable and meadow land, for three lives,
with reversion to the see, on condition that they
would be good friends and protectors to the chapter[2].   It is likewise probable that even if no settled, legal share of the plunder were his of right,
still his opportunities of enriching himself in his
capacity of general were not inconsiderable : he
must for instance have had the ransom of all pri-
soners of any distinction, or the price of their sale.
And lastly in his public capacity he must always
have had a sufficient supply of convict as well
as voluntary labour at command, to ensure the
profitable cultivation of his land, and the safe
keeping of his flocks and herds.   There cannot be

---

[1] Cod. Dipl. No. 279.   [2] Ibid. No. 339.

the slightest doubt that he also possessed all the regalia in his own lands whether public or private, and that thus, wreck, treasure-trove, fines for harbouring of outlaws, and many other bóts or legal amerciaments passed into his hands. There are even slight indications that he, like many of the bishops, possessed the right to coin money; and in every case, he must have had the superintendence of the royal mint, and therefore probably the forfeiture of all unlicensed moneyers. In addition to all this, we cannot doubt that his power and influence pointed him out as the lord who could best be relied upon for protection and favour; and we may therefore conclude that commendation of estates to him was not unusual, from all which estates he would receive not only recognitory services, and yearly *gafol* or rent in labour and produce, but in all probability also fines on demise or alienation.

Thus the position which his nobility, his power and his wealth secured to the ealdorman was a brilliant one. In fact the whole executive government may be considered as a great aristocratical association, of which the ealdormen were the constituent members, and the king little more than the president. They were in nearly every respect his equals, and possessed the right of intermarriage with him [1]: it was solely with their consent that

[1] This would follow from their original nobility, which made them of equal birth with the king : but there is a case which seems to show that the rank itself of ealdorman sufficed to give this privilege. Eádríc ealdorman of Mercia, who is said to have been of low extraction, married a sister of Cnut ; and Eádweard the Confessor had a daughter of earl Godwine to wife. The other case was common : "And Æðel-

he could be elected or appointed to the crown, and by their support, co-operation and alliance that he was maintained there. Without their concurrence and assent, their license and permission, he could not make, abrogate or alter laws : they were the principal witan or counsellors, the leaders of the great gemót or national inquest, the guardians, upholders and regulators of that aristocratical power of which he was the ultimate representative and head. The wergyld and oath of an ealdorman were in proportion to this lofty position : at first no doubt, he ranked only with the general class of nobles in this respect, and the Kentish law does not distinguish him from them : but at a later period, when the aristocratical hierarchy had somewhat better developed itself, we find him rated on the same level with the bishop, and above the ordinary nobles. From the chapter concerning wergylds [1], we find that the Northumbrian law rated the ealdorman at something more than thirty times the value of the ceorl, while in Mercia we hear only of thanes or twelve-hynde men, worth six times the ceorl or two-hynde man : and in Kent the eorl seems to have exceeded the ceorl by three times only.

But the value of the wergyld was not the only

flǽd æt Domerhamme, Ælfgáres dohtor ealdormannes, wæs ðá his cwen," *i. e.* Eádmund's. Chron. Sax. an. 946. " Eádgár cyning-genam Ælfðrýðe him tó cwene; heó wæs Ordgáres dohtor ealdormannes." Chron. Sax. 965. The Anglosaxon kings were in fact very rarely married to foreign princesses, though several of their beautiful daughters found husbands on the continent.

[1] Thorpe, i. 187. An ealdorman or bishop=8000 thryms: a ceorl only 266.

measure of the ealdorman's dignity. His oath bore
the same proportion to that of the ceorl, and I
think we may assume that this relative proportion
was maintained throughout all ranks. The law respecting oaths declares that the oath of a twelve-
hynde shall be equal to those of six ceorlas, because
if one would avenge a twelve-hynde it can be fully
done upon six ceorlas, and his wergyld is equal to
their six [1]. His house was in some sort a sanctuary,
and any wrong-doer who fled to it had three days'
respite [2]; if any one broke the peace therein, he
was liable to a heavy fine [3]; his burhbryce, or the
mulct for violation of his castle, was eighty shillings [4], which however the law of Ælfred reduces
to sixty [5]; for a breach of his borh or surety, and
his mundbyrd or protection, a fine of two pounds
was imposed [6]; his Fihtwíte, or the penalty imposed upon the man who drew sword and fought
in his presence, was one hundred shillings [7], which
was increased to one hundred and twenty if the offence was committed in the open court of justice [8].
The only person who enjoys a higher state, beside
the king, is the archbishop; and this pre-eminence
may probably have once been due to the heathen
high-priest; just as, indeed, the equality of the
bishop and ealdorman may have been traditionally
handed down from a period when the priesthood

---

[1] Thorpe, i. 182.
[2] Leg. Æðelst. iii. § 6, but seven days Æðelr. vii. § 5; iv. 4.
[3] Leg. Ini, § 6.   [4] Leg. Ini, § 45.   [5] Leg. Ælfr. § 40.
[6] Ibid. § 3. Leg. Cnut, Sec. § 69. Æðelr. vii. § 11.
[7] Leg. Ælfr. § 15. Æðelr. vii. § 12.   [8] Leg. Ælfr. § 38.

and the highest nobility formed one body. There
is no very distinct intimation of any peculiar dress
or decoration by which the ealdorman was distinguished, but he probably wore a beáh or ring upon
his head, the fetel or embroidered belt, and the
golden hilt which seems to have been peculiar to
the noble class. The staff and sword were probably borne by him as symbols of his civil and
criminal jurisdiction.

The method then by which this rank was attained becomes of some interest. And first it is necessary to inquire whether it was hereditary or not ;
whether it was for life, or only *durante beneplacito,*
or *benemerito.* That it was not strictly hereditary
appears in the clearest manner from the general
fact that the appointments recorded in the Chronicle and elsewhere are given to nobles unconnected
by blood with the last ealdorman. There are very
few instances of an ealdorman's rank being held in
the same county by a father and son in succession.
This occurred indeed in Mercia, where in 983 Ælfríc succeeded his father Ælfhere : Harald followed
Godwine in his duchy, and at the same period,
Leófríc and Sigeweard succeeded in establishing a
sort of succession in their families. But when this
did take place, it must be looked upon as a departure from the old principle, and as a thing which in
practice would have been carefully avoided, during
the better period of Anglosaxon history, for which
the feeble reign of Æðelred offers no fair pattern.
Under his weak and miserable rule the more powerful nobles might venture upon usurpations which

would have been impossible under his father. And Cnut's system of administration was favourable to the growth of an hereditary order of dukes. A further examination of our history shows that in general the dignity was held for life; we very rarely, if ever, hear of an ealdorman removed or promoted from one shire to another, and the entries in the Chronicle as well as the signatures to the charters attest that many of their number enjoyed their dignity for a very large number of years, in spite of the chances of an active military life. But we do find, and not unfrequently, that ealdormen have been expelled from their offices for treason and other grave offences. In the later times of Æðelred, when traitorous dealings with the Danish enemy offered the means of serving private or family hostility, the outlawry of the ealdorman who led the different conflicting parties in the state was common, and similar events accompanied the struggles of Godwine's party against the family of Mercia, for the conduct of public affairs in England[1]. But at a much earlier period we hear of ealdormen losing their offices and lands: in 901, Eádweard gave to Winchester ten hides at Wiley, which duke Wulfhere had forfeited by leaving his king and country without licence [2].

---

[1] See the Chronicle *passim*.

[2] "Ista vero praenominata tellus primitus fuit praepeditus a quodam duce, nomine Wulfhere, et eius uxore, quando ille utrumque et suum dominum regem Ælfredum et patriam ultra iusiurandum quam regi et suis omnibus optimatibus iuraverat sine licentia dereliquit. Tunc etiam, cum omnium iudicio sapientium Gewissorum et Mercensium, potestatem et haereditatem dereliquit agrorum." Cod. Dipl. No. 1078.

But if the dignity of ealdorman did not descend by regular succession, are we to conclude that it was attained by popular election? Such is the doctrine of the laws commonly attributed to Eádweard the Confessor. In these we are thus told:—

" There were also other authorities and dignities established throughout all the provinces and countries, and separate counties of the whole realm aforesaid, which among the Angles were called Heretoches, being to wit, barons, noble, of distinguished wisdom, fidelity and courage: but in Latin these were called *ductores exercitus*, leaders of the army, and among the Gauls, Capital Constables, or Marshals of the army. They had the ordering of numerous armies in battle, and placed the wings as was most fitting, and to them seemed most con· ducive to the honour of the crown and the utility of the realm. Now these men were elected by common counsel for the general weal, throughout all the provinces and countries, and the several counties, in full folkmote, as the sheriffs of the provinces and counties ought also to be elected: so that in every county there was one heretoch elected to lead the array of his county, according to the precept of our lord the king, to the honour and advantage of the crown of the realm aforesaid, whenever need should be in the realm[1]."

To this doctrine I deeply regret that I cannot subscribe. Whatever rémembrance of the earliest periods and their traditions may have lurked in

[1] Thorpe, i. 456.

L 2

the mind of the writer, I am compelled to say that his description is not applicable to any period comprehended in authoritative history. A real election of a duke or ealdorman by the folcmót may have been known to the Germans of Tacitus, but I fear not to those who two centuries later established themselves in England. There cannot, I imagine, be the slightest doubt that the ealdormen of the several districts were appointed by the crown, with the assent of the higher nobles, if not of the whole witena gemót. But it is also probable that in the strict theory of their appointment, the consent of the county was assumed to be necessary; and it is possible that, on the return of the newly appointed ealdorman to his shire, he was regularly received, installed and inaugurated by acclamation of the shire-thanes, and the oath of office administered in the shiremoot, whose co-operation and assent in his election was thus represented. Whatever may have been his original character, it seems certain that at no time later than the fifth century could the ealdorman have been the people's officer, but on the contrary that he was always the officer of that aristocratical association of which the king was the head[1].

Still I do not think that in general the choice of the witan could be a capricious or an unconditional one. There must have been in every shire certain powerful families from whose members alone the selection could be made; the instincts of all

[1] As the king and his witan could unquestionably depose or remove the ealdorman, we can scarcely doubt their power to appoint him.

aristocracies, as well as the analogy of other great Anglosaxon dignities, render it certain that the ealdormannic families, as a general rule, retained this office among themselves, although the particular one from which the officer should at any given time be taken were left undecided, for the determination of the Witan. It was almost necessary policy to place at the head of the county one of the most highly connected, trustworthy, powerful and wealthy of its nobles,—less necessary, however usual, *now* than then, when the functions of the Lord Lieutenant and the High Sheriff were united in the same person. It even appears probable, although the difficulty of tracing the Anglosaxon pedigrees prevents our asserting it as a positive fact, that the ducal families were in direct descent from the old regal families, which became mediatized, to use a modern term, upon the rise of their more fortunate compeers. We know this to have been the case with Æðelred, duke and viceroy of Mercia under Ælfred and Eádweard. In the ninth century we find Oswulf, ealdorman of East Kent, calling himself " Dei gratia dux ; " and Sigewulf and Sigehelm, who appear in the tenth also among the dukes of Kent, were very probably descendants of Sigeræd, a king of that province.

The new Constitution introduced by Cnut reduced the ealdorman to a subordinate position : over several counties was now placed one eorl, or earl, in the northern sense a jarl, with power analogous to that of the Frankish dukes. The word ealdorman itself was used by the Danes to denote a class, gentle indeed, but very inferior to the princely officers who had previously borne that title: it is under Cnut, and the following Danish kings that we gradually lose sight of the old ealdormen; the king rules by his earls and his Húscarlas, and the ealdormen vanish from the counties. From this time the king's writs are directed to the earl, the bishop and the sheriff of the county, but in no one of them does the title of the ealdorman any longer occur; while those sent to the towns are directed to the bishop and the portgeréfa or præfect of the city. Gradually the old title ceases altogether except in the cities, where it denotes an inferior judicature, much as it does among ourselves at the present day.

CHAPTER V.

THE GERE'FA.

THE most general name for the fiscal, administrative and executive officer among the Anglosaxons was Geréfa, or as it is written in very early documents geróefa[1] : but the peculiar functions of the individuals comprehended under it, were further defined by a prefix compounded with it, as scír-geréfa, the reeve of the shire or sheriff: túngeréfa the reeve of the farm or bailiff. The exact meaning and etymology of this name have hitherto eluded the researches of our best scholars, and yet perhaps few words have been more zealously investigated[2] : if I add another to the number of attempts to solve the riddle, it is only because I believe the force of the word will become much more

---

[1] Cod. Dipl. No. 235. The Chronicle even calls Cæsar's Tribune, Labienus, geréfa.

[2] The laws of Eádweard the Confessor show at how early a period the word was unintelligible. " Greve autem nomen est potestatis; apud nos autem nichil melius videtur esse quam praefectura. Est enim multiplex nomen; greve enim dicitur de scira, de wæpentagiis, de hundredo, de burgis, de villis: et videtur nobis compositum esse e griÐ anglice, quod est *pax* latine, et *ve* latine, videlicet quod debet facere griÐ, i. e. pacem, ex illis qui inferunt in terram ve, i. e. miseriam vel dolorem..... Frisones et Flandrenses comites suos meregrave vocant, quasi majores vel bonos pacificos; et sicut modo vocantur greves, qui habent praefecturas super alios, ita tunc temporis vocabantur eldereman, non propter senectutem, sed propter sapientiam." Cap. xxxii.

evident when we have settled its genuine derivation; and that philology has yet a part to play in
history which has not been duly recognized.   One
of the oldest and most popular opinions was that
which connected the name with words denoting
seniority; thus, with the German adjective *grau*,
Anglosaxon *grǽg*, grey.   There was however little
resemblance between geréfa and grǽg, the Anglosaxon forms, and the whole of this theory was
applicable only to the Latino-Frankish form graphio, or gravio.   The frequent use of words denoting advanced age, as titles of honour,—among
which ealdor *princeps*, senior *seigneur*, ठa yldestan
primates, and many others, will readily occur to
the reader,—favoured this opinion, which was long
maintained: but especially in Germany, it has
been entirely exploded by Grimm in his Rechts-
alterthümer [1], and proof adduced that there cannot be the slighest connection between *graf* and
grau.

More plausibility lay in the etymology of geréfa
adopted by Spelman; this rested upon the assumption that geréfa was equivalent to gereáfa, and that
it was derived from reáfan, to plunder; this view
was strengthened by the circumstance of the word
being frequently translated by *exactor*, the levying
of fines and the like being a characteristic part of
a reeve's duties.   But this view is unquestionably
erroneous: in the first place geréfa could not have
been universally substituted for the more accurate

Page 753.   [2] Gloss. *in voc.* Grafio.

gereáfa, which last word never occurs, any more than on the other hand does réfan for reáfan. Secondly, an Anglosaxon geréfa, if for gereáfa, would necessarily imply a High-dutch garaupjo, a word which we not only do not find, but which bears no sort of resemblance to krávo and grávo which we do find[1]. Lambarde's derivation of geréfa from gereccan, *regere*, may be consigned to the same storehouse of blunders as Lipsius's *graf* from γράφειν. Again, as words compounded with *ge-* and ending in -*a*, often denote a person who participates with others in something expressed by the root, geréfa has been explained to be one who shares in the roof, *i. e.* the kings roof: and this has been sup ported by the fact that graf is equivalent to *comes*, and that at an early period the comites are found occupying the places of geréfan. But a fatal objection to this etymon lies in the omission of the *h* from geréfa, which would not have been the case had hróf really been the root. Grimm says, "I will venture another supposition. In old High-dutch rávo meant *tignum, tectum* (Old Norse ræfr, *tectum*), perhaps also *domus, aula*; garávjo, girávjo, girávo, would thus mean *comes, socius*, like gistallo, and gisaljo, gisello (Gram. ii. 736)[2]." There is however a serious objection to this hypothesis: were it admitted, the Anglosaxon word must have been

---

[1] Grimm seems to think the word was originally Frankish, and only borrowed by the Alamanni, Saxons, and Scandinavians. Rechtsalt. p. 753. I am disposed to claim it for the Frisians and Saxons as well as the Franks.

[2] Rechtsalt. p. 753.

geræfa, not geréfa for geróefa, that is, the vowel in
the root must have been a long æ, not a long é,
springing out of and representing a long ó. I am
naturally very diffident of my own opinion in a case
of so much obscurity, and where many profound
thinkers have failed of success; still it seems to me
that geréfa may possibly be referable to the word
róf, *clamor*, róf, *celeber*, *famosus*, and a verb rófan or
réfan, *to call aloud:* if this be so, the name would
denote *bannitor*, the summoning or proclaiming officer, him by whose summons or proclamation the
court and the levy of the freemen were called together; and this suggestion answers more nearly
than any other to the nature of the original office:
in this sense too, a reeve's district is called his
mánung, *bannum* [1]. In this comprehensive genera-
lity lay the possibility of so many different degrees
of authority being designated by one term ; so that
in the revolutions of society we have seen the German markgraf and burggraf assuming the rank of
sovereign princes, while the English borough-reeve
has remained the chief magistrate of a petty corporation, or the pinder of a village has been designated by the title of a hogreeve.

Whatever were the original signification of the
word, I cannot doubt that it is of the highest antiquity, as well as the office which it denotes. In all
probability it was borne by those elected chiefs
who presided over the freemen of the Gá in their
meetings, and delivered the law to them in their

---

[1] Æðelst. v. 8. § 2, 3, 4.

districts [1]. Throughout the Germanic constitutions,
and especially in this country, the geréfa always
appears in connexion with judical functions [2]: he
is always the holder of a court of justice: thus:—
"Eádweard the king commandeth all the reeves;
that ye judge such just dooms, as ye know to be
most righteous, and as it in the doombook standeth.
Fear not, on any account, to pronounce folkright;
and let every suit have a term, when it may be
fullfilled, that ye may then pronounce." Again:—
"I will that each reeve have a gemót once in every
four weeks; and so act that every man may have
his right by law; and every suit have an end and
a term when it shall be brought forward."

Upon this point it is unnecessary to multiply
evidence, and I shall content myself with saying
that wherever there was a court there was a reeve,
and wherever there was a reeve, he held some sort
of court for the guidance and management of persons for whose peaceful demeanour he was responsible. From this it is to be inferred that the geréfan were of very different qualities, possessed very
different degrees of power, and had very different
functions to perform, from the geréfa who gave
law to the shire, down to the geréfa who managed
some private landowner's estate. It will be con-

---

[1] "Eliguntur in iisdem conciliis et principes, qui iura per pagos
vicosque reddunt." Tac. Germ. xii. Some tribes may have called these
principes by one name, some by another: ealdorman, æsaga, lahmon,
are all legitimate appellations for a geréfa.

[2] Leg. Eádw. i. § 1.   Thorpe, i. 158.   Leg. Eádw. i. § 2.   Thorpe, i.
160.   Leg. Eádw. i. §. 11.   Thorpe, i. 164.   See also Inst. Polity, § xi.
Thorpe, ii. 318.

venient to take the different classes of geréfan *seria-tim*, and collect under each head such information as we can now obtain from our legal or historical monuments.

HEA'HGERE'FA.—In general the word coupled with geréfa enables us to judge of the particular functions of the officer; but this is not the case with the heáhgeréfa or *high reeve*, a name of very indefinite signification, though not very rare occurrence. It is obvious that it really denotes only a reeve of high rank, I believe always a royal officer ; but it is impossible to say whether the rank is personal or official; whether there existed an office called the heáhgeréfscipe (highreevedom) having certain duties; or whether the circumstance of the shire- or other reeve being a nobleman in the king's confidence gave to him this exceptional title. I am inclined to believe that they are exceptional, and perhaps in some degree similar to the Missi of the Franks,—officers dispatched under occasional commissions to perform functions of supervision, hold courts of appeal, and discharge other duties, as the necessity of the case demanded ; but that they are not established officers found in all the districts of the kingdom, and forming a settled part of the machinery of government. In this particular sense, our judges going down upon their several circuits, under a commission of jail delivery, are the heáhgeréfan of our day.

We are told in the Saxon Chronicle that in the year 778, Æðelbald and Heardberht of Northum-

berland slew three heáhgeréfan, namely Ealhwulf
the son of Bosa, Cynewulf and Ecga: and the immediate consequence of this appears to have been
the expulsion of Æ∂elred, and the succession of
Ælfwold to the throne of Northumberland. These
high-reeves were therefore probably military officers
of Æ∂elred, and Simeon of Durham, in recording
the events of the same year calls them dukes, *duces*.

Again, in 780, Simeon mentions Osbald and
Æ∂elheard as dukes, but the Chronicle calls them
heáhgeréfan[1].

In a preceeding chapter I have shown that the
dux is properly equivalent to the ealdorman, but
this can hardly have been the case with the heáhgeréfa. Again, in 1001, the Chronicle mentions
three high-reeves, Æ∂elweard, Leófwine and Kola,
and apparently draws a distinction by immediately naming Eádsige, the king's reeve, not his
high-reeve. In 1002 the Chronicle again mentions
Æfïc, a high-reeve, who though a great favourite
of the king, certainly never attained the rank of
a duke or ealdorman, or, as far as we know, ever
performed any public administrative functions. He
was a minion of Æ∂elred's, but not an officer of
the Anglosaxon state.

SCI'RGERE'FA OR SHERIFF.—The Scírge-
réfa is, as his name denotes, the person who stands

---

[1] The instances cited are Northumbrian, and it is remarkable that
the chapter on Wergylds, § 4, reckons the heáhgeréfa as a separate
rank, having a high wergyld, but inferior to that of the ealdorman. I
am much inclined to think that these were sheriffs.

at the head of the shire, *pagus* or county: he is also called Scírman or Scírigman[1]. He is properly speaking the holder of the county-court, scírgemót or folcmót, and probably at first was its elected chief. But as this geréfa was at first the people's officer, he seems to have shared the fate of the people, and to have sunk in the scale as the royal authority gradually rose: during the whole of our historical period we find him exercising only a concurrent jurisdiction, shared in and controlled by the ealdorman on the one hand and the bishop on the other. The latter interruption may very probably have existed from the very earliest periods, and the heathen priest have enjoyed the rights which the Christian prelate maintained: but the intervention of the ealdorman appears to be consistent only with the establishment of a central power, exercised in different districts by means of resident superintendents, or occasional commissioners especially charged with the defence of the royal interests. In the Anglosaxon legislation even of the eighth century, the ealdorman is certainly head of the shire[2]; but there is, as far as I know, no evidence of his sitting in judgment in the folcmót without the sheriff, while there is evidence that the sheriff sat without the ealdorman. Usually the court was held under the presidency of the ealdorman and bishop, and of the scírgeréfa,

---

[1] Leg. Ini, § 8. Æðelst. v. c. 8. § 2, 3, 4. Æðelwine scírman. Cod. Dipl. No. 761, but Æðelwine scírgeréfa. Ibid. No. 732. Wulfsige preóst scirigman; and Wulfsige se scírigman. Ibid. No. 1288. Ufegeát scíreman. Ibid. No. 972. Leófríc scíresman. Ibid. No. 929.

[2] Leg. Ini, § 36.

who from his later title of vicecomes, vicedominus, was probably looked upon as the ealdorman's deputy,—a strange revolution of ideas. The shiremoot at Ægelnóðes stán in the days of Cnut was attended by Æðelstán, bishop of Hereford, Ranig the ealdorman, Eádwine his son, Leófwine and Đurcytel the white, Tofig the king's *missus* or messenger, and Bryning the scírgeréfa[1]. But in a celebrated trial of title to land at Wouldham in Kent, where archbishop Dunstán himself was a party concerned, the case seems to have been disposed of by Wulfsige the shireman or sheriff alone [2]. The bishop of Rochester, being in some sort a party to the suit, could probably not take his place as a judge, and the ealdorman is not mentioned at all. Again in an important trial of title to land at Snodland in Kent, there is no mention whatever of the ealdorman: the king's writ was sent to the archbishop; and the sheriff Leófríc and the thanes of East and West Kent met to try the cause at Canterbury [3]. It may then be concluded that the presence of the sheriff was necessary in any case, while that of the ealdorman might be dispensed with [4]. By the provisions of our later kings it appears that the scírgemót or sheriff's court for the county was to be holden twice in the year, and before this were

[1] Cod. Dipl. No. 755.   [2] Ibid. No. 1288.
[3] Ibid. No. 729.
[4] The law of Æðelstán, i. § 12 (Thorpe, i. 206) assumes the presence of the reeves in the folcmót as a matter of course; but this does not particularise the shire-reeves, though these are probably included in the general term. See also Æðelst. iv. § 1. Thorpe, i. 220.

brought all the most important causes, and such as exceeded the competence of the hundred [1].

But the judicial functions of the scírgeréfa were by no means all that he had to attend to. It is clear that the execution of the law was also committed to his hands. The provisions of the council of Greatanleah conclude with these words:—" But if any of my reeves will not do this, and care less about it than we have commanded, let him pay the fine for disobeying me, and I will find another reeve who will do it [2]; " where reference is generally made to all the enactments of the council. And the same king requires his bishops, ealdormen and reeves (the principal shire-officer) to maintain the peace upon the basis laid down in the Judicia civitatis Londoniae, that is to put in force the enactments therein contained, on pain of fines and forfeiture [3]. In pursuance also of this part of their duty, they were commanded to protect the abbots on all secular occasions [4], and to see the church dues regularly paid; viz. the tithes, churchshots, soulshots and plough alms [5]. And Eádgár, Æðelred and Cnut arm them with the power to levy for tithe and inflict a heavy forfeiture upon those who

---

[1] Leg. Eádg. ii. 5. Cnut, ii. 18. Thorpe, i. 268, 386.

[2] Æðelst. i. § 26. So again Æðelst. iii. § 7; iv. § 1. Thorpe, i. 212, 219, 222.

[3] Æðelst. v. § 11. Thorpe, i. 240.

[4] " And the king enjoins the reeves in every place to protect the abbots in all their worldly needs, as best ye may." Æðelred, ix. § 32. Thorpe, i. 346.

[5] Æðelst. i. Introd. Thorpe, i. 194, 196.

withhold it [1]. It is also very clear from several passages in the Laws that the sheriff might be called upon to witness bargains and sales, so as to warrant them afterwards if necessary. Æðelstán enacts [2] : —" Let no man exchange any property, without the witness of the reeve, or the mass-priest, or the landlord, or the treasurer, or some other credible man : " and though the scírgeréfa is not particularly mentioned here, it is obvious that he is meant, for a subsequent law of Eádmund, following this enactment of Æðelstán, directs that no one shall bargain or receive strange cattle without the witness of the highest reeve (" summi praepositi "), the priest, the treasurer or the port-reeve [3]. He was further to exercise a supreme police in his county : it is declared by Æðelred [4],—" If there be any man who is untrue to all the people, let the king's reeve go and bring him under surety, that he may be held to justice, to them that accused him. But if he have no surety, let him be slain, and laid in the foul,"—that is, I presume, not buried in consecrated ground.

From this also it appears probable that the geréfa was the officer to conduct the execution of criminals in capital cases, as he remains to this day ; but as far as I remember, there is no instance of this duty recorded. The regulations respecting mints

---

[1] Eádg. i. § 3. Æðelr. ix. § 8. Cnut, i. § 8. Thorpe, i. 262, 342, 366.

[2] Æðelst. i. § 10. Thorpe, i. 204.

[3] Eádm. iii. § 5. Thorpe i. 253. This law uses the word *ordalii*, which I believe to be an error for *hordere*, as in Æðelstán's law, and have rendered it accordingly.

[4] Leg. Æðelr. i § 4. Thorpe, i. 282.

and coinage seem also to show that this part of the
public service was under the superintendence of the
scírgeréfa [1]. As the principal political officer, and
chief of the freemen in the shire, it was further his
duty to promulgate the laws enacted by the king
and his witena gemót, and take a pledge from the
members of the county, to observe these : and it is
to be concluded that this was solemnly done in the
county-court [2].

The scírgeréfa was also the principal fiscal officer
in the county. It was undoubtedly his duty to
levy all fines that accrued to the king from offenders,
and to collect such taxes as the land paid for public
purposes. We have unhappily no *pipe-rolls* of the
Anglosaxon period, which would have thrown the
greatest light upon the social condition of England;
but we have a precept of Cnut, addressed to Æðelríc the sheriff of Kent, and the other principal officers and thanes of the county, commanding that
archbishop Æðelnóð shall account only as far as
he had done before Æðelríc becaem sheriff, and
ordering that in future no sheriff shall demand
more of him [3]. From this it appears that even the
lands of the archbishop himself were not exempt
from the sheriff's authority in fiscal matters, although there can be little doubt that at this period
the prelate had a grant of sacu and sócn, or com-

---

[1] Cnut, ii. § 8. Thorpe, i. 380.

[2] Æðeist. v. § 10. Thorpe, i. 238.

[3] Cod. Dipl. No. 1323. This writ is directed in the usual form, to
the archbishop, the bishop of Rochester, the abbot of St. Augustine's,
the sheriff and the thanes of Kent.

plete immunity from the sheriff's power in judicial questions. And we shall have little difficulty in admitting that, if he possessed this authority in the case of the archbishop, he exercised it in that of other less distinguished landowners. It has been already shown that the king possessed certain profitable rights in, and received contributions from, the estates of folcland in private hands: these were exercised and collected by the scírgeréfa. It is probable that the zeal of this officer had sometimes overstepped the bounds of the law, and induced him to burthen the free landowner for the benefit of the crown; for we find Cnut enacting[1]: " This is the alleviation which it is my pleasure to secure to all the people, of that which hath heretofore too much oppressed them. First, I command all my reeves that they justly provide for me on my own, and maintain me therewith; and that no man need give them anything, as farm-aid, unless he choose. And if after this any one demand a fine, let him be liable in his wergyld to the king."

The law then goes on to regulate the king's rights in case of intestacy, the amount of heriot payable by different classes, the freedom of succession in the wife and children, and the freedom of marriage both for widow and maiden. And as all these laws, numbered respectively from § 70 to 75, appear to be dependent upon one another, and to form a chapter of alleviations by themselves, I conclude

---

[1] Cnut. ii. § 70. Thorpe, i. 412. *Feorm* is the king's farm or support: and *feormfultum* a benevolence in aid of the same. It had become compulsory in some cases, and this is what Cnut forbids.

that the sheriffs had been guilty of exaction in confiscating the estates of intestates, demanding extravagant heriots and reliefs, and imposing fines for licence to marry,—extortions familiar enough under the Norman rule. It was moreover the sheriff's duty to seize into the king's hands all lands and chattels belonging to felons, which would, in the event of a conviction become forfeit to the crown: of this we have instances. About A.D. 900, one Helmstán was guilty of theft; Eanwulf Penhearding, who was then sheriff, immediately seized all the property he had at Tisbury, except the land which Helmstán could not forfeit, as it was only Ordláf's lǽn or *beneficium* [1]. At the close of the tenth century, Æscwyn a widow had become implicated in the theft of some title-deeds by her own son: judgment was given against her in one of the royal courts, whereby all her property became forfeited to the king: Wulfstán the sheriff of Kent accordingly seized Bromley and Fawkham, her manors [2]. There is of course every probability that the sheriff was charged with certain disbursements, required by the public service, and that he rendered a periodical account both of receipts and expenditure, to the officers who then represented the royal exchequer; but upon this part of the subject we are unhappily without any evidence.

The sheriff was naturally the leader of the militia, posse comitatus, or levy of the free men, who served under his banner, as the different lords with their de-

---

[1] Cod. Dipl. No. 328.   [2] Ibid. No. 1258.

pendents served under the royal officers, the church vassals under the bishop's or abbot's officer, and all together under the chief command of the ealdorman or duke. It was his business to summon them, and to command them in the field, during the period of their service: and he thus formed the connecting link between the military power of the king and the military power of the people, for purposes both of offence and defence.

In the earliest periods, the office was doubtless elective, and possibly even to the last the people may have enjoyed theoretically, at least, a sort of concurrent choice. But I cannot hesitate for a moment in asserting that under the consolidated monarchy, the scírgeréfa was nominated by the king, with or without the acceptance of the county-court, though this in all probability was never refused[1]. The language of the laws which continually adopt the words, *our* reeves, where none but the sheriffs are intended, clearly shows in what relation these officers stood to the king: and as the latter indisputably possessed the power of removing, he probably did not want that of appointing them[2].

[1] In the Council of Baccanceld, Wihtred is made to say:—"It is the duty of kings to appoint eorls and ealdormen, scírgeréfan and doomsmen." Chron. Sax. an. 694. "Illius autem est comites, duces, optimates, principes, praefectos, iudices saeculares statuere." Cod. Dipl. No. 996. The charter is an obvious forgery, but it shows the tendency of opinion in the Anglosaxon times.

[2] In some of the writs addressed to the shires, the place properly filled by the scírgeréfa is given to noblemen of the king's household, as Eádnóð steallere in Hampshire. Cod. Dipl. No. 845. Esgár steallere in Hertfordshire, Kent and Middlesex. Nos. 827, 843, 864. Rodbeard steallere in Essex. No. 859. I believe these persons to have been really the sheriffs, but to have been named by their familiar, and in their own view, higher designations, as officers of the court.

On one occasion indeed Æðelstán distinctly declares, that if his sheriffs neglect their duty, *he*, the king, will find others to do it[1]. The means by which the dignity of the sheriff was supported are similar to those noticed in the case of the ealdorman. He received a proportion of the fines payable to the king: he was, we may presume, always a considerable landowner in the shire; indeed, several of those whom we know to have held the office, were amongst the greatest landowners in their respective districts[2]. It is even possible that there may have been some provision in land, attached to the office, for I meet occasionally with such words as geréf-land, geréf-mæd, where the form of the composition denotes, not the land or meadow of some particular sheriff, but of the sheriff generally. As leader of the *shire-fyrd* or armed force, the geréfa would have a share of the booty; and it is not unreasonable to suppose that his influence and good-will were secured at times by the voluntary offerings of neighbours and dependents.

The writs of the kings, touching judicial processes, and other matters connected with the public service, were directed to the ealdorman, bishop and sheriff of the district, as a general rule. From these writs, which are numerous in the eleventh century, we learn some of the names of the gentlemen who filled the office at that period: and as

[1] Conc. Greatanl. Æðelst. 1. § 26.

[2] Tofig Pruda, whom we recognize as scírgeréfa in Somersetshire, is elsewhere described as "vir praepotens." See Flor. Wig. an. 1042.

these names are not without interest I have collected from such documents as we possess a list of sheriffs for different counties.

Berks . . . . . Cyneweard[1].
Gódric[2].
Devonshire . . . Hugh the Norman[3].
Dorsetshire . . . Ælfred[4].
Essex . . . . . Leófcild[5].
Rodbeard steallere[6].
Hampshire . . . Eádsige[7].
Eádnóð steallere[8].
Herefordshire . . Ælfnóð[9].
Bryning[10].
Osbearn[11].
Ulfcytel[12].
Hertfordshire . . Ælfstán[13].
Esgár steallere[14].
Huntingdonshire . Ælfríc[15].
Cyneríc[16].
Kent . . . . . Æðelríc[17].
Æðelwine[18].
Esgár steallere[19].
Leófríc[20].
Osweard[21].

[1] Cod. Dipl. No. 948.
[2] Ibid. No. 840.
[3] Flor. Wig. an. 1008.
[4] Cod. Dipl. No. 871.
[5] Ibid. Nos. 788, 869, 870.
[6] Ibid. No. 859.
[7] Ibid. No. 1337.
[8] Ibid. No. 845.
[9] Chron. Sax. 1056.
[10] Cod. Dipl. No. 755.
[11] Ibid. No. 833.

[12] Ibid. No. 802.
[13] Ibid. No. 945.
[14] Ibid. No. 864.
[15] Ibid. No. 903.
[16] Ibid. No. 906.
[17] Ibid. Nos. 1323, 1325.
[18] Ibid. Nos. 731, 732.
[19] Ibid. No. 827.
[20] Ibid. No. 929.
[21] Ibid. Nos. 847, 854.

Kent	Wulfsige preóst [1].
	Wulfstán [2].
Lincolnshire. . .	Osgód [3].
Middlesex . . .	Ælfgeát [4].
	Esgár steallere [5].
	Ulf [6].
Norfolk	Eádríc [7].
Norfolk and Suffolk	Tolig [8].
Northampton . .	Marleswegen [9].
	Norðman [10].
Somersetshire . .	Godwine [11].
	Tofig [12].
	Tauid or Touid [13].
Suffolk	Ælfríc [14].
	Tolig [15].
Warwickshire . .	Uua [16].
Wiltshire. . . .	Eánwulf Penhearding [17].
Worcestershire . .	Leófríc [18].

[1] Cod. Dipl. No. 1288. This is contrary to the provision of archbishop Ecgberht's Poenitential, iii. § 8 : he says that a priest or deacon ought not to be a geréfa, or a wícnere, or to have any concern with secular business. "Nis nánum mæsse-preóste álýfed ne diacone, æt hí geréfan beón né wícneras, né ymbe náne worldbysgunga ábysgode beón, búton mid ðære ðe hig tó getitolode beóð." Thorpe, ii. 198. Perhaps however Ecgberht's rule was construed to mean private, not public, geréfan, when in process of time it might become useful to have the assistance of priests learned in the law, as judges; especially as in the tenth century the importance of missionary labours was less strongly felt than in the eighth.

[2] Cod. Dipl. No. 1258.
[3] Ibid. No. 1319.
[4] Ibid. No. 858.
[5] Ibid. No. 855.
[6] Ibid. No. 843.
[7] Ibid. No. 785.
[8] Ibid. Nos. 853, 875, 880, 881, 883, 908, 911.
[9] Ibid. Nos. 806, 808.
[10] Ibid. Nos. 863, 904.
[11] Ibid. Nos. 834, 835, 836, 838.
[12] Ibid. No. 821.
[13] Ibid. Nos. 837, 839, 917, 926, 976.
[14] Ibid. Nos. 832, 842.
[15] Ibid. Nos. 874, 905.
[16] Ibid. No. 493.
[17] Ibid. No. 328.
[18] Ibid. Nos. 757, 898, 923.

It is possible that increased research may extend this list of sheriffs, and much to be regretted that our information is so scanty as it is. We have no means of deciding whether the office was an annual one, or how its duration was limited. The Kentish list shows that the clergy were neither exempt nor excluded from its toils or advantages: and the position of Wulfsige the priest and sheriff recalls to us the earlier times when priest and judge may have been synonymous terms among the nations of the north [1]. I now proceed to a third class, the

CYNINGES GERE'FA, or Royal Reeve.— There is some difficulty with regard to this officer, because in many cases where the cyninges geréfa is mentioned, it is plain that the scírgeréfa is meant. For example, Ælfred twice mentions the cyninges geréfa as sitting in the folcmót and administering justice there [2], which is hardly to be understood of any but the sheriff. However it is consistent with the general principles of Teutonic society that as there was a scírgeréfa to do justice between freeman and freeman, so also there should be a cyninges geréfa, before whom the king's tenants should ultimately stand to right, and who more particularly administered the king's sacu and

---

[1] " Si iudex vel sacerdos reperti fuerint nequiter iudicasse," etc. Leg. Visigoth. ii. c. l. § 33.

[2] " Gif mon on folces gemóte cyninges geréfan ge-yppe eofot," etc. § 22. " And gebrengen beforan cyninges geréfan on folcgemóte .... gecýðe in gemótes gewitnesse cyninges geréfan." § 34. See also Æðelred, iii. § 13. Cnút, ii. § 8, 33. Thorpe, i. 76, 82, 380, 396. In Cod. Dipl. No. 789, appears a king's reeve Wulfsige: but is not this the same Wulfsige as we find sheriff of Kent at the same period?

sócn in his own private lands. To this officer, under the ealdorman, would belong the investigation of those causes which the king's manorial courts could not decide: perhaps he might possess some sort of appellate jurisdiction: and it cannot be doubted that it was his duty to superintend the management of the king's private domains, and to lead the array of the king's private tenants in the general levy. It is therefore not unlikely that this officer may be identical with the heáhgeréfa already noticed. But in many cases where a king's reeve is mentioned, and where we cannot understand the term of the scírgeréfa, it is clear that a wícgeréfa or burh- or túngeréfa are intended, and that they are called royal officers merely because the wíc, burh or tún happened to be royal property. The Chronicle under the year 787 mentions a geréfa who was slain by the Northmen:—" This year king Beorhtríc took to wife Eádburh, king Offa's daughter: and in his time first came three ships of Northmen from Hæretha land. And then the geréfa rode to the place, and would have driven them to the king's tún, for he knew not who they were: and there on the spot they slew him. These were the first Danish ships that ever sought the land of the English."

Now Florence of Worcester under the same date tells us that this officer was " regis praepositus," that is, a king's reeve: and Henry of Huntingdon improves him into a sheriff[1], " praepositus regis illius provinciae:" Æðelweard however, who is

---

[1] Hen. Hunt. lib. iv.

obviously much better acquainted with the details of the story than his Norman successors, records that this officer's name was Beadoheard, and that he was the royal burggrave in Dorchester [1].

In 897 again we hear of the death of Lucemon, in battle against the Danes : the Chronicle calls him " ðæs cyninges geréfa: " but Henry of Huntingdon, " praepositus regalis exercitus [2]," which may merely mean the officer appointed to lead the *royal* force, that is a king's reeve in the sense which I have attempted to establish on a preceding page. Other king's reeves mentioned, are Ælfweard, (Chron. Sax. an. 1011), and Ælfgár (Cod. Dipl. No. 693).

It may admit of doubt whether in the parts of England which were subject to Danish rule, and only re-annexed to the Westsaxon crown by conquest, the same institutions prevailed as in the rest of the country. In the laws of Æðelred [3] we hear of a king's reeve in the Wapentake and in the community of the Five Burgs. These are not sheriffs; the former rather resembling the Hundredman ; the latter a Burhgeréfa, but with extended powers, perhaps approaching those of a sheriff, or the Northumbrian heáhgeréfa already alluded to in this chapter.

THE BURHGEREFA.—In a fortified town, which I take to be the strict meaning of *burh*, there

---

[1] Æðelw. lib. iii. " Exactor regis, iam morans in oppido, quod Dorceastre nuncupatur." Gaimar calls him " un senescal al rei : " l. 2069.
[2] Hen. Hunt. lib. v.
[3] Æðelr. iii. § 1, and iii. § 3. Thorpe, i. 292, 294.

was an officer under this title. We know but little of his peculiar powers; but there is every reason to conclude that they were similar to those of other geréfan, according to the circumstances in which he was placed. If the town were free, it is possible that he may have been the popular officer, a sort of sheriff where the town is itself a county. But this is improbable, and it is much more likely that the burhgeréfa was essentially a royal officer, charged with the maintenance and defence of a fortress. Such a one I take Badoheard to have been in Dorchester; similarly we hear of Godwine, praepositus civitatis Oxnafordi[1], Æðelwig praepositus in Bucingaham[2], and Wynsige also praepositus in Oxnaforda[2], Osulf and Ylcærðon both praepositi in Padstow[3]; and finally Ælfred, the reeve of Bath[4]. It was this officer's duty to preside in the burhgemót, which was appointed to be held thrice in the year[5], and he was most likely the representative of the towns-people, so far as these were unfree, in the higher courts. It is also probable that he was their military leader, and that he was expected to be present at sales and exchanges in order to be able to warrant transactions, if impeached. Lastly he was to see that tithes were duly rendered from his fellow-citizens[6]. From a very interesting document just now cited[7], it may be inferred that he possessed considerable power

[1] Cod. Dipl. No. 950.
[2] Ibid. No. 1289.
[3] Ibid. No. 981.
[4] Chron. Sax. an. 906.
[5] Leg. Eádg. ii. § 5.
[6] Æðelst. i. § 1. Thorpe, i. 194.
[7] See Note [2] in this page.

in his district, and that persons of rank and wealth
were clothed with the office.   We there find the
reeves of Buckingham and Oxford granting the rites
of Christian burial to some Saxon gentlemen who
had perished in a brawl brought on by an attempt
at theft; and the intervention of the king himself
seems to have been necessary to prevent the execution of their decree.   The burhgeréfa may perhaps be said to have had some of the rights of the
Aedile and Praetor urbanus under the old, or those
of the duumvir under the later, provincial constitution of Rome.   Still he seems to have been in some
degree subject to the supervision of the ealdorman.   I have sometimes thought that he might be
compared in part with the Burggraf, in part with
the Vogt of the German towns under the Empire;
but unfortunately we know too little of our ancient municipal constitution to enable us to carry
out this enquiry.   We have no means now of
ascertaining the duration of his office, the nature
of his appointment, or the actual extent of his
powers.

PORTGERE'FA.—The Portgeréfa is in many
respects similar to the Burhgeréfa : but as it appears
that *Port* is applied rather to a commercial than a
fortified town, there are differences between the two
offices.   In some degree these will have depended
upon the comparative power, freedom and organization of the citizens themselves, and I can readily
believe that the portreeves of London were much
more important personages than the burhreeves of

Oxford or Bath. In the smaller towns, it is probable that the court of the portreeve was a sort of pie-powder court; but in the larger, it must have had cognizance of offences against the customs laws, the laws affecting the mint, and the general police of the district. As a general rule I imagine the portgeréfa to have been an elective officer: perhaps in the large and important towns he required at least the assent of the king. In London he holds the place of the sheriff, and the king's writs are directed to the earl, the bishop and the portreeve [1]. There are two cities in which we hear of portreeves, viz. London and Canterbury: in the former we have Swétman [2], Ælfsige [3], Ulf [4], Leófstán [5], and the great officer of the royal household, Esgár the steallere [6], which alone would be sufficient evidence of the importance attached to the post. In Canterbury we read of Æðelred [7], Leofstán [8], and Gódric [9], occupying the same station. Again we have Ælfsige portgeréfa in Bodmin [10], and Leófcild portgeréfa in Bath [11]. It is worthy of remark that the

---

[1] Cod. Dipl. vol. iv. *passim.* There is not the slightest reason to suppose that there ever was a special ealdorman of London, as Palgrave imagines. The city was governed by Portreeves, usually two at once, until long after the Conquest, when it obtained mayors, like many other towns.

[2] Cod.Dipl. Nos. 857, 861. [3] Cod. Dipl. No. 856.

[4] Ibid. No. 872. [5] Ibid. Nos. 857, 861.

[6] Ibid. No. 872. [7] Ibid. No. 929.

[8] Ibid. No. 799. [9] Ibid. No. 789.

[10] Ibid. No. 981.

[11] Cod. Dipl. No. 933. This evidence that the officer in Bath was a portreeve and not a burhreeve may suggest the possibility of those persons whom I have cited under the former head, belonging rather to the present one. The Latin *praepositus civitatis* will denote either one or the other office, and indeed it is difficult to prove any difference between them by direct testimony.

two, Ælfsige and Leófstán, served the office together in London, and that Ulf also occurs, as sheriff of Middlesex. In the smaller towns especially it must have been a principal part of the portreeve's duty to witness all transactions by bargain and sale[1]. A portion of his subsistence at least was probably derived from the proceeds of tolls, and fines levied within his district.

WI'CGERE'FA.—The Wícgeréfa was a similar officer, in villages, or in such towns as had grown out of villages without losing the name of a village. I presume that he was not concerned with the freemen, but was a kind of steward of the manor, and that his dignity varied with the rank of his employer and the extent of his jurisdiction. However there is so much difficulty in making a clear distinction between Port and Wíc, that we find wícgeréfa applied to officers who ruled in large and royal cities. Thus the Saxon Chronicle mentions Beornwulf under the title of Wícgeréfa in Winchester[2], whom Florence in the same year calls Praepositus Wintoniensium. And in the laws of Hloðhere and Eádríc[3], the same title is given to the king's officer in London, Cyninges wícgeréfa. In general I should be disposed to construe the word strictly as a village-reeve, and especially in any case where the village was not royal, but ducal or episcopal property. Many places may indeed

---

[1] Leg. Eádw. § 1.　Thorpe, i. 158.　Eádm. iii. § 5.　Thorpe, i. 253. Æðelst. i. § 12.　Thorpe, i. 206
[2] Chron. Sax. an. 897　　　　　　　　[3] § 16. Thorpe, i. 34.

have once been called by the name of *Wíc* which afterwards assumed a much more dignified appellation, together with a much more important social condition.

TU'NGERE'FA.—The Túngeréfa is literally the reeve of a tún, enclosure, farm, vill or manor : and his authority also must have fluctuated with that of his lord. He is the *villicus* or bailiff of the estate, and on the royal farms was bound to superintend the cultivation, and keep the peace among the cultivators. In London he appears to have been subordinate to the portgeréfa, and was probably his officer [1]; it was his business to see that the tolls were paid. Ælfred commands, in case a man is committed to prison in the king's tún, that the reeve shall feed him, if necessary [2]. This I suppose to be the túngeréfa, the officer on the spot who would be responsible for his security. So Eádgár forbids his reeves to do any wrong to the other men of the tún, in respect to the tracking of strange cattle [3]. Here the túngeréfa represents the king, among the class that would in earlier times have formed a court of free markmen. That the túngeréfa was the manager of a royal estate appears plainly from an ordinance of Æðelstán, respecting the doles or charities which were to issue from the various farms' domain [4]. " I Æðelstán, with the consent of Wulfhelm my archbishop, and all my other bishops and

---

[1] Æðelr. iv. § 3.　　　　　　[2] Ælfr. § 1. Thorpe, i. 61.
[3] Eádg. Supp. § 13. Thorpe, i. 276.
[4] Æðelst. i. § 1. Thorpe, i. 196.

God's servants, command all you my reeves, within
my realm, for the forgiveness of my sins, that ye
entirely feed one poor Englishman, if ye have him,
or that ye find another. From every two of my
farms, be there given him monthly one amber of
meal, and one shank of bacon, or a ram worth four
pence, and clothing for twelve months every year.
And ye shall redeem one wíteþeów: and let all
this be done for the Lord's mercy, and for my
sake, under witness of the bishop in whose diocese
it may be. And if the reeve neglect this, let him
make compensation with thirty shillings, and let
the money be distributed to the poor in the tún
where this remains unfulfilled, by witness of the
bishop."

Lastly, in the law of Æðelred[1] I find the Tun-
gravius, decimales homines, and presbyter charged
with the care of seeing certain alms bestowed and
fasts observed; which seems to denote a special
authority exercised by the Túngeréfa together with
the heads of the tithings. The geréfa in a royal vill
may easily have been a person of consideration:
if the Æðelnóð who in 830 was reeve at Eastry in
Kent[2], were such a one, we find from his will that
he had no mean amount of property to dispose of.

SWA'NGERE'FA.—The Swángeréfa, as his name
denotes, was reeve of that forest-court which till a
late period was known in England as the *swain-
moot*. It was his business to superintend the swánas

---

[1] Æðelr. viii. § 2. Thorpe, i. 338.   [2] Cod. Dipl. No. 191.

or swains, the herdsmen and foresters, to watch over
the rights of pasture, and regulate the use which
might be made of the forests. It is probably one
of the oldest constitutional offices, and may have
existed by the same name at a time when the organization in Marks was common all over England.
From a trial which took place in 825, we find that
he had the supervision of the pastures in the shire-
wood or public forest[1], and from this also it appears
that he was under the immediate superintendence
and control of the ealdorman. The extended organization which the swána gemót attained under
Cnut, may be seen in that prince's Constitutions
de Foresta[2]. It is probable that there were Holt-
geréfan and Wudugeréfan, holtreeves and wood-
reeves among the Saxons, having similar duties to
those of the Swángeréfa, but I have not yet met
with these names. They are, I believe, by no means
extinct in many parts of England, any more than
the Landreeve, a designation still current in Devonshire, and probably elsewhere.

WEALHGERE'FA.—The last officer whom I
shall treat of particularly is the Wealhgeréfa or
Welsh-reeve. This singular title occurs in an entry of the Saxon Chronicle, *anno* 897. "The same
year died Wulfríc, the king's horse-thane, who was
also Wealhgeréfa." There can be no dispute as to
the meaning of the word, but the functions of the
officer designated by it are far from clear. It de-

[1] Cod. Dipl. No. 219. [2] Thorpe, i. 426.

notes a reeve who had the superintendence of the
Welsh; but the question where this superintendence was exercised is a very important one. If in
the king's palace, Wulfríc was set over a certain
number of unfree Britons, *laeti* or even serfs, as
their judge and regulator: or he may have had the
superintendence of property belonging to Ælfred
in Wales, which is somewhat less probable: or
lastly he may have been a margrave, whose mission it was to watch the Welsh border, and defend
the Saxon frontier against sudden incursions. This
I think the least probable of all, inasmuch as I find
no traces of margraves (mearcgeréfan) in Anglosaxon history. On the contrary the marches in
this country seem to have been always committed
to the care of a duke or ealdorman, not a geréfa.
Wulfríc's rank however, which was that of a maris-
calcus or marshal, is not inconsistent with so great
and distant a command. On the whole therefore I
am disposed to believe that he was a royal reeve to
whose care Ælfred's Welsh serfs were committed,
and who exercised a superintendence over them in
some one or in all of the royal domains.

　　The geréfa was not necessarily a royal officer:
on the contrary we find bishops, ealdormen, nay
simple nobles with them upon their establishment.
Of course the moment an immunity of sacu and
sócn existed upon any estate, the lord appointed a
geréfa to hold his court and do right among his
men, as the scírgeréfa held court for the freemen
in the shire. And if any proof of this were necessary, we might find it in the title *socnereve* (sócne

geréfa) which occurs at page 12 of the valuable book known as 'Liber de antiquis Legibus,' but which would have been much more justly entitled Annals of the Corporation of London. We may be assured that in every vill belonging to a bishop or a lay lord, in every city where there was a cathedral or a castle, there was found a bisceopes or an ealdormannes geréfa, as the case might be, performing such functions for the prelate or the noble, as the king's geréfa exercised for him; and if there were an immunity, performing every function that the royal officer performed. Thus in some towns I can conceive it very possible that the king's, ealdorman's and bishop's reeves may have met side by side and exercised a concurrent jurisdiction: and as the bishop's geréfa must have led his armed retainers, (at least whenever it pleased the prelate to remember the canons of his church,) this officer may be compared to the Vogt, Advocatus, Vicedominus or Vidame, who fulfilled that duty on the continent. The bishop's reeve is empowered by the king to aid the sheriff in the forcible levy of tithe[1]; he is recognised in the law of Wihtræd as an intermediary between a dependent of the bishop and the public courts of justice[2]; the thane's or nobleman's reeve was allowed on various occasions to act as his attorney: the great landowner was admonished to appoint reeves over his dependents, to preserve the peace and represent them before the law; and lastly so necessary a part of a

---

[1] Æðelr. i. § 1. Cnut, ii. § 30.   [2] Wihtr. § 22. Thorpe, i. 43.

nobleman's establishment is the geréfa considered to be, that Ini enacts[1], " whithersoever a noble journeys, thither may his reeve accompany him." Of course in many cases these geréfan would be merely stewards[2], but in nearly all we must consider them to have been judges in various courts of greater or less importance, public or private as it might chance to be. This one original character distinguishes all alike; whether it be the scírgeréfa of a county-court, the burhgeréfa of a corporation, the swán-geréfa of a woodland moot, the mótgeréfa[3] of *any court* in which plea could be holden, or the tún-geréfa of a vill or dependent settlement, the ancient steward of a manorial court.

---

[1] Ini. § 63.　　　　　　　　　　[2] Cod. Dipl. No. 931.

[3] " Swá ðæt nán scírgeréfa oððe mótgeréfa hæbbe ænige sócne oððe mót, búton ðæs abbudes ágen híése ꝺ unne." Cod. Dipl. No. 841. The law of Eadweard which commands the reeve to hold his court once a month, and which can only apply to the hundred, makes it probable that as the scírgeréfa was in some places called scírman, so the hundred-man may in some places have been called hundred-geréfa : I have already alluded to the geréfa in the Wapentake; and the law of Eadweard the Confessor (§ 31) shows that in the counties where there were Triðingas or Ridings, there existed also a Triðing-geréfa.

CHAPTER VI.

THE WITENA GEMÓT.

THE conquest of the Roman provinces in Europe was accomplished by successive bands of adventurers, ranged under the banners of various leaders, whom ambition, restlessness or want of means had driven from their homes. But the conquest once achieved, the strangers settled down upon the territory they had won, and became the nucleus of nations: in their new settlements they adopted the rules and forms of institutions to which they had been accustomed in their ancient home, subject indeed to such modifications as necessarily resulted from the mode of the conquest, and their new position among vanquished populations, generally superior to themselves in the arts of civilized life. If we carefully examine the nature of these ventures, we shall I think come to the conclusion that they were carried on upon what may be familiarly termed the joint-stock principle. The owner of a ship, the supplier of the weapons or food necessary to set the business on foot, is the great capitalist of the company: the man of skill and judgment and experience is listened to with respect and cheerfully obeyed: the strong arms and unflinching courage of the multitude complete the work: and when the prize is won, the profits are justly divided among the winners, according to the value of each man's contribution to the general utility[1]. But in such voluntary associations as these, it is clear that every man retains a certain amount of free will, that he has a right to consult, discuss and advise, to assent to or dissent from the measures proposed to be adopted: even the council of war of such a band must differ very much from what in our day goes by that name; where a few officers of high rank decide, and the mass of the army blindly execute their plans. It cannot then surprise us that in such cases everything should be done with the counsel, consent and leave of the associated adventurers. The bands were then not too numerous for general consultation: there was no fear lest treachery or weakness should betray the plans to an enemy : the necessities of self-preservation guaranteed the faith of every individual; for, camped among hostile and exasperated populations, ignorant of their tongue, and remote from them in manners, the German straggler, captive or deserter could look forward to nothing save a violent death or a life of weary slavery. Mutual participation in danger must have given rise to mutual trust.

Again the principle upon which the settlement of the land was effected, was that of associations for common benefits, and a mutual guarantee of

---

[1] This is not hypothetical or imaginary. The settlements in Iceland were positively made upon this principle, and by it the subsequent divisions of the land were regulated.

peaceful possession [1]. Each man stood engaged to his neighbour, both as to what he would himself avoid, and as to what he would maintain. The public weal was the immediate interest of every individual member of the state; it came home to him at every instant of his life, directly, pressing him either in his property, his freedom or his peace, not through a long and accidental chain of distant causes and results. Moreover in an association based upon the individual freedom of the associates, each man had a right to guard the integrity of the compact to which he was himself a party; and not only a right, but a strong interest in exercising it, for in proportion to the smallness of the state, is the effect which the conduct of any single member may produce upon its welfare. But wherever free men meet on equal terms of alliance, the will of the majority is the law of the state. If the minority be small it must submit, or suffer for rebellion: if large, and capable of independent action and subsistence, it may peaceably separate from the majority, renounce its intimate alliance, and emigrate to new settlements, where it may at its own leisure, and in its own way, develop its peculiar views of

[1] The Acts, if we may so call them, of an Anglosaxon parliament, are a series of *treaties of peace*, between all the associations which make up the state; a continual revision and renewal of the alliances offensive and defensive, of all the free men. They are universally mutual contracts for the maintenance of the frið or peace. Those who chose to do so, might withdraw from this contract, but they must take the consequence. The witan had no money to vote, except in very rare and extreme cases; consequently their business was confined to regulating the terms on which the frið could be maintained.

polity, leaving to fortune or to the gods to decide
the abstract question of right between itself and
its opponents. How then is the will of the majority
to be ascertained? Where the number of citizens
is small, the question is readily answered: by the
decision of a public meeting at which all may be
present.

Now such public meetings or councils we find in
existence among the Germans from their very first
appearance in history. The graphic pen of Tacitus
has left us a lively description of their nature and
powers, and in some degree their forms of business.
He says[1],—"In matters of minor import, the chiefs
take counsel together; in weightier affairs, the
whole body of the state: but in such wise, that the
chiefs have the power of discussing and recommending even those measures, which the will of
the people ultimately decides. They meet, except
some sudden and fortuitous event occur, on fixed
days, either at new or full moon . . . . This inconvenience arises from their liberty, that they do not
assemble at once, or at the time for which they are
summoned, but a second or even a third day is wasted
by the delay of those who are to meet. They sit
down, in arms, just as it suits the convenience of
the crowd. Silence is enjoined by the priests, who,
on these occasions, have even the power of coercion. Then the king, or the prince, or any one,
whom his age, nobility, his honours won in war or
his eloquence may authorise to speak, is listened

---

[1] Germ. xi. xii. xiii.

to, more through the influence of persuasion than
the power of command. If his opinion do not
please them, they reject it with murmurs : if it do,
they dash their lances together. The most honourable form of assent is adoption by clashing of arms.
It is lawful also to bring accusations, and prosecute
capitally before the council. The punishment varies
with the crime. Traitors and deserters they hang
on trees ; cowards, the unwarlike, and infamous of
body they bury alive in mud and marsh, with a
hurdle cast over them : the difference of the penalty
has this intention as it were, that crimes should
be made public, but infamous vices hidden, while
being punished. . . . . In the same councils also,
princes are elected, to give law in the shires and villages. Each has a hundred comrades from among
the people, both to advise him and add to his authority. They transact no business either of a public or private nature, without their weapons. But
it is not the custom for any one to begin wearing
them, before the state has approved of him as likely
to be an efficient citizen. Then, in the public
meeting itself, either one of the chiefs, or his father
or a kinsman, decorates the youth with a shield
and javelin. This is their *Toga ;* this is the first
dignity of their youth : before this they appear part
of a household,—after it, of a state."

Such then was the nature of a Teutonic parliament as Tacitus had learnt that it existed in his
time ; nor is there the least doubt that he has
described it most truly. And such were all the popular meetings of later periods, whether shiremoots,

markmoots, or the great *placita* of kingdoms, folk-moots in the most extended sense of the term. Such, at least in theory, and to a great extent in practice, were the meetings of the Franks under the Merwingian kings, and even under the Carolings. It will not be uninteresting or without advantage to compare with this account the description which Hincmar, archbishop of Rheims, gives of the institution as recognised and organized by Charlemagne, a prince by nature not over well disposed to popular freedom, and by circumstances placed in a situation to be very dangerous to it[1].

Charlemagne held Reichstage or Parliaments twice a year, in May and again in the autumn, for the general arrangement of the public business. The earlier of these was attended by the principal officers of state, the ministers as we should call them, both lay and clerical, the administrators of the public affairs in the provinces, and other persons engaged in the business of government. These, who are comprehended under the titles of Maiores, Seniores, Optimates, may possibly have had the real conduct of the deliberations; but there is no doubt that the freemen were also present, first because the general armed muster or Hereban took place at the same time,—the well-known Campus Madius or Champ de Mai,—and partly because we know that all new capitularies added to the existing law were subjected to their approval[2]. We may

---

[1] What follows is abstracted from Hincmar, Epistola de ordine Palatii, as cited and commented upon by Dönniges, p. 74, etc.

[2] " Ut populus interrogetur de capitulis quae in lege noviter addita

therefore conclude that they were still possessed of a share in the business of legislation, although it may have only amounted to a right of accepting or rejecting the propositions of others. The king had his particular curia, court or council, the members of which were chosen ("eligebantur"), though how or by whom we know not, from the laity and the clergy : probably both the king and the people had their share in the election. The Seniores, according to Hincmar, were called "propter consilium ordinandum," to lead the business; the Minores, "propter idem consilium suscipiendum," to accept the same; but also "interdum pariter tractandum," sometimes to take a part also in the discussions, "and to confirm them, not indeed by any inherent power of their own, but by the moral influence of their judgment and opinion."

The second great meeting comprised only the seniores and the king's immediate councillors[1]. It appears to have been concerned with questions of revenue as well as general policy. But its main object was to prepare the business and anticipate the necessities of the coming year. It was a deliberative assembly[2] in which questions afterwards to be submitted to the general meeting were discussed and agreed upon. The members of this council were bound to secrecy. When the public

---

sunt. Et postquam omnes consenserint, subscriptiones suas in ipsis capitulis faciant." Pertz, iii. 115, § 19.

[1] Hincmar, c. 30.

[2] These persons were in the strictest sense of the word $\pi\rho o\beta o\acute{u}\lambda o\iota$, and their acts $\pi\rho o\beta o\upsilon\lambda\epsilon\acute{u}\mu a\tau a$. No doubt their body comprised the principal officers engaged in the administration of the State.

business had been concluded, they formed a court of justice and of appeal, for the settlement of litigation in cases which transcended the powers or skill of the ordinary tribunals [1].

The general councils were held, in fine weather, in the open air, or, if occasion required, in houses devoted to the purpose. The ecclesiastics and the magnates, for so we may call them, sat apart from the multitude; but even they had separate chambers, in which the clergy could deliberate upon matters purely ecclesiastical, the magnates upon matters purely civil: but when the object of their enquiry was of a mixed character, they were called together [2]. Before these chambers the questions were brought which had been prepared at the preceding meeting, or arose from altered circumstances: the opinion of the members was taken upon them, and when agreed to they were presented

---

[1] Hincmar, c. 33.

[2] "Sed nec illud praetermittendum, quomodo, si tempus serenum erat, extra, sin autem intra, diversa loca distincta erant; ubi et hi abundanter segregati semotim, et caetera multitudo separatim residere potuissent, prius tamen caeterae inferiores personae interesse minime potuissent. Quae utraque seniorum susceptacula sic in duobus divisa erant, ut primo omnes episcopi, abbates, vel huiusmodi honorificentiores clerici, absque ulla laicorum commixtione congregarentur; similiter comites vel huiusmodi principes sibimet honorificabiliter a caetera multitudine primo mane segregarentur, quousque tempus, sive praesente sive absente rege, occurrerent. Et tunc praedicti Seniores more solito, clerici ad suam, laici vero ad suam constitutam curiam, subselliis similiter honorificabiliter praeparatis, convocarentur. Qui cum separati a caeteris essent, in eorum manebat potestate, quando simul, vel quando separati resident, prout eos tractandae causae qualitas docebat, sive de spiritalibus, sive de saecularibus, seu etiam commixtis. Similiter, si propter aliquam vescendi [? noscendi] vel investigandi causam quemcunque vocare voluissent, et [? an] re comperta discederet, in eorum voluntate manebat." Hincmar, c. 35.

to the king, who agreed or disagreed in turn, as the case might be. While the new laws or administrative regulations were under discussion, the king, unless especially invited to be present at the deliberations, occupied himself in mixing with the remaining multitude, receiving their presents, welcoming their leaders, conversing with the new comers, sympathizing with the old, congratulating the young, and in similar employments, both in spirituals and temporals, says Hincmar[1]. When the prepared business had been disposed of, the king propounded detailed interrogatories to the chambers, respecting the state of the country in the different districts, or what was known of the intentions and actions of neighbouring countries; and these having been answered or reserved for consideration, the assembly broke up. When any new chapters, hence called Capitula, had been added to the ancient law or folkright, special messengers (*missi*) were dispatched into the provinces to obtain the assent and signatures of the free men, and the chapters thus ratified became thenceforth the law of the land. Is it unreasonable to suppose that the proposals of the princes were also presented to the assembled freemen, the *reliqua multitudo*, in arms upon the spot, and that in the old German fashion they carried them by acclamation ?

---

[1] " Interim vero, quo haec in regis absentia agebantur, ipse princeps reliquae multitudini in suscipiendis muneribus, salutandis proceribus, confabulando rarius visis, compatiendo senioribus, congaudendo iunioribus, et caetera his similia tam in spiritalibus, quamque et in saecularibus occupatus erat. Ita tamen, quotienscunque segregatorum voluntas esset, ad eos veniret," etc. Hincmar, c. 35.

While the district whose members attend the folk-moot is still small, there is no great inconvenience in this method of proceeding. In the empire of Charlemagne attendance upon the Campus Madius, whether as soldier or councillor must have been a heavy burthen. Nor can we conceive it to have been otherwise here, as soon as counties became consolidated into kingdoms, and kingdoms into an empire. In a country overrun with forests, inter-sected with deep streams or extensive marshes, and but ill provided with the means of internal commu-nication, suit and service even at the county-court must have been a hardship to the cultivator; a duty performed not without danger, and often vex-atiously interfering with agricultural processes on which the hopes of the year might depend. Much more keenly would this have been felt had every freeman been called upon to attend beyond the limits of his own shire, in places distant from, and totally unknown to him : how for example would a cultivator from Essex have been likely to look upon a journey into Gloucestershire[1] at the severe sea-

[1] Easter and Christmas were usual times for the meetings of the Witan, and during the Mercian period, Cloveshoo was frequently the place where they assembled. Doubts have been lavished upon the si-tuation of this place, which I do not share. In 804 Æðelríc the son of Æðelmund was impleaded respecting lands in Gloucestershire, and stood to right at Cloveshoo. Now it is clear that trial to those lands could properly be made only in the hundred or shire where they lay ; and as the brotherhood of Berkeley were claimants, and the whole business appertained to *Westminster*, I am disposed to seek Cloveshoo somewhere in the hundred of that name in the county of Gloucester, and therefore not far from Deerhurst, Tewksbury and Bishop's Cleeve; not at all improbably in Tewksbury itself, which may have been called Clofeshoas, before the erection of a noble abbey at a later period gave it the name it now bears. Cod. Dipl. No. 186.

son of Christmas[1], or the, to him, important farm-
ing period of Easter ? What moreover could he care
for general laws affecting many districts beside the
one in which he lived, or for regulations applying
to fractions of society in which he had no interest ?
for the Saxon cultivator was not then a politician ;
nor were general rules which embraced a whole
kingdom of the same moment to him, as those
which might concern the little locality in which his
alod lay.   Or what benefit could be expected from

---

[1] These were usual periods for holding the gemót.   " Actum Win-
toniae in publica curia Natalis Christi, in die festivitátis sancti Sylves-
tri," etc. Cod. Dipl. No. 815.   The old folcmót probably met three times
in the year at the unbidden Ðing or *placitum*: so did the followers of
the first Norman kings at least, and it is remarkable enough that the
barons at Oxford should have returned to this arrangement, 42 Hen. III.
anno 1258.   " Fait a remembrer qe lez xxiiii ount ordeignez qe trois
parlementz seront par an, le primere az octaues de seint Michel, le
seconde lendimayn de le chaundelour, le tierce le primer iour de Juyn
ceste asauoir trois semayns deuant le seint Johan ; et a ces troiz parlementz vendront lez conseillours le roi eluz tut ne seyent il pas mandez
pur vere lestat du roialme, et pur treter les communes busoignes du
reaume et del roi ensement et autrefoitz ensembleront quant mester sera
par maundement le roi." Prov. Oxon., Brit. Mus., Cotton MS., Tiberius B.
iv. folio 213.   According to the later custom Parliaments were to be, at
least, annual, and were frequently admitted so to be by law, until the Tu-
dor times. See 5 Ed. II. an. 1311.   "Nous ordenoms qe le Roy tiegne Parlement vne foiz par an ou deux fois se mestre soit, et ceo en lieu conve-
nable," etc.: which ordinance of the Lords was passed into an act of Parliament 4 Ed.III. cap. 14.   Some years later the Commons petitioned the
same king, that for redress of grievances and other important causes,
" soit Parlement tenuz au meinz chescun an en la seson que plerra au
Roy." Rot. Parl. 36 Ed. III. n. 25.   To which the king answered that
the ancient statute thereupon should be held.   This petition the Commons found it necessary to repeat fourteen years later, " qe chescun
an soit tenuz un Parlement," etc.: to which the answer was, " Endroit
du Parlement chescun an, il y aent estatuz et ordenances faitz les queux
soient duement gardez et tenuz." Rot. Parl. 50 Ed. III. n. 186: and
the same thing took place at the accession of Richard the Second.
Rot. Parl. 1 Ric. II. n. 95. 2 Ric. II. n. 2. Triennial parliaments were,
I believe, first agreed to by Charles the First.

his attendance at deliberations which concerned parts of the country with whose mode of life and necessities he was totally unacquainted? Lastly, what evil must not have resulted to the republic by the withdrawal of whole populations from their usual places of employment, and the congregating them in a distant and unknown locality? If we consider these facts, we shall find little difficulty in imagining that any scheme which relieved him from this burthen and threw it upon stronger shoulders, would be a welcome one, and the foundation of a representative system seems laid *à priori*, and in the nature of things itself. To the rich and powerful neighbour whose absence from his farms was immaterial, while his bailiffs remained on the spot to superintend their cultivation; to the scírgeréfa, the ealdorman, the royal reeve, or royal thane, familiar with the public business, and having influence and interest with the king; to the bishop or abbot, distinguished for his wisdom as well as his station; to any or all of these he would be ready to commit the defence of his small, private interests, satisfied to be virtually represented if he were not compelled to leave the business and the enjoyments of his daily life [1].

On the other hand, to whom could the king look with greater security, than to the men whose sympathies were all those of the ruling caste; many

---

[1] The establishment of the Scabini or Schöffen in the Frankish empire was intended to relieve the freemen from the inconvenience of attending gemóts, which the counts converted into an engine of extortion and oppression.

of whom were his own kinsmen by blood or marriage, more of whom were his own officers ; men, too, accustomed to business, and practically acquainted with the wants of their several localities? Or how, when the customs and condition of widely different social aggregations were to be considered and reconciled, could he do better than advise with those who were most able to point out and meet the difficulties of the task? Thus, it appears to me, by a natural process did the folkmót or meeting of the nation become converted into a witena gemót or meeting of councillors. Nor let it be imagined by this that I mean the king's councillors only: by no means ; they were the witan or councillors of the nation, members of the great council or inquest, who sought what was for the general good, certainly not men who accidentally formed part of what we in later days call the king's council, and who might have been more or less the creatures of his will: they were leódwitan, þeódwitan, general, popular, universal councillors: only when they chanced to be met for the purpose of advising him could they bear the title of the cyninges þeahteras or cyninges witan. Then no doubt the Leódwitan became ðæs cyninges witan (*the* king's, not king's, councillors) because without their assistance he could not have enacted, nor without their assistance executed, his laws. Let it be borne in mind throughout that the king was only the head of an aristocracy which acted with him, and by whose support he reigned ; that this aristocracy again was only a higher order of the

freemen, to whose class it belonged, and with many
of whose interests it was identified; that the clergy,
learned, active and powerful, were there to mediate
between the rulers and the ruled; and I think we
shall conclude that the system which I have faintly
sketched was not incapable of securing to a great
degree the well-being of a state in such an early
stage of development as the Saxon Commonwealth.
At what exact period the change I have attempted
to describe was effected, is neither very easy to
determine nor very material. It was probably very
gradual, and very partial; indeed it may never have
been formally recognised, for here and there we
find evident traces of the people's being present
at, and ratifying the decisions of the witan. Much
more important is it to consider certain details
respecting the composition, powers and functions of
the witena gemót as we find it in periods of ascertained history. The documents contained in the
Codex Diplomaticus Ævi Saxonici enable us to do
this in some degree. In that collection there are
several grants which are distinctly stated to have
been made in such meetings of the witan, by and
with their consent, and the signatures to which
may be assumed to be those of members present
on the occasion. Among these we find the king,
frequently the æðelings or princes of the blood,
generally the archbishops and all or some of the
bishops and abbots; all or some of the dukes or
ealdormen; sometimes priests and deacons; and
generally a large attendance of milites, ministri or
thanes, many of whom must unhesitatingly be as-

o 2

serted to be royal officers, geréfan and the like, in
the shires[1]. From one document it is evident that

[1] It has always been a question of deep interest in this country, what
persons were entitled to attend the Gemót: and in truth very important constitutional doctrines depend upon the answer we give to it. The
very first and most essential condition of truth appears to me, that we
firmly close our eyes to everything derived from the custom of Parliaments, under the Norman, the Angevine or the English kings: the
practice of a nation governed by the principles of Feudal law, is totally
irreconcileable with the old system of personal relations which existed
under the earlier Teutonic law. The next most important thing is, that
we use no words but such as the Saxons themselves used : the moment
we begin to talk of Tenants in capite, Vavassors, Vassals, and so forth,
we introduce terms which may involve a *petitio principii*, and must
lead to associations of ideas tending to an erroneous conclusion. One
of these fallacies appears to me to lie in the assertion that a landed
qualification was required for a member of the Witena gemót. One of
the most brilliant, if not the most accurate, commentators on our constitutional history, Sir F. Palgrave, has raised this question. According
to his view no one could be a member of that singular body which he
supposes the Anglosaxon Parliament to have been, unless he had forty
híds of land, four thousand acres at least according to the popular doctrine. But this whole supposition rests upon a series of fine-drawn
conclusions, in my opinion, without sound foundation, and totally inconsistent with every feeling and habit of Saxon society. The monkish writer of the history of Ely—a very late and generally ill-informed
authority—says that a lady would not marry some suitor of hers, because not having forty híds he could not be counted among the Proceres ; and this is the whole basis of this parliamentary theory,—*proceres* being assumed, without the slightest reason, to mean members of
the witena gemót,—and the witena gemót to be some royal council,
some Curia Regis, and not at all the kind of body described in this
chapter. I confess I cannot realize to myself the notion of an Anglosaxon woman nourishing the ambition of seeing her husband a member of Parliament. The passage no doubt implies that a certain amount
of land was necessary to entitle a man to be classed in a certain high
rank in society : and this becomes probable enough as we find a landed
qualification partially insisted on with regard to the ceorl who aspired
to be ranked as a thane. But this is a negative condition altogether:
it is intended to repress the pretensions of those who, in spite of their
ceorlish birth, assumed the weapons and would, if possible, have assumed the rights of thanes. In the Saxon custumal, called " Ranks,"
it is said :—"And if a thane throve so that he became an eorl, he was

the sheriffs of all the counties were present[1] : and
in a few cases we meet with names accompanied
by no special designation. Now it appears that a
body so constituted would have been very competent to advise for the general good ; and I do not
scruple to express my opinion that under such a
system the interests of the country were very fairly
represented ; especially as there were then no parliamentary struggles to make the duration of mi-
nistries dependent upon the counting up of single
votes ; and contests for the representation of counties or boroughs would have been as much without an object in those days, as they are important in our own ; above all, since there was then
no systematic voting of money for the public
service.

thenceforth worthy of eorl-right." Thorpe, i. 192. On this the learned
editor of the Ancient Laws and Institutes observes :—" It is to this law
that the historian of Ely seems to allude in the following passage, and
not to any qualification for a seat in the witena gemót, as has been so
frequently asserted. ' Habuit (sc. Wulfricus abbas) enim fratrem Gud-
mundum vocabulo, cui filiam praepotentis viri in matrimonium coniungi
paraverat, sed quoniam ille quadraginta hidarum terrae dominium minime obtineret, licet nobilis esset [that is, a thane] inter proceres tunc
nominari non potuit, eum puella repudiavit.' Gale, ii. c. 40. If we
refer to the Dooms of Cnut, c. 69, we shall see that the heriots of an
eorl and of a lesser thane were in the proportion of from one to eight,
—a rule which may have been supposed to have arisen from a somewhat similar relation between the quantities of their respective estates ;
and as the possession of five hides conferred upon a ceorl the rights of
a thane, the possession of forty (5×8) in all probability raised a thane
to the dignity of an eorl." This opinion is only a confirmation of that
which I had myself formed on similar grounds long before Mr. Thorpe's
work was published : and it was apparently so understood by Phillips
before either of us wrote. See Angels. Recht. p. 114, note 317. Göt-
tingen, 1825.

[1] Leg. Æðelst. v. § 10.

Among the charters from which we derive our information as to the constituent members of the gemót, one or two appear to be signed by the queen and other ladies, always I believe, ecclesiastics of rank and wealth. I do not however, on this account, argue that such women formed parts of the regular body. In many cases it is clear that when a grant had been made by the king and his witan, the document was drawn up, and offered for attestation to the principal persons present or easily accessible. When the queen had accompanied her consort to the place where the gemót was held, or when, as was usual, the gemót attended the king at one of his own residences to assist in the hospitalities of Christmas and Easter, it was natural that the first lady of the land should be asked to witness grants of land, and other favours conferred upon individuals : it was a compliment to herself, not less than to him whom she honoured with her signature. But I know no instance where the record of any solemn public business is so corroborated ; nor does it follow that the document which was drawn up in accordance with the resolution of a gemót should necessarily be signed in the gemót itself. It may have been executed subsequently at the king's festal board, and in presence of the members of his court and household. The case of abbesses, if not disposed of by the arguments just advanced, must be understood of gemóts in which the interests of the monastic bodies were concerned. Here it is possible that ladies of high rank at the head of nunneries may have attended to watch the proceedings of the synod and attest its acts. Again, where the gemót acted as a high court of justice, which often was the case, a lady who had been party to a cause might naturally be called upon to sign the record of the judgment. The instances however in which the signatures of women occur are very rare.

Although the members of the gemót are called in Saxon generally by the name of *witan*[1], they are decorated with very various titles in the Latin documents. Among these the most common are Maiores natu, Sapientes, Principes, Senatores, Primates, Optimates, Magnates, and in three or four charters they are designated Procuratores patriae[2], which last title however seems confined to the thanes, geréfan or other members below the rank of an ealdorman. In the prologue to the laws of Wihtræd they are called ða eádigan, for which I know no better translation than the Spanish *Ricos hombres*, where the wealth of the parties is certainly not the leading idea. But whatever be their titles they are unquestionably looked upon as representing the whole body of the people, and consequently the national will: and indeed in one charter of Æðelstán, an. 931, the act is said to have been confirmed "tota plebis generalitate ovante," with

---

[1] I write *wita* not *wíta*. The vowel is short, and the noun is formed either upon the plural participle of *witan* to know, or upon a noun *wit*, *intellectus*, previously so formed. The quantity of the vowel is ascertained by the not uncommon spelling weota, where eo = i (see Cod. Dipl. No. 1073), and the occurrence in composition of the form *uta*, which is consonant to the analogy of wudu, wuduwe, wuce for widu, widuwe, wice, but excludes the possibility of a long í.

[2] Cod. Dipl. Nos. 361, 1102, 1105, 1107, 1108.

the approbation of all the people[1]; and the act of a similar meeting at Winchester in 934, which was attended by the king, four Welsh princes, two archbishops, seventeen bishops, four abbots, twelve dukes, and fifty-two thanes, making a total of ninety-two persons, is described to have been executed "tota populi generalitate[2]." On one occasion a gemót is mentioned of which the members are called the king's heáhwitan, or high councillors[3]: it is impossible to say whether this is intended to mark a difference in their rank. If it were, it might be referred to the analogy of the autumnal meetings in Charlemagne's constitution, but nothing has yet been met with to confirm this hypothesis, which, in itself, is not very probable.

The largest amount of signatures which I have yet observed is 106, but numbers varying from 90 to 100 are not uncommon, especially after the consolidation of the monarchy[4]. In earlier times, and smaller kingdoms, the numbers must have been much less: the gemót which decided upon the reception of Christianity in Northumberland was held in a room[5], and Dunstan met the witan of England in the upper floor of a house at Calne[6]. Other meetings, which were rather in the nature of conventions, and were held in the presence of armies, may have been much more numerous and tumul-

---

[1] Cod. Dipl. No. 1103.   [2] Cod. Dipl. No. 364.
[3] Chron. Sax. an. 1009.
[4] See Cod. Dipl. Nos. 353, 364, 1107. There is one document signed by 121 persons (Cod. Dipl. Nos. 219, 220), but I have some doubt whether all the signitaries were members of the gemót.
[5] Beda, H. E. ii. 13.   [6] Chron. Sax. an. 978.

tuary,—much more like the ancient armed folk-moot or the famous day which put an end to the Merwingian dynasty among the Franks[1].

That the members of the witena gemót were not elected, in any sense which we now attach to the word, I hold to be indisputable: elective witan ceased together with elective scírgeréfan or ealdor-men[2]. But in a system so elastic as the Saxon, it is conceivable that an ealdorman, bishop or other great wita may have occasionally carried with him to the gemót some friend or dependent whose wisdom he thought might aid in the discussions, or whom the opinion of the neighbourhood designated as a person well calculated to advise for the general good,—a slight trace, but still a trace, of the

---

[1] Such perhaps was the gemót which after Eádmund írensída's death elected Cnut sole king of England, or that in which Earl Godwine and his family were outlawed.

[2] This is not altogether devoid of strangeness, because we know that among the Oldsaxons of the continent there was a regulated system of elective representatives, including even those of the servile class. Huc-bald, in his life of Lebuuini, tells us: "In Saxonum gente priscis tem-poribus neque summi coelestisque regis inerat notitia, ut digna cultui eius exhiberetur reverentia, neque terreni alicuius regis dignitas et honorificentia, cuius regeretur providentia, corrigeretur censura, de-fenderetur industria: sed erat gens ipsa, sicuti nunc usque consistit, ordine tripartito divisa. Sunt denique ibi, qui illorum lingua *edilingi*, sunt qui *frilingi*, sunt qui *lassi* dicuntur, quod in latina sonat lingua, nobiles, ingenuiles atque serviles. Pro suo vero libitu, consilio quoque, ut videbatur, prudenti, singulis pagis principes praeerant singuli. Sta-tuto quoque tempore anni semel ex singulis pagis, atque ab eisdem ordinibus tripartitis, singillatim viri duodecim electi, et in unum col-lecti, in media Saxonia secus flumen Wiseram et locum Marklo nuncu-patum, exercebant generale concilium, tractantes, sancientes et propa-lantes communis commoda utilitatis, iuxta placitum a se statutae legis. Sed etsi forte belli terreret exitium, si pacis arrideret gaudium, con-sulebant ad haec quid sibi foret agendum." Pertz, Monum. ii. 361, 362.

ancient popular right to be present at the settlement of public business. To this I attribute the frequent appearance of priests and deacons, who probably attended in the suite of prelates, and would be useful assessors when clerical business was brought before the council. Generally, I imagine, the witan after having once been called by writ or summons, met like our own peers, as a matter of course, whenever a parliament was proclaimed; and that they were summoned by the king, either *pro hac vice*, or generally, can be clearly shown. Æðelstán, speaking of the gemóts at Greatanleá, Exeter, Feversham and Thundersfield, says that the consultations were made, before the archbishop, the bishops, and the witan present, *whom the king himself had named:* " Swá Æðelstán cyng hit geræd hæfð, ꝺ his witan, ǽrest æt Greátanleá, ꝺ eft æt Exanceastre, ꝺ syððám æt Fæfreshám, ꝺ feorðan síðe æt Đunresfelda, beforan ðám arcebiscope, ꝺ eallum ðám bisceopan, ꝺ his witum, ðe se cyng silf namode, ðe ðǽron wǽron [1]." How these appointments took place is not very material, but as the witan were collected from various parts of England, it is not unreasonable to suppose that it was by the easy means of a writ and token, *gewrit and insigel.* The meeting was proclaimed some time in advance, at some one of the royal residences [2].

---

[1] Æðelst. v. § 10. Thorpe, i. 240.

[2] " Đonne beád mon ealle witan tó cynge, and man sceólde ðonne rǽdan, hú man ðisne eard werian sceólde." Chron. an. 1010. *Beódan* is to *proclaim.*

See also Chron. Sax. 1048. Hist. Eliens. 1, 10, etc.

The proper Saxon name for these assemblies was witena gemót [1], literally the meeting of the witan; but we also find, micel gemót, the great meeting; sinoðlíc gemót, the synodal meeting; seonoð, the synod. The Latin names are concilium, conventus, synodus, synodale conciliabulum, and the like. Although synodus and seonoð might more properly be confined to ecclesiastical conventions, the Saxons do not appear to have made any distinction; probably because ecclesiastical and secular regulations were made by the same body, and at the same time. But it is very probable that the Frankish system of separate houses for the clergy and laity prevailed here also, and that merely ecclesiastical affairs were decided by the king and clergy alone. There are some acts in which the signatures are those of clergymen only, others in which the clerical signatures are followed and, as it were, confirmed by those of the laity; and in one remarkable case of this kind, the king signs at the head of each list, as if he had in fact affixed his mark successively in the two houses, as president of each [2].

[1] "And se cyng hæfde ðær on morgen witena gemót, ꝧ cwæð hine útlage." Chron. Sax. an. 1052. "And wæs ðá witena gemót." Ib. an. 1052. "Ða hæfde Eádwerd cyning witena gemót on Lundene." Ib. an. 1050.

[2] Cod. Dipl. No. 116. It is probable that even in strictly ecclesiastical synods, the king had a presidency at least, as head of the church in his dominious. In Willibald's life of Boniface we are told:—"Regnante Ini, Westsaxonum rege, subitanea quaedam incubuerat, nova quadam seditione exorta, necessitas, et statim synodale a primatibus aecclesiarum cum consilio praedicti regis servorum Dei factum est concilium; moxque omnibus in unum convenientibus, saluberrima de hac recenti dissentione consilii quaestio inter sacerdotales aecclesiastici ordinis gradus sapienter exoritur, et prudentiori inito consultu, fideles in

A more important question for us is, what were the powers of the witena gemót? It must be answered by examples in detail.

1. *First, and in general, they possessed a consultative voice, and right to consider every public act, which could be authorised by the king.* This has been attempted to be denied, but without sufficient reason. Runde, who is one of the upholders of the erroneous doctrine on this subject, appeals to the introduction of Christianity into Kent, which he perhaps justly declares to have been made without the assent of the witan [1]. But it does not at all follow that the first reception of Augustine by Æðelberht is to be considered a public act, or that it had any immediate consequences for the public law. Nor is it certain that at a later period, a meeting of the witan may not have ratified the private proceeding of the king. Æðelberht, who had some experience of Christianity from the doctrine and practice of his Frankish consort Beorhte, may have chosen to trust to the silent, gradual working of the missionaries, without courting the opposition of a heathen witena gemót, till assured of success: his court were already accustomed to the sight of a Christian bishop and clergy in Beorhte's suite, and

---

Domino legatos ad archiepiscopum Cantuariae civitatis, nomine Berchtwaldum, destinandos deputarunt, ne eorum praesumptione aut temeritati adscriberetur, si quid sine tanti pontificis agerent consilio. Cumque omnis senatus et universus clericorum ordo, tam providenti peracta conlatione, consentirent, confestim rex cunctos Christi famulos adlocutus est, ut cui huius praefatae legationis nuntium inponerent, sciscitarent," etc. Pertz, ii. 338.

[1] Runde, Abhandlung vom Ursprung der Reichsstandschaft der Bischöfe und Aebte. Gött. 1775, p. 35, etc.

Augustine with his company might easily pass for a mere addition to that department of the royal household. Indeed Augustine himself does not appear to have been at all ambitious of martyrdom, and probably preferred trying the chances of a gradual progress to a stormy and perhaps fatal collision with a body of barbarians, led by a pagan and rival priesthood. The words of Beda therefore can prove nothing in the matter, except indeed what is most important for us, viz. that Æðelberht at first refused to interfere as king, that is, would not make a public question of Augustine's mission[1]. But Runde seems to have forgotten that Æðelberht's laws, which must be dated between 596 and 605, do most emphatically recognise Christianity and the Christian priesthood; and as Beda declares him to have enacted these laws " cum consilio sapientum[2]," we shall hardly be saying too much if we affirm that the introduction of Christianity was at least ratified by a solemn act of the witan. Runde's further remarks upon the conversion of Northumberland seem to prove that he really never read through the passages he himself cites, so completely do they refute his own arguments[3].

2. *The witan deliberated upon the making of new laws which were to be added to the existing folcriht*[4], *and which were then promulgated by their own*

---

[1] Hist. Eccl. i. 26.   [2] Ibid. ii. 5.

[3] See Phillips, Geschichte des Angelsächsischen Rechts. Gött. 1825, p. 71.

[4] Hloðhære and Eádríc, kings of the men of Kent, *augmented* the laws which their forefathers had made before them, by these dooms. Prol. to Leg. Hloð. et Ead. Thorpe, i. 26. See also the Prologue to Wihtræd's laws in the text.

and the king's authority [1]. Beda, in a passage just
cited, says of Æðelberht :—" Amongst other benefits which consulting, he bestowed upon his nation, he gave her also, with the advice of his witan,
decrees of judgments, after the example of the
Romans : which, written in the English tongue,
are yet possessed and observed by her [2]." And
these laws were enacted by their authority, jointly
with the king's. The Prologue to the law of Wihtræd declares :—"These are the dooms of Wihtræd,
king of the men of Kent. In the reign of the
most clement king of the men of Kent, Wihtræd, in

[1] This is the case throughout the Teutonic legislation, where there
is a king at all. "Theodoricus rex Francorum, cum esset Cathalaunis,
elegit viros sapientes, qui in regno suo legibus antiquis eruditi erant :
ipso autem dictante, iussit conscribere legem Francorum, Alemannorum
et Baiuvariorum," etc. Eichhorn, i. 273. "Incipit Lex Alamannorum, quae temporibus Illodharii regis (an. 613–628) una cum principibus suis, id sunt xxxiii episcopis, et xxxiv ducibus, et lxii comitibus,
vel caetero populo constituta est." Eichhorn, i. 274, note a. "In
Christi nomine, incipit Lex Alamannorum, qui temporibus Lanfrido
filio Godofrido renovata est. Convenit enim maioribus natu populo
allamannorum una cum duci eorum lanfrido vel citerorum populo adu-
nato ut si quilibet," etc. About beginning of eighth century. Eichhorn. i. 274, note c. The Breviarium of Alaric the Visigoth (an. 506)
was compiled by Roman jurists, but submitted to an assembly of prelates and noble laymen. In the authoritative rescript which accom-
panies this work, it is said the object was, " Ut omnis legum Romana-
rum, et antiqui iuris obscuritas, adhibitis sacerdotibus ac nobilibus
viris, in lucem intelligentiae melioris deducta resplendeat. . . . .
Quibus omnibus enucleatis atque in unum librum prudentium electione
collectis, haec quae excerpta sunt, vel clariori interpretatione composita,
venerabilium Episcoporum, vel electorum provincialium nostrorum ro-
boravit adsensus." Eichhorn, i. 280, note bb. Gundobald the Burgundian, whose laws must have been promulgated before 515, says
that he was aided by the advice of his optimates. Again he says,
"Primum habito consilio comitum, procerumque nostrorum," etc.
Eichhorn, i. 265, note c.

[2] Hist. Eccl. ii. 5. He cites a passage which identifies these dooms
with those which yet go under Æðelberht's name.

the fifth year of his reign, the ninth indiction [1], the
sixth day of the month Rugern, in the place which
is called Berghamstead [2], where was assembled a
deliberative convention of the great men [3]; there
was Brihtwald the high-bishop [4] of Britain, and the
aforenamed king; also the bishop of Rochester;
the same was called Gybmund, he was present; and
every degree of the church in that tribe, spake
in unison with the obedient people [5]. There the
great men decreed, with the suffrages of all, these
dooms, and added them to the lawful customs of
the men of Kent, as hereafter is said and declared [6]."

The prologue to the laws of Ini establishes the
same fact for Wessex; he says,—"Ini, by the grace
of God, king of the Westsaxons, with the advice
and by the teaching of Cénred, my father, and of
Hedde my bishop, and Ercenwold my bishop, with
all my ealdormen, and the most eminent witan of
my people, and also with a great assemblage of
God's servants [7], have been considering respecting
our soul's heal, and the stability of our realm; so
that right law, and right royal judgments might
be settled and confirmed among our people; so that

---

[1] A.D. 696. The month is unknown, but probably in autumn.

[2] Now Berstead, near Maidstone, in Kent, certainly not Berkhamp-
stead in Hertfordshire, as Clutterbuck affirms in his history of that
county.

[3] "Eádigra geþeahtendlíc ymcyme." See Thorpe, i. 36, note c.

[4] Archbishop of Canterbury.

[5] The people subject to their charge. Were the people, that is, the
freemen, present at this gemót in their divisions as parishes or ecclesiastical districts?

[6] Thorpe, i. 36.   [7] The clergy especially.

none of our ealdormen, nor of those who are subject unto us, should ever hereafter turn aside these our dooms [1]."

And this is confirmed in more detail by Ælfred. This prince, after giving some extracts from the Levitical legislation, and deducing their authority through the Apostolical teaching, proceeds to engraft upon the latter the peculiar principle of bót or compensation which is the characteristic of Teutonic legislation [2]. He says,—"After this it happened that many nations received the faith of Christ; and then were many synods assembled throughout all the earth, and among the English race also, after they had received the faith of Christ, of holy bishops, and also of their exalted witan. They then ordained, out of that mercy which Christ had taught, that secular lords, *with their leave*, might without sin take for almost every misdeed— for the first offence—the bót in money which they then ordained ; except in cases of treason against a lord, to which they dared not to assign any mercy ; because Almighty God adjudged none to them that

[1] Thorpe, i. 102.

[2] Ælfred makes a marked exception in the case of treason, and repeats it in strong terms in § 4 of his laws, "be hláford syrwe." These despotic tendencies of a great prince, nurtured probably by his exaggerated love for foreign literature, may account to us for the state of utter destitution in which his people at one time left him. His strong personality, and active character, coupled with the almost miraculous, at any rate most improbable, event, of his ascending the throne of Wessex, may have betrayed him in his youth into steps which his countrymen looked upon as dangerous to their liberties. Nothing can show Ælfred's antinational and un-Teutonic feeling more than his attributing the system of bóts or compensations to the influence of Christianity.

despised him, nor did Christ, the son of God, adjudge any to him that sold him unto death: and he commanded that a lord should be loved like oneself[1]. They then, in many synods, decreed a bót for many human misdeeds; and in many synodbooks they wrote, here one doom, there another.

" Then I, Ælfred the king, gathered these together, and commanded many of those which our forefathers held, and which seemed good to me, to be written down; and many which did not seem good to me, I rejected by the counsel of my witan, and commanded them in other wise to be holden; but much of my own I did not venture to set down in writing, for I knew not how much of it might please our successors. But what I met with, either of the time of Ini my kinsman, or of Offa, king of the Mercians, or Æðelberht who first of the English race received baptism, the best I have here collected, and the rest rejected. I then, Ælfred king of the Westsaxons, showed these to all my witan, and they then said, that it liked them well so to hold them."

The laws of Eádweard like those of Hloðhere and Eádríc have no proem: next in order of time are those of Æðelstán. The council of Greatley opens with an ordinance which the king says was framed by the advice of Wulfhelm, archbishop of Canterbury and his other bishops: no other witan are mentioned. Now it is remarkable enough that this ordinance refers exclusively to tithes, and other

---

[1] This is Mr. Thorpe's version, i. 59. But the words may be as strictly construed, " should be loved like *himself*," viz. God.

ecclesiastical dues, and works of charity. But the secular ordinances which follow conclude with these words : " All this was established in the great synod at Greátanleá ; in which was archbishop Wulfhelm, with all the noblemen and witan whom Æðelstán the king [commanded to] gather together [1]."

The witan at Exeter, under the same king, are much more explicit as to their powers : in the preamble to their laws, they say : " These are the dooms which the witan at Exeter decreed, with the counsel of Æðelstán the king, and again at Feversham, and a third time at Thundersfield, where the whole was settled and confirmed together [2]."

The concurrence of these witan is continually appealed to in the Saxon laws which follow [3], and which are supplementary to the three gemóts mentioned. But in a chapter (§ 7) concerning ordeals, the regulation is said to be by command of God, the archbishop and all the bishops, and the other witan are not mentioned; probably because the administration of the ordeal was a special, ecclesiastical function. Again in the Judicia Civitatis Londoniae the joint legislative authority of the king and the witan is repeatedly alluded to [4].

Eádmund commences his laws by stating that he had assembled a great *synod* in London at Easter, at which the two archbishops, Oda and Wulfstan, were present, together with many bishops and persons of ecclesiastical as well as secular condi-

---

[1] Thorpe, i. 214.   [2] Ibid. i. 207.
[2] Æðelst. iv.   Thorpe, i. 220, 224.
[4] Æðelst. v. § 10, 11, 12.   Thorpe, i. 238, 240.

tion[1]. And having thus given the authority by
which he acted, he proceeds to the details of his
law, which he again declares to have been promulgated, after deliberation with the council of his
witan, ecclesiastical and lay[2]. The council of Culinton, held under the same prince, commences
thus: "This is the decree which Eádmund the
king and his bishops, with his witan, established
at Culinton, concerning the maintenance of peace,
and taking the oaths of fidelity."

Next comes Eádgár, whose law commences in
these words: "This is the ordinance which Eádgár
the king, with the counsel of his witan, ordained,
to the praise of God, his own honour, and the benefit of all his people[3]."

In like manner, Æðelred informs us that his law
was ordained, "for the better maintenance of the
public peace, by himself and his witan at Woodstock, in the land of the Mercians, according to
the laws of the Angles[4]." In precisely similar terms
he speaks of new laws made by himself and his
witan at Wantage[5]. In a collection of laws passed
in 1008, under the same prince, we find the following preamble[6]: "This is the ordinance which
the king of the English, with his witan, both clerical and lay, have chosen[7] and advised;" and every
one of the first five paragraphs commences with

---

[1] Thorpe, i. 244.   [2] Ibid. i. 246.
[3] Ibid. i. 262 ; see also pp. 270, 272, 276.
[4] Ibid. i. 280.   [5] Ibid. i. 292.   [6] Ibid. i. 304.
[7] The word *ceósan*, to elect or choose, is the technical expression
in Teutonic legislation for ordinances which have been deliberated
upon.

the same solemn words, viz. "This is the ordinance of our lord, and of his witan," etc.

But far more strongly is this marked in the provisions of the council of Enham, under the same miserable prince. These are not only entitled, "ordinances of the witan[1]," but throughout, the king is never mentioned at all, and many of the chapters commence, "It is the ordinance of the witan," etc. If it were not for one or two enactments referring to the safety of the royal person, and the dignity of the crown, we might be almost tempted to imagine that the great councillors of state had met, during Æðelred's flight from England, and passed these laws upon their own authority, without the king. The laws of 1014 commence again with the words so often repeated in this chapter[2], and such also usher in the very elaborate collection which Cnut and his witan compiled at Winchester[3].

Now I think that any impartial person will be satisfied with these examples, and admit that whoever the witan may have been, they possessed a legislative authority, at least conjointly with the king. Indeed of two hypothetical cases, I should be far more inclined to assert that they possessed it without him, than that he possessed it without them: at least, I can find no instance of the latter; while I have shown that there was at least a probability of the former: and even Æðelred himself says, twice: "Wise in former days were those

---

[1] Thorpe, i. 314, 316, 318.   [2] Ibid. i. 340, 342, 350.
[3] Ibid. i. 358, 376.

secular witan [1] who first added secular laws to the just divine laws, for bishops and consecrated bodies; and reverenced for love of God holiness and holy orders, and God's houses and his servants firmly protected." Again [2]: " Wise were those secular witan who to the divine laws of justice added secular laws for the government of the people; and decreed bót to Christ and the king, that many should thus, of necessity, be compelled to right."

Is it not manifest that he, like Ælfred, really felt the legislative power to reside in the witan, rather than in the king?

3. *The witan had the power of making alliances and treaties of peace, and of settling their terms.*

The defeat of the Danes by Ælfred, in 878, was followed, as is well known, by the baptism of Guðorm Æðelstán, and the peaceful establishment of his forces in portions of the ancient kingdoms of Mercia, Essex, Eastanglia and Northumberland. The terms of this treaty, and the boundaries of the new states thus constituted were solemnly ratified, perhaps at Wedmore [3]; the first article of this important public act, by which Ælfred obtained a considerable accession of territory, runs thus [4]: " This is the peace that Ælfred the king, and Gyðrum the king, and the witan of all the English nation, and all the people that are in Eastanglia, have all ordained and confirmed with oaths, for themselves and for their descendants, born and unborn, who

---

[1] Woroldwitan. Æðelr. vii. § 24.   Thorpe, i. 334.
[2] Æðelr. ix. § 36.   Thorpe, i. 348.
[3] Chron. Sax. an. 878. Asser, *in anno.*   [4] Thorpe, i. 152.

desire God's favour or ours. First, concerning our land-boundaries," etc. In like manner the treaty which Eádweard entered into with the same Danes, is said to have been frequently (" oft and unseldan ") renewed and ratified by the witan[1].

We still have the terms of the shameful peace which Æðelred bought of Olafr Tryggvason and his comrades in 994. The document, which was probably signed at Andover[2], commences with the following words : " These are the articles of peace and the agreement which Æðelred the king and all his witan have made with the army which accompanied Anlaf, and Justin and Guðmund, the son of Stegita[3]."

Many other instances might be cited, as for example the entry in the Chronicle, anno 947, where it is stated that Eádred made a treaty of peace with the witan of Northumberland at Taddenes scylf, which was broken and renewed in the following year : but further evidence upon this point seems unnecessary[4].

4. *The witan had the power of electing the king.*

The kingly dignity among the Anglosaxons was partly hereditary, partly elective : that is to say, the kings were usually taken from certain qualified families, but the witan claimed the right of choosing the person whom they would have to reign. Their history is filled with instances of occasions when

---

[1] Thorpe, i. 166.   [2] Chron. Sax. an. 994.   [3] Thorpe, i. 284.
[4] See Chron. Sax. an. 1002, 1004, 1006, 1011, 1012. The solemn partition of the kingdom between Eádmund írensída and Cnut was effected by the witan, at Olney in Gloucestershire. Chron. Sax. an. 1016.

the sons or direct descendants of the last king
have been set aside in favour of his brother or
some other prince whom the nation believed more
capable of ruling: and the very rare occurrence
of discontent on such occasions both proves the
authority which the decision of the witan carried with it, and the great discretion with which
their power was exercised. Only here and there,
when the witan were themselves not unanimous,
do we find any traces of dissensions arising out of
a disputed succession [1]. On every fresh accession,
the great compact between the king and the people was literally, as well as symbolically, renewed,
and the technical expression for ascending the
throne is being " gecoren and áhafen tó cyninge,"
elected and raised to be king: where the *áhafen*
refers to the old Teutonic custom of what we still
at election times call chairing the successful can-
didate; and the *gecoren* denotes the positive and
foregone conclusion of a real election. Ælfred's
own accession is a familiar instance of this fact:
he was chosen, to the prejudice of his elder brother's children; but the nation required a prince
capable of coping with dangers and difficulty, and
Asser tells us that he was not only received as
king by the unanimous assent of the people, but
that, had he so pleased, he might have dethroned

---

[1] I speak now of periods subsequent to the consolidation of the monarchy: while England was full of kinglets, disputes were not infre-
quent. Northumberland and Wessex (previous to Beorhtríc's alliance
with Offa) furnish examples. But here the competitors were numerous,
and the witan themselves split into parties, generally maintaining the
interests of *different* royal families.

his brother Æðelred and reigned in his place[1]. His words are: " In the same year (871) the aforesaid Ælfred, who hitherto, during the life of his brother, had held a secondary place, immediately upon Æðelred's death, by the grace of God, assumed the government of the whole realm, with the greatest goodwill of all the inhabitants of the kingdom; which indeed, even during his aforesaid brother's life, he might, had he chosen, have done with the greatest ease, and by the universal consent; truly, because both in wisdom and in all good qualities he much excelled all his brothers; and moreover because he was particularly warlike, and successful in nearly all his battles[2]."

Not one word have we here about his nephews, or any rights they might possess: and Asser seems to think royalty itself a matter entirely dependent upon the popular will, and the good opinion entertained by the nation of its king. I shall conclude this head by citing a few instances from Saxon documents of the intervention of the witan in a king's election and inauguration.

In 924, the Chronicle says: " This year died Eádweard the king at Fearndún, among the Mercians . . . . and Æðelstán was chosen king by the Mercians, and consecrated at Kingston."

Florence of Worcester, an. 959, distinctly asserts

---

[1] Asser, an. 871.

[2] Simeon of Durham uses equally strong terms on the occasion. " Ælfredus a ducibus et a praesulibus totius gentis eligitur, et non solum ab ipsis, verumetiam ab omni populo adoratur, ut eis praeesset, ad faciendam vindictam in nationibus, increpationes in populis." An. 871.

that Eádgár was elected by all the people of England,—" ab omni Anglorum populo electus . . . regnum suscepit."

In 979, the Chronicle again says: " This year Æðelred took to the kingdom ; and he was soon after consecrated king at Kingston, with great rejoicing of the English witan."

In 1016, the election of Eádmund írensída is thus related: " Then befel it that king Æðelred died . . . . and then after his death, all the witan who were in London, and the townsmen, chose Eádmund to be king." Again in 1017: " This year was Cnut elected king."

In 1036 again we have these words: " This year died Cnut the king at Salisbury . . . and soon after his decease there was a gemót of all the witan ('ealra witena gemót') at Oxford: and Leófríc the eorl, and almost all the thanes north of the Thames, and the *lithsmen* in London chose Harald to be chief of all England; to him and his brother Hardacnut who was in Denmark." This election was opposed unsuccessfully by Godwine and the men of Wessex.

The Chronicle contains a very important entry under the date 1014. Upon the death of Swegen, we are told that his army elected Cnut king: " But all the witan who were in England, both clerical and lay, decided to send after king Æðelred[1]; and they declared that no lord could be dearer to them than their natural lord, if he would

---

[1] He had fled to Normandy.

rule them more justly than he had done before. Then the king sent his son Eádweard hither, with his messengers, and commanded them to greet all his people[1]; and he said that he would be a loving lord to them, and amend all those things which they all abhorred ; and that everything which had been said or done against him should be forgiven, on condition that they all, with one consent and without deceit, would be obedient to him. Then they established full friendship, by word and pledge on either side, and declared every Danish king an outlaw from England for ever."

Cnut nevertheless succeeded ; but after the extinction of his short-lived dynasty, we are told that all the people elected Eádweard the Confessor king. " 1041. This year died Hardacnut . . . . And before he was buried, all the people elected Eádweard king, at London." Another manuscript reads :— " 1042. This year died Hardacnut, as he stood at his drink . . And all the people then received Eádweard for their king, as was his true natural right."

One more quotation from a manuscript of the Saxon Chronicle shall conclude this head:—" 1066. In this year was hallowed the minster at Westminster on Childermas-day (Dec. 28th). And king Eádweard died on the eve of Twelfth-day, and he was buried on Twelfth-day in the newly consecrated church at Westminster. And Harald the earl

---

[1] Leóde and leódscipe, the words used in the Chronicle, *may* possibly mean only the great officers or ministerials, the Frankish *Leudes*. But the balance of probability is in favour of its representing *the whole people:* leódscipe, which is the reading of the most manuscripts, having a more general sense than leóde.

succeeded to the kingdom of England, even as the king had granted it unto him, and men also had elected him thereto.   And he was consecrated king on Twelfth-day."

The witan of England had met to aid in the consecration of Westminster Abbey, and, as was their full right, proceeded to elect a king, on Eádweard's decease.

5. *The witan had the power to depose the king, if his government was not conducted for the benefit of the people.*

It is obvious that the very existence of this power would render its exercise an event of very rare occurrence.   Anglosaxon history does however furnish one clear example.   In 755, the witan of Wessex, exasperated by the illegal conduct of king Sigeberht, deposed him from the royal dignity, and elected his relative Cynewulf in his stead.   The fact is thus related by different authorities.   The Chronicle[1] says very shortly :—" This year, Cynewulf and the witan of the Westsaxons deprived his kinsman Sigeberht of his kingdom, except Hampshire[2], for his unjust deeds."

Florence tells the same story, but in other words[3] :—" Cynewulf, a scion of the royal race of Cerdic, with the counsel of the Westsaxon *primates*, removed their king Sigeberht from his realm, on account of the multitude of his iniquities, and

---

[1] Chron. Sax. an. 755.

[2] Perhaps his own, ancestral kingdom.   Does not all this look very much as if Wessex was still only a confederation of petty principalities, with one elective and paramount head ?

[3] Flor. Wig. an. 755.

reigned in his place: however he granted to him one province, which is called Hampshire."

Æðelweard[1], whose royal descent and usual pedantry conspire to make his account of the matter somewhat hazy, says :—" So, after the lapse of a year from the time when Sigeberht began to reign, Cynewulf invaded his realm and took it from him ; and he drew the *sapientes* of all the western country after him, apparently, on account of the irregular acts of the said king," etc.

The fullest account however of the whole transaction is given by Henry of Huntingdon[2], who very frequently shows a remarkable acquaintance with Saxon authorities which are now lost, but from which he translates and quotes at considerable length. These are his words :—" Sigeberht, the kinsman of the aforesaid king, succeeded him, but he held the kingdom for a short time only : for being swelled up and insolent through the successes of his predecessor, he became intolerable even unto his own people. But when he continued to ill-use them in every way, and either twisted the laws to his own advantage, or turned them aside for his advantage, Cumbra, the noblest of his ealdormen, at the petition of the whole people, brought their complaints before the savage king. Whom, for attempting to persuade him to rule his people more mercifully, and setting his inhumanity aside to show himself an object of love to God and man, he shortly after commanded to be put to an impious

---

[1] Æðelw. an. 755, lib. ii. c. 17.
[2] Hen. Hunt. Hist. Ang. lib. iv.

death : and becoming still more fierce and intolerable to his people, he aggravated his tyranny.   In the beginning of the second year of his reign, Sigeberht the king continuing incorrigible in his pride and iniquity, the princes and people of the whole realm collected together ; and by provident deliberation and unanimous consent of all he was expelled from the throne. But Cynewulf, an excellent young prince, of the royal race, was elected to be king [1]."

I have little doubt that an equally formal, though hardly equally justifiable, proceeding severed Mercia from Eádwig's kingdom, and reconstituted it as a separate state under Eádgár [2]; and lastly from Simeon of Durham we learn that the Northumbrian Alchred was deposed and exiled, with the counsel and consent of all his people [3].

6. *The king and the witan had power to appoint prelates to vacant sees.*

As many of the witan were the most eminent of the clergy, and the people might be fairly considered

---

[1] " Sigebertus rex, in principio secundi anni regni sui, cum incorrigibilis superbiae et nequitiae esset, congregati sunt proceres et populus totius regni, et provida deliberatione, et unanimi consensu omnium expulsus est a regno.   Kinewulf vero, iuvenis egregius de regia stirpe oriundus, electus est in regem."

[2] Flor. Wig. an. 957.

[3] " Eodem tempore, Alcredus rex, consilio et consensu omnium suorum, regiae familiae principum destitutus societate, exilio imperii mutavit maiestatem." Sim. Dun. an. 774. Other Germanic tribes did the same thing. "Sed cum Aldoaldus eversa mente insaniret, de regno eiectus est." Paul. Diac. Langob. iv. 43. Among the Burgundians, " generali nomine rex appellatur Hendinos, et *ritu veteri*, potestate deposita removetur, si sub eo fortuna titubaverit belli, vel segetum copiam negaverit terra." Amm. Marc. xxxiii. 5.

to be represented by the secular members of the body, these elections were perhaps more canonical than the Frankish, and assuredly more so than those which take place under our system by *congé d'élire*. The necessary examples will be found in the Saxon Chronicle, an. 971, 995, 1050. But one may be mentioned at length. In 959 Dúnstán was elected archbishop of Canterbury " consilio sapientum [1]."

7. *They had also power to regulate ecclesiastical matters, appoint fasts and festivals, and decide upon the levy and expenditure of ecclesiastical revenue.*

The great question of monachism which convulsed the church and kingdom in the tenth century, was several times brought before the consideration of the witan, who, both clerical and lay, were very much divided upon the subject. This perhaps is a sufficient reason why no formal act of the gemót was ever passed on the subject, and the solution of the problem was left to the bishops in their several cathedrals : but no reader of Saxon history can be ignorant that it was frequently brought before the gemót, and that it was the cause of deep and frequent dissensions among the witan [2]. The festival days of St. Eádweard and St. Dúnstán were fixed by the authority of the witan on the 15th Kal. April and 14th Kal. June respectively [3]; and the

---

[1] " Dehinc beatus Dunstanus, Æthelmi archiepiscopi ex fratre nepos, Glæstaniæ abbas, post Huicciorum et Londoniensium episcopus, ex respectu divino et sapientum consilio, primae metropolis Anglorum primas et patriarcha." Flor. Wig. an. 959.

[2] Flor. Wig. an. 975, says, " Et in synodo constituti, se nequaquam ferre posse dixerunt, ut monachi eiicerentur de regno."

[3] Æðelr. v. § 16.   Cnut, i. § 17.   Thorpe, i. 310, 370.

laws contain many provisions for the due keeping of the Sabbath, and the strict celebration of fasts and festivals[1]. The levying of church-shots, soul-shots, light-alms, plough-alms, tithes, and a variety of other church imposts, the payment of which could not be otherwise legally binding upon the laity, was made law by frequently repeated chapters in the acts of the witan : these are much too numerous to need specification. They direct the amount to be paid, the time of payment, and the penalties to be inflicted on defaulters : nay, they actually direct the mode in which such payments when received should be distributed and applied by the receivers[2]. They establish, as law of the land, the prohibitions to marry within certain degrees of relationship : and lastly they adopt and sanction many regulations of the fathers and bishops, respecting the life and conversation of priests and deacons, canons, monks and religious women. On all these points it is sufficient to give a general reference to the laws, which are full of regulations even to the minutest details.

8. *The king and the witan had power to levy taxes for the public service.*

I have observed in an earlier chapter of this work that the estates of the freeman were bound to make certain settled payments. These may at some time or other have been voluntary, but there can be no doubt that they did ultimately become compulsory

---

[1] For example, Cnut, i. § 14, 15, 16. Thorpe, i. 368, etc.
[2] For example, Æðelr. ix. § 6. Thorpe, i. 342. Æðelr. vi. § 51. Thorpe, i. 328, etc.

payments. They are the cyninges gafol, payable on the hide, and may possibly be the cyninges útware, and cyninges geban of the laws, the *contributions directes* by which a man's station in society was often measured. Now in the time of Ini, we find the witan regulating the amount of this tax or gafol, in barley, at six pounds weight upon the hide[1]. Again, under the extraordinary circumstances of the Danish war under Æðelred, when it became almost customary to buy off the invaders, we find them authorising the levy of large sums for that purpose[2], and also for the maintenance of fleets[3]: these payments, once known by the name of Danegeld, and which in 1018 amounted to the enormous sum of 82,500 pounds[4], were after thirty-nine years' continuance finally abolished by Eádweard[5].

9. *The king and his witan had power to raise land and sea forces when occasion demanded.*

The king always possessed of himself the right to call out the ban or armed militia of the freemen: he also possessed the right of commanding at all times the service of his comites and their vassals: but the armed force of the freemen could only be

[1] Ini, § 59. Thorpe, i. 140. Wyrhta like the factus (=Mansus) of the Franks appears to be the Mansio or Hide. But the amounts do not concern us at present.

[2] Chron. Sax. an. 1006. The sum raised was thirty-six thousand pounds. Chron. an. 1012. In this year forty-eight thousand pounds were paid.

[3] Chron. Sax. an. 1008. A ship from every three hundred hides; and a helmet and coat-of-mail from every eight hides,—a very heavy amount of shipmoney.

[4] Chron. Sax. an. 1018.   [5] Ibid. an. 1052.

kept on foot for a definite period, and probably within definite limits. It seems therefore that when the pressure of extraordinary circumstances called for more than common efforts, and the nation was to be urged to unusual exertions, the authority of the witan was added to that of the king ; and that much more extensive levies were made than by merely calling out the *hereban* or *landsturm*. And this particularly applies to naval armaments, which were hardly a part of the constitutional force, at all events not to any great extent [1]. Accordingly we find in the Chronicle that the king and the witan commanded armaments to be made against the Danes in 999, and at the same time directed a particular service to be sung in the churches. We learn distinctly from another event that the disposal of this force depended upon the popular will : for when Svein, king of the Danes, made application to Eádweard the Confessor for a naval force in aid of his war against Magnus of Norway, and Godwine recommended compliance, we find that it was refused because Earl Leófríc of Coventry, and all the people, with one voice opposed it [2].

10. *The witan possessed the power of recommending, assenting to, and guaranteeing grants of lands, and of permitting the conversion of folcland into bócland, and vice versâ.*

With regard to the first part of this assertion, it will be sufficient to refer to any page of the Codex

---

[1] The Butsecarls or shipmen of the seaports may possibly have been obliged to find shipping and serve on board.

[2] Flor. 1047, 1048. Compare Chron. Sax. *in an. cit.*

Diplomaticus Ævi Saxonici : it is impossible almost to find a single grant in that collection which does not openly profess to have been made by the king, '' cum consilio, consensu et licentia procerum,'' or similar expressions. And the necessity for such consent will appear intelligible when we consider that these grants must be understood, either to be direct conversions of folcland (fiscal or public property) into bócland (private estates), beneficiary into hereditary tenure ; or, that they contain licences to free particular lands from the ancient, customary dues to the state. In both cases the public revenue, of which king and witan were fiduciary administrators, was concerned : inasmuch as nearly every estate, transferred from folcland to bócland, became just so much withdrawn from the general stock of ways and means. Only in the case where lands were literally exchanged from one category into the other, did the state sustain no loss. Of this we have evidence in a charter of the year 858[1]. The king and Wulfláf his thane exchanged lands in Kent, Æ'ðelberht receiving an estate of five plough-lands at Mersham and giving five plough-lands at Wassingwell. The king then freed the land at Wassingwell in as ample degree as that at Mersham had been freed; that is, from every description of service, or impost, except the three inevitable burthens, of military service, and repair of fortifications and bridges. And having done so, he made the land at Mersham, folcland, i. e., imposed the burthens upon it.

[1] Cod. Dipl. No. 281.

That this is a just view of the powers of the witan in respect to the folcland, further appears from instances where the king and the witan, on one part, as representatives of the nation for that purpose, make grants to the king in his individual capacity. In 847, a case of this kind occurred: Æðelwulf of Wessex obtained twenty hides of land at Ham, as an estate of inheritance, from his witan[1]. The words used are very explicit: " I Æðelwulf, by God's aid king of the Westsaxons, with the consent and licence of my bishops and my princes, have caused a certain small portion of land, consisting of twenty hides, to be described by its boundaries, to me, as an estate of inheritance." And again: " These are the boundaries of those twenty hides which Æðelwulf's senators granted to him at Ham." We learn that Offa, king of the Mercians, had in a similar manner caused one hundred and ten hides in Kent to be given to him and his heirs as an estate of bócland[2], which he had afterwards left to the monastery at Bedford. And this is a peculiarly valuable record, because it was only by conquest that Offa and his witan could have obtained a right to dispose of lands beyond the limits of his own kingdom. Between 901 and 909 the witan of the Westsaxons booked a very small portion of land to Ælfred's son Eádweard, for the site of his monastery at Winchester[3]. In 963 we have another instance: Eádgár caused five hides to be given him at Peatanige as an estate of

---

[1] Cod. Dipl. No. 260.　　　　[2] Ibid. No. 1019.
[3] Ibid. No. 1087.

inheritance. The terms of the document are un-usual: he says, " I *have* a portion of land," etc., but he frees it from all burthens but the three, and renders it heritable. The rubric says: " This is the charter of five hides at Peatanige, which are Eádgár's the king's, during his day and after his day, to have, or to give to whom it pleaseth him best[1]." Again in 964, the same prince gave to his wife Ælfðrýð ten hides at Aston in Berkshire, as an estate of inheritance, " consilio satellitum, pon-tificum, comitum, militum[2]." It is obvious that in all these cases the grants were made out of public land, and were not the private estates of the king.

11. *The witan possessed the power of adjudging the lands of offenders and intestates to be forfeit to the king.*

This power applied to bócland, as well as folc-land, and was exercised in cases which are by no means confined to the few enumerated in the laws. Indeed the latter may very probably refer to no-thing but the chattels or personal property of the offender; while the real estate might be transferred to the king, by the solemn act of the witan. A few examples will make this clear.

Ælfred, condemned for treason or rebellion against Æðelstán, lost his lands by the judgment of the witan, who bestowed them upon the king[3]. In 1002 a lady forfeited her lands for her inconti-

---

[1] Cod. Dipl. No. 1246. " Aliquam terrae particulam [h]abeo, id est quinque mansas. . . . æt Peatanige, quatinus bene perfruar, ac perpetu-aliter possideam, vita comite, et post me cuicunque voluero perhenniter haeredi derelinquam in aeternam haereditatem," etc.

[2] Cod. Dipl. No. 1253.   [3] Ibid. No. 1112.

nence ; the king became seised of them, obviously
by the act of the gemót, for he calls it *vulgaris traditio* [1]. Again, the lands of certain people which
had been forfeited for theft, are described as having been granted to the king, " iusto valde iudicio
totius populi, seniorum et primatum [2]."

The case of intestacy is proved by a charter of
Ecgberht in 825. He gave fifteen hides at Aulton
to Winchester, and made title in these words.
" Now this land, a very faithful reeve of mine called
Burghard formerly possessed by my grant : but he
afterwards dying childless, left the land without a
will, and he had no survivors : and so the land
with all its boundaries was restored to me, its former possessor, by judicial decree of my *optimates* [3]."

Other examples may be found in the quotations
given in page 52 of this volume ; to which I may
add a case of forfeiture for suicide [4].

12. *Lastly, the witan acted as a supreme court
of justice, both in civil and criminal causes.*

The fact of important trials being decided by the
witena gemót is obvious from a very numerous list
of charters recording the result of such trials, and
printed in the Codex Diplomaticus. It is perfectly
unnecessary to give examples ; they occur continually in the pages of that work. The documents
are in great detail, giving the names of the parties,
the heads of the case, sometimes the very steps in
the trial, and always recording the place and date

---

[1] Cod. Dipl. No. 1295.   [2] Ibid. No. 374.   [3] Ibid. No. 1035.
[4] The charter which furnishes the evidence of this fact will appear
in the seventh volume of the Codex Diplomaticus. It is in the archives
of Westminster Abbey, and its date is the time of Eádgár. [The death
of Mr. Kemble in 1857 prevented the publication of this seventh volume.]

of the gemót, and the names of those who presided therein.

The proceedings of the witan as a court of criminal jurisprudence, are well exemplified in the case of earl Godwine and his family during their patriotic struggle for power with the foreign minions of Eádweard, and the northern earls, the hereditary enemies of their house. Eustace the count of Boulogne, then on a visit to Eádweard, having with a small armed retinue attempted violence against some of the inhabitants of Dover, was set upon by the townsmen, and after a severe loss hardly succeeded in making his escape. He hastened to Gloucester, where Eádweard then held his court, and laid his complaint before the king. Godwine, as earl of Kent, was commanded to set out with his forces, and inflict summary punishment upon the burghers who had dared to maltreat a relative of the king. But the stern old statesman saw matters in a very different light: he probably found no reason to punish the inhabitants of one of his best towns, for an act of self defence, especially one which had read a severe lesson to the foreign adventurers, who abused the weakness of an incapable prince, and domineered over the land. He therefore flatly refused, and withdrew from Gloucester to join his sons Harald and Swegen who lay at Beverston and Langtree with a considerable power. The king being reinforced by a well-appointed contingent from the northern earldoms, affairs threatened to be brought to a bloody termination. The conduct of Godwine and his family had been repre-

sented to Eádweard in the most unfavourable co-
lours, and the demand they made that the obnoxious
strangers should be given up to them, only aggravated his deep resentment. However for a time
peace was maintained, hostages were given on
either side, and a witena gemót was proclaimed,
to meet in London, at the end of a fortnight, September 21st, 1048. On the arrival of the earls in
Southwark, they found that a greatly superior force
from the commands of Leofríc, Sigeward and
Raulf awaited them : desertion thinned their numbers, and when the king demanded back his hostages, they were compelled to comply. Godwine and
Harald were now summoned to appear before the
gemót and make answer to what should be brought
against them. They demanded, though probably
with little expectation of obtaining, a safe conduct to and from the gemót, which was refused;
and as they very properly declined under such circumstances to appear, five days were allowed them
to leave England altogether.

It is probable that the strictly legal forms were
followed on this occasion, although the composition of the gemót was such that justice could not
have been done. The same observation will apply
to another witena gemót holden in London, after
Godwine's triumphant return to England, though
with a very different result. Before this assembly
the earl appeared, easily cleared himself of all
offences laid to his charge, and obtained the outlawry and banishment from England of all the
Frenchmen whose pernicious councils had put dis-

sension between the king and his people. Other examples might be given of outlawry, and even heavier sentences, as blinding, if not death, pronounced by the high court of the witan. But as these are all the result of internal dissensions, they resemble rather the violence of impeachments by an irresistible majority, than the calm, impassive judgments of a judicial assembly [1].

Such were the powers of the witena gemót, and it must be confessed that they were extensive. Of the manner of the deliberations or the forms of business we know little, but it is not likely that they were very complicated. We may conclude that the general outline of the proceedings was something of the following order. On common occasions the king summoned his witan to attend him at some royal vill, at Christmas, or at Easter, for festive and ceremonial as well as business purposes. On extraordinary occasions he issued summonses according to the nature of the exigency, appointing the time and place of meeting. When assembled, the witan commenced their session by attending divine service [2], and formally professing their adherence to the catholic faith [3]. The king then brought his propositions before them, in the Frankish manner [4], and after due deliberation they were accepted, modified, or rejected. The reeves, and perhaps on occasion officers specially desig-

---

[1] At a gemót in 1055, earl Ælfgár was outlawed. At a gemót in 1066 at Oxford, earl Tostig was outlawed, etc.

[2] See vol. i. p. 145 note.   [3] Cod. Dipl. No. 1019.

[4] I conclude this from the Prologue to Ælfred's Laws.

nated for that service [1], carried the chapters down into the several counties, and there took a *wed* or pledge from the freemen that they would abide by what had been enacted. This last fact, important to us in more respects than one, is substantiated by the following evidence. Toward the close of the Judicia Civitatis Londoniae (cap. 10), passed in the reign of Æðelstán, and subsidiary to the acts of various gemóts held by him, we find:—" All the witan gave their pledges together to the archbishop at Thundersfield, when Ælfheáh Stybb and Brihtnóð, Odda's son, came to meet the gemót by the king's command, that each reeve should take the pledge in his own shire, that they would all hold the frið, as king Æðelstán and the witan had counselled it, first at Greátanleá, and again at Exeter, and afterwards at Feversham, and the fourth time at Thundersfield," etc.

We have also a very remarkable document addressed to the same king, apparently upon receipt of the acts of the council at Feversham, by the men of Kent, denoting their acceptance of the same. They commence by saying:—" Dearest! Thy bishops of Kent, and all the thanes of Kentshire, earls and churls [2], return thanks to thee their

---

[1] The Franks and the church were familiar with such officers, who under the name of *Missi* were dispatched into the provinces for special purposes. Perhaps the Ælfheáh and Brihtnóð mentioned in the Judicia Civitatis were the Missi who were to be employed on this commission.

[2] Mr. Hallam, in his Supplemental Notes, p. 229, remarks upon this important document: " It is moreover an objection to considering this a formal enactment by the witan of the shire, that it runs in the names of 'thaini, comites et villani.' Can it be maintained that the ceorls ever formed an integrant element of the legislature in the kingdom of

dearest lord, for what thou hast been pleased to ordain respecting our peace, and to enquire and Kent ? It may be alleged that their name was inserted, though they had not been formally consenting parties, as we find in some parliamentary grants of money much later. But this would be an arbitrary conjecture, and the terms ' omnes thaini,' etc. are very large."

If the ceorls ever did form an integral part of the legislature in the kingdom of Kent, the whole question is settled. But I do not contemplate the thanes in Kent acting here as a legislative body : that is, I do not believe Æðelstán's witan in Wessex to have passed a law, and then his witan in Kent to have accepted or confirmed it. I believe his witan from all England to have made certain enactments, which the proper officers brought down to the various shires, and in the shiremoots there took pledge of the shire-thanes that they accepted and would abide by the premises ; just as in the case quoted on the preceding page. And this is the more striking because there is every reason to suppose that the witena gemót whose acts the shire-thanes of Kent thus accepted was actually holden at Feversham in that county. But it is further to be observed that the document we possess is a late Latin translation of the original sent to Æðelstán : I will venture to assert that in that original the words used were, " ealle scírþegnas on Cent, ge eorl ge ceorl," or perhaps " ge twelfhynde ge twihynde." Again, there is no reason to suppose that the ceorls did *not* form an integrant part of the shiremoot, the representative of the ancient, independent legislature. A full century later than the date of the council of Feversham, they continued to do so in the same kingdom or, at that period, earldom : and it will be readily admitted that during those hundred years the tendency of society was not to increase the power or improve the condition of the ceorl. Between 1013 and 1020 we thus find Cnut addressing the authorities in Kent (Cod. Dipl. No. 731) :—" Cnut the king sends friendly greeting to archbishop Lýfing, bishop Godwine, abbot Ælfmær, Æðelwine the sheriff, Æðelríc, and all my thanes, both twelve-hundred and two-hundred men,—ealle míne þegnas twelfhynde and twihynde : "—in other words, both eorl and ceorl, nobilis and ignobilis, or as the witan of Æðelstán have it, in the Norman translation, comites et villani. The nature of Cnut's writ, which is addressed to the authorities of the county, the archbishop and sheriff, shows clearly that the thanes in question are not those royal officers called cyninges þegnas—who could never be two-hundred men—but the scírþegnas. These are of frequent occurrence in Anglosaxon documents. The scírgemót at Ægelnóðes stán (about 1038) was attended by Æðelstán the bishop, Ranig the ealdorman, Bryning the sheriff and all the thanes in Herefordshire. Cod. Dipl. No. 755. A sale by Stigand was witnessed by all the scírþegenas in Hampshire ; that is, it was a public instrument

consult concerning our advantage, since great was
the need thereof for us all, both rich and poor.

completed in the shiremoot. Cod. Dipl. No. 949.   Again a grant of
Stigand was witnessed about 1053 by various authorities in Hampshire,
including Eádsige the sheriff and all the scírþegnas. Cod. Dipl. No.
1337: and similarly a third of the same prelate, Cod. Dipl. No. 820.
About the same period Wulfwold abbot of Bath makes title to lands,
which he addresses to bishop Gisa, Tofig the sheriff and all the thanes
of Somersetshire. Cod. Dipl. No. 821. In the year 1049, Þurstán
granted lands at Wimbush by witness of a great number of persons,
among whom are Leófcild the sheriff and all the thanes of Essex.
Cod. Dipl. No. 788: and about the same time Gódríc bought lands at
Offham, in a shiremoot at Wii, before all the shire. Cod. Dipl. No. 789.
Lastly, Leófwine bought land, by witness of Ulfcytel the sheriff and all
the thanes in Herefordshire. Cod. Dipl. No. 802. The relation of these
thanes to the gódan men or dohtigan men (good men, doughty men,
boni et legales homines, Scabini, Rachinburgii, etc.) will be examined
in a subsequent Book, when I come to treat of the courts of justice : but
I will here add one example, which is illustrative of the subject of this
note.   The marriage-ccvenants of Godwine, arranged before Cnut, by
witness of archbishop Lyfing and others, including Æðelwine the sheriff, and various Kentish landowners, are stated to be in the knowledge
(gecnǽwe) of every *doughty man* in Kent and Sussex (where the lands
lay) both thane and churl. Cod. Dipl. No. 732. There was nothing
whatever to prevent a man from being a scírþegn, whether eorlcund or
ceórlcund, as long as he had land in the scír itself : without land, even
a cyninges þegn could certainly not be a scírþegn.   It is true that a
man might be of síðcund rank, that is noble, without owning land (see
Leg. Ini, § 51), and there were king's thanes who had no land (Æðelst.
v. § 11); but such a one could assuredly not represent himself in the scírgemót.   There is a common error which runs through much of what
has been admitted on this subject : the ceorl is universally represented
in a low condition.   This is not however necessarily the case : some
ceorls, though well to do in the world, may have preferred their independence to the conventional dignity of thaneship. We may admit, as
a general rule, that the thanes were a wealthier class than the ceorls;
indeed, without becoming a thane, a ceorl had little chance of getting
a grant of folcland or bócland, but some of them may have, through
various circumstances, inherited or purchased considerable estates : as
late as the year 984, I find an estate of eight hides (that is 264 acres
according to my reckoning) in the possession of a *rusticus*, obviously a
ceorl :—" Illud videlicet rus quod Æðeríc quidam rusticus prius ha-
buisse agnoscitur." Cod. Dipl. No. 1282.

And this we have taken in hand, with all the diligence we could, by the aid of those witan [*sapientes*] whom thou didst send unto us," etc [1].

It is plain from the preceding passage that the witan gave their *wed* to observe, and cause to be observed, the laws they had enacted [2]. Eádgár says, "I command my geréfan, upon my friendship, and by all they possess, to punish every one that will not perform this, and who by any neglect shall break the *wed* of my witan." This seems to imply that the people were generally bound by the acts of the witan, and their pledge or *wed*; and if it were so, it would naturally involve the theory of representation. But this deduction will not stand.

The whole principle of Teutonic legislation is, and always was, that the law is made by the constitution of the king, and the consent of the people [3]: and we have seen one way in which that consent was obtained, viz. by sending the *capitula* down into the provinces or shires, and taking the *wed* in the shiremoot. The passage in the text seems to presuppose an interchange of oaths and

---

[1] Thorpe, i. 216. Æðelstán complains on another occasion that the oaths and *weds* which had been given *to the king and his witan* were all broken: "quia iuramenta et vadia, quae regi et sapientibus data fuerunt, semper infracta sunt et minus observata quam Deo et saeculo conveniant." Æðelst. iii. § 3. Thorpe, i. 218. Again: Æðelstán the king makes known, that I have learned that our peace is worse kept than is pleasing to me, or as was ordained at Greatley; and my witan say that I have borne with it too long. . . . Because the oaths, and weds, and *borhs* are all disregarded and broken which on that occasion were given, etc. Æðelst. iv. § 1. Thorpe, i. 220.

[2] Conc. Wihtbordes stán. Eádg. Supp. § 1. Thorpe, i. 272.

[3] "Lex consensu populi fit, et constitutione regis." Edict. Pistense. an. 864. Pertz, iii. 490, § 6.

pledges between the king and witan themselves;
and even those who had no standing of their own
in the folcmót or scírgemót, were required to be
bound by *personal* consent. The lord was just as
much commanded to take oath and pledge of his
several dependents (the hired men, *familiares*, or
people of his household), as the sheriff was required
to take them of the free shire-thanes [1]. Of course
this excludes all idea of representation in our modern sense of the word, because with us, promulgation by the Parliament is sufficient, and the constituent is bound without any further ceremony by
the act of him whom he has sent in his own place.
But the Teutons certainly did not elect their representatives as we elect ours, with full power to judge,
decide for, and bind us, and therefore it was right
and necessary that the laws when made should be
duly ratified and accepted by all the people.

Although the dignified clergy, the ealdormen
and geréfan, and the þegnas both in counties and
boroughs, appear to have constituted the witena
gemót properly so called, there is still reason to
suppose that the people themselves, or some of
them, were very often present. In fact a system
gradually framed as I suppose that of our forefathers to have been, and indebted very greatly to
accident for its form, must have possessed a very
considerable elasticity. The people who were in
the neighbourhood, who happened to be collected
in arms during a sitting of the witan, or who
thought it worth while to attend their meeting,

---

[1] Æðelst. v. § 11.   Thorpe, i. 240.

were very probably allowed to do so, and to exercise
at least a right of conclamation [1],—a right which
must daily become rarer, as the freemen gradually
disappeared, and the number of landowners, dependent upon and represented by lords, as rapidly
increased. In conclusion a few passages may be
cited, which seem to render it probable that the
people, when on the spot, did take some part in
the business, as I have already mentioned with
respect to the Frankish levies in the Campus Ma
dius of Charlemagne. But it must also be borne in
mind that such a case ought to be looked upon as
accidental, rather than necessary, and that a meeting of the witan did not require the formality of
an acceptance by the people on the spot, to render
its acts obligatory. It was enough that the thanes
of the gemót should pass, and the thanes of the scír
accept the law. Indeed it could not be otherwise;
for as the heads of all the more important social
aggregations of the free, and the lords whose men
were represented by them even in courts of justice,
were the members of the gemót, their decisions
must have been, strictly considered, the real decisions of the *populus*, or franchise-bearing people.

Beda, relating the discussion which took place

---

[1] There is evidence of their doing this on a somewhat less solemn
occasion, though perhaps it was a shiremoot. Æðelstán, a duke,
booked land to Abingdon, by witness of bishop Cynsige, archbishop
Wulfhelm, Hroðweard, and other prelates. The boundaries were
solemnly led, and then the assembled bishops and abbots excommunicated any one who should dispossess the monastery : and all the people that stood round about cried " So be it ! So be it ! " " And cwæð
ealle ðæt folc ðe ðær embstód, Sý hit swá. Amen. Amen." " Et dixit
omnis populus qui ibi aderat, Fiat, Fiat. Amen." Cod. Dipl. No. 1129.

respecting the celebration of Easter, and which was
held in the presence of Oswiu and Alhfri𐍃 of Northumberland, and Wilfri𐍃's successful defence of the
Roman custom, adds : " When the king had said
these words, all who sat or stood around assented :
and abandoning the less perfect institution, they
hastened to adopt what they recognized as a better
one [1]." Again the deposition of Sigeberht is stated
to have taken place in an assembly of the *proceres*
and *populus*, the princes and people of the whole
realm [2]. A doubtful charter of Ini, A.D. 725, is
said to be consented to " cum praesentia popula-
tionis [3]," by which words are meant either the witan
or the people of Wessex. In 804 Æ𐍃elríc's title-
deeds were confirmed before a gemót at Clofesho :
the charter recites that archbishop Æ𐍃elheard gave
judgment, with the witness of king Cóenwulf and
his *optimates*, before all the synod or meeting :
whence it is clear that others were present besides
the *optimates* or witan strictly so called [4]. On the
28th of May 924 a gemót was held at Winchester, " tota populi generalitate," as the charter witnesses [5], and in 931 another at Wor𐍃ig, " tota plebis generalitate [6]." Æ𐍃elstán in 938 declares that
certain lands had been forfeited for theft, by the
just judgment of all the people, *and* the Seniores
and Primates ; and that the original charters were
cancelled by a decree of all the people [7].

---

[1] Hist. Eccl. iii. c. 25.
[2] Hen. Hunt. lib. iv.
[3] Cod. Dipl. No. 73.
[4] Cod. Dipl. No. 186.
[5] Ibid. No. 364.
[6] Ibid. No. 1103.
[7] " Iusto valde iudicio totius populi, et seniorum et primatum," etc.
" Ideoque decretum est ab omni populo," etc.   Cod. Dipl. No. 374.

But whether expressions of˚this kind were intended to denote the actual presence of the people on the spot; or whether *populus* is used in a strict and technical sense—that sense which is confined to those who enjoy the full franchise, those who form part of the πολίτευμα,—or finally whether the assembly of the witan making laws is considered to represent in our modern form an assembly of the whole people,—it is clear that the power of self-government is recognized in the latter.

In order to facilitate reference to the important facts with which this chapter deals, I have added to it a list of witena gemóts, with here and there a few remarks upon the business transacted in them. They do not nearly exhaust the number that must have been held, but still they form a respectable body of evidence; and we may perhaps be justly surprised, not that so little, but that so much has survived. We need not lament that the present forms and powers of our parliament are not those which existed a thousand years ago, as long as we recognize in them only the matured development of an old and useful principle. We shall not appeal to Anglosaxon custom to justify the various points of the Charter; but we may still be proud to find in their practice the germ of institutions which we have, throughout all vicissitudes, been taught to cherish as the most valuable safeguards of our peace as well as our freedom. Truly there are few nations whose parliamentary history has so ample a foundation as our own.

THE WITENA GEMÓTS OF THE SAXONS.

ÆÐELBERT OF KENT, A.D. 596–605.—The promulgation of the laws of Æðelberht took place during the life of Augustine. This fixes their date between 596, when he arrived in England, and 605, when he died. Beda tells us that these laws were enacted by the advice of the witan, "cum consilio sapientium[1]." We may therefore conclude that a gemót was held in Kent for the purpose : and from the contents of the laws themselves, it is obvious that the Roman clergy filled an important place therein. They had probably stepped into the position of the Pagan priesthood, and improved it.

EA′DUUINI OF NORTHUMBERLAND, A.D. 627. —The first witena gemót of which we have any detailed record was holden in 627, near the city of York, wherein no less important business was discussed than the desertion of Paganism and reception of Christianity, by the people of Northumberland. From Beda[2] we learn that this step was not ventured without the gravest deliberation ; and that Eáduuini had taken good care to sound the most influential of his nobles, before he called a public meeting to decide upon the question. Indeed the parts in this great drama appear to have been arranged beforehand. The interesting account given by Beda[3] is to this effect. Eáduuini had determined to embrace Christianity, but still he was not contented, or would not venture, to do this alone. He wished to extend the blessings of the new faith to his

[1] Hist. Eccl. ii. 5.   [2] Ibid. ii. 9.   [3] Ibid. ii. 13.

subjects; perhaps also to avoid the difficulties which might result from his conversion, while the rest of the people remained pagans. To the exhortations of the missionary Paulinus he rejoined, "suscipere quidem se fidem quam docebat, et velle, et debere . . . . verum adhuc cum amicis, principibus et consiliariis suis, sese de hoc collaturum esse dicebat; ut si illi eadem cum illo sentire vellent, omnes pariter in fonte vitae Christo consecrarentur. Et annuente Paulino, fecit ut dixerat. Habito enim cum sapientibus consilio, sciscitabatur singillatim ab omnibus, qualis sibi doctrina haec eatenus inaudita, et novus divinitatis qui praedicabatur cultus videretur." The chief of his priests, Cóefi, immediately commenced an attack upon the ancient religion, and was followed by other nobles, one of whose speeches, the earliest specimen of English parliamentary eloquence, is yet on record[1]. " His similia et caeteri maiores natu ac regis consiliarii, divinitus admoniti, prosequebantur." Paulinus was now invited to expound at greater length the doctrines which he recommended. At the close of his address Cóefi declared himself a convert, and proposed the destruction of the ancient fanes. Eáduuini now professed himself a Christian, and in turn demanded whose duty it was to profane the pagan altars. This Cóefi at once assumed to himself, and taking the most conspicuous means to demonstrate to the people (who, the historian says, thought him mad,) his apostasy from the old creed, hurled his lance into the sacred enclosure, and commanded its immediate destruction. The scene of this daring act was Godmundingahám, not far from the British Delgovitia, and now Godmundham or Goodmanham. The king then as speedily as possible, " citato opere," built a wooden basilica in the city of York, in which he was solemnly baptized on the twelfth of April, being Easter-day. And thus, says the historian, Eáduuini

---

[1] Beda, Hist. Eccl. ii. 13.

became a Christian, " cum cunctis gentis suae nobilibus ac plebe perplurima[1]."

WULFHARI OF MERCIA, A.D. 657.—In this year a witena gemót was probably held for the endowment and consecration of Saxwulf's monastery at Peterborough. This the king is stated to have done by the advice, and with the consent, of all the witan of his kingdom, both clerical and lay[2]. The charter in the Saxon Chronicle is a late forgery, but throws no well-grounded doubt upon the fact.

O'SUUIU OF NORTHUMBERLAND, A.D. 662.— A meeting was held this year at Streoneshalh, to bring about uniformity of Paschal observance, tonsure, and other ecclesiastical details. It was presided over by Osuuiu and Alhfri∂[3].

ECGBERHT OF KENT, A.D. 667.—A gemót was probably held in Kent, and Wighard was elected archbishop of Canterbury[4].

ARCHBISHOP THEODORE, A.D. 673.—In this year was held the synod or gemót of Hertford[5]. Beda has preserved its ecclesiastical acts. The seventh provision is an important one, viz. that similar meetings should be held twice in every year. But this appearing inconvenient, it was agreed that there should be one, on the first of August yearly at Clofeshoas.

ARCHBISHOP THEODORE, A.D. 680.—In this year was held the gemót at Hæ∂feld, in the presence of the kings of Northumberland, Mercia, Eastanglia and Kent. Its ecclesiastical acts are preserved[6]: they are particularly directed against the heresy of Eutyches. But

[1] Beda, Hist. Eccl. ii. 14.
[2] Chron. Sax. an. 657. Cod. Dipl. No. 984.
[3] Beda, Hist. Eccl. iii. 25.   [4] Beda, Hist. Eccl. iii. 29.
[5] Beda, Hist. Eccl. iv. 5. Chron. Sax. an. 673.
[6] Beda, Hist. Eccl. iv. 17. Chron. Sax. an. 675, 680. Cod. Dipl. No. 991.

there was a witena gemót at the same time, probably to sanction the decision of the clergy.

ECGFRIÐ OF NORTHUMBERLAND, A.D. 684.— There was a gemót at Twyford, on the river Alne, and Cúðberht was elected bishop of Hexham[1].

ÆÐELRED OF MERCIA, A.D. 685.—A gemót was held on the thirtieth of July at Berhford, now Burford in Gloucestershire. Berhtwald the subregulus and Æðelred were probably both present[2].

WIHTRAED OF KENT, A.D. 696.—Immediately upon Wihtraed's accession[3] he held a great council, "mycel consilium," or gemót of his witan, to settle the ecclesiastical and secular difficulties which had arisen during the civil wars of his predecessors and his own struggle for the throne. The gemót was held at Beorganstede, now Berstead in Kent. Its acts are extant in the laws which yet go under Wihtraed's name[4]. Another gemót of Wihtraed's, said by the Chronicle[5] to have been held in 694 at Baccanceld, now Bapchild, in Kent, confirmed the liberties of the Kentish clergy.

INI OF WESSEX, A.D. 704.—A witena gemót was held by Ini at Eburleáh, in which, with the consent of his witan, he gave certain privileges to the monasteries of Wessex[6]. Its acts were signed by the principes, senatores, iudices and patricii present. We learn also from a charter of Aldhelm[7], that before 705, a council had been held upon the banks of the river Woder, which is possibly the "synodus suae gentis" mentioned by Beda[8].

---

[1] Beda, Hist. Eccl. iv. 28.   Cod. Dipl. No. 25.

[2] Cod. Dipl. No. 26.

[3] The Saxon Chronicle, which often errs in its dates by two years, puts this in 694. But the year 696 is ascertained by the indiction, which was the ninth.

[4] Thorpe, i. 36.   [5] Chron. Sax. an. 694. Cod. Dipl. No. 996.

[6] Cod. Dipl. Nos. 50, 51.   [7] Ibid. No. 54.

[8] Hist. Eccl. v. 18.

O'SRAED OF NORTHUMBERLAND, A.D. 705.—
Upon the death of Aldfriꝺ in 705, a gemót was held upon
the banks of the Nidd, and after long debates bishop Wil-
friꝺ was restored to his see and possessions[1].

A.D. 710.—In this year a gemót appears to have been
held, in which Sussex was erected into a separate see, and
severed from the diocese of Winchester[2].

ARCHBISHOP NO'ÐHELM, A.D. 734–737.—Difficulties having arisen about the possession and patronage
of certain monasteries, the case was referred to and decided
by a synod, "sancta sacerdotalis concilii synodus," which
must have met between 734–737. It seems to have been
purely ecclesiastical, and its acts are signed only by the
bishops who were present[3]. Yet as its judgment involved
a question of property, and title to lands, I presume that
the case was laid before a mixed gemót, sitting very possibly in different chambers. If so, the record we have is
that of the clerical house only.

ÆÐELBALD OF MERCIA, A.D. 742.—In this year
a great council, "magnum concilium," was held at Clofeshoas, under Æꝺelbald, and Cúꝺbeorht, archbishop of Canterbury. It took into consideration the state of the church;
but it was clearly a witena gemót, and its acts are signed
by clerks and laymen indifferently[4].

ÆÐELBALD OF MERCIA, A.D. 749.—A witena
gemót was held at Godmundes leáh in this year. Ecclesiastical liberties were again provided for[5].

A.D. 755.—A witena gemót in Wessex must have been
held in this year, for the deposing of Sigebeorht and election of Cynewulf to the throne[6].

---

[1] Beda, Hist. Eccl. v. 19.   [2] Beda, Hist. Eccl. v. 18.
[3] Cod. Dipl. No. 82.   [4] Cod. Dipl. No. 87.
[5] Cod. Dipl. No. 99.
[6] Chron. Sax. an. 755. Flor. Wig. 755. Æꝺelw. ii. 17. Hen. Hunt.
lib. iv. See the remarks in the text, p. 219 *seq.* of this volume.

OFFA OF MERCIA, A.D. 780. — A gemót called
" synodale conciliabulum " was held this year at Brentford.
It transacted various business of a secular character[1].

A.D. 782.—A gemót was held at Acleáh, now Ockley in
Surrey[2].

OFFA OF MERCIA, A.D. 785.—In this year was
held the stormy synod of Cealchȳð, in which the province
of Canterbury was partitioned, and the archbishopric of
Lichfield founded[3]. It was clearly a witena gemót, as
Offa caused his son Ecgferhð to be elected king by the
meeting.

A.D. 787.—In this year there was another gemót, "synodalis conventus," at Ockley[4].

OFFA OF MERCIA, A.D. 788.—A gemót was held
at Cealchȳð[5]. And in the same year, according to the
Chronicle and Florence[6], but one year sooner according
to Simeon Dunelmensis[7], was held the synod of Pincan-
healh in Northumberland.

OFFA OF MERCIA, A.D. 789.—In this year another
gemót was held at Cealchȳð, where a good deal of secular
business was transacted[8]. In the second document cited
in the note it is called "pontificale conciliabulum," and
this charter is signed only by the king and the bishops.

Another gemót is also said to have been held at Ockley[9]; but the known error of two years in the dates of the
Chronicle may make us suspect that this really met in
791.

OFFA OF MERCIA, A.D. 790.—A great gemót was
held this year in London, on Whitsunday[10].

[1] Cod. Dipl. Nos. 139, 140, 143.   [2] Chron. Sax. an. 782.
[3] Chron. Sax. an. 785.   Flor. Wig. 785.
[4] Cod. Dipl. No. 151.   [5] Cod. Dipl. No. 153.
[6] Chron. Sax. an. 788.   Flor. Wig. 788.
[7] Sim. Dunelm. 787.   [8] Cod. Dipl. Nos. 155, 156, 157.
[9] Chron. Sax. an. 789.   [10] Cod. Dipl. No. 159.

OFFA OF MERCIA, A.D. 793.—A gemót at Cealc-hȳð, called "conventus synodalis"[1]. Also about this time a gemót at Verulam, "concilium episcoporum et optimatum[2]."

OFFA OF MERCIA, A.D. 794.—A gemót at Clofeshoas, called "synodus," and "concilium synodale"[3]

ECGFERHÐ OF MERCIA, A.D. 796.—A gemót at Cealchȳð, called probably in consequence of Offa's death, and for reformation of affairs in the church[4].

CE′NWULF OF MERCIA, A.D. 798.—A gemót, called "synodus," the place of which is not known. The business recorded is merely secular[5]. Before the signatures occur the words : " Haec sunt nomina episcoporum ac principum qui hoc mecum in synodo consentientes subscripserunt." The signatures comprise the names of several laics,—a plain proof that the word *synodus* is not confined to ecclesiastical meetings. Another, or perhaps the same, at Baccanceld, Bapchild, in Kent, where the clergy made a declaration of liberties[6]. Another and very solemn one at Clofeshoas[7].

CE′NWULF OF MERCIA, A.D. 799.—A gemót of the witan was held this year at Colleshyl, probably Coleshill in Berkshire[8].

CE′NWULF OF MERCIA, A.D. 799–802.—Between these two years there was a gemót, called "synodale conciliabulum," at Cealchȳð, in which secular business was transacted. The signature of the king to one of its acts is double; first at the head of the clergy, and then again at the head of the lay nobles[9].

---

[1] Cod. Dipl. No. 162. [2] Rog. Wend. i. 257.
[3] Cod. Dipl. Nos. 164, 167.
[4] Chron. Sax. an. 796. Cod. Dipl. Nos. 172, 173.
[5] Cod. Dipl. No. 175. [6] Ibid. No. 1018.
[7] Ibid. No. 1019. [8] Ibid. No. 176.
[9] Ibid. No. 116. Another act, Ibid. No. 1023.

CE′NWULF OF MERCIA, A.D. 803.—In the year 803 was held a memorable synod at Clofeshoas, which lasted from the ninth till the twelfth of October. Affairs of great importance were discussed. The principal object of the meeting was to restore the ancient splendour of Canterbury by the abrogation of the archiepiscopal see at Lichfield, and further to secure the liberties of the church. We have two solemn acts, dated on the twelfth of October[1]: the signatures are exclusively those of clerics. The second of those documents deserves the highest attention, as the signatures may be taken to represent the members of a full convocation of the clergy, called for a most important purpose. But it is nevertheless certain that a general meeting of the witan took place at the same time, for on the sixth of October they heard and determined causes relating to landed property, and various laymen signed the acts[2]. Moreover an archbishopric established by a witena gemót could only be abrogated by another,—not by a mere assemblage of clergymen, however dignified and influential they might be.

CE′NWULF OF MERCIA, A.D. 804.—There was a "synodus" in this year at Clofeshoas, the nature of the business transacted in which and before whom transacted, appears from these words following[3] :—" Anno ab incarnatione Christi 804, indictione duodecima, ego Æðelríc filius Æðelmundi cum conscientia synodali invitatus ad synodum, et in iudicio stare, in loco qui dicitur Clofeshoh, cum libris et ruris, id est, æt Westmynster, quod prius propinqui mei tradiderunt mihi et donaverunt, ibi Æðelheardus archiepiscopus mihi regebat atque iudicaverat, cum testimonio Coenwulfi regis, et optimatibus eius, coram omni synodo, quando scripturas meas perscrutarent, ut liber essem terram meam atque libellos dare quocumque volui." He

---

[1] Cod. Dipl. Nos. 185, 1024.   [2] Ibid. Nos. 183, 184.
[3] Cod. Dipl. No. 186.

had been regularly summoned to appear before the synodus, as a court of justice.

CE'NWULF OF MERCIA, A.D. 805.—A witena gemót was held at Ockley, a favourite locality[1].

CE'NWULF OF MERCIA, A.D. 810.—Another gemót, "sancta synodus," sat at Ockley, and decided a lawsuit between Æ∂elhelm, and Beorn∂ry∂, the widow of O'swulf, duke of Kent[2].

CE'NWULF OF MERCIA, A.D. 811.—A great gemót, "concilium pergrande," was held this year in London[3]. In the same year a great gemót was collected at Wincelcumbe, Winchcomb in Gloucestershire, for the dedication of Cénwulf's new abbey there[4].

CE'NWULF OF MERCIA, A.D. 815.—In this year a gemót assembled at Cealchý∂[5].

BEORNWULF OF MERCIA, A.D. 824.—At a meeting held this year at Clofeshoas, there attended a considerable number of laymen, as well as prelates : the gemót however is called " pontificale et synodale conciliabulum[6]." In 824 there was also a gemót of Wessex at Ockley in Surrey. Ecgberht gave Meon to Wulfward his praefectus or geréfa. The act is signed by four geréfan[7].

BEORNWULF OF MERCIA, A.D. 825.—A gemót was held also at Clofeshoas in 825 ; this is called " siono∂-líc gemót "[8], and it is stated that there were assembled the bishops, ealdormen, and all the weotan of the nation : one act of this gemót[9] declares it to have consisted of the king, bishops, abbots, dukes, "omniumque dignitatum optimates, aecclesiasticarum vel saecularium personarum[10]."

---

[1] Cod. Dipl. No. 190.   [2] Ibid. No. 256.   [3] Ibid. Nos. 196, 220.
[4] Ibid. No. 197.   Chron. MS. Wincelc. an. 811.
[5] Cod. Dipl. No. 208.   [6] Ibid. No. 218.   [7] Ibid. No. 1031.
[8] Ibid. No. 219.   [9] Ibid. No. 220 : see also No. 1034.
[10] In some Saxon original, no doubt, " and eal dúgo∂, ge cyriclíces ge woroldlíces hádes."

The acts of this council are signed by no less than one hundred and twenty-one persons, of whom ninety-five are clerical, embracing all ranks from bishops to deacons. But one reason for this large attendance is, that as some cases of disputed title were to be decided by the gemót, these monks and clerks attended in order to make oath to the property in dispute.

ECGBERHT OF WESSEX, A.D. 826.—In 825 Ecgberht had taken the field against the Welsh. He seems to have made various grants while *in hoste*. These were afterwards confirmed and reduced to writing by a gemót held in 826 at Southampton[1].

ECGBERHT OF WESSEX and ÆÐELWULF OF KENT, A.D. 838.—In this year there was a council at Kingston, under these kings, Ceólnóð the archbishop, and the prelates of his province. Secular affairs of great importance were settled on this occasion, and a regular treaty of peace and alliance agreed between the Kentish clergy and the kings[2]. At first this was signed only by Ceólnóð and the clergy ; but for further confirmation it was taken to king Æðelwulf at the royal vill of Wilton, and there executed by the king, his dukes and thanes. Another document exists in which the clergy of Winchester enter into similar engagements with the kings[3].

ÆÐELWULF OF WESSEX, A.D. 839.—The treaty mentioned in the last article was read in a council of all the southern bishops, held at Astra[4].

ÆÐELWULF OF WESSEX, ÆÐELSTA'N OF KENT, A.D. 844.—A gemót at Canterbury, attended by the kings, the archbishop, the bishop elect of Rochester, " cum principibus, ducibus, abbatibus, et cunctis generalis dignitatis optimatibus[5]."

ÆÐELWULF OF WESSEX, A.D. 851.—The very

---

[1] Cod. Dipl. Nos. 1035, 1036, 1038. [2] Ibid. No. 240.
[3] Ibid. No. 1044.   [4] Ibid. No. 240.   [5] Ibid. No. 256.

questionable authority of Ingulph mentions a witena gemót this year at Cyningesbyrig[1].

BURHHRED OF MERCIA, A.D. 853.—This year, the Chronicle says[2], a formal application was made by the Mercian king Burhhred and his witan for military aid, in order to the subjugation of the Northern Britons. This seems to imply a regular meeting in Mercia.

ÆÐELWULF OF WESSEX, A.D. 855.—In this year there was a gemót at Winchester[3].

BURHHRED OF MERCIA, A.D. 868.—In this year the Mercian witan applied to those of Wessex for aid against the Danes. We may conclude that gemóts were held both in Mercia and Wessex[4].

A.D. 866–871.—We learn from king Ælfred himself that there was a witena gemót at Swinbeorh in some year between these limits, wherein the successions to lands, among the members of the royal family, were settled, and placed under the guarantee of the witan[5].

ÆLFRED OF WESSEX, A.D. 878.—In this year there was a gemót, very probably at Wedmore[6], where the Dane Guðorm made his submission to Ælfred, and where the articles of peace between the Saxons and Danes were settled[7].

ÆLFRED OF WESSEX, A.D. 880–885.—A gemót sat at Langandene between these two years, and the affairs of Ælfred's family were again considered. The validity of king Æðelwulf's will was admitted, and Ælfred's settlement of his lands guaranteed[5].

ÆÐELRED, DUKE OF MERCIA, A.D. 883.—In this year the witan of Mercia met at Risborough, under

[1] Cod. Dipl. No. 265.
[2] Chron. Sax. an. 853.
[3] Cod. Dipl. No. 275.
[4] Chron. Sax. an. 868.
[5] Cod. Dipl. No. 314.
[6] Chron. Sax. an. 878. Flor. Wig. 878.
[7] Thorpe, i. 152 seq.

Æðelred their duke[1]: an interesting circumstance, inasmuch as it shows that the union with Wessex did not abrogate the ancient rights, or interfere with the independent action of the Mercian witan.

ÆÐELRED, DUKE OF MERCIA, A.D. 888.—This gemót was held at Saltwíc in Worcestershire, to consult upon affairs both ecclesiastical and secular. The witan assembled from far and near[2].

ÆÐELRED, DUKE OF MERCIA, A.D. 896.—Another gemót of the Mercians was held this year at Gloucester, whose interesting acts are yet preserved[3].

ÆÐELRED, DUKE OF MERCIA, A.D. 878–899.— At a gemót held between these years, and very likely at Worcester, Æðelred and Æðelflǽd commanded a burh or fortification to be built for the people of that city, and the cathedral to be enlarged. The endowments and privileges which are granted by the instrument are extensive and instructive[4].

EA'DWEARD OF WESSEX, A.D. 901.—The death of Ælfred, and Eádweard's election probably caused an assembly of witan at Winchester in this year[5], and it is likely that we still possess one of its acts[6]. This is the more probable because Æðelwald, Eádweard's cousin, disputed the succession, and not only seized upon the royal vill of Wimborne, which he is said to have done without the consent of the king and his witan, but broke into open rebellion, and after being acknowledged king in Essex, joined the Danes in Northumberland, and perished in an unsuccessful battle against his countrymen.

ÆÐELRED, DUKE OF MERCIA, A.D. 904.—In this year a Mercian gemót was held, and duke Æðelfrið obtained permission to have new charters written, his own

[1] Cod. Dipl. No. 1066.   [4] Ibid. No. 1075.
[2] Ibid. Nos. 327, 1068.   [5] Chron. Sax. an. 901.
[3] Ibid. No. 1073.   [6] Cod. Dipl. No. 1087.

having perished by fire[1]. And a gemót of the Westsaxon witan was held at the king's hunting-seat of Bicanleáh[2]. About the same period a gemót of Wessex was held at Exeter by Eádweard[3].

EA'DWEARD OF WESSEX, A.D. 909.—A gemót of Wessex was held in 909 : its acts are signed by fifty of the witan[4].

EA'DWEARD OF WESSEX, A.D. 910.—A gemót was held in Wessex this year[5]. And there appears to have been another at Aylesford in Kent, in which the witan gave judgment in the suit between Góda and queen Eádgyfu[6].

EA'DWEARD OF WESSEX, A.D. 911.—In this year a gemót was probably held, in which terms of peace were offered to the Danes in Northumberland[7]. But this may possibly be only the last-named gemót in 910, as we know that Eádweard was in Kent in 911.

ÆÐELSTA'N, A.D. 925 or 926.—About this date a gemót was held by Æðelstán at Ham near Lewes, and the suit between Góda and Eádgyfu was again decided by public authority[8].

ÆÐELSTA'N, A.D. 928.—A solemn gemót was held this year at Exeter[9].

ÆÐELSTA'N, A.D. 930.—In this year the gemót met at Nottingham. It was attended by three Welsh princes, the archbishops and sixteen bishops, thirteen dukes, twelve thanes, twelve untitled persons, " et plures alii milites quorum nomina in eadem carta inseruntur." There are fifty-eight signatures[10].

[1] Cod. Dipl. No. 338.
[2] Ibid. Nos. 1082, 1084.
[3] Leg. Eádw. § 4. Thorpe, i. 162.
[4] Cod. Dipl. No. 1091.
[5] Ibid. No. 1096.
[6] Ibid. No. 499.
[7] Chron. Sax. an. 911.
[8] Cod. Dipl. No. 499.
[9] Ibid. No. 1101.
[10] Ibid. No. 352.

ÆÐELSTA'N, A.D. 931.—In this year several gemóts were held. First, one at Luton in Bedfordshire, signed by 106 persons[1]. One at Worðig, "cum tota plebis generalitate[2]." One at Colchester[3], and one at Wellow in Wilts[4].

ÆÐELSTA'N, A.D. 932.—There was a gemót at Amesbury, said to be attended by the dukes, bishops, abbots and "patriae procuratores"[5]. Also one at Middleton, in which the same words occur: the signatures amount to ninety, and comprise four Welsh princes, nineteen archbishops and bishops, fifteen dukes, four abbots, and forty-seven ministri or thanes[6].

ÆÐELSTA'N, A.D. 934.—A gemót was held in London on the seventh of June[7]; but on the twenty-eighth of May there was a great meeting at Winchester, "tota populi generalitate." The total number of names is ninety-two[8]. Again on the twelfth of September, the king was at Buckingham, and there held a gemót, "tota magnatorum generalitate[9]."

ÆÐELSTA'N, A.D. 935.—On the twenty-first of September in this year there was a gemót at Dorchester, "tota optimatum generalitate[10]."

ÆÐELSTA'N, A.D. 937.—A gemót was held, "archiepiscopis, episcopis, ducibus et principibus Anglorum insimul pro regni utilitate coadunatis[11]."

An undated charter of Æðelstán[12] records a meeting of witan at Abingdon: a grant was made to the abbey. The archbishop, bishops and abbots present solemnly excommunicated any one who should disturb the grant; to which

---

[1] Cod. Dipl. No. 353.
[2] Ibid. No. 1103.
[3] Ibid. No. 1102.
[4] Ibid. No. 1105.
[5] Ibid. No. 361.
[6] Ibid. Nos. 1107, 1108.

[7] Ibid. No. 361.
[8] Ibid. No. 364.
[9] Ibid. No. 365.
[10] Ibid. Nos. 367, 1112.
[11] Ibid. No. 1113.
[12] Ibid. No. 1129.

all the people present exclaimed, " So be it ! Amen." " Et dixit omnis populus qui ibi aderat, Fiat, Fiat. Amen." " And cwæð ealle ðæt folc ðe ðǽr embstód, Sy hit swá. Amen. Amen."

Gemóts of Æðelstán's, the dates of which are uncertain, were held at Witlanburh[1], Greátanleá[2], Fevershám[3], Thundersfield[4], and Exeter[5].

EA'DMUND, before A.D. 946.—This prince held at least two gemóts, one at London, one at Culintún, but in what years is uncertain[6].

EA'DRED, A.D. 946.—This year there was a gemót at Kingston, and king Eádred was crowned[7].

EA'DRED, A.D. 947.—In this year there was at least one witena gemót, in which the terms of peace with the Northumbrian witan were arranged[8]. There were others also in Mercia, and I have little doubt that all the charters bearing that date in the Codex Diplomaticus are really acts of such meetings.

EA'DRED, A.D. 948.—In this year the witan of Northumberland having elected a king Eirik, Eádred marched into their country and plundered it ; upon which · they again made a formal submission to him[9].

Between 960–963.—In one of these years a gemót was held, but the place is unknown, and Eádgyfu ultimately succeeded in putting an end to the pretensions of Goda's family[10].

EA'DGA'R, A.D. 966.—A gemót in London[11].

---

[1] Thorpe, i. 240.
[2] Ibid. i. 194.
[3] Thorpe, i. 216.
[4] Ibid. i. 217.
[5] Ibid. i. 220. This however may have been in 926, when Æðelstán was in that city.
[6] Leg. Eádm. Thorpe, i. 244, 252.
[7] Cod. Dipl. No. 411.
[8] Chron. Sax. an. 947.
[9] Chron. Sax. an. 948.
[10] Cod. Dipl. No. 499.
[11] Ibid. No. 528.

EA'DGA'R, A.D. 968.—A gemót was held at some place unknown[1].

EA'DGA'R, A.D. 973.—A great gemót was held in St. Paul's church, London[2].

EA'DGA'R, A.D. 977.—After Easter (April 8th), there was held a great gemót, "ðæt mycele gemót," at Kirtlington in Oxfordshire[3].

EA'DGA'R, A.D. 978.—In this year was held the celebrated gemót at Calne in Wiltshire, when the floor gave way and precipitated the witan to the ground[4]. There was another gemót at Ceodre, now Cheddar in Somersetshire[5].

In addition to these Eádgár held at least two gemóts, one at Andover in Hants, one at a place called Wihtbordesstán, which we cannot now identify. In both of these meetings laws were passed[6].

ÆÐELRED, A.D. 979.—A gemót was held at Kingston for the coronation of Æðelred[7].

ÆÐELRED, A.D. 992.—In this year there were probably several witena gemóts for the prosecution of the Danish war[8].

ÆÐELRED, A.D. 993.—In this year there was at least one gemót at Winchester[9].

ÆÐELRED, A.D. 994.—A witena gemót met this year at Andover[10].

ÆÐELRED, A.D. 995.—A gemót at Ambresbyrig, now Amesbury, where Ælfríc was elected archbishop of Canterbury in the place of Sigeríc[11]. There seems to have

[1] Cod. Dipl. Nos. 1265, 1266.
[2] Ibid. No. 580.
[3] Chron. Sax. an. 977.
[4] Ibid. an. 978.
[5] Cod. Dipl. No. 598.
[6] Thorpe, i. 272.
[7] Chron. Sax. an. 979.
[8] Ibid. an. 992.
[9] Cod. Dipl. No. 684.
[10] Chron. Sax. an. 994. Ll. Æðelr. 11. Thorpe, i. 284.
[11] Chron. Sax. an. 995.

been another meeting in the same year, one of whose acts we still possess[1].

ÆÐELRED, A.D. 996.—In this year a gemót was held at Cealchýð[2].

ÆÐELRED, A.D. 997.—This year a gemót was held in the palace at Calne : " collecta haud minima sapientium multitudine, in aula villae regiae quae nuncupative a populis Et Calnæ vocitatur[3]." A few days later we find the gemót assembled at Waneting or Wantage ; and here they promulgated laws which we yet possess[4]. There is a charter also, passed at this gemót[5]. A previous gemót of uncertain year had been held at Brómdún[6], and another at Woodstock[7].

ÆÐELRED, A.D. 998.—A gemót was held this year in London[8]; and another apparently at Andover[9], where conditions of peace were ratified with Anláf or Olaf Tryggvason[10].

ÆÐELRED, A.D. 999.—At least one gemót was held this year, to concert measures of defence against the Danes[11].

A.D 996–1001.—Between these years there was a gemót at Cócham, now Cookham in Berks, which was attended by a large assemblage of thanes from Wessex and Mercia, both of Saxon and Danish descent[12].

ÆÐELRED, A.D. 1002.—In this year the witan met and paid tribute to the Danes[13]. We have still an evident act of such a gemót in this year[14].

ÆÐELRED, A.D. 1004.—In this year a meeting of the

[1] Cod. Dipl. No. 692.
[2] Ibid. No. 696.
[3] Ibid. No. 698.
[4] Thorpe, i. 292.
[5] Cod. Dipl. No. 698.
[6] Thorpe, i. 280, 294.
[7] Ibid. i. 280.

[8] Cod. Dipl. No. 702.
[9] Chron. Sax. an. 998.
[10] Thorpe. i. 284.
[11] Chron. Sax. an. 999.
[12] Cod. Dipl. No. 704.
[13] Chron. Sax. an. 1002.
[14] Cod. Dipl. No. 707.

Eastanglian witan, under earl Ulfcytel, took place. From the description I do not think it could have been an ordinary scírgemót. It shows, at any rate, that the witan were resident in the shires, and not permanently attached to the royal person or household[1].

ÆÐELRED, A.D. 1006.—Another gemót was held this year, somewhere in Shropshire, for the melancholy and shameful purpose of buying peace from the Danes[2].

ÆÐELRED, A.D. 1008.—A gemót was held, one of whose acts we have still[3].

ÆÐELRED, A.D. 1009.—In this year we are told that the king and his heáhwitan met; but the place is unknown[4].

ÆÐELRED, A.D. 1010.—In this year a gemót was proclaimed, to concert measures of defence against the Danes[5]. "Ðonne beád man eallan witan tó cynge, and man sceólde ðonne rædan hú man ðisne eard werian sceólde."

ÆÐELRED, A.D. 1011.—A gemót was again held for the shameful purpose of buying peace[6].

ÆÐELRED, A.D. 1012.—At Easter (April 13th) there was a great meeting at London, and tribute was paid to the Danes[7].

ÆÐELRED, A.D. 1014.—In this year was holden that important gemót, perhaps we might say convention, which has been mentioned in the text; when the witan, upon the death of Swegen, consented again to receive Æðelred as king, upon promises of amendment[8].

ÆÐELRED, A.D. 1015.—In this year was the great

---

[1] Chron. Sax. an. 1004.
[2] Ibid. an. 1006.
[3] Cod. Dipl No. 1305.
[4] Chron. Sax. an. 1009.
[5] Chron. Sax. an. 1010.
[6] Ibid. an. 1011.
[7] Ibid. an. 1012.
[8] Ibid. an. 1014.

gemót of Oxford, "ðæt mycel gemót," and Sigeferð and Morcar the powerful earls of the north were slain[1].

It is uncertain in what years we must place the promulgation of Æðelred's laws[2], at Enham, and Haba[3]; and others without date or place.

EA'DMUND I'RENSI'DA, A.D. 1016.—In this year there must have been various meetings of the witan, if tumultuous and armed assemblages can claim the name of witena gemóts at all. The witan in London elected Eádmund king; and there was a meeting at Olney, near Deerhurst, where the kingdom was partitioned[4].

A.D. 1016–1020.—Probably between these years was the great gemót at Winchester, in which Cnut promulgated his laws[5].

CNUT, A.D. 1020.—In this year was a great gemót at Cirencester[6].

HARALD HARANFOT, A.D. 1036.—Upon the death of Cnut, there was a gemót at Oxford, and Harald was elected king[7].

HARDACNUT, A.D. 1042.—In this year there was probably a gemót at Sutton[8]. And another on Hardacnut's death, when all the people chose Eádweard the Confessor to be king[9].

---

[1] Chron. Sax. an. 1015.   [2] Thorpe, i. 314.
[3] Thorpe, i. 366.   [4] Chron. Sax. an. 1016.
[5] Thorpe, i. 358.   [6] Chron. Sax. an. 1020.
[7] Chron. Sax. an. 1036.   [8] Cod. Dipl. Nos. 765, 766.
[9] Chron. Sax. an. 1042. At Gillingham. Will. Malm. i. 332, § 197.
" Nihil erat quod Edwardus pro necessitate temporis non polliceretur, ita, utrinque fide data, quicquid petebatur sacramento firmavit. Nec mora Gillingcham congregato concilio, rationibus suis explicitis, regem effecit (Godwinus) hominio palam omnibus dato: homo affectati leporis, et ingenue gentilitia lingua eloquens, mirus dicere, mirus populo persuadere quae placerent. Quidam auctoritatem eius secuti, quidam muneribus flexi, quidam etiam debitum Edwardi amplexi."

EA'DWEARD, A.D. 1043.—A witena gemót was held at Winchester, April 3rd, and Eádweard was crowned[1].

EA'DWEARD, A.D. 1044.—There was a gemót, "generale concilium," in London; the only business recorded is the election of Manni, abbot of Evesham[2]; but there is a charter[3].

EA'DWEARD, A.D. 1045.—There seems to have been a gemót this year[4].

EA'DWEARD, A.D. 1046.—A gemót, the place of which is unknown[5].

EA'DWEARD, A.D. 1047.—On the 10th of March this year there was "mycel gemót" in London[6].

EA'DWEARD, A.D. 1048.—A gemót sat on the 8th of September at Gloucester[7]; and on the 21st of September, another met in London, and outlawed the family of earl Godwine.

EA'DWEARD, A.D. 1050.—There was a great gemót in London[8].

EA'DWEARD, A.D. 1052, 1053.—A gemót, place unknown[9].

EA'DWEARD, A.D. 1055.—A gemót in London[10].

EA'DWEARD, A.D. 1065.—There was a great gemót at Northampton[11], Another was held at Oxford on the 28th of October[11], and lastly at Christmas in London[11]. At this Eádweard dedicated Westminster Abbey, and dying on the 5th of January, 1066, the assembled witan elected Harald king.

---

[1] Chron. Sax. an. 1043.
[2] Flor. Wig. an. 1044.
[3] Cod. Dipl. Nos. 776, 777.
[4] Ibid. Nos. 779, 783.
[5] Ibid. No. 786.
[6] Chron. Sax. an. 1047.

[7] Chron. Sas. an. 1048.
[8] Ibid. an. 1050.
[9] Cod. Dipl. No. 799.
[10] Chron. Sax. an. 1055.
[11] Ibid. an. 1065.

Having now completed this list, which must be confessed to be but an imperfect one, I do not scruple to express my belief that every charter in the Codex Diplomaticus, which is not merely a private will or private settlement, is the genuine act of some witena gemót: and that we thus possess a long and interesting series of records, enabling us to follow the action of the Saxon Parliaments from the very cradle of our monarchy.

CHAPTER VII.

THE TOWNS.

We have now arrived at that point of our enquiry at which it behoves us to bestow our attention upon the origin and growth of towns among the Anglosaxons; and to this end we shall find it expedient to carry our researches to a still earlier period, and investigate, though in a slight degree, the condition of their British and Roman predecessors in this respect. At first sight it would seem natural to suppose that where a race had long possessed the outward means and form of civilization, —a race among whom great military and civil establishments had been founded, who had clustered round provincial cities, the seats of a powerful government, and whose ports and harbours had been the scenes of active commerce,—there need be little question as to the origin of towns and cities among those who conquered and dispossessed them. It might be imagined that the later comers would have nothing more to do than seize upon the seats from which they had expelled their predecessors, and apply to their own uses the established instruments of convenience, of wealth or safety. Further enquiry however proves that this induction would be erroneous, and that the Saxons did not settle in

the Roman towns. The reason of this is not difficult to assign: a city is the result of a system
of cultivation, and it is of no use whatever to a
race whose system differs entirely from that of the
race by whom it was founded. The Curia and
the temple, the theatre and thermae, house joined
to house and surrounded by a dense quadrangular
wall, crowding into a defined and narrow space the
elements of civilization, are unintelligible to him
whose whole desire centres in the undisturbed enjoyment of his éðel, and unlimited command of
the mark. The buildings of a centralized society are
as little calculated for his use as their habits and
institutions: as well might it have been proposed
to him to substitute the jurisdiction of the *praetor
urbanus* for the national tribunal of the folcmót.
The spirit of life is totally different: as different
are all the social institutions, and all the details
which arise from these and tend to confirm and
perpetuate them.

Nevertheless we cannot doubt that the existence
of the British and Roman cities did materially influence the mode and nature of the German settlements; and without some slight sketch of the growth
and development of the former, we shall find it
impossible to form a clear notion of the conditions
under which the Anglosaxon polity was formed.

If we may implicitly trust the report of Caesar,
a British city in his time differed widely from what
we understand by that term. A spot difficult of
access from the trees which filled it, surrounded
with a rampart and a ditch, and which offered a

refuge from the sudden incursions of an enemy, could be dignified by the name of an *oppidum*, and form the metropolis of Cassivelaunus[1]. Such also among the Slavonians were the *vici*, encircled by an *abbatis* of timber, or at most a paling, proper to repel not only an unexpected attack, but even capable of resisting for a time the onset of practised forces: such in our own time have been found the stockades of the Burmese, and the Pah of the New Zealander: and if our skilful engineers have experienced no contemptible resistance, and the lives of many brave and disciplined men have been sacrificed in their reduction, we may admit that even the *oppida* of Cassivelaunus, or Caratac or Galgacus, might, as fortresses, have serious claims to the attention of a Roman commander. But such an *oppidum* is no town or city in the sense in which those words are contemplated throughout this chapter: by a town I certainly intend a place enclosed in some manner, and even fortified: but much more those who dwell together in such a place, and the means by which they either rule themselves, or are ruled. I mean a metaphysical as well as a physical unit,—not exclusively what was a collection of dwellings or a fortification, but a centre of trade and manufacture and civilization.

If the Romans found none such, at least they left

---

[1] Bell. Gall. v. 21. Caesar stormed it, and had therefore good means of knowing what it was. His further information was probably derived from his British ally Comius. Strabo gives a very similar account: πόλεις δ' αὐτῶν εἰσιν οἱ δρυμοί· περιφράξαντες γὰρ δένδρεσι καταβεβλημένοις εὐρυχωρῆ κύκλον καλυβοποιοῦνται, καὶ τὰ βοσκήματα κατασταθμεύουσιν, οὐ πρὸς πολὺν χρόνον. lib. iv.

them, in every part of Britain. The record of their gradual and successive advance shows that, partly with a politic view of securing their conquests, partly with the necessary aim of conciliating their soldiery, they did establish numerous *municipia* and *coloniae* here, as well as military stations which in time became the nuclei of towns.

It is however scarcely possible that Caesar and Strabo can be strictly accurate in their reports, or that there were from the first only such towns in Britain as these authors have described. It is not consonant to experience that a thickly peopled and peaceful country[1] should long be without cities. A commercial people[2] always have some settled stations for the collection and interchange of commodities, and fixed establishments for the regulation of trade. Caesar himself tells us that the buildings of the Britons were very numerous, and that they bore a resemblance to those of the Gauls[3], whose cities were assuredly considerable. Moreover a race so conversant with the management of horses as to use armed chariots for artillery, are not likely to have been without an extensive system of roads, and where there are roads, towns will not long be wanting. Hence when, less than eighty years after the return of the Romans to Britain, and scarcely forty after the complete subjugation of the

---

[1] "Hominum est infinita multitudo." Bell. Gall. v. 12. Εἶναι δὲ καὶ πολυάνθρωπον τὴν νῆσον....βασιλεῖς τε καὶ δυνάστας πολλοὺς ἔχειν, καὶ πρὸς ἀλλήλους κατὰ τὸ πλεῖστον εἰρηνικῶς διακεῖσθαι. Diodor. Sicul. v. 21.

[2] Οὐενέτοι....χρώμενοι τῷ ἐμπορίῳ. Strabo, lib. iv.

[3] "Creberrima aedificia, fere Gallicis consimilia." Bell. Gall. v. 12

island by Agricola, Ptolemy tells us of at least fifty-six cities in existence here[1], we may reasonably conclude that they were not all due to the efforts of Roman civilization.

Caesar says indeed nothing of London, yet it is difficult to believe that this was an unimportant place, even in his day. It was long the principal town of the Cantii, whom the Roman general de-

---

[1] Ptolemy at the commencement of the second century (*i. e.* about A.D. 120) mentions the following πόλεις, which surely are *towns*:—

District.	Towns.	District.	Towns.
Novantae	Loucopibia.	Parisi	Petuaria.
	Rhetigonium.	Ordovices	Mediolanium.
Selgovae	Carbantorigum.		Brannogenium.
	Uxelum.	Cornabii	Deuana.
	Corda.		Viroconium.
	Trimontium.	Coritavi	Lindum.
Damnii	Colania.		Rhage.
	Vanduara.	Catyeuchlani	Salenae.
	Coria.		Urolanium.
	Alauna.	Simeni	Venta.
	Lindum.	Trinoantes	Camudolanum.
	Victoria.	Demetae	Luentinium.
Otadeni	Curia.		Maridunum.
	Bremenium.	Silures	Bullaeum.
Vacomagi	Banatia.	Dobuni	Corinium.
	Tameia.	Atrebatii	Nalkua.
	The Winged Camp.	Cantii	Londinium.
	Tuesis.		Darvenum.
Venicontes	Orrhea.		Rhutupiae.
Texali	Devana.	Rhegni	Naeomagus.
Brigantes	Epeiacum.	Belgae	Ischalis.
	Vinnovium.		The Hot Springs.
	Caturhactonium.		Venta.
	Calatum.	Durotriges	Dunium.
	Isurium.	Dumnonii	Voliba.
	Rhigodunum.		Uxela.
	Olicana.		Tamare.
	Eboracum.		Isca.
	Camunlodunum.		

scribes as the most polished of the inhabitants of
Britain; and as we know that there was an active
commercial intercourse between the eastern coast
of England and Gaul, it is at least probable that a
station, upon a great river at a safe yet easy distance from the sea, was not unknown to the foreign
merchants who traded to our shores[1]. One hundred and sixteen years later it could be described
as a city famous in a high degree for the resort of
merchants and for traffic[2]: but of these years one
hundred had been spent in peace and in the natural
development of their resources by the Britons, undisturbed by Roman ambition; and we have therefore ample right to infer that from the very first

---

[1] It is clear that Caesar was not greatly harassed in his march towards the ford of the Thames near Chertsey; and if, as is probable, his
advance disarmed the Cantii generally, or compelled the more warlike
of their body to retire upon the force of Cassivelaunus, concentrated on
the left bank of the river, we can understand what would otherwise
seem a very dangerous movement,—a march into Surrey, leaving London unoccupied on the right flank. Thus it seems to me that the fact
of Caesar's not noticing the city may be more readily explained by its
not lying within the scope of his manœuvres, than by its not existing in his time. And indeed it is probable that just here some portion of his memoirs has been lost: for in the nineteenth chapter of the
fifth book, he distinctly says: "Cassivelaunus, *ut supra demonstravi-
mus*, omni deposita spe contentionis," etc.; but nothing now remains
in what we possess, to which these words can possibly be referred.
Caesar's Commentaries were the private literary occupation of the great
soldier in peaceful times, and we cannot attribute this contradiction
in his finished work to carelessness.

[2] "At Suetonius mira constantia medios inter hostes Londinium
perrexit, cognomento quidem coloniae non insigne, sed copia negotia-
torum et commeatuum maxime celebre." Tacit. Ann. xiv. 33. "Not a
colonia," seems to me equivalent to saying, a British city.—Twenty
years after the return of the Romans to Britain, *seventy thousand* citizens and allies perished during Boadicea's rebellion in London, Verulam and Colchester. (Ibid.)

Cair Lunden had been a place of great commercial importance. The Romans on their return found and kept it so, although they did not establish a colonia there. The first place which received this title with all its corresponding advantages was Camelodunum, probably the British Cair Colun, now Colchester in Essex[1].

As the settlement of the nations, and their reduction under a centralizing system, followed the victories of the legions, municipia and coloniae arose in every province, the seats of garrisons and the residences of military and civil governors: while as civilization extended, the Britons themselves, adopting the manners and following the example of their masters, multiplied the number of towns upon all the great lines of internal communication. It is difficult now to give from Roman authorities only a complete list of these towns; many names which we find in the *itineraria* and similar documents, being merely post-stations or points where subordinate provincial authorities were located; but the names of fifty-six towns have been already quoted from Ptolemy, and even tradition may be of some service to us on this subject[2].

---

[1] This was long supposed to be Maldon, but it seems difficult to resist Mannert's reasoning in favour of Colchester. See Geograph. der Griech. u. Röm. p. 157.

[2] In the third century Marcianus reckons, unfortunately without naming them, fifty-nine celebrated cities in Britain: ἔχει δὲ ἐν αὐτῇ ἔθνη λγ, πόλεις ἐπισήμους νθ, ποτάμους ἐπισήμους μ, ἀκρωτήρια ἐπίσημα ιδ, χερσόνησον ἐπίσημον ἕνα, κόλπους ἐπισήμους ε, λίμενας ἐπισήμους γ. Marcian. Heracleot. lib. i. Nor will this surprise us when we bear in mind that about this period the Britons enjoyed such a reputation for building as to find employment in Gaul. " Civitas Aeduorum....

Nennius sums up with patriotic pride the names of thirty-four principal cities which adorned Britain under his forefathers, and many of these we can yet identify: amongst them are London, Bristol, Canterbury, Colchester, Cirencester, Chichester, Gloucester, Worcester, Wroxeter, York, Silchester, Lincoln, Leicester, Doncaster, Caermarthen, Carnarvon, Winchester, Porchester, Grantchester, Norwich, Carlisle, Chester, Caerleon on Usk, Manchester and Dorchester[1]. To these from other sources we may add Sandwich, Dover, Rochester, Nottingham, Exeter, Bath, Bedford, Aylesbury and St. Alban's.

Whatever the origin of these towns may have been, it is easy to show that many of them comprised a Roman population: the very walls by which some of them are still surrounded, offer conclusive evidence of this; while in the neighbourhood of others, coins and inscriptions, the ruins of theatres, villas, baths, and other public or private buildings, attest either the skill and luxury of the conquerors, or the aptness to imitate of the con-

plurimos, quibus illae provinciae redundabant, accepit artifices," etc. Eumen. Const. Paneg. c. 21.

[1] Henry of Huntingdon copies Nennius and aids in the identification. Asser adds to the list Nottingham, in British Tinguobauc, and Cair Wisc now Exeter. The Saxon Chronicle records Anderida, Bath, Bedford, Leighton, Aylesbury, Bensington and Eynesham. Among the places unquestionably Roman may be named Londinium, Verulamium, Colonia, Glevum (Gloucester), Venta Belgarum (Winchester), Venta Icenorum (Norwich), Venta Silurum (Cair Gwint) Durocornovium or Corinium (Cirencester), Calleva Atrebatum (Silchester), Eboracum (York), Uxella (Exeter), Aquæ Solis (Bath), Durnovaria (Dorchester), Regnum (Chichester), Durocovernum (Canterbury), Uriconium (Wroxeter) and Lindum (Lincoln).

quered[1]. But a much more important question arises; viz. how many of them were ruled freely, like the cities of the old country, by a municipal body constituted in the ancient form: what provision, in short, the Romans made or permitted for the education of their British subjects in the manly career of citizenship and the dignity of self-government[2].

The constitution of a provincial city of the empire, in the days when the republic still possessed virtue and principle, was of this description, at all events from the period of the Social, Marsic or Italian war, when the cities of Italy wrested isopolity, or at least isotely, from Rome. The state consisted of the whole body of the citizens, without distinction, having a general voice in the management of their own internal affairs. The administrative functions however resided in a privileged

[1] The walls of Chichester still offer an admirable example in very perfect condition. The remains at Lincoln and Old Verulam enable us to trace the ancient sites with precision, and in the immediate neighbourhood of the latter town the foundations of a large theatre are yet preserved. The plough still brings to light the remains of Roman villas and the details of Roman cultivation throughout the valley of the Severn. It is impossible here to enumerate all the places where the discovery of coins, inscriptions, works of art and utility or ruins of buildings attest a continued occupation of the site and a peaceful settlement. Many archæological works, the result of modern industry, may be beneficially consulted; and among these I would call particular attention to the Map of Roman Yorkshire, published by Mr. Newton, with the approbation of the Archæological Institute of Great Britain and Ireland.

[2] The following lines contain a very slight sketch of the municipal institutions of a Roman city. It is not necessary to burthen the reader's attention with the deeper details of this special subject. A general reference may be given to Savigny's Geschichte des Römischen Rechts the leading authority on all such points.

class of those citizens, commonly called *Curiales*, *Decuriones*, *Ordo Decurionum* (or sometimes *Ordo* alone), and occasionally *Senatus*. They were in fact to the whole body of the citizens what the Senatus under the Emperors was to the citizens of Rome[1], and their rights and privileges seem in general to have varied very much as did those of the higher body. They were hereditary, but, when occasion demanded an increase of their numbers, self-elected. Out of this college of Decuriones the *Magistratus* or supreme executive government proceeded. In the better days I believe these were always freely chosen for one year, by the whole community, but exclusively from among the members of the Ordo: and after Tiberius at Rome transferred the elections from the Comitia to the Senate, the Decuriones in the provinces may have become the sole electors, as they were the only persons capable of being elected. The Magistratus had the supreme jurisdiction, and were the completion of the communal system: they bore different names in different cities, but usually those of Duumviri or Quatuorviri, from their number. Sometimes, but very rarely, they were named Consules. In fact the general outline of this constitution resembled as much as possible that of Rome itself, which was only the head of a confederation embracing all the cities of Italy.

---

[1] If we adopt an old legal phrase, the Decuriones were *cives optimo iure*, or full burghers; the rest of the citizens were *non optimo iure*, not full burghers, not having a share in the advantages possessed by the members of the corporation.

A somewhat similar arrangement was introduced into the cities of the various countries which, under the name of provinces, were brought within the influence of the Roman power: only that in these the communal organization was throughout subordinated to the regulation and control of the Consularis, the Legatus, Procurator, and other officers military and fiscal, who administered the affairs of the province.   A principal point of distinction between the free communities of Italy and the dependent provincial corporations lay in this; that in the latter, the magistrates were indeed elected by the Ordo or Curia, but upon the nomination of the Roman governor: their jurisdiction in suits was consequently very limited, while political functions were for the most part confined to the civil and military officers of the empire.

As long as the condition of the imperial city itself was tolerably easy, and the provinces had not yet been flooded with the vice, corruption and misery which called for and rendered possible the victories of the barbarians, the condition of the provincial decurions was on the whole one of honour and advantage.   They formed a kind of nobility, a class distinguished from their fellow-citizens by a certain rank and privileges, as they were assuredly also distinguished from them by superior wealth: they resembled in fact an aristocracy of county families at this day, with its exclusive possession of the magistrature and other local advantages. On the other hand they were responsible for the public dues, the levies, the annona or victualling of forces, the *tributum* or raising of the assessed taxes; and thus they were rendered immediately subject to the exactions of the fiscal authorities, and especially exposed to the caprice and illegal demands of the Roman officials[1]—a class univer-

[1] Tacitus gives us an insight into some of the gratuitous insults and vexations inflicted upon the British provincials, while he describes the reforms introduced by Agricola into these branches of the public service. "Ceterum animorum provinciae prudens, simulque doctus per aliena experimenta, parum profici armis, si iniuriae sequerentur, causas bellorum statuit excidere. . . . Frumenti et tributorum exactionem aequalitate munerum mollire, circumcisis, quae in quaestum reperta, ipso tributo gravius tolerabantur: namque per ludibrium adsidere clausis horreis, et emere ultro frumenta, ac vendere pretio cogebantur : devortia itinerum et longinquitas regionum indicebatur, ut civitates a proximis hybernis in remota et avia deferrent, donec, quod omnibus in promtu erat, paucis lucrosum fieret." Tac. Agric. xix. The same grave historian attributes the fierce insurrection under Boadicea to the tyrannous conduct of the Legati and Procuratores of the province, and the insolent conduct of their subordinates. "Britanni agitare inter se mala servitutis, conferre iniurias et interpretando accendere : 'nihil profici patientia, nisi ut graviora, tanquam ex facili tolerantibus, imperentur : singulos sibi olim reges fuisse, nunc binos imponi : e quibus Legatus in sanguinem, Procurator in bona saeviret. Aeque discordiam Praepositorum, aeque concordiam subiectis exitiosam, alterius manus, centuriones alterius, vim et contumelias miscere. Nihil iam cupiditati, nihil libidini exceptum." Tac. Agric. xv. It is obviously with reference to the same facts that he describes the Britons as peaceable and well disposed to discharge the duties laid upon then, if they are only spared insult. Tac. Agric. xiii. Xiphilinus, who though a late writer is valuable inasmuch as he represents Dio Cassius, describes some of the intolerable atrocities which drove the Iceni into rebellion, destroyed Camelodunum and Verulamium, and led in those cities and in London to the slaughter of nearly seventy thousand citizens and allies. Deep as was the wrong done to the family of Prasutagus, he is no doubt right in attributing the general exasperation mainly to the confiscation of the lands which Claudius Caesar had granted to the chiefs, and which the procurator Catus Decianus attempted to call in. Πρόφασις δὲ τοῦ πολέμου ἐγένετο ἡ δήμευσις τῶν χρημάτων (publicatio bonorum), ἃ Κλαύδιος τοῖς πρώτοις αὐτῶν ἐδεδώκει· καὶ ἔδει καὶ ἐκεῖνα, ὥς γε Δεκιανὸς Κάτος ὁ τῆς νήσου ἐπιτροπεύων ἔλεγεν, ἀναπόμπιμα γενέσθαι. Boadicea is made to declare that they were charged with a poll-tax, so severely exacted

sally infamous for tyrannical extortion in the provinces : and in yet later times, when the land itself
frequently became deserted, through the burthen of
taxation and exaction[1], they were compelled to undertake the cultivation of the relinquished estates,
that the fiscus might be no loser. Gradually as the
bond which held the fragments of the empire together was loosened, and as limb after limb dropped
away from the mouldering colossus, the condition of a Decurion became so oppressive that it
was found necessary to press citizens by force into
the office : some committed suicide, others expatriated themselves, in order to escape it. The state

that an account was required even of the dead : οὐδὲ γὰρ τὸ τελευτῆσαι
παρ᾽ αὐτοῖς ἀζήμιόν ἐστιν, ἀλλ᾽ ἴστε ὅσον καὶ ὑπὲρ τῶν νεκρῶν τελοῦμεν·
παρὰ μὲν γὰρ τοῖς ἄλλοις ἀνθρώποις καὶ τοὺς δουλεύοντάς τισιν ὁ θάνατος
ἐλευθεροῖ, Ῥωμαίοις δὲ δὴ μόνοις καὶ οἱ νεκροὶ ζῶσι πρὸς τὰ λήμματα.
These accusations put into the mouths of the personages themselves,
must not be taken to be exaggerated statements without foundation :
they are the confessions of the historians, which sometimes perhaps they
lacked courage to make in another form. The sudden and violent
calling in of large sums which Seneca had forced upon the British
chiefs in expectation of enormous interest, was another cause of the war:
διά τε οὖν τοῦτο, καὶ ὅτι ὁ Σενέκας χιλίας σφίσι μυριάδας ἄκουσιν ἐπὶ
χρησταῖς ἐλπίσι τόκων δανείσας, ἔπειτ᾽ ἀθρόας τε ἅμα αὐτὰς καὶ βιαίως
εἰσέπρασσεν. The Roman mortgages in Britain were enormous, yet
easily explained. The procurator made an extravagant demand : the
native state could not pay it ; but the procurator had a Roman friend
who would advance it upon good security, etc. Similar things have
taken place in *Zemindaries* of later date than the British. For the
references above see Joan. Xiphil. Epitome Dionis, *Nero* vi.

[1] This not only appears from the digests, but from numerous merely
incidental notices in the authors of the time. The population were
crowded into cities, and the country was deserted. This was not the
result of a healthy manufacturing or commercial movement, but of a
state of universal distraction and insecurity. Had the cultivation of
the land ceased through a prudent calculation of political economy,
we should not have heard of compulsory tillage.

was obliged to forbid by law the sale of property for the purpose of avoiding it; freemen went into the ranks, or subjected themselves to voluntary servitude, as a preferable alternative; nay at length vagabonds, people of bad character, even malefactors, were literally condemned to it[1]. This tends perhaps more than any fact to prove the gradual ruin of the municipal as well as the social fabric, and the miserable condition of the provinces under the later emperors.

However, in the better days of Vespasian, Trajan and the Antonines we are not to look for such a state of society; and in the provinces, the Ordo, though exposed to many harsh and painful conditions, yet held a position of comparative dignity and influence. I have compared them to a county aristocracy, but there is perhaps a nearer parallel, for in the Roman empire it is difficult to distinguish the county from the town. The position of the Decurions can hardly be made clearer than by a reference to the Select (that is self-elected) Vestries of our great metropolitan parishes before the passing of Sir John Hobhouse's Acts; or to the town-councillors and aldermen of our country-towns, before the enactment of the Municipal Corporations' Bill. Whoso remembers these bodies with their churchwardens on the one hand, their mayors, borough-reeves and aldermen on the other,—their exclusive jurisdiction as a magistracy,—their exclusive possession of corporation property, tolls,

---

[1] Savigny, Röm. Recht. i. 23 *seq.*

rents and other sources of wealth,—their private rights in the common land, held by themselves or delegated to their *clients*,—their custody of the public buildings, and sole management of civic or charitable funds,—their patronage as trustees of public institutions,—their franchise as electors,— their close family alliances, and the methods by which they contrived to recruit their diminished numbers, till they became a very aristocracy among a people of commoners[1],—whoso, I say, considers these phænomena of our own day, need have little difficulty not only in understanding the condition of a Decurion in the better days of the Roman empire : but, if he will cast his thought back into earlier ages, he may find in them no little illustration of the nature, rights and policy of the Patriciate, under the Republic.

Other cities of a less favoured description were governed directly as præfectures, by an officer sent from Rome, who centred in himself all the higher branches of administration : in these cities the functions of the Ordo were greatly curtailed ; little was left them but to attend to the police of the town and markets, the determination of trifling civil suits, the survey of roads or buildings ; and, in conjunction with the heads of the guilds (" collegia opificum ") the vain and mischievous attempt to regulate wages and prices. On the other hand a few cities had what was called the Jus Italicum, or right to form a free corporation, in every respect

[1] Cives optimo iure, optimates, senatus, patricii, rachinburgi, boni homines,—these are all more or less equivalent terms.

identical with those of the cities of Italy, that is to say identical in plan with that of Rome itself. The provinces of the Roman empire must have contained many of these privileged states which thus enjoyed a valuable pre-eminence over their neighbours, the reward of public services: but history has been sparing of their names, and in western Europe, three only, Cologne, Vienne and Lyons are particularly mentioned[1]. In all the cities which had not this privilege, after the close of the fourth century we find a particular officer called the Defensor, who was not to be one of the curiales, who was to be elected by the whole body of the citizens and not by the curiales only, and who must therefore be looked upon in a great degree as the representative of the popular against the aristocratic element, as the support of the Cives against the Senatus and Duumvir. In the cities of Gaul, the bishops for the most part occupied this position, which necessarily led to results of the highest importance, from the peculiar relation in which it placed them to the barbarian invaders[2]. From all these details it appears that very different measures of municipal freedom were granted under different circumstances.

We have considered the general principles of Roman provincial government, and we now ask, how were these applied in the case of Britain? The

---

[1] Savigny, Röm. Recht. i. 53.

[2] The Bishops were the most valuable allies of Clovis in his aggressive wars. Without their co-operation that savage Merwing would perhaps never have established the Frankish pre-eminence in the Gauls.

answer is much more difficult to give than might be imagined. Wealthy as this country was, and capable of conducing to the power and well-being of its masters, it seems never to have received a generous, or even fair treatment from them. The Briton was to the last, as at the first, " penitus toto divisus orbe Britannus," and his land, always " ultima Thule," was made indeed to serve the avarice or ambition of the ruler, but derived little benefit to itself from the rule. " Levies, Corn, Tribute, Mortgages, Slaves "—under these heads was Britain entered in the vast *ledger* of the Empire. The Roman records do not tell us much of the details of government here, and we may justly say that we are more familiar with the state of an eastern or an Iberian city than we are with that of a British one. A few technical words, perfectly significant to a people who, above all others, symbolized a long succession of facts under one legal term, are all that remain to us; and unfortunately the jurists and statesmen and historians whose works we painfully consult in hopes of rescuing the minutest detail of our early condition, are satisfied with the use of general terms which were perfectly intelligible to those for whom they wrote, but teach us little. " Ostorius Scapula reduced the hither Britain to the form of a province [1],"—conveyed ample information to those who took the institutions of the Empire for granted wherever its eagles flew

---

[1] " Consularium primus Aulus Plautius praepositus, ac subinde Ostorius Scapula, uterque bello egregius : redactaque paulatim in formam provinciae proxima pars Britanniae." Tac. Agric. xiv.

abroad: to us they are nearly vain words, a detailed explanation of which would be valuable beyond all calculation, for it would contain the secret of the weakness and the sudden collapse of the Empire. But what little we can gather from ancient sources does not induce us to believe that Britain met with a just or enlightened measure of treatment at the hands of her victors. Violence on the one hand, seduction on the other, were employed to destroy the spirit of resistance, but we do not learn that submission and docility were rewarded by the communication of a fair share of those advantages which spring from peace and cultivation. Agricola, whose information his severe and accomplished son-in-law must be considered to reproduce, tells us that, on the whole, the Britons were not difficult subjects to rule, as long as they were not insulted by a capricious display of power: " The Britons themselves are not backward in raising the levies and taxes, or filling the offices[1], if they are only not exposed to insult in doing it. Insult they will not submit to; for we have beaten them into obedience, but by no means yet into

---

[1] Agric. xiii. Offices under the Empire were *honores* or *munera:* the former, places of dignity and some power, duumvirates and the like: the latter, places of much labour and great responsibility, coupled with but little distinction. The condition of a decurion already described will give some notion of a *munus;* and it is a painful thing to find Tacitus implying that the *munera* were troublesome and repulsive offices at so early a period; for this is clearly his meaning : he evidently intends to compliment the Keltic population on a disposition to behave well, if their Roman task-masters will only be content not to add insult to injury. The case would be nearly parallel if we made Heki a petty constable, and then held him responsible when a New-Zealand outlaw stole a sheep or burnt out a missionary.

slavery." In this peaceable disposition Agricola saw the readiest means of producing a complete and radical subjection to Rome; and on this basis he formed his plan of rendering resistance powerless. He entirely relinquished the forcible method of his predecessors and applied himself to break down the national spirit by the spreading of foreign arts and luxuries among the people; judging rightly that the seductive allurements of ease and cultivation would ere long prove more efficient and less costly instruments than the constant and dangerous exercise of military coercion. "Those who did not deeply sound the purposes of men, called this civilization; but it was part and parcel of slavery itself [1]." Temples there were, fora, porticoes, baths and luxurious feasts, Roman manners and Roman vices, and to support them loans, usurious mortgages and ruin. But we seek in vain for any evidence of the Romanized Britons having been employed in any offices of trust or dignity, or permitted to share in the really valuable results of civilization: there is no one Briton recorded of whom we can confidently

---

[1] "Sequens hyems saluberrimis consiliis absumpta: namque, ut homines dispersi ac rudes, eoque in bella faciles, quieti et otio per voluptates adsuescerent, hortari privatim, adiuvare publice, ut templa, fora, domus exstruerent, laudando promtos et castigando segnes: ita honoris aemulatio pro necessitate erat. Iam vero principum filios liberalibus artibus erudire, et ingenia Britannorum studiis Gallorum anteferre, ut qui modo linguam Romanam abnuebant, eloquentiam concupiscerent. Inde etiam habitus nostri honor et frequens toga: paullatimque discessum ad delinimenta vitiorum, porticus et balnea et conviviorum elegantiam: idque apud imperitos humanitas vocabatur, cum pars servitutis esset." Tac. Agric. xxi. " Quaedam civitates Cogidumno regi donatae ......vetere ac iam pridem recepta populi Romani consuetudine, ut haberet instrumenta servitutis et reges." Agric. xiv.

assert that he held any position of dignity and power under the imperial rule: the historians, the geographers, nay even the novelists (who so often supply incidental notices of the utmost interest), are here consulted in vain; nor in the many inscriptions which we possess relating to Britain, can we point out one single British name. The caution of Augustus and Tiberius had from the first detected the difficulties which would attend the maintenance of the Roman authority in Britain: the feeling at home was, that it would be much more profitable to raise a small revenue in Gaul upon the British exports and imports, than to attempt to draw tribute from the island, which would require a considerable military force for its collection[1]. During their administration therefore the island was left undisturbed; and even after Claudius had relinquished this wise moderation, and engaged the Roman arms in a career of unceasing struggles, Nero felt anxious to abandon a conquest which promised little to the state and could only be maintained by the most exhausting efforts. That this

---

[1] Strabo calculated it at not less than one legion, the cost of which establishment could hardly fail to swallow up all the profit. Νυνὶ μέντοι τῶν δυναστῶν τινες τῶν αὐτόθι, πρεσβεύσεσι καὶ θεραπείαις κατασκευασάμενοι τὴν πρὸς Καίσαρα τὸν Σεβαστὸν φιλίαν, ἀναθήματά τε ἀνέθηκαν ἐν τῷ Καπετωλίῳ, καὶ οἰκείαν σχεδόν τι παρεσκεύασαν τοῖς Ῥωμαίοις ὅλην τὴν νῆσον· τέλη τε οὕτως ὑπομένουσι βαρέα τῶν τε εἰσαγομένων εἰς τὴν Κελτικὴν ἐκεῖθεν καὶ τῶν ἐξαγομένων ἐνθένδε (ταῦτα δ᾽ ἐστὶν ἐλεφάντινα ψάλια, καὶ περιαυχένια, καὶ λυγγούρια, καὶ ὑαλᾶ σκεύη, καὶ ἄλλος ῥῶπος τοιοῦτος) ὥστε μηδὲν δεῖν φρουρᾶς τῆς νήσου· τοὐλάχιστον μὲν γὰρ ἑνὸς τάγματος χρῄζοι ἂν καὶ ἱππικοῦ τινος, ὥστε καὶ φόρους ἀπάγεσθαι παρ᾽ αὐτῶν· εἰς ἴσον δὲ καθίστατο πᾶν τὸ ἀνάλωμα τῇ στρατιᾷ τοῖς προσφερομένοις χρήμασιν· ἀνάγκη γὰρ μειοῦσθαι τὰ τέλη φόρων ἐπιβαλλομένων, ἅμα δὲ καὶ κινδύνους ἀπαντᾶν τινας, βίας ἐπαγομένης. Geogr. lib. iv. cap. 5, § 3.

reasonable object was defeated in part by the vanity of the Romans themselves is probable[1]: but a more cogent reason is to be found in the interests of the noble usurers, of which we have seen so striking an example in the philosophical Seneca. Against such motives even the moderation and justice of an Agricola could avail but little: and after his recall and disgrace by Domitian, it is easy to imagine that the Roman officials here would not be too anxious by their good government to attain a dangerous popularity. Selfish and thoroughly unprincipled as the Roman government was in all its dependencies, it is little to be thought that it would manifest any unusual tenderness in this distant, unprofitable and little known possession: and I think we cannot entertain the least doubt that the condition of the British aborigines was from the first one of oppression, and was to the very last a mere downward progress from misery to misery. But such a system as this—ruinous to the conquered, and beneficial even to the conquerors only as long as they could maintain the law of force— had no inherent vitality. It rested upon a crime,— a sin which in no time or region has the providence of the Almighty blessed,—the degradation of one class on pretext of benefiting another. And as the sin, so was also the retribution. The Empire itself might have endured here, had the Romans

---

[1] " Augendi propagandique imperii neque voluntate ulla neque spe motus unquam, etiam ex Britannia deducere exercitum cogitavit: nec nisi verecundia, ne obtrectare parentis gloriae videretur, destitit." Sueton. vi. 18.

taught the Britons to be men, and reconstituted a
vigorous state upon that basis, in the hour of ruin,
when province after province was torn away from
the city, and the curse of an irresponsible will in
feeble hands was felt through every quarter of the
convulsed and distracted body. But the Britons
had been taught the arts and luxuries of cultivation
that they might be enervated. Disarmed, except
when a jealous policy called for levies to be drafted
into distant armies,—congregated into cities on the
Roman plan, that they might forget the dangerous
freedom of their forests,—attracted to share and
emulate the feasts of the victors, that they might
learn to abhor the hard but noble fare of a squalid
liberty,—supported and encouraged in internal war,
that union might not bring strength, and that the
Roman slave-dealer might not lack the objects of
his detestable traffic,—how should they develop
the manly qualities on which the greatness of a
nation rests? How should they be capable of independent being, who had only been trained as
instruments for the ambition, or victims to the
avarice, of others? To crown all, their beautiful
daughters might serve to amuse the softer hours
of their lordly masters; but there was to be no
connubium, and thus a half-caste race inevitably
arose among them, growing up with all the vices
of the victors, all the disqualifications of the vanquished. Nor under such circumstances can population follow a healthy course of development,
and a hardy race be produced to recruit the power
and increase the resources of the state. No price

is indeed too great to pay for civilization,—the root of all individual and national power; but mere cultivation may easily be purchased far too dearly. It is not worth its cost if it is obtained only by the sacrifice of all that makes life itself of value.

Such, upon the severest and most impartial examination of the facts which we possess, seems to me to have been the condition of the British population under the Romans. No otherwise can we even plausibly account for the instantaneous collapse of the imperial authority : it fell, with one vast and sudden ruin, the moment the artificial supports upon which it relied, were removed. Had Britain not been utterly exhausted by mal-administration, had there remained men to form a reserve, and resources to victual an army, the last commander who received the mandate of recall, would probably have thrown off his allegiance, and proclaimed himself a competitor for empire. Many tried the perilous game ; all lost it, because the country was incapable of furnishing the means to maintain a contest: and in the meanwhile, the Saxons proceeded to settle the question in their own way. As such a state of society supplied no materials for the support of the Roman power, so it furnished no elements of self-subsistence when that power was removed ; when that hour at length arrived, the possibility of which the overweening confidence in the fortune of the city had never condescended to contemplate. Before the eyes of all the nations, and amidst the ruins of a world falling to pieces in confusion, was this awful lesson written in gigantic characters by the hand of God—that authority which rules ill, which rules for its own selfish ends alone, is smitten with weakness, and shall not endure.   It was then that a long-delayed, but not the less awful retribution burst at last upon the enfeebled empire. Goth and Vandal, Frank and Sueve and Saxon lacerated its defenceless frontiers ; the terrible Attila—the Scourge of God—ravaged with impunity its fairest provinces ; the eternal city itself twice owed its safety to the superstition or the contemptuous mercy of the barbarians whose forefathers had trembled at its name even in the depths of their forest fastnesses ; the legions, unable to maintain themselves, and called—but called in vain—to defend a state perishing by its own corruptions, left Britain exposed to the attack of fierce and barbarous enemies that thronged on every side. Without arms and discipline, and what is far more valuable than these, the spirit of self-reliance and faith in the national existence, the Britons perished as they stood : bowing to the inevitable fate, they passed only from one class of task-masters to another, and slowly mingled with the masses of the new conquerors, or fell in ill-conducted and hopeless resistance to their progress.

The Keltic laws and monuments themselves supply conclusive evidence of the justice of these general observations. Throughout all the ages during which these populations were in immediate contact with Rome, not a single ray of Keltic na-

tionality is able to penetrate. It is only among the
mountains of the Cymri, a savage race, as little
subjugated by the Romans, as even to this moment
by ourselves, that a trace of that nationality is to
be found. There indeed, guarded by fortresses
which nature itself made impregnable, the heart-
blood of Keltic society was allowed to beat; and
the barbarians whom policy affected or luxury could
afford to despise, grew up in an independence, features of which we can still recognize in their legal
and poetical remains. The pride of the invaders
might be soothed by the erection of a few castra, or
praesidia or castella in the Welsh marches; the iti-
nerary of an emperor might finish in a commercial
city on the Atlantic; but in Wales the Romans had
hardly a foot of ground which they did not over-
shadow with the lines of their fortresses ; and to
the least instructed eye, the chain of fortified
posts which guard every foot of ground to the east
of the Severn tells of a contemplated retreat and
defence upon the base of that strong line of entrenchments.

And yet how insufficient are the laws and triads
of the Cymri in point of mere antiquity! Let us
do all honour to the praiseworthy burst of Keltic
patriotism which has revived in our day: let us
even concede that some few of the triads may carry
us back to the sixth century : yet the earliest
Cymric laws of which the slightest trace can be
discovered, are those of Hywel in the tenth. And
even, if with a courteous desire to do justice to
the subject, we admit the historical existence of the

fabulous Dynwall and fabulous Marcia[1], who has even insinuated that a single sentence of their codes survive; or that, if even if such existed, they had currency a single foot to the eastward of the Severn? Who can imagine that such laws ever had authority beyond the boundaries of a solitary sept, more fortunate than the rest, inasmuch as its record has not, like those of others, perished?

More directly to the purpose is the information we derive from Gildas, whose patriotism is beyond suspicion, and whose antiquity gives his assertions some claim to our respect[2]. He tells us that on the final departure of the Romans, including the *armatus miles, militares copiae*, and *rectores immanes* (by which last words he may possibly intend the civil officers called *rectores provinciarum*), Britain was *omnis belli usu penitus ignara*, utterly ignorant of the practice of war[3]: the island was consequently soon overrun by predatory bands of Picts and Scots whose ravages reduced the inhabitants to the extremest degree of misery: and these incursions were followed at no great interval of time by so violent a pestilence that the living were hardly numerous enough to bury the dead[4]. Then having

---

[1] We may leave those, if any such there be, who still think Geoffrey of Monmouth an authority, to cite his proofs that Dynwall Moelmwd flourished four centuries before Christ; and that the Mercian laws of Offa, quoted by Ælfred, were those of the British princess Marcia.

[2] Gildas probably wrote within two centuries of the time when the Romans left Britain. Two hundred years it is true offer a large margin for imagination, especially when it is Keltic, and employed about national history: but Gildas's report, credible in itself, is confirmed by other evidence.

[3] Gild. Hist. xiv.   [4] Ibid. xxii.

briefly noticed the savage invasion of the Saxons, and a defeat which he says they sustained at Bath, and which is supposed to have been given them by Arthur in the year 520, he thus continues: " But not even now, as before, are the cities of my country inhabited; deserted and destroyed, they lie neglected even unto this day: for civil wars continue, though foreign wars have ceased [1]." We can easily imagine that a nation in anything like the state which Gildas describes, might suffer severely from the brigandage of banditti in the interior; and on the frontier, from raids and forays of the Picts and Scots. Attacks which even the disciplined soldiery of Rome found it necessary to bridle by means of such structures as the walls of Hadrian, Antonine and Severus, must have had terror enough for a disarmed and disheartened population; nor is it in the least degree improbable that the universal disorder, the withdrawal of the legions and some new immigration of Teutonic adventurers set in motion populations, which in various parts of the country had hitherto rested quietly under the nominal control of the Roman arms. But still it is not without surprise that we notice the absence of all evidence that the Britons even attempted to maintain the cities the Romans had left them, or to make a vigorous defence behind their solid fortifications, inexpugnable one would think by rude undisciplined assailants. It is true, we are told that

[1] Gild. Hist. xxvi. Foreign wars, those of the Britons and Saxons; —Civil wars, those of the Britons among themselves; perhaps those of the Saxon kings.

in half a century England had gone entirely out of cultivation, and that the land had again become covered with forests which alone supplied food for the inhabitants [1] : but if this were really the case —and it is not entirely improbable—it can only have had the effect of driving the population into the cities. That these were to a great extent still standing in the fifth century is certain, since Gildas, in the sixth, represents them as deserted and decaying; that the Saxons found them yet entire is obvious ; in the tenth and twelfth centuries their ancient grandeur attracted the attention of observant historians [2] ; and even yet their remains

---

[1] " Nam laniant seipsos mutuo, nec pro exigui victus brevi sustentaculo miserrimorum civium latrocinando temperabant : et augebantur extraneae clades domesticis motibus, quo et huiusmodi crebris direptionibus vacuaretur omnis regio totius cibi baculo, excepto venatoriae artis solatio." Gild. xix. Half a century in an unexhausted soil is ample time to convert the most flourishing district into thick brushwood and impervious *bush*. Beech and fir, which, though said by Strabo to be not indigenous, must have been plentiful in the fifth century, do not require fifty years to become large trees : the elm, alder and even oak are well-sized growths at that age. Even thorn, maple and bramble with such a course before them are very capable of making an imposing wilderness of underwood.

[2] Æðelweard says of the Romans : " Urbes etiam atque castella, necnon pontes plateasque mirabili ingenio condiderunt, quae usque in hodiernam diem videntur." Chron. lib. i. And William of Malmesbury argues how greatly the Romans valued Britain from the vast remains of their buildings extant when he wrote. " Romani Britanniam. . . . magna dignatione coluere ; ut et in annalibus legere, et in veterum aedificiorum vestigiis est videre." Gest. Reg. lib. i. cap. 1. The following is his account of the state in which the island was left : " Ita cum tyranni nullum in agris praeter semibarbaros, nullum in urbibus praeter ventri deditos reliquissent, Britannia omni patrocinio iuvenilis vigoris viduata, omni exercitio artium exinanita, conterminarum gentium inhiationi diu obnoxia fuit. Siquidem, e vestigio, Scottorum et Pictorum incursione multi mortales caesi, villae succensae, urbes sub

testify to the astonishing skill and foresight of their builders. I cannot therefore but believe that Britain really was, as described, disarmed and disheartened, and most probably so depopulated as to be incapable of any serious defence : a condition which throws a hideous light upon the nature of the Roman rule and the practices of Roman civilized life.

It is highly improbable that any large number of the Roman towns perished during the harassing period within which the Pictish invasions fall, at all events by violent means. The marauding forays of such barbarians are not accompanied with battering trains or supported by the skilful combinations of an experienced commissariat : wandering banditti have neither the means to destroy such masonry as the Romans erected, the time to execute, nor in general the motive to form such plans of subversion. One or two cities may possibly have fallen

rutae, prorsus omnia ferro incendioque vastata ; turbati insulani, qui omnia tutiora putarent quam praelio decernere, partim pedibus salutem quaerentes fuga in montana contendunt, partim sepultis thesauris, quorum plerique in hac aetate defodiuntur, Romam ad petendas suppetias intendunt." Gest. Reg. lib. i. cap. 2, 3. But Rome had then enough to do to defend herself, for those were the days of Alaric and Attila. The emptying the island of all the fighting men by Maximus is a very ancient fiction. Archbishop Usher makes him carry over to the continent thirty thousand soldiers, and one hundred thousand *plebeii*, which have settled in Armorica. Antiq. Eccles. Brittan. pp. 107, 108. We may admit the number of the soldiery ; the Roman force, with the levies, probably amounted to as many. But who were the *plebeii*? Beda gives a similar account of the condition of Britain : "Exin Brittania, *in parte* Brittonum, omni armato milite, militaribus copiis universis, tota floridae iuventutis alacritate, spoliata, quae tyrannorum temeritate abducta nusquam ultra domum rediit, praedae tantum patuit, utpote omnis bellici usus prorsus ignara." Hist. Eccl. i. 12. cf. Gild. xiv.

under the furious storm of the Saxons, and Anderida is recorded to have done so : more than this
seems to me unlikely : Keltic populations have generally been found capable of making a very good
defence behind walls, in spite of the ridiculous
accounts which Gildas gives of their ineffectual resistance to the Picts [1]. The Roman cities perished,
it is true, but by a far slower and surer process
than that of violent disruption ; they crumbled
away under the hand of time, the ruinous consequences of neglect, and the operation of natural
causes, which science finds no difficulty in assign-
ing. We may believe that the gradual impoverish-
ment of the land had driven the population to
crowd into cities, even before the retreat of the
legions ; and that the troublous era of the tyrants [2]
completely emptied the country into the towns.
But even if we suppose that citizens remained and,
what is rather an extravagant supposition, that
they remained undisturbed in their old seats, we

[1] According to him, the Britons suffered the Picts to pull them off
the wall with long hooks. " Statuitur ad haec in edito arcis acies, segnis
ad pugnam, inhabilis ad fugam, trementibus praecordiis inepta, quae
diebus ac noctibus stupido sedili marcebat. Interea non cessant unci-
nata nudorum tela, quibus miserrimi cives de muris tracti solo allide-
bantur." Gild. xix. Beda copies this statement almost verbatim. Hist.
Eccl. i. 12.

[2] Britain was at last, even as at first, *fertilis tyrannorum:* and in the
agony which preceded her dissolution more so than ever. Aurelius
Ambrosius, if a Briton at all, is said to have been born of parents *pur-*
pura induti: and this is possible at a period when it was unknown to
contemporary writers whether a partizan were *imperator* or only *latrun-*
culus. But I suspect that there were not many Britons of rank, or
importance in any way, in the fifth century, in those parts of the island
where the Romans held sway.

shall find that there are obvious reasons why they could not maintain themselves therein. There are conditions necessary to the very existence of towns, and without which it is impossible that they should continue to endure. They must have town-lands, and they must have manufactures and trade : in other words they must either grow bread or buy it : but to this end they must have the means of safe and ready communication with country districts, or with other towns which have this. It matters not whether that communication be by the sea, as in the case of Tyre and Carthage [1]; over the desert, as at Bagdad and Aleppo ; down the river or canal, along the turnpike road, or yet more compendious railway : easy and safe communication is the condition *sine qua non*, of urban existence.

Let us apply these principles to the case before us. Even supposing that Gildas and other authors have greatly exaggerated the state of rudeness into which the country had fallen, yet we may be certain that one of the very first results of a general panic would be the obstruction of the ancient roads and established modes of communication. It is certain that this would be followed at first by a considerable desertion of the towns; since every one would anxiously strive to secure that by which he could feed himself and his family ; in preference to continuing in a place which no longer offered

[1] Athens, though shut up within her walls, felt little inconvenience from the loss of her corn-fields and vegetable gardens, while her fleet still swept the Ægean. She fell only when she lost the dominion of the sea, and with it the means of feeding her population.

any advantages beyond those of temporary defence and shelter. The retirement of the Romans, emigration of wealthy aborigines, general discomfort and disorganization of the social condition, and ever imminent terror of invasion, must soon have put a stop to those commercial and manufacturing pursuits which are the foundation of towns and livelihood of townspeople. Internal wars and merciless factions which ever haunt the closing evening of states, increased the misery of their condition ; and a frightful pestilence, by Gildas attributed to the superfluity of luxuries, but which may far more probably be accounted for by the want of food, completed the universal ruin.

Still even those who fled for refuge to the land, could find little opportunity of improving their situation : there was no room for them in an island which was thenceforward to be organized upon the Teutonic principles of association. The Saxons were an agricultural and pastoral people: they required land for their alods,—forests, marshes and commons for their cattle : they were not only dangerous rivals for the possession of those estates which, lying near the cities, were probably in the highest state of cultivation, but they had cut off all communication by extending themselves over the tracts which lay between city and city. But they required serfs also, and these might now be obtained in the greatest abundance and with the greatest security, cooped up within walls, and caught as it were in traps, where the only alternative was

the extermination of its inhabitants, is the only re-slavery or starvation[1].   Nor can we reasonably ima-gine that such spoils as could yet be wrested from the degenerate inhabitants were despised by con-querors whose principle it was that wealth was to be won at the spear's point[2].

No doubt the final triumph of the Saxons was not obtained entirely without a struggle : here and there attempts at resistance were made, but never with such success as to place any considerable ob-stacle in the way of the invaders. Spirit-broken, and reduced both in number and condition, the islanders gradually yielded to the tempest; and with some allowance for the rhetorical exaggeration of the historian, Britain did present a picture such as Beda and Gildas have left.   Stronghold after stronghold fell, less no doubt by storm (which the Saxons were in general not prepared to effect) than by blockade, or in consequence of victories in the open field.   The sack of Anderida by Aelli, and

---

[1] "Sic enim et hic agente impio victore, immo disponente iusto iu-dice, proximas quasque civitates agrosque depopulans, ab orientali mari usque ad occidentale, nullo prohibente, suum continuavit incendium, totamque prope insulae pereuntis superficiem obtexit. Ruebant aedi-ficia publica simul et privata, passim sacerdotes inter altaria trucida-bantur, praesules cum populis, sine ullo respectu honoris, ferro pariter et flammis absumebantur ; nec erat qui crudeliter interemptos sepul-turae traderet. Itaque nonnulli de miserandis reliquiis, in montibus comprehensi acervatim iugulabantur; alii fame confecti procedentes manus hostibus dabant, pro accipiendis alimentorum subsidiis aeternum subituri servitium, si tamen non continuo trucidarentur : ali transma-rinas regiones dolentes petebant; alii perstantes in patria pauperem vitam in montibus, silvis vel rupibus arduis, suspecta semper mente, agebant." Beda, Hist. Eccl. i. 15.   See also Gildas, xxiv. xxv.

[2] " Mit géru scal man geba infahan," with the spear shall men win gifts. Hiltibrants Lied.

corded instance of a fortified city falling by violent breach, and in this case so complete was the destruction that the ingenuity of modern enquirers has been severely taxed to assign the ancient site. But when we are told [1] that Cúðwulf, by defeating the Britons in 571 at Bedford, gained possession of Leighton Buzzard, Aylesbury, Bensington and Ensham, I understand it only of a wide tract of land in Bedfordshire, Buckinghamshire, and Oxfordshire, which had previously been dependent upon towns in those several districts [2], and which perished in consequence. Again when we are told [3] that six years later Cúðwine took Bath, and Cirencester and Gloucester, the statement seems to me only to imply that he cleared the land from the confines of Oxfordshire to the Severn and southward to the Avon, and so rendered it safely habitable by his Teutonic comrades and allies. Thirty years later we find Northumbria stretching westward till the fall of Cair Legion became necessary : accordingly Æðelfrið took possession of Chester. Its present condition is evidence enough that he did not level it with the ground, or in any great degree injure its fortications.

The fact has been already noticed that the Saxons

---

[1] Chron. Sax.

[2] It seems difficult to take these statements *au pied de la lettre.* How could Cúðwulf possibly have manœuvred such a force as he commanded, so as to fight at Bedford, if, as we must suppose, he marched from Hampshire or Surrey? How in fact could he ever reach Bedford, leaving Aylesbury in his rear, Bensington and Ensham on his left flank, if those places were capable of offering any kind of resistance? If they were so, we must admit that the Britons richly merited their overthrow.

[3] Chron. Sax. an. 577.

did not themselves adopt the Roman cities, and
the reason for the course they pursued has been
given. They did not want them, and would have
been greatly at a loss to know what to do with
them. The inhabitants they enslaved, or expelled
as a mere necessary precaution and preliminary to
their own peaceable occupation of the land: but
they neither took possession of the towns, nor did
they give themselves the trouble to destroy them [1].
They had not the motive, the means or perhaps the
patience to unbuild what we know to have been so
solidly constructed. Where it suited their purpose
to save the old Roman work, they used it for their
own advantage: where it did not suit their views
of convenience or policy to establish themselves on
or near the old sites, they quietly left them to decay.
There is not even a probability that they in general
took the trouble to dismantle walls or houses to
assist in the construction of their own rude dwellings [2]. Boards and rafters, much more easily ac-

[1] Müller, in his treatise on the Law of the Salic Franks, expresses the
opinion that the German conquerors always destroyed the cities which
they found. But the arguments which he adduces appear to me insufficient in themselves, and to be refuted by the obvious facts of the case.
See his Der Lex Salica alter und Heimath, p. 160. The passages in
Tacitus (Germ. xvi.) and Ammianus (xvi. 2) only prove that the Germans did not themselves like living in cities, which no one disputes.

[2] This was left for later and more civilized times; witness St. Alban's
massive abbey, one of the largest buildings in England, constructed almost entirely of bond-tiles from ancient Verulam. Caen stone would
probably have been easier got and cheaper: but labour-rents must
never be suffered to fall in arrear. It is the only rent which cannot be
fetched up. Old Verulam was first dismantled because Ealdred, a
Saxon abbot, in the tenth century found its cellars and ruined houses
offered an asylum to bad characters of either sex: so runs the story.

cessible, and to them much more serviceable, much
more easy of transport than stones and bond-tiles,
they very likely removed : the storms, the dews,
the sunshine, the unperceived and gentle action of
the elements did the rest,—for desolation marches
with giant strides, and neglect is a more potent le-
veller than military engines.　Clogged watercourses
undermined the strong foundations; decomposed
stucco or the detritus of stone and brick mingled
in the deserted chambers with drifted silt, and dust
and leaves ; accumulations of soil formed in and
around the crumbling abodes of wealth and power;
winged seeds, borne on the autumnal winds, sunk
gently on a new and vigorous bed; vegetation
yearly thickening, yearly dying, prepared the genial
deposit; roots yearly matting deepened the crust;
the very sites of cities vanished from the memory
as they had vanished from the eye; till at length
the plough went and the corn waved, as it now
waves, over the remains of palaces and temples in
which the once proud masters of the world had revelled and had worshipped.　Who shall say in how
many unsuspected quarters yet, the peasant whistles
careless and unchidden above the pomp and luxury
of imperial Rome !

Many circumstances combined to make a distinction between the cities of Britain and those of the
Gallic continent.　The latter had always been in
nearer relation than our own to Rome : they had
been at all periods permitted to enjoy a much
greater measure of municipal freedom, and were
enriched by a more extensive commercial inter-

course.   England had no city to boast of so free as
Lugdunum, none so wealthy as Massilia.   Even in
the time of the Gallic independence they had been
far more advanced in cultivation than the cities of
the Britons, and in later days their organization
was maintained by the residence of Roman bishops
and a wealthy body of clergy.   Nor on the other
hand do the Franks appear to have been very
numerous in proportion to the land, a sufficient
amount of which they could appropriate without
very seriously confining the urban populations :
many of these still retained their communications
with the sea: and, lastly, before the conquerors,
slowly advancing from Belgium through Flanders,
had spread themselves throughout the populous
and wealthy parts of Gaul, their chiefs had shown
a readiness to listen to the exhortation of Christian teachers, to enter into the communion of the
Church, and recognize its rights and laudable customs.   So that in general, whether among the
Lombards in Italy, the Goths in Aquitaine, or the
Franks in Neustria, there was but little reason for
a violent subversion, or even gradual ruin, of the
ancient cities.   In these the old subsisting elements
of civilization were still tolerated, and continued to
prevail by the force of uninterrupted usage.   More
happy than the demoralized and dispossessed inhabitants of Britain, the Roman provincials under
the Frankish and Langobardic rule were still numerous and important enough to retain their own
laws, and the most of their own customs.   Skilful
in the character of counsellors or administrators,

wealthy and enterprising as merchant-adventurers, dignified and influential as forming almost exclusively the class of the clergy, they still retained their old seats, under the protection of the conquerors: and thus, for the most part their cities survived the conquest, and continued under their ancient character, till they slowly gave way at length in the numerous civil or baronial wars of the middle ages, and the frequent insurrections of the urban populations in their struggle for communal liberties.

It is natural to imagine that when once the Saxons broke up from their peaceful settlements and commenced a career of aggression, they would direct their marches by the great lines of roads which the Roman or British authorities had maintained in every part of the island. They would thus unavoidably be brought into the neighbourhood of earlier towns, and be compelled to decide the question whether they would attack and occupy them, or whether they would turn them and proceed on their march. If the views already expressed in this chapter be correct, it is plain that no very efficient resistance was to be feared by the invaders: they could afford to neglect what in the hands of a population not degraded by the grossest misgovernment would have offered an insuperable obstacle. But the locality of a town is rarely the result of accident alone: there are generally some conveniences of position, some circumstances affecting the security, the comfort or the interests of a people, that determine the sites of their seats: and these which

must have been nearly the same for each successive race, may have determined the Saxons to remain where they had determined the Britons or
Romans first to settle.   Yet even in this case, and
admitting Saxon towns to have gradually grown up
in the neighbourhood of ancient sites, there is no
reason to suppose that either the kings or bishops
made their ordinary residences in them ; and thus
in England, a very active element was wanting to
the growth and importance of the towns, which we
find in full force in other Roman provinces.   In
truth both king and bishop adopted for the most
part the old Teutonic habit of wandering from vill
to vill, from manor to manor, and in this country
the positions of cathedrals were as little confined
to principal cities as were the positions of palaces.
This is not entirely without strangeness, especially
in the case of the earliest bishops, seeing that we
might reasonably expect Roman missionaries to
choose by preference buildings ready for their purpose, and of a nature to which they had been accustomed in Italy.   Gregory had himself recommended that the heathen temples should if possible
be hallowed to Christian uses; and even if Christian temples were entirely wanting, which we can
scarcely imagine to have been the case [1], there were
yet basilicas in Britain, even as there had been in
Rome, which might be made to serve the purposes
of churches.   Nevertheless, whatever we do read

---

[1] We know that it was not the case in Canterbury.   Queen Beorhte's
bishop and chaplain, Liuthart, had restored a ruined church, and offici-
ated there before the arrival of Augustine.

teaches us that in general, on the conversion of a
people, structures of the rudest character were
erected even upon the sites of ancient civilization:
thus in York, Eádwine caused a church of wood to
be built in haste, " citato opere," for the ceremony
of his own baptism : thus too in London, upon the
establishment of the see, a new church was built
—surely a proof that Saxon London and Roman
London could not be the same place.   It is indeed
probable that the missionaries, yet somewhat uncertain of success, and not secure of the popular
good-will, desired to fix their residences near those
of the kings, for the sake both of protection and
of influence; and thus, as the kings did not make
their settled residence in cities whether of Saxon or
Roman construction, the sees also were not established therein [1].

The town of the Saxons had however a totally
independent origin, and one susceptible of an easy
explanation.   The fortress required by a simple
agricultural people is not a massive pile with towers
and curtains, devised to resist the attacks of reck-
less soldiers, the assault of battering-trains, the sap
of skilful engineers, or the slow reduction of fa-
mine. A gentle hill crowned with a slight earthwork,
or even a stout hedge, and capacious enough to

---

[1] York supplies a striking example of the facts stated in this chapter.
In the ninth century a Danish army pressed by the Saxons took refuge
within its entrenchments. The Saxons determined to attack them,
seeing the weakness of the wall: as Asser says, "Murum frangere
instituunt, quod et fecerunt; non enim tunc adhuc illa civitas firmos
et stabilitos muros illis temporibus habebat." An. 867. It seems quite
impossible that this should refer to the Roman city of York.

receive all who require protection, suffices to repress the sudden incursions of marauding enemies, unfurnished with materials for a siege or provisions to carry on a blockade [1]. Here and there such may have been found within the villages or on the border of the Mark, tenanted perhaps by an earl or noble with his comites, and thus uniting the characters of the mansion and the fortress : around such a dwelling were congregated the numerous poor and unfree settlers, who obtained a scanty and precarious living on the chieftain's land; as well as the idlers whom his luxury, his ambition or his ostentation attracted to his vicinity. Here too may have been found the rude manufacturers whose craft supplied the wants of the castellan and his comrades; who may gradually and by slow experience have discovered that the outlying owners also could sometimes offer a market for their productions; and who, as matter of favour, could obtain permission from the lord to exercise their skill on behalf of his neighbours. Similarly round the church or the cathedral must bodies of men have gathered, glad to claim its protection, share its charities and aid in ministering to its wants [2]. I

[1] Ida built Bebbanburh, Bamborough, which was at first enclosed by a hedge, and afterwards by a wall. Chron. Sax. an. 547.

[2] The growth of a city round a monastery is well instanced in the case of Bury St. Edmund's. The following passage is cited from Domesday (371, b) in the notes to Mr. Rokewode's edition of Jocelyn de Brakelonde. "In the town where the glorious king and martyr St. Edmund lies buried, in the time of king Edward, Baldwin the abbot held for the sustenance of the monks one hundred and eighteen men; and they can sell and give their land; and under them fifty-two bordarii, from whom the abbot can have help; fifty-four freemen poor

hold it undeniable that these people could not feed themselves, and equally so that food would find its way to them; that the neighbouring farmer,— instead of confining his cultivation to the mere amount necessary for the support of his household or the discharge of the royal dues,—would on their account produce and accumulate a capital, through which he could obtain from them articles of convenience and enjoyment which he had neither the leisure nor the skill to make. In this way we may trace the growth of barter, and that most important habit of resorting to fixed spots for commercial and social purposes. In this process the lord had himself a direct and paramount interest. If he took upon himself to maintain freedom of buying and selling, to guarantee peace and security to the

enough; forty-three living upon alms; each of them has one *bordarius*. There are now two mills and two store-ponds or fish-ponds. This town was then worth ten pounds, now twenty. It has in length one leuga and a half, and in breadth as much. And it pays to the geld, when payable in the hundred, one pound. And then the issues therefrom are sixty pence towards the sustenance of the monks; but this is to be understood of the town as it was in the time of king Edward, if it so remains; for now it contains a greater circuit of land, the which was then ploughed and sown; where, one with another, there are thirty priests, deacons and clerks, twenty-eight nuns and poor brethren who pray daily for the king and all Christian people; eighty less five bakers, brewers, seamsters, fullers, shoemakers, tailors, cooks, porters, serving-men; and these all daily minister to the saint, and abbot and brethren. Besides whom there are thirteen upon the land of the reeve, who have their dwellings in the same town, and under them five *bordarii*. Now there are thirty-four persons owing military service, taking French and English together, and under them twenty-two *bordarii*. Now in the whole there are three hundred and forty-two dwellings in the demesne of the land of St. Edmund, which was arable in the time of king Edward.' Chron. Joc. de Brakelonde, pp. 148, 149 (Camden Society). Similarly Durham and other towns grew up around cathedrals.

chapmen, going and coming, he could claim in return a slight recognition of his services in the shape
of toll or custom. If the intervention of his officers
supplied an easy mode of attesting the *bona fides* of
a transaction, the parties to it would have been
unreasonable had they resisted the jurisdiction
which thus gradually grew up. So that on all accounts we may be assured that the lord encouraged
as much as possible the resort of strangers to his
domain. In the growing prosperity of his dependents, his own condition was immediately and ex-
tensively concerned. Even their number was of
importance to his revenue, for a capitation-tax,
however light, was the inevitable condition of
their reception. Their industry as manufacturers
or merchants attracted traffic to his channels.
Lastly in a military, political and social view, the
wealth, the density and the cultivation of his
burgher-population were the most active elements
of his own power, consideration and influence.
What but these rendered the Counts of Flanders
so powerful as they were throughout the middle
ages? Let it now be only considered with what
rapidity all these several circumstances must tend
to combine and to develop themselves, as the class
of free landowners diminishes in extent and influence and that of the lords increases. Concurrent
with such a change must necessarily be the extension of mutual dependence, which is only another name for traffic, and, as far as this alone is
concerned, a great advance in the material well-
being of society. It is difficult to conceive a

more hopeless state than one in which every household should exactly suffice to its own wants, and have no wants but such as itself could supply. Fortunately for human progress, it is one which all experience proves to be impossible. There is no principle of social ethics more certain than this, that in proportion as you secure to a man the command of the necessaries of life, you awaken in him the desire for those things which adorn and refine it. And all experience also teaches that the attempt of any individual to provide both classes of things for himself and within the limits of his own household, will totally fail; that time is wanting to produce any one thing in perfection; that skill can only be attained by exclusive attention to one object; and that a division of labour is indispensable if society is to be enabled to secure, at the least possible sacrifice, the greatest possible amount of comforts and conveniences. The farmer therefore raises, stores and sells the abundance of the grain which he well knows how to gain from his fields; and, relinquishing the vain attempt to make clothes or hardware, ornamental furniture and articles of household utility or elegance, nay even ploughs and harrows,—the instruments of his industry,—purchases them with his superfluity. And so in turn with his superfluity does the mechanic provide himself with bread which he lacks the land, the tools and the skill to raise. But the cultivator and the herdsman require land and space: the mechanic is most advantageously situated where numbers concentrate, where his various materials can be brought together cheaply and speedily; where there is intercourse to sharpen the mind; where there is population to assist in processes which transcend the skill or strength of the individual man. The wealth of the cultivator, that is, his superabundant bread, awakens the mechanic into existence; and the existence of the mechanic, speedily leading to the enterprise of the manufacturer, and the venture of the distributor, broker, merchant, or shopman, ultimately completes the growth of the town. It is unavoidable that the first mechanics—beyond the heroical weapon-smith on the one hand, and on the other the poor professors of such rude arts as the homestead cannot do without,—the wife that spins, the husbandman that hammers his own share and coulter—should be those who have no land; that is, in the state of society which we are now considering,—the unfree. It is a mere accident that they should gather round this lord or that, on his extensive possessions, or that they should seek shelter, food and protection in the neighbourhood of the castle or the cathedral: but where they do settle, in process of time the town must come.

The conditions under which this shall constitute itself are many and various. For a long while they will greatly depend upon the original circumstances which accompanied and regulated the settlement. When a great manufacturing and commercial system has been founded, embracing states and not petty localities only, it is clear that petty local interests will cease to be the guiding principles: but this state of things transcends the limits of a rude

and early society. The liberties of the first cities
must often have been mere favours on the part of
the lords who owned the soil, and protected the
dwellers upon it. Later these liberties were the
result of bargains between separate powers, grown
capable of measuring one another. Lastly, they
are necessities imposed by an advanced condition
of human associations, in which the wishes, objects
and desires of the individual man are hurried re-
sistlessly away by a great movement of civilization,
in which the vast attraction of the mass neutra-
lizes and defeats all minor forces. It would indeed
be but slight philosophy to suppose that any one
set of circumstances could account for the infinite
variety which the history of towns presents : though
there are features of resemblance common to them
all, yet each has its peculiar story, its peculiar conditions of progress and decay ; even as the children
of one family, which bear a near likeness to each
other, yet each has its own tale of joy and sorrow,
of smiles and tears, of triumph and failure. Yet
there is probably no single element of urban prosperity more potent than situation, or which more
pervasively modifies all other and concurrent conditions of success. Let the most careless observer
only compare London, Liverpool and Bristol, I will
not say with Munich or Madrid, but even with
Warwick, Stafford or Winchester. If royal favour
and court gaieties could have made cities great, the
latter should have flourished; for they were the
residences of the rulers of Mercia and Wessex,
the scenes of witena gemóts, of Christmas festi-

vals and Easters when the king solemnly wore his
crown; while the *ceorls* or *mangeras* of Brigstow and
Lundenwíc were only cheapening hides with the
Esterlings, warehousing the foreign wines which
were to supply the royal table, or bargaining with
the adventurer from the East for the incense which
was to accompany the high mass in the Cathedral.
But Commerce, the child of opportunity, brought
wealth; wealth, power; and power led independence in its train.

Against the manifold relations which arose during the gradual development of urban populations,
the original position of the lord could not be maintained intact.   It is indeed improbable that in any
very great number of cases, the inhabitants of an
English town long continued in the condition of
personal serfage.   The lords were too weak, the
people too strong, for a system like that of the
French nobles and their towns ever to have become settled here; nor had our city populations,
like the Gallic provincials, the habit and use of
slavery.   The first settlers on a noble's land may
have been unfree; serfs and oppressed labourers
from other estates may have been glad to take
refuge among them from taskmasters more than ordinarily severe; but in this unmixed state they did
not long remain.   There is no doubt that freemen
gradually united with them under the lord's protection or in his alliance; that strangers sojourned
among them in hope of profits from traffic; and
hence that a race gradually grew up, in whom the
original feelings of the several classes survived in a

greatly modified form. To this, though generally so difficult to trace step by step in history, we owe the difference of the urban government in different cities,—distinctions in detail more frequent than is commonly supposed, and which can be unhesitatingly referred to the earliest period of urban existence, if not in fact, at least in principle,— institutions representing in a shadowy manner the distant conditions under which they arose, and for the most part separated in the sharpest contrast from the ordinary forms prevalent upon the land.

The general outline of an urban constitution, in the earlier days of the Saxons, may have been somewhat of the following character. The freemen, either with or without the co-operation of the lord, but usually with it, formed themselves into associations or clubs, called *gylds*. These must not be confounded either on the one side with the Hanses (in Anglosaxon Hósa), i. e. trading guilds, or on the other with the guilds of crafts ("collegia opificum") of later ages. Looking to the analogy of the country-gylds or Tithings, described in detail in the ninth chapter of the First Book, we may believe that the whole free town population was distributed into such associations; but that in each town, taken altogether, they formed a compact and substantive body called in general the *Burhwaru*, and perhaps sometimes more especially the *Ingang burhware*, or " burgher's club[1]." It is also certain

[1] The "Ingang burhware" may possibly be only a selected portion of the population; as, for example, the richer inhabitants, a special burgher's club. The argument in the text is no way affected by the pre-eminence of some particular association among the rest, and an

from various expressions in the boundaries of charters, as "Burhware mǽd," "burhware mearc," and
the like, that they were in possession of real property as a corporate body, whether they had any
provision for the management of corporation revenues, we cannot tell; but we may unhesitatingly
affirm that the gylds had each its common purse,
maintained at least in part by private contributions, or what we may more familarly term *rates*
levied under their bye-laws. These gylds, whether
in their original nature religious, political, or
merely social unions, rested upon another and
solemn principle: they were sworn brotherhoods
between man and man, established and fortified
upon "áð and wed," oath and pledge; and in them
we consequently recognize the germ of those sworn
communes, *communae* or *communiae*[1], which in the

"Ingang burhware," even if a distinct thing, only proves the existence
of a "burhwaru" besides. However it is probable that there was a
general disposition to admit as many members as possible into associations whose security and influence would greatly depend upon their
numbers.

[1] The word *communa* occurs at almost every page of the 'Liber de
antiquis Legibus,' to express the whole commonalty of the city of London. Glanville himself uses *communa* and *gyldae* as equivalent terms.
"Item si quis nativus quiete per unum annum et unum diem in aliquâ
villâ privilegiatâ manserit, ita quod in eorum *communiam*, scilicet
gyldam, tanquam civis receptus fuerit, eo ipso a villenagio liberabitur."
Lib. v. cap. 5. The reader may consult with advantage Thierry's
history of the Communes in France, in his 'Lettres sur l'histoire de
France,' a work which has not received in this country an attention
at all commensurate to its merits, or comparable to that bestowed upon
his far less sound production the 'Conquête de l'Angleterre par les
Normands.' At the same time it would be an error to apply the example of the French Communes to our own or those of Flanders,
which had frequently a very different origin. See Warnkönig, Hist.
de Flandre, par Gheldolf : Bruxelles, 1835, particularly vol. ii. with its
valuable appendixes.

times of the densest seigneurial darkness offered a
noble resistance to episcopal and baronial tyranny,
and formed the nursing-cradles of popular liberty.
They were alliances offensive and defensive among
the free citizens, and in the strict theory possessed
all the royalties, privileges and rights of independent government and internal jurisdiction. How
far they could make these valid, depended entirely
upon the relative strength of the neighbouring lord,
whether he were ealdorman, king or bishop. Where
they had full power, they probably placed themselves under a geréfa of their own, duly elected
from among the members of their own body, who
thenceforth took the name of Portgeréfa or Burhgeréfa, and not only administered justice in the
burhwaremót or husting, on behalf of the whole
state, but if necessary led the city trainbands to
the field. Such a civic political constitution seems
the germ of those later liberties which we understand by the expression that a city is a county of
itself,—words once more weighty than they now
are, when privilege has become less valuable before
the face of an equal law. Nevertheless there was
once a time when it was no slight advantage for a
population to be under a portreeve or sheriff of
their own, and not to be exposed to the arbitrary
will of a noble or bishop who might claim to exercise the comitial authority within their precincts.
Such a free organization was capable of placing a
city upon terms of equality with other constituted
powers ; and hence we can easily understand the
position so frequently assumed by the inhabitants

of London. As late as the tenth century, and
under Æðelstán, a prince who had carried the influence of the crown to an extent unexampled in
any of his predecessors, we find the burghers treat-
ing as power to power with the king, under their
portreeves and bishop : engaging indeed to follow
his advice, if he have any to give which shall be
for their advantage; but nevertheless constituting
their own sworn gyldships or commune, by their
own authority, on a basis of mutual alliance and
guarantee, as to themselves seemed good [1].

The rights of such a corporation were in truth
royal. They had their own alliances and feuds;
their own jurisdiction, courts of justice and power
of execution; their own markets and tolls; their own
power of internal taxation; their personal freedom
with all its dignity and privileges. And to secure
these great blessings they had their own towers
and walls and fortified houses, bell and banner,
watch and ward, and their own armed militia.

Such too were the rights which, in more than one
European country, the brave and now forgotten
burghers of the twelfth century strove to wring
from the territorial aristocracy that hemmed them
in; when ancient tradition had not lost its vigour,
though liberty had been trampled under the armed
hoof of power. If we admire and glory in these

---

[1] This truly interesting and important document will be found in an
appendix to this Book. In fact the principle of all society during the
Saxon period is that of free association upon terms of mutual benefit,
—a noble and a grand principle, to the recognition of which our own
enlightened period is as yet but slowly returning.

true fathers of popular freedom, firm in success, unbroken by defeat,—steadfast in council, steadfast in the field, steadfast even under the seigneurial gibbet and in the seigneurial dungeon,—let us yet give our meed of thanks to those still older assertors of the dignity of man, duly honouring the gyldsmen of the tenth century, who handed down their noble inheritance to the less fortunate burgesses of the twelfth. Few pictures from the past may the eye rest upon with greater pleasure than that of a Saxon portreeve looking down from his strong gyld-hall upon the well-watched walls and gates that guard the populous market of his city [1]. The fortified castle of a warlike lord may frown upon the adjacent hill; the machicolated and crenelated walls of the cathedral close, with buttress and drawbridge, may tell of the temporal power and turbulence of the episcopate; but in the centre of the square stands the symbolic statue which marks the freedom of jurisdiction and of commerce [2]; balance in hand, to show the right of unimpeded traffic; sword in hand, to intimate the *ius gladii*, the right

[1] " Ealdredesgate et Cripelesgate, *i. e.* portas illas, observabant custodes." Inst. London. § 1. Thorpe, i. 300.

[2] In the cities of the Roman empire with Jus Italicum a statute of Marsyas or Silenus was erected in the forum. Servius ad Æneid. iv. 58. " Patrique Lyæo.—Urbibus libertatis est deus, unde etiam Marsyas, minister eius, per civitates in foro positus, libertatis indicium est; qui erecta manu testatur nihil urbi deesse." So also Æneid, iii. 20. The reader of Horace will remember the Marsyas in the Forum as symbolizing the magistrate's jurisdiction. Whether the Germanic populations derived their pillar, figure or statue from the Roman custom seems uncertain : certain however it is that the Rolandseule, the pillar or figure of Orlando, (and, as is sometimes said, of Charlemagne) denotes equally ' nihil urbi deesse."

to judge and punish, the right to guard with the weapons of men all that men hold dearest.

Again, no brighter picture than the present; when, drawing a veil over the miserable convulsions of a nearly millennial struggle, we can contemplate the mayor of the same town wandering with a satisfied eye over the space where those old walls once stood, but which now is covered with the workshop, the manufactory or the house, the reward of patient, peaceful industry.   Looking to the hill, crowned with its picturesque ruin, he sees the mansion of a noble citizen united with himself in zealous obedience to an equal law,—the peer who in the higher, or the burgess who in the lower house of parliament, consults for the weal of the community, and derives his own value and importance most from the trust reposed in him by his fellow-townsmen.   We can now contemplate this peaceful magistrate (elected because his neighbours honour his worth and the character won in a successful civic career,—not because he is a stout man-at-arms, or tried in perilous adventure,) when turning again to the ruined defences of the old cathedral, he sees streets instinct with life, where the ditch yawned of yore, walls picturesque with the ivy of uncounted ages, now carved out into quaint, prebendal houses; and while he admires the beauty of their architecture, wonders why the gates of cathedral closes should have been so strongly built, or bear so unnecessary a resemblance to fortresses. Still in the market-place stands the belfry, once dreaded by the neighbouring tyrant: but its bell calls no longer to the defence of a city, which now fears no enemy. The tenant of its dungeon is no more a turbulent man-at-arms, or well-born hostage: the dignity of the prisoner rises no higher than that of a petty market-pilferer, and the name of the belfry itself is forgotten in that of the " cage." Over the flesh- or fish-stalls perhaps yet stands the mysterious statue, inherited from earlier times, but without the meaning of the inheritance. The sword and balance are still there, but it is no longer Marsyas or Silenus or Orlando: flowing robes and bandaged eyes have transformed it into a harmless allegory; and where the warlike citizen, whose privileges were maintained with sweat and blood, erewhile looked upon it as the symbol—if not the talisman—of freedom, his modern successor, as his humour leads him, wonders whether *Justice* were ever wanting in that place, or smiles to think that her eyes are closed to the petty tricks of temporary stall-keepers.

Beyond all price indeed is this privilege of quiet inherited from our earnest forefathers, and great the debt of gratitude we owe to those whose wisdom laid, whose courage and patience maintained, its deep foundations.

Yet not in all cases can we draw so favourable a picture of the condition of an Anglosaxon town: in many of them, the unfree dwelt by the side of the freemen in their gylds, under the presidency of their lord's geréfa. And where the number of the unfree was greatly preponderant, and the power of the lord proportionally increased, we cannot but

believe that the freemen themselves were too often
deprived of their most cherished privileges. Without going quite so far as the custom in some mediæval towns, where the air itself was emphatically
said to be loaded with serfage,—where slavery was
epidemic [1],—it is but too evident that in many
places, the free settlers, while they retained their
wergyld and perhaps other personal rights, must
yet have been subject like their neighbours to servile dues and works, and compelled to attend the
lord's court. Let us only imagine a case which
was probably not uncommon ; where the lord, with
his own numerous unfree dependents, occupied
the post of the king's burggeréfa, the bishop's
or abbot's *advocatus*, and forced himself as their
geréfa upon the free. What refuge could there
be for these, if he determined to assimilate his
various jurisdictions, and subject all alike to the
convenient machinery of a centralized authority ?
They might in vain declare, as did the Northumbrians of old, that " free by birth and educated
as freemen, they scorned to submit to the ty
ranny of any duke," or count or geréfa,—but what
remedy had they, when once the defence of the
mutual guarantee was removed ? Theoretically of
course they were *cyre-lif*, that is, they could go
away and choose a lord elsewhere : but we may
fairly doubt whether they could practically do this.
New connexions are not easily formed in a state
which enjoys but little means of intercommunica-
tion : what would be sacrificed now without regret,

[1] " Die Luft macht eigen."

assumes a very disproportionate importance at a period when accumulation is slow, and acquisition difficult: nor could the expatriated chapman securely remove his valuables from one place to another; or even legally withdraw from the district where he felt himself aggrieved, without the consent of the very officer from whose unjust exactions he desired to escape. Under such circumstances of difficulty, it is to be supposed that, like the prædial freemen on the country estates, they were reduced to make the best bargain that they could; in other words, that they ultimately submitted to the customs of the place.

Moreover there may have been then, as there frequently were in the twelfth century, a plurality of lords each having *ban* or jurisdiction in particular localities [1], each having different customs to enforce, separate and conflicting interests to further, and a separate armament to dispose of. Often, as we pursue the history of mediæval cities, do we find king, count, and bishop, with perhaps one or more barons or castellans, claiming portions of the town as subject in totality or shares to their several jurisdictions, imposing heavy capitation-taxes on their own dependents, establishing hostile tolls or tariffs to the injury of internal traffic, warring with one another, from motives of pride or hate, ambition or avarice, and dragging their reluctant quotas of the city into internecine hostilities, ruinous to the interests of all. And then, if strong

---

[1] *Banlieu,* banni leuca, or according to some etymologists, banni locus.

enough, among them all subsists a corporation of
burgesses, perhaps a turbulent mob of handicrafts,
distributed in gylds or mysteries, with their deacons, common-chests, banners, and barricades :—
freer than the old serfs were, but unfree still as
regards the corporation : for the full burgesses have
made alliances with the nobles, have enrolled the
nobles as burgesses in their *Hanse*, and have become themselves an aristocracy as compared with
the democracy of the crafts.   Or the corporation of
freemen may have elected a noble *advocatus*, *Vogt*
or Patron, to be the constable of their castle, and to
lead their militia against his brethren by birth and
rivals in estate.   Or they may have coalesced with
the crafts in a bond of union for general liberation:
—unhappily too rare a case, for even those old burgesses sometimes forgot their own origin, and blun-
dered into the belief that liberty meant privilege[1].

The misery and mischief of this state of things
were not so prominent among the Anglosaxons,
because the subdivision of powers was much less
than where the principles of feudality prevailed,
and the lords and castellans were not numerous.
Nor were the guarantees which the tithings and
gyldships offered, and which were secured by the
popular election of officers, at any time entirely
devoid of their original force.   History therefore

---

[1] Slight as this sketch is, it may serve to throw some light upon the
fortunes of the Flemish and Italian cities.   Dönniges gives a most interesting and instructive account of Regensburg in very early times,
with its three fortified quarters,—the Count's (Palatium, Pfalz or Imperial *banlieu*), the Bishop's, and the Burghers' or Merchants' quarter.
Deut. Staatsr. p. 250, *seq.*

records no instances of such painful struggles as marked the progress of the continental cities, or even of our own subsequent to the Norman conquest. But we are nevertheless not without examples of towns in which the powers of government were unequally divided: where the king, the bishop and the burgesses, or the king and bishop alone, shared in the civil and criminal jurisdiction. In these the burh, properly so called, or fortification, often formed part of the city walls, or commanded the approaches to the market. In it sat the royal burhgeréfa and administered justice to the freemen; while the unfree also appeared in his court, and became gradually confounded with the free in his sócn or jurisdiction. On the other hand the bishop, through his sócnegeréfa, judged and taxed and governed his own particular dependents: unless the power of the king had been such as to unite all the inhabitants in one body under the authority of the royal thane who exercised the palatine functions. Even in the burgmót of the freemen did the royal and episcopal reeves appear as assessors, to watch over the interests of their respective employers, and add a specious, but little suspected, show of authority to the acts of the corporation.

We are still fortunately able to give some account of the growth of various English towns, which seem to have arisen after the close of the Danish wars, and the successive victories of Ælfred's children, Eádweard king of Wessex, and Æðelflǽd, duchess of Mercia.

By the treaty of peace between Ælfred and Guð-

orm, a very considerable tract of country in the
north and east of England was surrendered to the
latter and his Scandinavian allies. It is clear that
from very early periods this district had contained
important cities and fortresses, but many of these
had probably perished during the wars which expelled the Northumbrian and Mercian kings, and
finally reduced their territories under the arms of
the Danish invaders. The efforts of Ælfred had
indeed succeeded in saving his ancestral kingdoms
of Wessex and Kent, and by the articles of Wed-
mor he had become possessed of a valuable part of
Mercia, between the Severn, the Ouse, the Thames
and the Watling-street. To the east and north of
these lines however, the Scandinavians had settled,
dividing the lands, for the most part denuded of
their Saxon population, or occupied by Saxons who
had submitted to the invader and made common
cause with him, against a king of Wessex to whom
they owed no allegiance. The Eastanglians and a
portion of the Northumbrians had adopted the
kingly form of government; but there were still
independent populations in those districts following their national Jarls, and in the North was a
powerful confederation of five Burghs or cities,
which sometimes included seven, comprising in one
political unity, York, Lincoln, Leicester, Derby,
Nottingham, Stamford and Chester[1]. The power of

---

[1] The "Five Burghs" were Lincoln, Nottingham, Derby, Leicester
and Stamford. Chester and York could only be joined in a more distant alliance, but still when there was a common action among them,
they were called the "Seven Burghs."

the Scandinavians however was frittered away in internal quarrels, and those two children of Wessex, Eádweard and his lion-hearted sister, determined upon carrying into the country of the Pagans the sufferings which they had so often inflicted upon others. A career of conquest was commenced from the west and the south ; place after place was cleared of the intruding strangers, by men themselves intruders, but gifted with better fortune ; the Scandinavians were either thrown back over the Humber, or compelled to submit to Saxon arms ; and the country wrested from them was secured and bridled by a chain of fortresses erected and garrisoned by the victors.

In the course of this victorious career we learn that Æðelflǽd erected the following fortresses[1] :— In 910, the burh at Bremesbyrig : in 912, those at Scargate and Bridgnorth : in 913, those at Tamworth and Stafford : in 914, those at Eddisbury and Warwick : in 915, the fortresses of Cherbury, Warborough and Runcorn. In 917 she took the fortified town of Derby ; and in 918, Leicester : and thus, upon the submission of York, in the same year, broke up the independent organization of the " Seven Burhs."

The evidences of Eádweard's activity are yet more numerous. The following burhs or towns are recorded to have been built by him. In 913,

---

[1] These statements are taken from the Saxon Chronicle, Florence of Worcester, Simeon, and other authorities, under the years quoted. For the sake of illustration I have added in the Appendix a list of Anglosaxon towns, whose origin we have some means of tracing.

the northern burh at Hertford, between the rivers Mimera, Benefica and Lea : a burh at Witham, and soon after another on the southern bank of the Lea. In 918, he constructed burhs, or fortresses, on both sides of the river at Buckingham. In 919 he raised the burh on the southern bank of the Ouse at Bedford. In 921 he fortified Towchester with a stone wall; and in the same year he rebuilt the burhs at Huntingdon and Colchester, and built the burh at Cledemouth. The following year he built the burh on the southern bank of the river at Stamford, and repaired the castle of Nottingham. In 923 he built a fortress at Thelwall, and repaired one at Manchester. In 924 he built another castle at Nottingham, on the south bank of the Trent, over against that which stood on the northern bank, and threw a bridge between them. Lastly he went to Bakewell in Derbyshire, where he built and garrisoned a burh.

A large number of these were no doubt merely castles or fortresses, and some of them, we are told, received stipendiary garrisons, that is literally, king's troops, contradistinguished on the one hand from the free landowners who might be called upon under the *hereban* to take a turn of duty therein, and on the other from the unfree tenants, part of whose rent may have been paid in service behind the walls. But it is also certain that the shelter and protection of the castle often produced the town, and that in many cases the mere sutler's camp, formed to supply the needs of the permanent garrison, expanded into a flourishing centre of commerce, guarded by the fortress, and nourished by the military road or the beneficent river. It is also probable enough that on many of their sites towns, or at least royal vills, had previously existed, and that the population whom war and its concomitant misery had dispossessed, returned to their ancient seats, when quiet seemed likely to be permanently restored.

It cannot be doubted that those who were already congregated, or for the sake of security or gain did afterwards collect in such places, were subject to the authority of the burhgeréfa or castellan, and that thus the burh by degrees became a Palatium or Pfalz in the German sense of the word. In truth *burh* does originally denote a castle, not a town; and the latter only comes to be designated by the word, because a town could hardly be conceived without a castle,—a circumstance which favours the account here given of their origin in general.

It is certain that the free institutions which have been described in an earlier part of this chapter, could not be found in towns, the right to which must be considered to have been based on conquest, or which arose around a settlement purely military. In such places we can expect to find no mint, except as matter of grant or favour: if there was watch and ward, it was for the fortress, not the townsmen: toll there might be—but for the lord to receive: jurisdiction,—but for the lord to exercise: market,—but for the lord to profit by: armed militia,—but for the lord to command. Yet while the lord was the king, and the town was,

through its connexion with him, brought into close
union with the general state, its own condition was
probably easy, and its civic relations not otherwise
than beneficial to the republic. In such circumstances a town is only one part of a system; nor
is a royal landlord compelled to rack the tenants
of a single estate for a fitting subsistence: the
shortcoming of one is balanced by the superfluity of other sources of wealth. The owner of
the small flock is ever the closest shearer. But
even on this account, when once the towns became
seigneurial, their own state was not so happy, nor
was their relation to the country at large beneficial to the full extent. But all general observations of this character do not explain or account
for the separate cases. It is clear that everything
which we have to say upon this subject will depend
entirely upon what we may learn to have been the
character of any particular person or class of persons at any given time. The lord or Seigneur may
have ruled well; that is, he may have seen that
his own best interests were inseparably bound up
with the prosperity, the peace and the rational
freedom of his dependents; and that both he and
they would flourish most, when the mutual well-
being was guarded by a harmonious common action, founded upon the least practicable sacrifice
of individual interests. Thus he may have contented himself with the legal capitation-tax, or even
relinquished it altogether: he may have exacted
only moderate and reasonable tolls, trusting wisely
to a consequent increase of traffic, and rewarded by

a rapid advance in wealth and power: he may have given a just and generous protection in return for submission and alliance; have supported his townsmen in their public buildings, roads, wharves, canals, and other laudable undertakings. Nay, when the re-awakened spirit of self-government grew strong, and the whole mighty mass of mediæval society heaved and tossed with the working of this all-pervading leaven, we have even seen Seigneurs aiding their serf-townsmen to swear and maintain a " Communa,"—that institution so detested and savagely persecuted by popes, barons and bishops, — so hypocritically blamed, but so lukewarmly pursued by kings, who found it their gain to have the people on their side against the nobles [1].

But unhappily there is another side to the picture: the lord may have ruled ill, and often did so rule, for class-prejudices and short-sighted selfish views of personal interest drove him to courses fatal to himself and his people. When this was the case, there was but one miserable alternative, revolt, and ruin either for the lord, the city, or both,—in the

---

[1] History furnishes notable instances of what has been put here merely hypothetically. The earls of Flanders were honourably distinguished among all the European potentates by the liberal manner in which they treated their subjects. The appendix to this chapter contains some of the earliest charters which they granted to their towns, and these fully explain the wealth, power and happiness of Flanders in the twelfth and thirteenth centuries. And notwithstanding what I have said in the text, and which is justified by the conduct of the bishops in some parts of Europe, it must be admitted that the clergy were generally just and merciful lords, as far as the material well-being of their dependents was concerned. The German proverb says: " 'Tis good to live under the crozier."

former case possibly, in the latter always and certainly a grievous loss to the republic. But before this final settlement of the question, how much irreparable mischief, how much of credit and confidence shaken, of raw material wasted and destroyed, of property plundered, of security unsettled, of internecine hostility engendered, class set against class, family against family, man against man! Verily, when we contemplate the misery which such contests caused from the twelfth to the fifteenth centuries, we could almost join in the cry of the Jacquerie, and wish, with the prædial and urban serfs of old, that the race of Seigneurs had been swept from the face of the earth; did we not know that gold must be tried in the fire, that liberty could grow to a giant's stature only by passing through a giant's struggles.

But from this painful school of manhood it pleased the providence of the Almighty to save our forefathers; nor does Anglosaxon history record more than one single instance of those oppressions or of that resistance, which make up so large and wretched a portion of the history of other lands[1].

---

[1] Even under the Norman kings, the condition of this country seems to have been comparatively easy. Its darkest moments were during the wars of Stephen and Henry Plantagenet. The position then assumed by the seigneurs or castellans and its results are thus well described by an old chronicler:—" Sane inter partes diu certatum est, alternante fortuna; sed tunc quodammodo remissiores motus esse coeperunt: quod tamen Angliae non cessit in bonum, eo quod tot erant reges quot domini castellorum, habentes singuli numisma proprium et more regis subditos iudicantes. Et quia magnates terrae sic invicem excellere satagebant, eo quod nullus in alterum habebat imperium, mox inter se disceptantes rapinis et incendiis clarissimas regiones corruperunt, in

Suffering enough they had to bear, but it was at the hands of invading strangers, not of those who were born beneath the same skies and spake with the same tongue. The power of the national institutions was too general, too deeply rooted, to be shaken by the efforts of a class; nor does it appear that that class itself attempted at any time an undue exercise of authority. One ill-advised duke did indeed raise a fierce rebellion by his misgovernment; but even here national feeling was probably at work, and the Northumbrians rose less against the bad ruler, than the intrusive Westsaxon: the interests of Morcar's family were more urgent than the crimes of Tostig. Yet these may have been grave, for he was repudiated even by those of his own class, and the strong measure of his deprivation and outlawry was concurred in by his brother Harald.

In addition to the natural mode by which the authority of a lord became established in a town built on his demesne, the privileges of lordship

---

tantum quod omne robur panis fere deperiit." Walt. Hemingburh, vulgo Gisseburne, i. 74. " Castella quippe studio partium per singulas provincias surrexerant crebra; erantque in Anglia tot quodammodo reges, vel potius tyranni, quot castellorum domini, habentes singuli percussuram proprii numismatis, et potestatem dicendi subditis regio more iura." Annal. Trivet. 1147, p. 25. The contemporary Saxon chronicler gives the most frightful account of the tyrannous exactions of the castellans, and the tortures they inflicted on the defenceless cultivators. And this miserable condition of the country is only too obvious in the words with which the contemporary author of the life of Stephen commences his work. Gest. Stephani, p. 1 seq. Nor can this surprise us, when we learn that at this period not less than eleven hundred and fifteen castles had been built in England. Rog. Wendov. an. 1153, Coxe's edit. ii. 256.

were occasionally transferred from one person to another. Like other royalties, the rights of the crown over taxation, tolls or other revenues, might be made matter of grant. The following document illustrates the manner in which a portion of the seigneurial rights was thus alienated in favour of the bishop of Worcester. It is a grant made by Æðelræd and Æðelflæd to their friend Werfrið, about the end of the ninth century[1].

"To Almighty God, true Unity and holy Trinity in heaven, be praise and glory and rendering of thanks, for all his benefits bestowed upon us! Firstly for whose love, and for St. Peter's and the church at Worcester, and at the request of Werfrið the bishop, their friend, Æðelræd the ealdorman and Æðelflæd commanded the *burh* at Worcester to be built, and eke God's praise to be there upraised. And now they make known by this charter that of all the rights which appertain to their lordship, both in market and in street, within the byrig and without, they grant half to God and St. Peter and the lord of the church; that those who are in the place may be the better provided, that they may thereby in some sort easier aid the brotherhood, and that their remembrance may be the firmer kept in mind, in the place, as long as God's service is done within the minster. And Werfrið the bishop and his flock have appointed this service, before the daily one, both during their lives and after, to sing at matins, vespers and ' un-

---

[1] Cod. Dipl. No. 1075.

dernsong,' the psalm De Profundis, during their lives; and after their death, Laudate Dominum; and every Saturday, in St. Peter's church, thirty psalms, and a mass for them whether alive or dead. Æðelræd and Æðelflæd proclaim, that they have thus granted with good-will to God and St. Peter, under witness of Ælfred the king and all the *witan* in Mercia; excepting that the wain-shilling and load-penny[1] are to go to the king's hand, as they always did, from Saltwíc: but as for everything else, as *landfeoh*[2], *fihtwite, stalu, wohceápung*, and all the customs from which any fine may arise, let the lord of the church have half of it, for God's sake and St. Peter's, as it was arranged about the market and the streets; and without the market-place, let the bishop enjoy his rights, as of old our predecessors decreed and privileged. And Æðelræd and Æðelflæd did this by witness of Ælfred the king, and by witness of those witan of the Mercians whose names stand written hereafter; and in the name of God Almighty they abjure all their successors never to diminish these alms which they have granted to the church for God's love and St. Peter's!"

A valuable instrument is this, and one which supplies matter for reflection in various ways. The

---

[1] There can be no doubt that Wænscilling, written erroneously in the MS. pægnsilling, is what is meant by *statio* et *inoneratio plaustrorum* in another charter. Cod. Dipl. No. 1066. It is custom or toll upon the standing and loading of the salt-waggons. See p. 71 of this volume.

[2] *Landfeoh,* land-fee, probably a recognitory rent for land held under the burh or city. *Fihtwite,* fine for brawling in the city. *Stalu,* fine or mulct for theft. *Wohceápung,* fine for buying or selling contrary to the rules of the market.

royalties conveyed are however alone what must occupy our attention here. These are, a land-tax, paid no doubt from every hide which belonged to the jurisdiction of the burhgeréfa, and which was thus probably levied beyond the city walls, in small outlying hamlets and villages, which were not included in any territorial hundred, but did suit and service to the burhmót. And next we find the lord in possession of what we should now call the police, inflicting fines for breaches of the peace, theft, and contravention of the regulations laid down for the conduct of the market.   And this market in Worcester was not the people's, but the king's, seeing that not only are the bishop's rights, beyond its limits, carefully distinguished, but that Æ‍ðelred grants half the customs within it, that is, half the tolls and taxes, to the bishop.   In this way was an authority established concurrent with the king's or duke's, and exercised no doubt by the biscopes geréfa, as the royal right was by the cyninges or ealdormannes burhgeréfa.   Nor were its results unfavourable to the prosperity of the city: there is evidence on the contrary that in process of time, the people and their bishop came to a very good understanding, and that the Metropolis of the West grew to be a wealthy, powerful and flourishing place: so much so that, when in the year 1041 Hardacnut attempted to levy some illegal or unpopular tax, the citizens resisted, put the royal commissioners to death, and assumed so determined an attitude of rebellion, that a large force of *Húscarlas* and *Hereban*, under the principal military chiefs

of England, was found necessary to reduce them.
Florence of Worcester, who relates the occurrence
in detail[1], says that the city was burnt and plundered. From his narrative it seems not improbable that the whole outbreak was connected with
the removal of a popular bishop from his see in the
preceding year.

There is another important document of nearly
the same period as the grant to Werfrið, by which
Eádweard the son of Ælfred gave all the royal rights
of jurisdiction in Taunton to the see of Winchester[2]. He freed the land from every burthen, except
the universal three, whether they were royal, fiscal,
comitial or other secular taxations: he granted
that all the bishop's men, noble or ignoble, resiant upon the aforesaid land, should have every

[1] 1041. "Hoc anno rex Anglorum Hardecanutus suos huscarlas
misit per omnes regni sui provincias ad exigendum quod indixerat tributum. Ex quibus duos, Feader scilicet et Turstan, Wigornenses provinciales cum civibus, seditione exorta, in cuiusdam turris Wigornensis
monasterii solario, quo celandi causa confugerant, quarto Nonas Maii,
feria secunda peremerunt. Unde rex ira commotus, ob ultionem necis
illorum, Thurum Mediterraneorum, Leofricum Merciorum, Godwinum
Westsaxonum, Siwardum Northimbrorum, Ronum Magesetensium, et
caeteros totius Angliae comites, omnesque ferme suos huscarlas, cum
magno exercitu....illo misit; mandans ut omnes viros, si possint, oc-
ciderent, civitatem depraedatam incenderent, totamque provinciam de-
vastarent. Qui, die veniente secundo Iduum Novembrium, et civitatem
et provinciam devastare coeperunt, idque per quatuor dies agere non
cessaverunt: sed paucos vel e civibus vel provincialibus ceperunt aut
occiderunt, quia praecognito adventu eorum, provinciales quoque locorum fugerant. Civium vero multitudo in quandam modicam insulam,
in medio Sabrinae fluminis sitam, quae Beverege nuncupatur, confugerant; et munitione facta, tam diu se viriliter adversus suos inimicos
defenderunt, quoad pace recuperata, libere domum licuerit eis redire.
Quinta igitur die, civitate cremata, unusquisque magna cum praeda
rediit in sua; et regis statim quievit ira." Flor. Wig. 1041.

[2] Cod. Dipl. No. 1084. Anno 904.

privilege and right which was enjoyed by the king's men, resiant in his royal fiscs[1], and that all secular jurisdiction should be administered for the bishop's benefit, as fully as it was elsewhere executed for the king's. Moreover he attached for ever to Winchester the market-tolls (" villae mercimonium, quod anglice ðæs túnes cýping adpellatur "), together with every civic *census*, tax or payment. Whatsoever had heretofore been the king's was henceforth to belong to the bishop of Winchester. And that these were valuable rights, producing a considerable income, must be concluded from the large estates which bishop Denewulf and his chapter thought it advisable to give the king in exchange, and which comprised no less than sixty hides of land in several parcels. The bishops, it is to be presumed, henceforth governed Taunton by their own geréfa, to whom the grant itself must be construed to have conveyed plenary jurisdiction, that is the *blut-ban* or *ius gladii*, the supreme criminal as well as civil justice.

These examples will suffice to show in what manner seigneurial rights grew up in certain towns, and how they were exercised. From the account thus given we may also see the difference which existed between such a city and one founded originally upon a system of free gylds. These associations placed the men of London in a position to maintain their own rights both against king and bishop, and indeed it is evident from the ' Judicia

[1] Lands held immediately of the king, and administered by his own officers. People resident about the royal vills.

Civitatis' itself, that the bishops united with the citizens in the establishment of their free communa under Æðelstán. We are not very clearly informed what was the earliest mode of government in London; but, from a law of Hloðhære, it is probable that it was presided over by a royal reeve, in the seventh century. The sixteenth chapter of that prince's law provides that, when a man of Kent makes any purchase in Lundenwíc, he is to have the testimony of two or three credible men, or of the king's wícgeréfa[1]. In the ninth century, when Kent and its confederation had passed into the hands of the royal family of the Gewissas, London may possibly have vindicated some portion of independence. It had previously lain within the nominal limits at least of the Mercian authority[2]: but the victories of Ecgberht and the subsequent invasions of the Northmen destroyed the Mercian power, and in all likelihood left the city to provide for itself and its own freedom. We know that it suffered severely in those invasions, but we have slight record of any attempt to relieve it from their assaults, which might imply an interest in its welfare, on the part of any particular power. In the year 886 however, we learn, Ælfred, victorious on every point, turned his attention to London, whose fortifications he rebuilt, and which he re-annexed

[1] Leg. Hloð. § 16.   Thorpe, i. 34.

[2] Asser considers London to belong locally to Essex: he states that the Danes plundered it in 851. Vit. Ælfr. *in anno.* Berhtwulf of Mercia made an unsuccessful attempt to relieve it; so that it must be considered to have been a Mercian town at that period. Later it seems to have been left to itself, till Ælfred restored it in 886.

to Mercia, now constituted as a duchy under Æðel-red[1]. On the death of this prince, Eádweard seized Oxford and London into his own hands, and it is reasonable to suppose that he governed these cities by burhgeréfan of his own[2]. But very shortly after we find the important document, which I have already mentioned, the so-called ' Judicia Civitatis,' or Dooms of London, which proves clearly enough the elasticity of a great trading community, the readiness with which a city like London could recover its strength, and the vigour with which its mixed population could carry out their plans of self-government and independent existence. Henceforward we find the citizens for the most part under portgeréfan or portreeves of their own[3], to whom the royal writs are directed, as in counties they are to the sheriffs. We must not however suppose that at this early period constitutional rights were so perfectly settled as to be beyond the possibility of infringement. Circumstances, whose record now escapes us, may sometimes have occurred which abridged the franchise of particular cities: we cannot conclude that the Portgeréfa was always

[1] " Gesette Ælfred cyning Lundenburg......and he ðá befæste ða burg Æðerede aldormen tó healdanne." Chron. Sax. an. 886. "Eodem anno Ælfred, Angulsaxonum rex, post incendia urbium, stragesque populorum, Londoniam civitatem honorifice restauravit, et habitabilem fecit : quam generi suo Æðeredo, Merciorum comiti, commendavit servandam." Asser, Vit. Ælf. an. 886. In 880 the Danes wintered at Fulham, and may then have ruined London, if they had not done so before.

[2] Chron. Sax. an. 912.

[3] Swétman, portgeréfa. Cod. Dipl. No. 857. Ælfsige, ibid. Nos. 858, 861. Ulf. ibid. No. 872. The first mayor of London was elected probably in 1187. See Lib. de Ant. Legib. p. 1 seq.

freely elected by the citizens; for in some places
we hear of " royal " portreeves[1], from which it may
be argued either that the king had made the
appointment by his own authority, or, what is
far from improbable, that he had concurred with
the citizens in the election. Moreover the direction of writs to noblemen of high rank, even in
London, seems to imply that, on some occasions,
either the king had succeeded in seizing the liberties of the city into his own hand, or that the elected
officers were sometimes taken from the class of
powerful ministerials, having high rank and station in the royal household[2]. Where there existed
clubs or gylds of the free citizens, we may also believe that similar associations were established by
the lords and their dependents, either as a means of
balancing the popular power, or at least of sharing
in the benefits of an association which secured the
rights and position of the free men ; and thus, the
same document which reveals to us the existence of the " Ingang burhware " or " burghers'
club " of Canterbury, tells us also of the " Cnihta
gyld," or " Sodality of young nobles " in the same
city[3].

[1] " Cyninges geréfa binnan port," the king's reeve within the city.
Leg. Æðelst. iii. § 7 ; iv. § 3. Canterbury appears to have had both a
cyninges geréfa and a portgeréfa. The signatures of both these officers
are appended to the same instrument. Cod. Dipl. No. 789.

[2] The document De Institutis Londoniae, which is considered to date
from the time of Æðelræd, that is the commencement of the eleventh
century, gives the fine for burhbryce to the king; and inflicts a further bót of thirty shillings, for the benefit of the city, if the king will
grant it, "si rex hoc concedat nobis." Inst. Lond. § 4. Thorpe, i. 301.

[3] Cod. Dipl. No. 293.

Two points necessarily arrest our attention in considering the case of every city; the first of these is the internal organization, on which the freedom of the inhabitants itself depends: the second is the relation the city stands in to the public law, that is to say, its particular position toward the state. The Anglosaxon laws do contain a few provisions destined to regulate the intercourse between the townspeople and the country: for example we may refer to the laws which regulate the number of mints allowed to each city. In the tenth century it was settled that each burh might have one,— and from this very fact it is clear that "burh" was then a legal term having a fixed and definite meaning,—while a few cities were favoured with a larger number. The names of the places so distinguished are preserved, and from the regulations affecting them in this respect we may form a conclusion as to their comparative importance. Under Æðelstán we find the following arrangement:—At Canterbury were to be seven moneyers; four for the king, two for the bishop, one for the abbot. At Rochester three; two for the king, one for the bishop. At London eight. At Winchester six. At Lewes, Hampton, Wareham, Exeter and Shaftsbury, two moneyers to each town. At Hastings, Chichester, and at the other burhs, one to each town[1].

It is right to observe that all these places are in Æðelstán's peculiar kingdom, south of the Thames,

---

[1] Leg. Æðelst. i. § 14. Thorpe, i. 206.

and that his legislation takes no notice of the Mercian, Eastanglian or Northumbrian territories. But half a century later, it was ordered that no man should have a mint save the king, and that any person who wrought money without the precincts of a burh, should be liable to the penalties of forgery. The inconvenience of this was however too great, and by the 'Instituta Londoniae,' each principal city ("summus portus") was permitted to have three, and every other burh one moneyer [1].

Again, the difficulty of guarding against theft, especially in respect to cattle, the universal vice of a semi-civilized people,—led to more than one attempt to prohibit all buying and selling except in towns; and this of itself seems to imply that they were numerously distributed over the face of the country. But this provision, however beneficial to the lords of such towns, was too contrary to the general convenience, and seems to have been soon relinquished as impracticable. The enactments on the subject appear to have been abrogated almost as soon as made [2]: but the machinery by which it was proposed to carry their provisions into effect are of considerable interest. In each burh, according to its size, a certain number of the townspeople were to be elected, who might act as witnesses in every case of bargain and sale,—whom both parties on occasion would be bound to call to warranty, and whose decision or *veredictum* in the premises

[1] Leg. Æðelr. iii. § 8, 16; iv. § 5, 9. Thorpe, i. 296, 298, 301, 303.
[2] Leg. Eádw. § 1. Æðelst. i. § 12, 13; iii. § 2; v. § 10. Thorpe, i. 158, 206, 218, 240.

would be final. It was intended that in every larger burh ("summus portus") there should be thirty-three such elective officers, and in every hundred twelve or more, by whose witness every bargain was to be sanctioned, whether in a burh or a wapen-take. They were to be bound by oath to the faith-ful discharge of their duty. The law of Eádgár says: "Let every one of them, on his first election as a witness, take an oath that, neither for profit, nor fear, nor favour, will he ever deny that which he did witness, nor affirm aught but what he did see and hear. And let there be two or three such sworn men as witnesses to every bargain [1]."

The words of this law seem to imply that the appointment was to be a permanent one; and it is only natural to suppose that these "geæðedan men," *jurati,* or jurors, would become by degrees a settled urban magistracy. We see in them the germ of a municipal institution, a sworn corpo-ration, assessors in some degree of the geréfa or the later mayor [2]. They were evidently the "boni et legales homines," the "testes credibiles," "ða gódan men," "dohtigan men," and so forth, of various documents, the "Scabini," "Schoppen" or "Echevins," so familiar to us in the history of mediæval towns, which had any pretensions to freedom. They necessarily constituted · a magis-tracy, and gradually became the centre round

---

[1] Leg. Eádgár. Supp. § 3, 4, 5. Thorpe, i. 274.

[2] "Hoc anno [A.D. 1200] fuerunt xxv electi de discretioribus civi-tatis, et iurati pro consulendo civitatem una cum Maiore." Lib. de Antiq. Legib. *in anno.*

which the rights and privileges of the municipality clustered.

It is to be regretted that we have so little record of the internal organization of these municipal bodies, which must nevertheless have existed during the flourishing period of the Anglosaxon rule. Of Ealdormen in the towns, and in our modern sense, there naturally is, and could be, no trace : that dignity was very different from anything like the geréfscipe of a city, however wealthy and influential this might be: but the 'Instituta Londoniae' mention one or two subordinate officers: in these, beside the Portgeréfa, Burhgeréfa or Wícgeréfa,— names which all appear to denote one officer, the "praepositus civitatis,"—we are told of a Túngeréfa, who had a right to enquire into the payment of the customs[1]; and also of a Caccepol, catch-poll or beadle, who appears to have been the collector[2].

The archæologist, not less than the historian, has reason to lament that no remains from the past survive to teach us the local distribution of an Anglosaxon town. Yet some few hints are nevertheless supplied which enable us to form a faint image of what it may have been. It is probable that the different trades occupied different portions of the area, which portions were named from the occupations of their inhabitants. In the middle ages these several parts of the city were often fortified and served as strongholds, behind whose defences, or sallying forth from which, the crafts fought the

[1] Inst. Lond. § 3.   Thorpe, i. 301.   [2] Ibid.

battle of democracy against the burgesses or the neighbouring lords. We have evidence that streets, which afterwards did, and do yet, bear the names of particular trades or occupations, were equally so designated before the Norman conquest, in several of our English towns. It is thus only that we can account for such names as Fellmonger, Horsemonger and Fleshmonger, Shoewright and Shieldwright, Tanner and Salter Streets, and the like, which have long ceased to be exclusively tenanted by the industrious pursuers of those several avocations. Let us place a cathedral and a guildhall with its belfry in the midst of these, surround them with a circuit of walls and gates, and add to them the common names of North, South, East and West, or Northgate, Southgate, Eastgate and Westgate Streets,—here and there let us fix the market and its cross, the dwellings of the bishop and his clergy, the houses of the queen and perhaps the courtiers, of the principal administrative officers and of the leading burghers [1],—above all, let us build a stately fortress, to overawe or to defend the place, to be the residence of the geréfa and his garrison, and the site of the courts of justice,—and we shall have at least a plausible representation of a principal Anglosaxon city. Much as it is to be regretted

---

[1] The not unfrequent occurrence of such names as Kinggate, Queengate and Bishopgate Street, imply something of this kind : for we cannot suppose such names to have been assigned capriciously or without sufficient cause. It is likely that the streets so called led to the dwellings and were literally the property of the several parties : that is, that offences committed upon them belonged to the several jurisdictions.

that we now possess no ancient maps or plans which would have thrown a valuable light upon this subject, yet the guidance here and there supplied by the names of the streets themselves, and the foundations of ancient buildings yet to be traced in them, coupled with fragmentary notices in the chroniclers, do sometimes enable us to catch glimpses as it were of this history of the past. The giant march of commercial prosperity has crumbled into dust almost every trace of what our brave and good forefathers looked upon with pardonable pride : but the principles which animated them, still in a great degree regulate the lives of us their descendants ; and if we exult in the conviction that our free municipal institutions are the safeguard of some of our most cherished liberties, let us remember those to whom we owe them, and study to transmit unimpaired to our posterity an inheritance which we have derived from so remote an ancestry.

CHAPTER VIII.

THE BISHOP.

WHATEVER variety of form the heathendom of the Anglosaxons may have assumed in different districts, we are justified in asserting that a sacerdotal class existed, and that there were different grades of rank within it. We hear of priests, and of chief priests; and it is not unnatural to conclude that to the latter some pre-eminence in dignity, if not in power, was conceded over their less-distinguished colleagues. Similarly, the necessities of internal government and regulation, and the analogy of secular administration, had gradually supplied the Christian communities with a well-organized system of hierarchy, which commencing with the lower ministerial functions, passed upward through the presbyterate, the episcopal and metropolitan ordinations, and found its culminating point and completion in the patriarchates of the eastern and western churches. The paganism of the Old World, which admitted the participation of different classes in the public rites of religion, if it did not cause, could at least easily reconcile itself to, this systematic division. Our own heathen state is not well known enough to enable us to affirm as much of our forefathers; but the immediate foundation of

an episcopal church in all the newly-converted Teutonic countries, seems to show that no difficulty
existed or was apprehended as to its ready reception.   In England, as elsewhere, the introduction
of Christianity was immediately followed by the
establishment of bishops.   But it is necessary to
draw a distinction between the effects of this establishment in England and in various parts of the
continent.   As we pursue the inquiries which necessarily meet us in investigating the history of
conversion in the West, we are led to a remarkable
fact, viz. that the power of the Roman see was,
generally speaking, most substantially founded by
the efforts and energy of Teutonic prelates; while
a much more steady opposition to its triumph was
offered by the provincials who usually filled the
episcopal office in the cities of Gaul.

The apparent strangeness of this however soon
vanishes, when we consider the many grounds upon
which the Gallic churches contested the immediate
supremacy of Rome.   The archbishop of Vienne
long claimed the patriarchal authority in Gaul, upon
the same grounds as the bishops of Rome and Constantinople claimed it in those cities[1].   Many of
the provincial churches boasted an antiquity hardly
inferior to the Roman, and a foundation not less
illustrious; many had shown in persecution and
suffering a spirit of Christian perseverance and a
steadfastness of faith, which the City itself had not
exceeded in her own hour of trial.   Above all,
there continued to exist a vigorous nationality in

[1] Hüllmann, 'Origine de l'organisation de l'Eglise au Moyen Age,' p. 30.

Gaul, however oppressed and bridled by the energy
of the Frankish conquerors, especially in Neustria
or the northern portion of modern France. To this
spirit of nationality, based upon ancient descent
and long familiarity with the civilization of the
Roman empire, and fed in turn by a great amount
of material prosperity, we must refer the complete
dissolution of the Carolingian empire itself, and
the establishment of the counts of Paris as kings
in the western districts of that unwieldy body.

It is true that the Western Church did not lay
definite claim to any such total independence as
Cyprian vindicated for his African communities:
the good offices and arbitration of St. Peter's successor were sought in disputed and doubtful cases,
even if we cannot admit of positive appeals to the
Roman curia: the bishops of Burgundy, Provence
and Spain, early found that union with the oldest
and most respected church of the West offered an
important defence of orthodoxy threatened by the
Arian and semi-Arian dogma of the barbarians who
had wrested those fine provinces from the empire:
and the popes were not unwilling to encourage a
tendency which helped to realize the idea of a pre-
eminence in their church over all the Christian
communities[1]. The institution of Missi, or special
commissioners, was familiar: they adopted it, and

---

[1] This was strongly asserted by Romanus against Cyprian, and never
lost sight of by the Roman controversialists, whatever opposition it
encountered in other churches. But while Rome really was the first
city of the world, it was consonant to the analogy of the other episcopal relations that her prelate should claim the primacy. The founding
it either on St. Peter's peculiar principality, or on pretended decrees of
the Roman emperors, was quite a different thing, and an afterthought.

at a very early period we find papal vicars exercising some sort of authority in Gaul, and perhaps even in Britain.

The conversion of Clovis to the orthodox faith, instead of that which he might have learned from his Arian neighbours, was not only a source of power and importance to the Catholic bishops of Gaul, but ultimately of the greatest moment to the bishop of Rome. We must admit that under the Merwingian kings, the popes enjoyed some authority and great consideration in Gaul, though not enough to endanger the independence and freedom of the Gallican church : but under the family of Pipin they necessarily occupied a very different position. For during the earlier years of the imperial constitution, Rome was a city, and its bishop to a certain extent an officer, of the empire, and the power and influence of the popes was advanced by the Frankish emperor as best might suit his own purposes. It is assuredly not true that under Charlemagne those bishops ventured upon any of the usurpations which they succeeded in substantiating under later emperors.

During the reign of Hluduuig indeed, a pious but weak prince, they obtained various concessions which in process of time bore fruit of power[1]. It

---

[1] But, as yet, no independence. Pope Paschal in 823, being accused by the Romans of participation in various homicides, Hluduuig sent his Missi,—Adalung a presbyter and abbot, and Hunfrid duke of Rhætia (or Coire) to investigate the affair. Paschal appeared before them, and cleared himself by oath. " Qui supradictus Pontifex cum iuramento purificavit se in Lateranensi patriarchio coram supradictis legatis et populo Romano, cum episcopis 34, et presbyteris et diaconibus quinque." Thegan. Vit. Hludov. Imp. Pertz, ii. 597.

was reserved for later days to witness the triumph of Roman independence through the combination of communal with priestly tendencies. This combination first darkly arose when the nationality of Rome itself burst forth, encouraged by the vigour with which the bishop made head against the invading Saracens in Italy, supported the orthodox prelates of the southern kingdoms, Arles, Burgundy and Spain against Arian dukes and governors, and regulated the internal affairs of the city, neglected by its Frankish patricians and missi. At this time too Rome had no competitor: Africa had fallen, Constantinople had abdicated her imperial position, the cities and the sees of the East had vanished together; Rome—at least one of the oldest—was now unquestionably the most powerful of the Christian churches. She had all the prestige of the old empire, and all the support of the new one which she had helped to found upon the ruins of the old.

But this gradual advance and this commanding power could not at first have been contemplated. It is a common error to suppose that great results, which seem necessarily produced by a long series of combined causes, have from the first been prepared and foreseen. The spectator in his own struggle after a logical unity rejects the accidental and accessory facts, to fix his eyes upon the apparently essential development; and supposes everything to have been grasped together, because his intellect cannot conceive the whole variety of occurrences without so grasping them. The relations of Rome with the Franks were hardly the consequence of any deliberate or well-considered plan. The Frankish kings had been selected as patrons merely because they could afford the protection which was looked for in vain from Constantinople, or indeed any other quarter; and had Italy not been overrun by Germanic invaders of various race, from whose power there seemed no refuge, save in other and still more barbarous Germanic defenders, the Western empire might never have been restored: but when once it was so restored,—from the moment when Pope Leo and the Roman municipality agreed to place the command of the city, and the rights of the ancient Caesars, in the hands of a barbarian king,—but one capable of appreciating and securing all the advantages of his great position,—Rome itself became not only identified with the new views, but necessary to their fulfilment [1]. Had the new emperor been a Roman, or

---

[1] No sooner was Charlemagne crowned as emperor by Leo III. (Dec. 25th, 800) than he caused an oath of fidelity to be administered to all his subjects who were above the age of twelve years. See on this subject Dönniges, p. 2, etc. He thus obtained all the rights of the ancient emperors over the church and the Roman provincials, in addition to the powers as a German king, which in his vigorous hands assumed a consistency and compass unknown to his predecessors. Charlemagne required all the aid of the Pope against the great Frankish families, who might have given him a mayor of the palace, as they had given his own progenitors to the Merwingian kings. The following important passage will show in what spirit he considered the imperial authority which he had assumed. "A.D. 802. Eo anno demoravit domnus Caesar Carolus apud Aquis palatium quietus cum Francis sine hoste ; sed recordatus misericordiae suae de pauperibus, qui in regno suo erant et iustitias suas pleniter [h]abere non poterant, noluit de infra palatio pauperiores vassos suos transmittere ad iustitias faciendum propter munera, sed elegit in regno suo archiepiscopos et reliquos episcopos et abbates cum ducibus et comitibus, qui iam opus non [h]abebant super

had he selected Rome as his residence, and thus made it the local as well as real and political centre of his power, the Papacy would probably never have attained its territorial authority. But the Frankish king remained true to the habits of his people and of his predecessors, resided in peaceful times at Ingleheim or Aix la Chapelle, and spent years in wandering from one royal vill to another, or in the duties of active warfare upon the several confines of his empire; and thus the government of the eternal city practically fell into the hands of Frankish officers, dukes, missi, counts palatine, and

innocentes munera accipere, et ipsos misit per universum regnum suum, ut ecclesiis, viduis et orfanis et pauperibus, et cuncto populo iustitiam facerent. Et mense Octimbrio congregavit universalem synodum in iam nominato loco, et ibi fecit episcopis cum presbyteris seu diaconibus relegi universos canones quas sanctus synodus recepit, et decreta pontificum, et pleniter iussit eos tradi coram omnibus episcopis, presbyteris et diaconibus. Similiter in ipso synodo congregavit universos abbates et monachos qui ibi aderant, et ipsi inter se conventum faciebant, et legerunt regulam sancti patris Benedicti, et eam tradiderunt sapientes in conspectu abbatum et monachorum; et tunc iussu eius generaliter super omnes episcopos, abbates, presbyteros, diaconos seu universo clero facta est, ut unusquisque in loco suo iuxta constitutionem sanctorum patrum, sive in episcopatibus seu in monasteriis aut per universas sanctas ecclesias, ut canonici, iuxta canones viverent, et quicquid in clero aut in populo de culpis aut de negligentiis apparuerit, iuxta canonum auctoritate emendassent; et quicquid in monasteriis seu in monachis contra regulam sancti Benedicti factum fuisset, hoc ipsud iuxta ipsam regulam sancti Benedicti emendare fecissent. Sed et ipse imperator, interim quod ipsum synodum factum est, congregavit duces, comites et reliquo christiano populo cum legislatoribus, et fecit omnes leges in regno suo legi, et tradi unicuique homini legem suam, et emendare ubicumque necesse fuit, et emendatam legem scribere, et ut iudices per scriptum iudicassent, et munera non accepissent; sed omnes homines, pauperes et divites, in regno suo iustitiam habuissent." Annal. Laresham, xxv. Pertz, i. 38. In the theory of that great man, the imperial title was no empty name.

ministerials, who gradually proved no match for the enlightened skill, unwearied diplomacy and increasing power of the pontiffs, the Roman aristocratic families, and the resuscitated municipality: yet the popes had hardly succeeded in attaining to a complete independence of the German Caesars, when the son of Hugues, called Capet, expelled the last Caroling from the soil of France; though in the course of a policy long inexorably pursued, they had gone far to prepare for a dismemberment of the empire which was to be of more important consequence to the world than even that separation[1]. In 956—the year in which Eádwig, the mark of monkish calumny, came to the throne of England, the Patrician Octavian, son of Alberic of Spoleto, and through him grandson of the scandalous Marozia, caused himself to be elected Pope; and thus united the highest worldly and spiritual authorities in the city, concentrating in his own person all the rights both of the empire and the papacy [2].

Three hundred and sixty years earlier, Gregory, then bishop of Rome, had despatched a missionary adventure to this country.

[1] A.D. 987. See Dönniges, p. 197 *seq.* Thierry, Lettres sur l'Histoire de France, let. xii.

[2] Since A.D. 924 there had been in fact no Emperor of Germany, and the empire itself might seem to have been resolved anew into its original and discordant elements. From the year 904, when the elder Theodora succeeded in placing Sergius the Third upon the papal throne, the faction of that profligate woman and her daughters had completely disposed of all the dignities of the city, and the bed of the Theodoras or Marozia was the best introduction to the Chair of St. Peter.

The zeal of modern polemics has dealt more hardly with Gregory than justice demands [1]. Who shall dare to attribute to him, or to any other man, entire freedom from human error, or total absence of those faults which, for the very happiness of man, are found to chequer the most perfect of human characters? But even if we admit that he shared, to not less than the usual degree, in the weakness and selfishness of our nature, it is impossible to withhold the meed of our admiration from the man whose intellect could combine, whose prudence could direct, and whose courage could cope with, all the details of a conversion such as that of Saxon England. Let us only consider the circumstances under which he found himself placed at home, and we shall the better comprehend the power of mind which could devise and execute the vast design of a spiritual colonization, a transplantation of religion as it were from Rome the centre, to Britain the extreme, the least known, and most barbarous point of the ancient empire [2]. Temporal as well as spiritual ruler of the city, abandoned by those miserable intriguers who inherited from the emperors nothing but their title and their vices, and pressed on every side by the vigorous advance of the Langobardic arms, it was

[1] See Soames, Anglos. Church, p. 40 seq., and Latin Church during Anglos. Times, p. 12 seq., 19 seq. On the other side, Schrödl, Das erste Jahrhundert der Englischen Kirche, p. 10 seq.

[2] It must not be forgotten that the Southerns shuddered at the Saxons, as the most savage and barbarous of all the Germanic tribes. However unjust the opinion might be, it was the fashionable one at Rome.

Gregory's fate or fortune to pass in the midst of political excitement a life which he had hoped to devote to pious meditation. But he possessed a character capable of moulding itself to all the exigencies of his situation ; whether reluctantly or not, he flung himself into the gap, and comprehended, with a perfect singleness of insight, that to whom belongs the post of greatest honour, on him lies also the burthen of the greatest toil and greatest danger. By turns soldier, captain, negotiator, and priest,—now wielding the pen to instruct, now the sword to protect or to chastise,—now pouring passionate exhortations from his pulpit, now providing for the resources of his commissariat, or superintending the builders engaged on the material defences of his walls,—we see in him one of those men whom troublous times have often educated to cope with themselves, and whose names have thus justly become the very landmarks and pivots of history.

A great writer, who sometimes suffers his hostility against Christianity and its professors to outweigh the calmer judgment of the historian, has left us this graphic account of the condition of Rome at the end of the sixth century[1].

" Amidst the arms of the Lombards, and under the despotism of the Greeks, we again inquire into the fate of Rome[2], which had reached, about the

---

[1] Gibbon, Dec. and Fall, chapter 45.

[2] "The passages of the Homilies of Gregory, which represent the miserable state of the city and country, are transcribed in the Annals of Baronius, A.D. 590, No. 16 ; A.D. 595, No. 2. etc."

close of the sixth century, the lowest period of her
depression. By the removal of the seat of empire,
and the successive loss of the provinces, the sources
of public and private opulence were exhausted ; the
lofty tree, under whose shade the nations of the
earth had reposed, was deprived of its leaves and
branches, and the sapless trunk was left to wither
on the ground. The ministers of command and
the messengers of victory no longer met on the
Appian or Flaminian Way, and the hostile approach of the Lombards was often felt and continually feared. The inhabitants of a potent and
peaceful capital, who visit without an anxious
thought the garden of the adjoining country, will
faintly picture in their fancy the distress of the
Romans ; they shut or opened their gates with a
trembling hand, beheld from the walls the flames
of their houses, and heard the lamentations of their
brethren, who were coupled together like dogs, and
dragged away into distant slavery beyond the sea
and the mountains. Such incessant alarms must
annihilate the pleasures and interrupt the labours
of a rural life ; and the Campagna of Rome was
speedily reduced to the state of a dreary wilderness,
in which the land is barren, the waters are impure,
and the air is infectious. Curiosity and ambition
no longer attracted the nations to the capital of the
world : but if chance or necessity directed the steps
of a wandering stranger, he contemplated with hor-
ror the vacancy and solitude of the city, and might
be tempted to ask, Where is the senate, and where
are the people ? In a season of excessive rains,

the Tiber swelled above its banks, and rushed with irresistible violence into the valleys of the seven hills. A pestilential disease arose from the stagnation of the deluge, and so rapid was the contagion, that fourscore persons expired in an hour in the midst of a solemn procession, which implored the mercy of heaven [1]. A society in which marriage is encouraged and industry prevails, soon repairs the accidental losses of pestilence and war; but as the far greater part of the Romans was condemned to hopeless indigence and celibacy, the depopulation was constant and visible, and the gloomy enthusiasts might expect the approaching failure of the human race [2]."

It was in the midst of scenes such as these that Gregory found time to organize the mission of Augustine to Britain. In the absence of definite information, derived from his own account, or the relations of his friends and contemporaries, it is impossible to penetrate the motives which led the pontiff to this step. They have been variously interpreted by the zeal of opposing historians, who have construed them by the light of their own prejudices, in favour of the conflicting interests of their respective churches. Nor, with such insuffi-

---

[1] "The inundation and plague were reported by a deacon, whom his bishop, Gregory of Tours, had despatched to Rome for some relics. The ingenious messenger embellished his tale and the river with a great dragon and a train of little serpents." Greg. Turon. lib. x. cap. 1.

[2] "Gregory of Rome (Dialog. 1. ii. c. 15) relates a memorable prediction of St. Benedict. ' Roma a gentilibus non exterminabitur sed tempestatibus, coruscis turbinibus et terrae motu in semetipsa marcescet.' Such a prophecy melts into true history, and becomes the evidence of the fact after which it was invented."

cient means, do we attempt to reconcile their differences: human motives are rarely unmixed,
rarely all good or all evil: it is possible that there
may be some truth in all the conflicting views
which have been taken of this great act; that while
an earnest missionary spirit, and deep feeling of
responsibility, led the Pope to carry the blessings
of an orthodox Christianity to the distant and
benighted tribes of Britain, he may have contemplated—not without pardonable complacency—the
growth of a church immediately dependent upon
his see for guidance and instruction. It may be
that some lingering whispers of vanity or ambition
spoke of the increase of wealth or dignity or power
which might thus accrue to the patriarchate of the
West. Nay, who shall say that, looking round in
his despair upon Rome itself and the disject members of its once mighty empire, he may not even
have thought that England, inaccessible from its
seas, and the valour of its denizens, might one day
offer a secure refuge to the last remains of Roman
faith and nationality, and their last, but not least
noble, defender ?

To the pontiff and the statesman it was not unknown that the Britannic islands were occupied
by two populations different alike in their descent
and in their fortunes ; the elder and the weaker,
of Keltic blood; the younger and the conquering
race, an offshoot of that great Teutonic stock,
whose branches had overspread all the fairest provinces of the empire, and had now for the most
part adopted something of the civilization, together

with the profession, of Christianity. He was aware
that commercial intercourse, nay even family alliances, had already connected the Anglosaxons
with those Franks, who, in opposition to the Arian
Goths, Burgundians and Langobards, had accepted
the form of faith considered orthodox by the Roman
See [1]. The British church, he no doubt knew, in
common with others which claimed to have been
founded by the Apostles [2], still retained some rites
and practices which had either never been sanctioned or were now abandoned at Rome: but still
the communion of the churches had been maintained as well as could be expected between such
distant establishments. British bishops had appeared in the Catholic synods [3], and thè church of
the Keltic aborigines reverenced with affectionate
zeal the memory of the missionaries whom it
was the boast of Rome to have sent forth for her

---

[1] " I cannot bear to see the finest provinces of Gaul in the hands of
those heretics," cried Clovis, with all the zeal of a new convert. The
clergy blessed the pious sentiment, and the orthodox barbarian was
rewarded with a series of bloody victories, which mainly tended to
establish the predominance of the Frank over all the other elements in
Gaul.

[2] If traditions could be construed into good history, Britain was
abundantly provided with apostolical converters: Joseph of Arimathea,
Aristobulus, one of the seventy, St. Paul himself, have all had their
several supporters. Nay even St. Peter has been said to have visited
this island : Ἔπειτα [ὁ Πέτρος].... εἰς βρεττανίαν παραγίνεται· Ἔνθα
δ ἡ χειροτριβήσας καὶ πολλὰ τῶν ἀκατονομάτων ἐθνῶν εἰς τὴν τοῦ Χριστοῦ
πίστιν ἐπισπασάμενος.... ἐπιμείνας τε τοῖς ἐν βρεττανίᾳ ἡμέρας τινὰς,
καὶ πολλοὺς τῷ λόγῳ φωτίσας τῆς χάριτος, ἐκκλησίας τε συστησάμενος,
ἐπισκόπους τε καὶ πρεσβυτέρους καὶ διακόνους χειροτονήσας, δωδεκάτῳ
ἔτει τοῦ Καίσαρος αὖθις εἰς Ῥώμην παραγίνεται. Menolog. Graec. xvi.
Mart.

[3] At Arles in 314, Sardica in 347, and Rimini in 359.

2 A 2

instruction or confirmation in the faith [1]. On the other hand, it had reached the ears of the Pope, that the Germanic conquerors themselves yearned for the communication of the glad tidings of salvation ; that tolerance was found in at least one court,—and that, one of preponderating influence ; while an unhappy instinct of national hatred had induced the British Christians to withhold all attempts to spread the Gospel among their heathen neighbours [2].

[1] Not to speak of Ninian, Palladius and Patricius, we may refer to Germanus of Auxerre, who is stated to have been sent as Papal Vicar to England, to arrest the progress of Pelagianism, at the beginning of the fifth century. Schrödl asserts this in the broadest terms : " Auf Bitten der Britischen Bischöfe, und gesendet von Pabst Cölestin, besuchte der Bischof Germanus von Auxerre in der Eigenschaft eines päbstlichen Vicars, zweimal Britannien," etc. Erste Jahrh. p. 2. Lingard is somewhat less decided : he says, "Pope Celestine, at the representation of the deacon Palladius, commissioned Germanus of Auxerre to proceed in his name to Britain," etc. Ang. Church, i. 8. Both these authors refer to Prosper, in Chron. *anno* 429. " Papa Coelestinus Germanum Autisiodorensem episcopum *vice sua* mittit, et deturbatis haereticis Britannos ad Catholicam fidem dirigit." Prosper was not only a contemporary of the facts he relates, but at a later period actually became secretary to Celestine : his authority therefore is of much weight. Still it is observable that Beda, in his relation, does not attribute the mission of Germanus to the Pope. He says, that the Britons having applied for aid to the prelates of Gaul, these held a great synod, and *elected* Germanus and Lupus to proceed to England. Hist. Eccl. i. 17. Beda's account is taken from the life of Germanus written by Constantius of Lyons, about forty years after the bishop's death. He says as little of the Vicariate in his account of the second mission. However, even supposing Prosper, whose means of judgment were certainly the best, to be right, it only follows that Celestine dispatched Germanus as his Vicar, but not that the British prelates formally received him in that capacity. It does not seem to me that the passage contains any satisfactory proof that the Roman See enjoyed a *right* of appointing Vicars in England at the period in question, however it may have desired, or tried practically, to establish one.

[2] Beda, H. E. i. 22.

Under these circumstances, in the year 596, at the very moment when the ancient metropolis of the world seemed on the point of falling under the yoke of the Langobards, Augustine and his forty companions set out to carry the faith to the extreme islands of the West,—a deed as heroic as when Scipio marched for Zama, and left the terrible Carthaginian thundering at the gates of the city. Furnished with letters of introduction to facilitate their passage through Gaul, where they were to provide themselves with interpreters, and where, in the event of success, Augustine was to receive episcopal consecration, the adventurers finally landed in Kent, experienced a gentle reception from Æ☧elberht, and obtained permission to preach the faith among his subjects. In an incredibly short space of time—if we may credit the earliest historian of the Anglosaxon church—their efforts were crowned with success in the more important districts of the island; Canterbury, Rochester and London received the distinction of episcopal sees; swarms of energetic missionaries from Rome, from Gaul, from Burgundy, followed on their track, eager to aid their labours, and share their triumph; and at length the Keltic Scots themselves, emulous of their successes, or awakened, though late, to a sense of their own culpable neglect, entered vigorously upon the vacant field, and preached the Gospel to the pagan tribes north of the Humber, and in the central provinces of England. The progress of the new creed was not,

however, one unchequered triumph: in Wales and
Scotland the embittered Kelts refused not only
canonical submission to the missionary archbishop,
but even Catholic communion with his neophytes[1].
In Eastanglia, Essex, nay Kent itself, apostacy followed upon the death of the first converted kings;
while Wessex remained true to its ancient paganism; and Penda of Mercia, tolerant of Christianity
although himself no Christian, was dangerous
through his very indifference, his ambition, and the
triumphs of his arms over successive Northumbrian princes. Still the great aim of Gregory was
not to be vain, and despite kings and peoples, nay
even despite the faintheartedness and "little faith"
of the missionaries, the work of conversion did go
on and prosper, until it embraced every portion of
the island, and every part of England made at least
an outward profession of Christianity.

No sooner had the new creed found a reception

---

[1] "Scottos vero per Daganum episcopum in hanc, quam superius
memoravimus, insulam (sc. Britanniam) et Columbanum abbatem in
Gallis venientem, nihil discrepare a Brittonibus in eorum conversatione
didicimus. Nam Daganus episcopus ad nos veniens, non solum cibum
nobiscum, sed nec in eodem hospitio quo vescebamur, sumere voluit."
Such is the account Laurentius, Mellitus and Justus give in their
epistle to the Scottish prelates themselves. Beda, Hist. Eccl. ii. 4.
And the Keltic example is answered in an equally intolerant spirit
by Theodore:—"Qui ordinati sunt Scottorum vel Brittonum episcopi,
qui in Pascha vel tonsura catholicae non sunt adunati aecclesiae, iterum
a catholico episcopo manus impositione confirmentur. Licentiam quoque non habemus *eis poscentibus* chrisma vel eucharistiam dare, nisi
ante confessi fuerint velle nobiscum esse in unitate aecclesiae. Et qui
ex eorum similiter gente, vel quicumque de baptismo suo dubitaverit,
baptizetur." Cap. Theod. Thorpe, ii. 64. See also Canones Sancti
Gregorii, cap. 145. Kunstmann, Poenit. p. 141.

among the Saxons than the establishment of bishoprics followed in every separate kingdom. The intention of Gregory had been to appoint two metropolitans, each with twelve suffragan bishops, one having his cathedral in London, the other in York. But political events prevented the execution of this plan: Canterbury retained the primacy of the greater part of England, and (except during a very few years) the rule over all the bishops on this side the Humber; while York, after receiving an archbishop in the person of Paulinus, remained for nearly a century after his death under a bishop only; and never succeeded in establishing more than four suffragan sees, which were finally reduced to two. This state of things naturally sprang from the circumstances under which the conversion took place. Had England been subject to one central power, or had the relinquishment of paganism taken place simultaneously in the several districts, a general system might have been introduced whose leading features might have been in accordance with Gregory's desire; but this was not the case. The work of conversion was subject to many difficulties which could not have been appreciated at Rome. The pope had probably but sparing knowledge of the relations which existed between the Anglosaxon kingdoms, and how little concert could be expected from their scattered and hostile rulers. Nor could he have anticipated a jealous and sullen resistance on the part of the Keltic Christians, which was perhaps not altogether unprovoked by the indiscreet pretensions of Augustine [1]. But the first bishops were in fact strictly missionaries,—as much so as the bishop of New Zealand among the Maori,—heads of various bodies of voluntary adventurers, who at their own great peril bore the tidings of salvation to the pagan inhabitants of distant and separate localities. Prudence indeed dictated the propriety of commencing with those whose authority might tend to secure their own safety, and whose example would be a useful confirmation of their arguments; whose own religious convictions also were less likely to be of a settled and bigotted character than those of the villagers in the Marks. Christianity, which in its outset commenced with the lowest and poorest classes of society, and slowly widened its circuit till it embraced the highest, thus reversed the process in England, and commenced with the courts and households of the kings.

Accordingly the conversion of a king was generally followed by the establishment of a see, the princes being apparently desirous of attaching a Christian prelate to their comitatus, in place of the Pagan high-priest who had probably occupied a similar position. Considerations of personal dignity, not less than policy, may have led to this result: the lurking remains of heathen superstition may

---

[1] This seems to follow from the relation of what passed at Augustine's interview with the Welsh prelates. At the same time we should judge very unwisely were we to believe missionary jealousies confined to the nineteenth century. In the distracted state of the British the bishops were almost the only possessors of a legal authority; and it is not at all probable that they would have looked with equanimity on those who came with an open proposal of subordination, even had it been unaccompanied with circumstances wounding to their self-love.

not have been without their weight: whatever were
the cause, we find at first a bishopric co-extensive
with a kingdom [1]. But this was obviously an insufficient provision in the larger districts, as Christianity continued its triumphant course, and towards the close of the seventh century, Theodore,
the first archbishop who succeeded in uniting all
the English church under his authority, finally accomplished the division of the larger sees. From
this period till the ninth century, when the invasions of the Northmen threw all the established
institutions into confusion, the English sees appear
to have ranked in the following order [2] :—

[1] Kent is probably only an apparent exception. Rochester can
hardly have been otherwise than the capital of a subordinate kingdom.

[2] I neglect temporary changes, such as that of John at Beverley,
Birinus at Dorchester, etc., and confine myself to the settled and usual
location of the sees, and what appears to have been the established
order of their precedence. One of the most solemn ecclesiastical acts
on record, namely that of archbishop Æðelheard's synod at Clofeshoo,
in 803, by which the integrity of the see of Canterbury was restored,
was signed by the following prelates in the order in which they stand,
and which usually prevails in the rest of the charters :—

    1. Æðelheard, archbishop of Canterbury.
    2. Aldwulf, bishop of Lichfield.
    3. Werenberht, bishop of Leicester.
    4. Eádwulf, bishop of Sidnacester (Lincoln).
    5. Deneberht, bishop of Worcester.
    6. Wulfheard, bishop of Hereford.
    7. Wigberht, bishop of Sherborne.
    8. Ealhmund, bishop of Winchester.
    9. Alhheard, bishop of Elmham.
   10. Tidfrið, bishop of Dunwich.
   11. Osmund, bishop of London.
   12. Wermund, bishop of Rochester.
   13. Wihthun, bishop of Selsey.—Cod. Dipl. No. 1024.
The archbishop of York, and his suffragans, it appears, did not care
to attend a synod which restored his rival of Canterbury to a predo-
minant authority in England.

Province of Canterbury.—1. Lichfield. 2. Leicester. 3. Lincoln. 4. Worcester. 5. Hereford. 6. Sherborne. 7. Winchester. 8. Elmham. 9. Dummoc. 10. London. 11. Rochester. 12. Selsey.

Province of York.—1. Hexham. 2. Lindisfarn. 3. Whiterne.

Thus, inclusive of Canterbury and York, there were seventeen sees. At a later period some of these perished altogether, as Lindisfarn, Hexham, Whiterne and Dummoc; while others were formed, as Durham for Northumberland, Dorchester for Lincoln; and in Wessex, Ramsbury (Hræfnesbyrig, Ecclesia Corvinensis) for Wilts, Wells for Somerset, Crediton for Devonshire, and during some time, St. Petroc's or Padstow for Cornwall.

The earliest bishops among the Saxons were necessarily strangers. Romans occupied the cathedral thrones of Canterbury, Rochester and London, and for a while that of York also. Northumberland next passed for a short time under the direction of Keltic prelates,—Scots as they were then called, —who held no communion with the Romish missionaries. Felix, a Burgundian, but not an Arian, evangelized Eastanglia; Birinus, a Frank, carried the faith to Wessex. But as these men gradually left the scene of their labours, which must have been much increased ·by the difficulty of teaching populations who spoke a strange language, by means of interpreters, their Saxon pupils addressed themselves to the work with exemplary zeal and earnestness; it was very soon found that the island could supply itself with prelates fully equal to all the duties of their position; and to a mere accident was the English church indebted at the end of the seventh century for a foreign metropolitan, in the person of Theodore of Tarsus. Although we may reasonably suppose the traditions of the heathen priesthood not to have been without some weight, we must not conclude that these alone will account for the number of noble Anglosaxons whom, from the earliest period, we find devoting themselves to the service of the church, and clothed with its highest dignities. It must be admitted that nowhere else did Christianity make a deeper or more lasting impression than in England. Not only do we see the high nobles and the near relatives of kings among the bishops and archbishops, but kings themselves—warlike and fortunate kings—suddenly and voluntarily renouncing their temporal advantages, retiring into monasteries, and abdicating their crowns, that they may wander as pilgrims to the shrines of the Apostles in Rome. We find princesses and other high-born ladies devoting themselves to a life of celibacy, or separating from their husbands to preside over congregations of nuns: well descended men cannot rest till they have wandered forth to carry the tidings of redemption into distant and barbarous lands; a life of abstinence and hardship, to be crowned by a martyr's death, seems to have been hungered and thirsted after by the wealthy and the noble,—assuredly an extraordinary and an edifying spectacle among a race not at all adverse to the pomps and pleasures of worldly life, a spectacle which compels us to believe in the deep, earnest, conscientious spirit of self-sacrifice and love of truth which characterized the nation.

The complete organization of the ecclesiastical power in England appears to have been effected by Theodore, who is distinctly affirmed to have been the first prelate whose authority the whole church of the Angles consented to admit [1]. There is reason to suppose that this was not accomplished without some difficulty, for it involved the division of previously existing dioceses, and the consequent diminution of previously existing power and influence. Theodore, like Augustine, had been despatched from Rome to England, under very peculiar circumstances. After the death of Deusdedit, archbishop of Canterbury, a difficulty appears to have arisen about the election of a successor, in consequence of which the see remained for some time without an occupant [2]. At length however Oswiú of Northumberland and Ecgberht of Kent undertook to put a period to a state of affairs which must have caused grave inconveniences [3], and ac-

---

[1] " Isque primus erat in archiepiscopis, cui omnis Anglorum aecclesia manus dare consentiret." Beda, H. E. iv. 2.

[2] Deusdedit died Nov. 28th, 664. The Saxon Chronicle and Florence assign 667 as the date of Wigheard's mission, but this is hardly reconcilable with the facts of the case, and appears to be an erroneous calculation founded on the circumstance that the see was vacant three years, and that Theodore arrived only in 668. Some time must have elapsed from Wigheard's departure for Rome, until the interchange of letters between Oswiú and Pope Vitalian, and the completion of the negotiations which resulted in Theodore's appointment.

[3] The want of an archbishop to give canonical ordination to bishops, seems to have forced itself upon their notice. "Hunc antistitem ordinandum Romam miserunt ; quatenus accepto ipso gradu archiepiscopa-

cordingly they took, with the election and consent
of the church, a presbyter of the late archbishop,
named Wigheard, and sent him to Rome for consecration. It is most remarkable that we hear
nothing of any co-operation on the part of Wessex
in this step, or of the powerful king of Mercia,
Wulfhere, who had succeeded in establishing the
independence of his country against all the efforts of Oswiú himself. Shortly after his arrival
in Rome Wigheard died, and after some correspondence with the English kings, Vitalian undertook
to provide a prelate for the vacant see [1]. Various
difficulties being finally overcome, his choice fell

tus, catholicos per omnem Britanniam aecclesiis Anglorum ordinare
posset antistites." Beda, H. E. iv. 29. It was at all events a good argument, though the difficulty was one which Gaul had often arranged.

[1] This event has naturally been discussed with very different views·
The Roman Catholics construe it to imply a recognized right in the
Roman See : the Protestants look upon it as rather a piece of skilful
manœuvring on the part of the Pope. Lappenberg (i. 172) says : "The
death of Wigheard was taken advantage of by the Pope to set over the
Anglosaxon bishops a primate devoted to his views." "This opportunity was not lost upon Italian subtlety. Vitalian, then Pope, determined upon trying whether the Anglosaxons would receive an archbishop nominated by himself." Soames, Anglos. Church, p. 78. Against
this, of course, Lingard has expatiated in his Hist. and Antiq. i. 75.
He attributes the selection of Theodore to a *request* of the two kings,
and adds in a note : " That such was their request is certain. Beda
calls Theodore, who was selected by Vitalian, ' the archbishop asked
for by the king'—episcopum quem petierant a Romano pontifice (Bed.
iv. c. 1)—and ' the bishop whom the country had anxiously sought '—
doctorem veritatis, quem patria sedula quaesierat. Id. Op. Min. p. 142.
Vitalian, in his answer to the two kings, reminds them that their letter
requested him to choose a bishop for them in the case of Wigheard's
death—' secundum vestrorum scriptorum tenorem.' Bed. iii. 29. Certainly these passages must have escaped the eye of Mr. Soames, who
boldly, and without an atom of authority for his statement, ascribes
the choice of a bishop by Vitalian to Italian subtlety." Mr. Churton
in his Early English Church, p. 67, inclines also to this view, which is

upon Theodore of Tarsus, who accordingly was despatched to England with the power of an archbishop, and solemnly enthroned at Canterbury in 668.

Hitherto there had been churches in England; henceforward there was a church,—and a body of clergy existing as a central institution, in spite of the separation and frequent hostility of the states to which the clergy themselves belonged. No doubt the common rank and interests of the bishops, as well as the necessity for canonical consecration had from the first produced some sort of union among them. But from the time of Theodore we find at

again combated by Soames in his Latin Church, etc. p. 80 *seq.*; but this author with a happy skill which he sometimes manifests of not seeing disagreeable data, says nothing of the "*quem petierant* a Romano pontifice." Yet in these words lies the matter of the whole dispute. It certainly does not appear from Vitalian's letter, that any such contingency as Wigheard's death was provided for by the kings; this is in itself extremely improbable, and the assertion is an evidence of Lingard's rashness where the interests of his party are concerned. But is it not on the other hand very probable that more letters passed between the kings and the pope than are now recorded? that Vitalian announced Wigheard's death, and that the kings, conscious of the difficulty of coming to any second settlement in such a state of society as their own (especially as they were but two of four very equally poised authorities), fairly asked him to solve the problem for them? I greatly doubt the strict adherence to canonical forms of election in the seventh century; and indeed throughout the history of the English church it appears that the kings dealt very much at their own pleasure in the appointment of bishops. It could hardly be otherwise with a clergy dispersed through so many heterogeneous fractions as then made up England: and if it is now much to be desired that the appointment by the central authority should spare the church the scandal which might ensue from the canonical election of bishops—strictly construed—(for acted upon strictly it never has been under any orderly and strong government, since Christianity began), it was much more necessary then, when the clergy belonged to hostile populations. That central authority was royalty, recognized wherever found.

least the southern prelates assembling in provincial synods, under the direction of the metropolitan, to declare the faith as it was found among them, establish canons of discipline and rules of ecclesiastical government, and generally to make such arrangements as appeared likely to conduce to the well-being of the church, without regard to the severance of the kingdoms. To these synods, which though not holden twice a year in accordance with Theodore's plan, and indeed with the ancient canons of the church, were yet of frequent occurrence, the bishops repaired, accompanied by some of their co-presbyters and monks, and when the business before them was completed, returned to promulgate in their dioceses the regulations of the council, and spread among their clergy the news of what was doing in other lands for the furtherance of the Gospel.

The respectful deference paid to the Roman See was thus naturally converted into a much closer and more intimate relation. Saxon England was essentially the child of Rome; whatever obligations any of her kingdoms may have been under to the Keltic missionaries,—and I cannot persuade myself that these were at all considerable,—she certainly had entirely lost sight of them at the close of the seventh and the commencement of the eighth centuries. Her national bishops, as the Kelts and disciples of the Kelts have been unjustifiably called, had either retired in disgust, like Colman, or been deposed like Winfrið, or apostatized like Cedd. It was to Rome that her nobles and prelates wan-

dered as pilgrims; it was the interests of Rome
that her missionaries preached in Germany [1] and
Friesland ; it was to her that the archbishops elect
looked for their pall [2]—the sign of their dignity:

[1] Boniface found an ancient church even in Germany. Vit. Bonif.
Pertz, ii. 341. He rendered it a papal one. It is no doubt difficult
to imagine how it could have been originally anything else; but at
all events his efforts brought it back into subjection to the Vatican.
" D'abord les églises de la Grand Bretagne et de l'Allemagne, fon-
dées par les missionaires du pape, furent toutes rattachées et sub-
ordonnées à l'épiscopat Romain. C'est surtout Saint Boniface, le
fondateur de l'église Allemande, mort en 755, qui reserra cette union.
Ou diminua partout les metropolitains, et les simples évêques de-
vinrent plus indépendans par leurs rapports directs avec Rome."
Warnkönig, Hist. du Droit Belgique, p. 163. The spirit in which
Boniface considered his mission, which he himself calls *apostolicae
sedis legatio* (Vita, Pertz, ii. 342) is apparent from the correspondence with Pope Gregory III. in 731. "Denuo Romam nuntii eius
venerunt, sanctumque sedis Apostolicae pontificem adlocuti sunt,
eique prioris amicitiae foedera, quae misericorditer ab antecessore suo,
Sancto Bonifatio eiusque familiae conlata sunt, manifestaverunt; sed
et devotam eius in futurum humilitatis apostolicae sedi subiectionem
narraverunt, et ut familiaritati ac communioni sancti pontificis atque
totius sedis apostolicae ex hoc devote subiectus communicaret, quem-
admodum edocti erant, praecabantur. Statim ergo sedis apostolicae
Papa pacificum profert responsum, et suam sedisque apostolicae familiaritatis et amicitiae communionem tam sancto Bonifatio quam etiam
sibi subiectis condonavit, sumptoque archiepiscopatus pallio, cum muneribus diversisque sanctorum reliquiis legatos honorifice remisit ad
patriam." Pertz, ii. 345. With such provocation, the Popes would
indeed have acted an unwise part in not availing themselves of the
ready service of their Anglosaxon converts !

[2] Mr. Soames very cursorily says : "Augustine received about the
same time from Gregory the insidious compliment of a pall. He was
charged also to establish twelve suffragan bishops, and to select an
archbishop for the see of York. Over this prelate, who was likewise to
have under his jurisdiction twelve suffragan sees, he had a personal
grant of precedence. After his death the two archbishops were to
rank according to priority of consecration." Anglosax. Church, p. 55.
The language, thus most carefully selected, is intended to meet any
argument which might be derived from the despatch of the pallium, in
token of assumption of authority by the Pope. But there can be little

to the Pope her prelates appealed for redress, or
for authority : in the eighth century we find one

doubt, whatever its original character may have been, that this distinction was both intended and accepted as a mark of the archiepiscopal
dignity, and as conveying powers which without it could not be exercised. This was obviously the way Beda understood it, and Gregory
meant it to be understood. In his answers to Augustine's questions,
one of which referred to the relations which were to subsist between
the Gallican and English churches, the pope thus refuses to give his
missionary any authority over the continental bishops :—"In Galliarum
episcopis nullam tibi auctoritatem tribuimus ; quia ab antiquis praedecessorum meorum temporibus pallium Arelatensis episcopus accepit,
quem nos privare auctoritate percepta minime debemus." Hist. Eccl.
i. 27. And in a subsequent letter to Augustine the same pope writes:—
" Et quia nova Anglorum aecclesia ad omnipotentis Dei gratiam, eodem
Domino largiente et te laborante, perducta est, usum tibi pallii in ea
ad sola missarum solemnia agenda concedimus : *ita ut* per loca singula
duodecim episcopos ordines, qui tuae subiaceant ditioni, quatenus Lun-
doniensis civitatis episcopus semper in posterum a synodo propria
debeat consecrari, atque honoris pallium ab hac sancta et apostolica,
cui Deo auctore deservio, sede precipiat. Ad Eburacam vero civitatem
te volumus episcopum mittere, quem ipse iudicaveris ordinare ; ita
duntaxat, ut si eadem civitas cum finitimis locis verbum Dei receperit,
ipse quoque duodecim episcopos ordinet, et metropolitani honore per-
fruatur ; *quia* ei quoque, si vita comes fuerit, pallium tribuere Domino
favente disponimus." Beda, Hist. Eccl. i. 29. On which Beda remarks :—" Misit etiam litteras in quibus significat se ei pallium di-
rexisse, simul et insinuat qualiter episcopos in Britannia constituere
debuisset." Thirty years later, Pope Honorius sent palls both to
Paulinus of York and Honorius of Canterbury, with letters to Eádwini of Northumberland ; in these he says :—" Duo pallia utrorumque
metropolitanorum, id est Honorio et Paulino direximus, ut dum quis
eorum de hoc saeculo ad Auctorem suum fuerit arcessitus, in loco ipsius
alter episcopum ex hac nostra auctoritate debeat subrogare." Hist. Eccl.
ii. 17. The reason of this Beda tells us was the inconvenience of going
to Rome for archiepiscopal ordination :—" Ne sit necesse ad Romanam
usque civitatem per tam prolixa terrarum et maris spatia pro ordinando
archiepiscopo semper fatigari." Hist. Eccl. ii. 18. We learn from
Honorius's letter to the archbishop of Canterbury, that this alleviation
was granted at the petition of the English kings and prelates :—" Et
tam iuxta vestram petitionem, quam filiorum nostrorum regum, vobis
per praesentem nostram praeceptionem, vice beati Petri apostolorum
principis, auctoritatem tribuimus, ut quando unum ex vobis Divina ad

pope sanctioning the formation of a third archiepiscopal see, in defiance of the metropolitan of
Canterbury; and in the first year of the ninth century we find this new arrangement abrogated by
the same authority. Lastly it was England that
gave to Rome Wilfri𝛿 and Willibrord and Adel-
berht, Boniface and Willibald, Anselm and Becket
and Robert of Winchelsea.

Although these facts will not suffice to establish
that sort of dependence *de iure*, which zealous Papal partizans have asserted as the normal condi-

se iusserit gratia vocari, is qui superstes fuerit, alterum in loco defuncti
debeat episcopum ordinare.   Pro qua etiam re singula vestrae dilectioni
pallia pro eadem ordinatione celebranda direximus, ut per nostrae prae-
ceptionis auctoritatem possitis Deo placitam ordinationem efficere: quia
ut haec vobis concederemus, longa terrarum marisque intervalla, quae
inter nos ac vos obsistunt, ad haec nos condescendere coegerunt."
Hist. Eccl. ii. 18.   The archiepiscopate in York ceased after Paulinus's
expulsion till 735, when it was restored, king Eádberht having succeeded
in obtaining a pall for his brother Ecgberht.   The short chronicle appended to Beda says:—" Ecgberhtus episcopus, accepto ab apostolica
sede pallio, primus post Paulinum in archiepiscopatum confirmatus
est; ordinavitque Fridubertum et Friduwaldum episcopos." See also
Chron. Sax. an. 735; Sim. Dunelm. an. 735. The following archbishops
are recorded to have received their palls from Rome :—

Canterbury :—Tátwine. Sim. Dun. an. 733.
         Nó𝛿helm. Chron. Sax. an. 736. Flor. Wig. an. 736.
         Cú𝛿berht. Rog. Wend. i. 227. an. 740.
         Eánberht. Chron. Sax. an. 764. Flor. Wig. an. 764.
         Wulfred. Chron. Sax. an. 804. Flor. Wig. an. 804.
         Rog. Wend. an. 806.
         Ceólnó𝛿. Chron. Sax. an. 831. Flor. Wig. an. 831.
York :—Ecgberht. an. 745. Rog. Wend. i. 228.
         Alberht. Sim. Dun. an. 773.
         Eánbald I. Chron. Sax. an. 780. Flor. Wig. an. 781.
         Sim. Dun. an. 780.
         Eánbald II. Chron. Sax. an. 797. Sim. Dun. an. 797.
         Oswald. Flor. Wig. an. 973.
At some period however, which our chroniclers do not note, the

tion of the English church, they do indisputably
prove that the example, advice and authority of
the See of Rome were very highly regarded among
our forefathers.   It was impossible that it should
be otherwise ; and there is not the slightest doubt
that—despite the Keltic clergy—the Anglosaxon
church looked with affection and respect to Rome
as the source of its own being.   Respect and high
regard were paid to Rome in Gaul long before
Theodore ; but not such submission as our countrymen, less acquainted no doubt with their danger,
were zealous to pay.   Indeed, when we consider

custom arose for the archbishop not to receive, but to fetch his pallium.   The following cases are recorded :—

Canterbury :—Ælfsige.   Flor. Wig. an. 959.
           Dúnstán.   Flor. Wig. an. 960.
           Sigeríc.   Chron. Sax. an. 990.
           Ælfríc.   Chron. Sax. an. 995.
           Ælfheáh.   Chron. Sax. an. 1007.
           Æðelnóð.   Chron. Sax. an. 1022.   Flor. Wig. an.1022.
           Rodbyrht.   Chron. Sax. an. 1048.
York :—Ælfríc.   Chron. Sax. an. 1026.   Flor. Wig. an. 1026.
      Aldred.   Rog. Wend. i. 502. an. 1061.

Wendover states that when Offa determined to erect Lichfield into an
archbishopric, he sent to Pope Adrian for a pall ; and that the pall
was accordingly dispatched. Rog. Wend. i. 138.

The avarice of the Roman See was thus fed fat : but the inconveniences were felt to be so intolerable, that in 1031 Cnut made them
the subject of an especial remonstrance to the Pope.   In his letter to
the Witan of England he says, writing from Rome :—" Conquestus
sum iterum coram domino papa et mihi valde displicere causabar, quod
mei archiepiscopi in tantum angariabantur immensitate pecuniarum
quae ab eis expetebatur, dum pro pallio accipiendo, secundum morem,
apostolicam sedem peterent ; decretumque est ne ita deinceps fieret."
Epist. Cnut. apud Flor. Wig. 1031.   The question is not whether the
Roman See had a right to make a demand, but whether—usurpation or
not—it was acquiesced in and admitted by the Anglosaxon church ;
and on that point there can be no dispute.

the position of the Roman See towards the North of Europe, during the interval from the commencement of the seventh till that of the ninth century, we can scarcely escape from the conclusion that England was the great basis of papal operations, and the ποῦ στῶ from which Rome moved her world. In the ninth century a continental author calls the English "maxime familiares apostolicae sedis[1]," and in the tenth century it was unquestionably England that made the greatest progress, even if it did not take the initiative with regard to the revival of monachism and the great question of clerical celibacy. In short, throughout, the most energetic and successful missionaries of Rome were Englishmen.

But England nevertheless retained in some sense a national church. Many circumstances combined to ensure a very considerable amount of independence in this country. On the continent of Europe the prelates and clergy whom the invasions of the barbarians found established in the cities were, in fact, Roman provincials; and this character continued for a very long time to modify their relations toward the conquerors: in Britain, either Christianity was never widely and generally spread, or it retreated before the steady advance of the pagan Saxons. It is remarkable that we nowhere hear of the existence of Christian churches before Augustine, except in the territory exclusively British,

---

[1] " Unde remur, aliquos venerabiles viros aut de Britannia, id est gente Anglorum, qui maxime familiares apostolicae sedis semper existunt," etc. Gest. Abb. Fontanellens. Pertz, ii. 289.

and in the household of Æðelberht's Frankish queen, the latter an exception of little moment.

But no sooner do the first missionary prelates vanish from the scene, than we find them replaced by Saxons belonging to the noblest and most powerful families, and thus connecting the clergy with the state by that most close and intimate tie which forms the strongest and least objectionable security for both. Berhtwald, the eighth archbishop of Canterbury, was a very near relative of the Mercian king Æðelred; Aldhelm was closely connected with the royal family of Wessex; and even down to the Conquest we find the scions of the royal and noble houses occupying distinguished stations in the ministry of the Church. It is obvious how much this near and intimate association with the national aristocracy must have tended to diminish the evils of a separate institution, having some kind of dependence upon a foreign centre; and when to this it is added that the principal clergy, as ministers of state and members of the Witena gemót, had a clear and distinct interest in the maintenance of good government, and a personal share in its administration, we can easily understand why the clergy were, generally speaking, kept better within bounds in England than in other contemporaneous states[1]. Guilty of extrava-

---

[1] Every wise and powerful government has treated with deserved disregard the complaint that the "Spouse of Christ" was in bondage. In this respect our own country has generally been honourably distinguished. Boniface—himself an Englishman, papal beyond all his contemporaries—laments that no church is in greater bondage than the English,—a noble testimony to the nationality of the institution, the common sense of the people, and the vigour of the State.

gancies the clergy were here, no doubt, as elsewhere; but on the whole their position was not
unfavourable to the harmonious working of the
state; and the history of the Anglosaxons is perhaps as little deformed as any by the ambition and
power, and selfish class-interests of the clergy[1].
On the other hand it cannot be denied that in England, as in other countries, the laity are under the
greatest obligations to them, partly for rescuing
some branches of learning from total neglect, and
partly for the counterpoise which their authority
presented to the rude and forcible government of
a military aristocracy. Ridiculous as it would be
to affirm that their influence was never exerted for
mischievous purposes, or that this institution was
always free from the imperfections and evils which
belong to all human institutions, it would be still
more unworthy of the dignity of history to affect
to undervalue the services which they rendered to
society. If in the pursuit of private and corporate
advantages they occasionally seemed likely to prefer the separate to the general good, they did no
more than all bodies of men have done,—no more
than is necessary to ensure the active co-operation
of all bodies of men in any one line of conduct.
But, whatever their class-interests may from time

---

[1] Though monks are not strictly speaking the clergy, so many prelates and presbyters were bound by monastic vows in this country,
that I might be supposed to have fallen into confusion here, and forgotten the troubles of Eádwig's reign. But it will be seen hereafter
that I attach little credit to the exaggerations of the monkish authors
respecting those events, and believe their clients to have done much
less mischief than they themselves have recorded, or than their modern
antagonists have credited.

to time have led them to do, let it be remembered
that they existed as a permanent mediating authority between the rich and the poor, the strong
and the weak, and that, to their eternal honour,
they fully comprehended and performed the duties
of this most noble position.   To none but themselves would it have been permitted to stay the
strong hand of power, to mitigate the just severity of the law, to hold out a glimmering of hope
to the serf, to find a place in this world and a
provision for the destitute, whose existence the
state did not even recognize.   That the church of
Christ does not necessarily and indispensably imply that form of ministration or constitution called
Episcopal, is certain; but on the other hand let
us not listen too readily to the doctrine which represents episcopacy as inconsistent with Christianity.   To put it only on the lowest grounds, there
is great convenience in it; and though there are
no peculiar priests under the Christian dispensation, it is very useful that there should be persons
specially appointed and educated to perform functions necessary to the moral and religious training
of the people, and superior officers charged with
the inspection over those persons.   It would be
difficult for the State to ascertain the condition of
its members, as regards the most important of all
considerations,—their moral capability of obedience
to the law,—without such a body of recognized
ministers and recognized inspectors.   Accordingly
the Anglosaxon State at once recognized the
Bishops as State officers.

The circumstances under which the establishment of Christianity took place naturally threw a great power of superintendence and interference into the hands of the kings: from the beginning we find them taking a very active part both in the formation of sees, the appointment of bishops, and other public measures touching the government of the church and—within this—the relation of the clergy to the state. The privileges and rights conceded to the clerical body were granted by the king and his witan, and enjoyed under their guarantee; and down to the last moment of the Anglosaxon monarchy we find the episcopal elections or appointments to have been controlled by them. Indeed as the clergy, the people and the state may be said to have been duly represented by the Witena gemót, an episcopal election made by them appears to possess in all respects the genuine character of a canonical election: and in times when there were no parliamentary struggles to make single votes valuable, there seems no reason whatever to question that this mode was found satisfactory. The loose manner in which the early writers mention the appointment of the bishops, hardly permits us to draw any very definite conclusions; yet it would seem natural that, where the whole missionary work depended upon the goodwill of the king, the latter, with or without his council, would exercise a paramount authority in all matters of detail. Accordingly, though we do meet with instances in which the free election of prelates may be assumed, we do far more frequently find them both appointed

and displaced by the mere act of the royal will[1].
The case of Wessex in the seventh century is instructive. Ægilberht, a Frank, had succeeded Birinus, the first missionary bishop; but, from some
cause or other, he lost the favour of the king[2], who

---

[1] See on this subject Lingard, Anglos. Church, i. 89 *seq.* His view
seems upon the whole satisfactory, and conformable to truth.

[2] Lingard attributes this to the intrigues of Wini, whose simoniacal
bargain for the see of London does certainly not give a favourable impression of his character. " The influence of the stranger was secretly
undermined by the intrigues of Wini, a Saxon ecclesiastic, who possessed the advantage of conversing with the king in his native tongue."
Anglos. Church, i. 90. But Beda says nothing of this : he merely
hints that Coinwalh was disgusted with the difficulties which arose
from Ægilberht's ignorance of the Anglosaxon language. The whole
transaction is thus related in the Hist. Eccl. iii. 7 :—"Cum vero
restitutus esset in regnum Coinwalch, venit in provinciam de Hibernia
pontifex quidam nomine Agilberctus, natione quidem Gallus, sed tunc
legendarum gratia Scripturarum in Hibernia non parvo tempore demo-
ratus, coniunxitque se regi, sponte ministerium praedicandi adsumens :
cuius eruditionem atque industriam videns rex rogavit eum, accepta
ibi sede episcopali, suae genti manere pontificem. Qui precibus eius
adnuens, multis annis eidem genti sacerdotali iure praefuit. Tandem
rex, qui Saxonum tantum linguam noverat, pertaesus barbarae loquelae,
subintroduxit in provinciam alium suae linguae episcopum vocabulo
Uini, et ipsum in Gallia ordinatum : dividensque in duas parochias
provinciam, huic in civitate Venta, quae a gente Saxonum Uintancestir
appellatur, sedem episcopalem tribuit; unde offensus graviter Agilberctus, quod hoc ipso inconsulto ageret rex, rediit Galliam, et accepto
episcopatu Parisiacae civitatis, ibidem senex et plenus dierum obiit.
Non multis autem annis post abcessum eius a Britannia transactis,
pulsus est Uini ab eodem rege de episcopatu ; qui secedens ad regem
Merciorum, vocabulo Uulfheri, emit pretio ab eodem sedem Lundoniae
civitatis, eiusque episcopus usque ad vitae suae terminum mansit."
Wessex then remained for some time without a bishop, till Coinwalh
sent to Ægilberht and invited him to return. The Frankish prelate
replied that he could not desert his church and see, but recommended
his nephew Lothaire, as a proper person to be ordained to Wessex :
and he was accordingly consecrated by Theodore : " Quo honorifice a
populo et a rege suscepto, rogaverunt Theodorum, tunc archiepiscopum
Doruvernensis ecclesiae, ipsum sibi antistitem consecrari." Hist. Eccl.
iii. 27. See also Will. Malm. de Gest. Pontif. lib. ii.

proposed to divide his diocese, which was too large in fact for one prelate, and to appoint Wini, a native Westsaxon, to the second see. Ægilberht then withdrew from England in disgust, and the king committed the undivided bishopric to Wini : but on some subsequent misunderstanding, this bishop was expelled from Wessex, and afterwards *purchased* the see of London from Wulfhari, king of the Mercians. Coinwalh then applied for and obtained another bishop from Gaul in the person of Liuthari or Lothaire, Ægilberht's nephew. Equally great irregularities seem to have been admitted in respect to the Northumbrian sees in the time of Wilfrið; and indeed throughout the Anglosaxon history it appears that the ruling powers, that is the king and the witan, did in fact succeed in retaining the nomination of the bishops in their own hands[1]. I have already mentioned instances of episcopal nominations by the witena gemót[2], and called attention to the significant fact of so many royal chaplains promoted to sees[3]. It is difficult no doubt to withstand a royal recommendation, and though in the case of the Anglosaxon prelates this does not always seem to have ensured the canonical virtues, it perhaps very sufficiently supplied their want. After the appointment or election had thus

[1] Throughout every difficulty the English kings never lost sight of this part of their prerogative, often as they were deceived in its exercise. A writer of the twelfth century very justly calls it " the custom of the realm." " Cum autem *iuxta regni consuetudinem*, in electionibus faciendis potissimas et potentissimas habeat partes," etc. Pet. Blesensis, Ep. de Henrico II. An. Trivet. 1154. p. 35.

[2] Page 221 of this volume.   [3] Page 115 of this volume.

been made, it was usual for the bishop elect to make his profession of faith to his metropolitan; then to receive episcopal consecration from him, assisted by such of his suffragans as he thought fit. He then most likely received seizin of the temporalities in the usual way by royal writ. The following is the instrument issued in 1060, for the temporalities of the see of Hereford, on the appointment of Walther, queen Eádgyfu's Lorraine chaplain. " Eadwardus rex saluto Haroldum comitem et Osbearnum, et omnes meos ministros in Herefordensi comitatu amicabiliter. Et ego notifico vobis quod ego concessi Waltero episcopo istum episcopatum hic vobiscum, et omnia universa illa quae ad ipsum cum iusticia pertinent infra portum et extra, cum saca et cum socna, tam plene et tam plane sicut ipsum aliquis episcopus ante ipsum prius habuit in omnibus rebus. Et si illic sit aliqua terra extra dimissa quae illuc intus cum iustitia pertinet, ego volo quod ipsa reveniat in ipsum episcopatum, vel ille homo ipsam dimittat eidem in suo praetio, si quis ipsam cum eo invenire possit. Et ego nolo ullum hominem licentiare quod ei de manibus rapiat aliquam suam rem quam ipse iuste habere debet, et ego ei sic concessi [1]."

As this is obviously, indeed professedly, a Latin translation, I subjoin copies of the similar writs issued on the occasion of Gisa's appointment to the see of Wells [2].

[1] Cod. Dipl. No. 833.
[2] Gisa was a chaplain of the king, and also of Lotharingen or Lorraine.

" ✠ Eadward king grét Harold erl and Aylnóð abbot and Godwine schýre réuen and alle míne þeynes on Sumerseten frendlíche; and ich kýðe eów ðæt ich habbe geunnen Gisan mínan préste ðes biscopríche hér mid eów and alre ðare þinge ðás ðe ðær mid richte tógebyrað, on wóde and on felde, mid saca and mid sócna, binnon porte and bútan, swó ful and swó forð swó Duduc biscop oð ány biscop hit firmest him tóforen hauede on ællem þingan. And gif hér áni land sý out of ðám biscopríche gedon, ich wille ðæt hit cume in ongeæn óðer ðæt man hit ofgo on hire gemóð swó man wið him bet finde mage. And ich bidde eóu allen ðæt ge him fulstan tó dríuan Godes gerichte lóck huer hit neod sý and he eówwer fultumes biðurfe. And ich nelle nánne man geðefien ðæt him úram honde teó ánige ðáre þinge ðás ðe ich him unnen habben[1]."

" ✠ Eadward king grét Harold erl, and Aylnóð abbot, and Godwine and ealle míne þeines on Sumerseten frendlíche; ich queðe eóu ðæt ich wille ðæt Gyse biscop beó ðisses biscopríches wrðe heerinne mid eóu. And álch ðáre þinge ðe ðás ðár mid richte tógebyrað binnan porte and bútan, mid saca and mid sócna, swó uol and swó uorð swó hit éni biscop

---

[1] The same in Latin. "✠ Eádwardus rex Haroldo comiti, Ailnodo abbati, Godwino vicecomiti, et omnibus ballivis suis Somersetae, salutem! Sciatis nos dedisse Gisoni presbytero nostro episcopatum hunc apud vos cum omnibus pertinentiis, in bosco et plano, et saca et socna, in villis et extra, ita plene et libere in omnibus sicut episcopus Dudocus aut aliqui praedecessorum suorum habuerunt; et si quid inde contra iustitiam fuerit sublatum, volumus quod revocetur, vel quod aliter ei satisfaciat. Rogamus etiam vos ut auxiliari eidem velitis ad Christianitatem sustinandam si necesse habuerit, nolumus autem ut ullus hominum ei auferat aliquid eorum quae ei contulimus." Cod. Dipl. No. 835.

him tóuoren formest haueð on ealle þing. And ich
bidde eóu alle ðæt ge him beón on fultome Cristen-
dóm tó sprekene, lóc whar hit þarf sẏ and eówer
fultumes beðurfe eal swó ich getrowwen tó eów
habben ðat ge him on fultume beón willen. And
gif what sẏ mid unlage out of ðán biscopríche
geydón s.ẏ hit londe óðer an oððer þinge ðár fulstan
him uor mínan luuen ðæt hit in ongeyn cume swó
swó ge for Gode witen ðat hit richt sẏ. God eú
ealle gehealde [1]."

The metropolitans themselves were to receive
consecration from one another, in order that the
expense and trouble of going to Rome might be
avoided: but during the abeyance of the archiepiscopate of York, the prelate elect of Canterbury
appears to have been sometimes consecrated in
Gaul, sometimes by a conclave of suffragan bishops
at home: thus in 731 Tátwine was consecrated at
Canterbury by Daniel, Ingwald, Aldwine and Ald-
wulf, the respective bishops of Winchester, London, Worcester and Rochester[2]; and Pope Gregory the Third either made or acknowledged this

---

[1] The same in Latin. "✠ Eádwardus rex Haroldo comiti, Ailnodo
abbati, Godwino, et omnibus ballivis suis Sumersetac, salutem! Signi-
ficamus vobis nos velle quod episcopus Giso episcopatum apud vos pos-
sideat cum omnibus dictum episcopatum in villis et extra de iure con-
tingentibus, cum saca et socna, adeo plene et libere per omnia sicut ullus
episcoporum praedecessorum suorum unquam habebat. Rogamus
etiam vos ut coadiutores ipsius esse velitis ad fidem praedicandam et
Christianitatem sustinendam pro loco et tempore, sicut de vobis fideliter
confidimus vos velle id ipsum. Et si quid de dicto episcopatu sive in
terris sive in aliis rebus contra iustitiam fuerit sublatum, adiuvetis eum
pro amore nostro ad restitutionem, prout iustum fuerit habendam. Con-
servet vos Dominus." Cod. Dipl. No. 838.

[2] Flor. Wig. an. 731.

consecration to be valid by the transmission of a
pall in 733. We have no evidence by whom the
consecrations were performed, in many cases, but
it is probable that the old rule was adhered to as
much as possible. In 1020, Æðelnóð was consecrated to Canterbury by archbishop Wulfstán: the
ceremony took place at Canterbury on the 13th of
November[1] in that year: and since in many cases
the ordination of archbishops is mentioned without
any details, but yet as preliminary to their going
to Rome for their palls, it is likely that the chroniclers tacitly assumed the custom of reciprocal
functions in Canterbury and York to be too well
known to require description.

When the nomination or election by the king
and his witan had taken place, it is probable that
a royal mandate was sent to the metropolitan, to
perform the ceremony of consecration. We have
yet the instrument by which Wulfstán of York
certifies to Cnut the performance of this duty in
the case of archbishop Æðelnóð[2]: the archbishop
says:—"Wulfstán the archbishop greets Cnut his
lord, and Ælfgyfu the lady, humbly: and I notify
to you both, dear ones, that we have done as notice

---

[1] Chron. Sax. an. 1020.

[2] Cod. Dipl. No. 1314. " ✠ Wulfstán arcebisceop grét Cnut cyning his hlaford, and Ælfgyfe ða hlæfdian eádmódlíce; and ic cýðe inc
leóf ðæt we habbað gedón swá swá ús swutelung fram eów com æt ðám
biscop Æðelnóðe, ðæt we habbað hine nú gebletsod. Nú bidde ic for
Godes lufon and for eallan Godes hálgan ðæt gewitan on Gode ðam
æðe and on ðám hálgan háde, ðæt he mote beón ðære þinga wyrðe ðe
óðre beforan wǽron, Dúnstán ðe gód wæs, and mænig óðer; ðæt ðes
mote beón eall swá rihta and gerysna wyrðe ðæt inc byð bám þearflíc
for Gode, and eác gerysenlíc for worolde."

came from you to us respecting bishop Æðelwold, namely that we have now consecrated him." He then prays that the new prelate may have all the rights and dues granted to him, which have been usual, and enjoyed by his predecessors: which perhaps is to be understood as a formal demand that the temporalities may be properly conferred upon him. There can be no manner of doubt as to the meaning of the word *swutelung*, which I have rendered by *notice*, and Lingard by *order*[1]: it is a legal notification, and the technical word in a writ is *swutelian*. But I do not believe that Cnut was any more imperative in this matter than his predecessors had been. An Anglosaxon archbishop would never have found it a very safe thing to neglect a royal command by ancient right[2].

The bishops were in fact officers of the administration, and whatever importance their ecclesiastical functions may have possessed, their civil character was not of less moment. It is abundantly

---

[1] Hist. and Antiq. i. 94. His whole account is well worth attention.

[2] We have but one instrument:—granted. But what proportion have we of instruments respecting matters which are entirely beyond doubt? Supposing a royal mandate of consecration had issued on the election of every bishop, between 802, when Ecgberht came to the throne, and 1066, there would have been once in existence 36 archiepiscopal and 224 episcopal writs, or a total of 260. But during the same period, in the 32 counties south of the Humber there would have been held 25,344 shiremoots or county-courts. I will deduct one half of this number to meet all conceivable accidents. Of the 12,672, of which beyond a doubt records once existed, we still possess *three* or at the utmost *four* instruments: but do we on that account doubt that shiremoots were held? When we look at these ratios of 1 : 260 and 4 : 12,672, we find the authority for the writ of consecration more than ten times as great as that for the existence of shiremoots.

obvious that men of such a class, possessing nearly
a monopoly of what learning existed, would be
necessarily called to assist in the national councils, and would be very generally employed in the
diplomatic intercourse with foreign countries : few
persons of equal rank would have been competent
to conduct a negotiation carried on in writing :
and there is no doubt that their high position in
the universal institution of the church rendered
them at that period the fittest persons to manage
those affairs which concerned the general family of
nations. Moreover a close alliance always existed
in England between the aristocracy and the clergy :
faithful service of the altar, like faithful service of
the state, gave rank and dignity and privileges ;
and the ecclesiastical authority and influence of
the bishop, as well as his habits of business, and
general aptitude to advance the interests of the
crown, frequently designated him to discharge the
somewhat indefinite, but weighty, duties of what
we now call a prime minister. Administration is
in truth of such far greater importance than constitution, that we can readily see how greatly the
social welfare of England did in reality depend upon
this class, to whom so much of administrative detail was committed : and it was truly fortunate for
the country that the clerical profession was one
that a gentleman could devote himself to without
disparagement, and therefore embraced so many
distinguished members of the ruling class.

The civil and ecclesiastical jurisdictions were, it
is well known, not separated in England until after

the Conquest. William the Norman was the first
to establish that most questionable division, the consequences of which were often so bitterly felt by his
successors. Previous to his reign the bishop had been
the assessor of the ealdorman in the scírgemót or
county-court, and ecclesiastical causes, except such
as were reserved for the decision of the episcopal
synods, were subjected, like those of the laity, to the
judgment of the scírþegnas or shire-thanes: thus
even probate of wills was given in the county-court.
This participation of bishops in the administration
of justice, useful and necessary in the early ages of
Christianity, was very probably derived from the
functions of their heathen predecessors, the priests
of the ancient gods. The old Germanic *placita*
were held, as is well known, under the presidency
of the priests, and these were courts of law as well
as courts of parliament. In fact there is no reason
whatever to doubt that, long before the introduction of Christianity, the public pleadings were
opened with religious ceremonies, and that the
course of procedure was regulated by religious
ideas[1]. The gods were present,—to secure the
peaceful administration of justice, to sanction the
finding of the freemen, to give a holy character to
the act of *doing right* between man and man,—to
terrify the perjurer and the criminal,—perhaps to
justify the extreme penalty of the law in extreme
cases; for it is probable that to the gods alone

[1] "Omnis itaque concionis illius multitudo ex diversis partibus coacta,
primo suorum proavorum servare contendit instituta, numinibus videlicet suis vota solvens ac sacrificia." Hucbald. Vit. Lebwini, cap. xii

could the life of a great wrongdoer be offered, as an atonement to the Law, of which God is the root and guardian. The institution of the ordeal by which it was superstitiously supposed that the Almighty would reveal the hidden truth or falsehood of men, further tended to connect, first the pagan and afterwards the Christian priesthood with the administration of justice. In that most solemn appeal to the omniscience and justice of God, the clergy necessarily took the prominent part; and although we cannot believe that they always resisted the temptation offered by that most strange juggle, it may charitably be asserted that their intervention not rarely saved the innocent from the penal consequences of an uncertain and painful test.

I have remarked in an earlier chapter[1] upon the union of the sacerdotal with the judicial power: at a very early stage of human society, the functions of the priest and the judge seem in general to have been inseparable; nor were they separated in fact upon the introduction of Christianity. In the very commencement of our æra, when the church really did exist as a brotherhood under the guidance of the first disciples, it was most natural that all contentions between members of the body should be settled by the arbitration of the whole church, or such as represented it. Litigation before the ordinary tribunals of the state, even could such have been resorted to by Christians, was little consonant with the doctrine of charity which was to prevail among

---

[1] Volume i. page 146.

the members of one mystical body, founded on almighty Love. Accordingly St. Paul himself[1] expressly forbids the disciples to carry their contentions before the secular authorities, implying that it is their duty to bring them to the consideration of their fellow-believers, that they may be amicably settled, in the spirit of forbearance and Christian moderation. And as persecution gradually threatened the terrified community, this course became unavoidable: it was impossible for the Christian to submit to the pagan forms of the tribunals, yet to refuse these was to proclaim the adoption of a proscribed and illegal association. The establishment of a hierarchy among the Christians themselves supplied some remedy for this difficulty, and it was soon decided that the disputes of the brotherhood were to be brought before the presbyter or bishop as a judge,—a course which in itself was natural in countries where the Romans had permitted the existence of some authority in the national tribunals, and had not insisted upon dragging every cause before their own officers. The peculiar situation of the Christians themselves as citizens of a new state—viz. the religious state—tended to consolidate this system. Christianity took cognizance of motives, of acts entirely beyond the reach of mere human law, and the community claimed a right to judge of the internal as well as the external state of its members. Immorality, not cognizable by any positive law, was a proper subject for the animadversion

---

[1] 1 Corinthians vi. 1–7.

of a body whose duty it was to exclude from communion all who pertinaciously refused to perform the
duties of their profession. It was thus that a two-
fold jurisdiction became lodged in the church,—and
in the bishop or presbyter, as its representative in
each particular locality,—long before the reception
of Christianity among the *religiones licitae* transformed the customs of an obscure sect into recognised laws of the empire. But no sooner had the
terms of the great alliance been arranged, than the
state hastened to give the imperial sanction to what
had hitherto been merely the bye-laws of a sodality:
and the decisions of a council, if confirmed by the
assent of the emperor, were at once raised to the rank
of imperial laws. Thus the council of Carthage in 397
had threatened with excommunication any clergyman who should pursue another before the secular
tribunals; and this decree, repeated in 451 by the
fourth general Council—that of Chalcedon—had received the sanction of Marcianus, and become part
of the law of the Roman empire. The jurisdiction of
the bishops in the affairs of the clergy was thus rendered legal; but it was at a later period extended so
as to include a much wider sphere. Justinian not
only commanded all causes in which monks were
concerned to be referred to the bishop of the diocese, but made him the only legal channel of proceedings even in cases where laymen had claims
against the clergy[1].

Arbitration by the bishop had thus grown up

[1] Novel. § 83.

into a custom, at first absolutely necessary, and afterwards always desirable, in a society like the Christian. Accordingly Constantine permitted all contentions to be so settled. But it was a rule of Roman law that there could lie no appeal whatever from a voluntary arbitration; and in pursuance of this rule, in the year 408, Arcadius and Honorius decreed that the sentences of bishops should be without appeal[1]. In this manner was the ecclesiastical jurisdiction founded in the Greek and Roman empires.

Happily for ourselves, this could not be admitted without modification in the Germanic states. Had it indeed been so, every trace of independence would long since have perished, and the whole civilized world have found itself subject to the principles and regulations of an effete scheme of jurisprudence. The antagonism of the Germanic customary right it was that saved us from the consequences which must have followed the universal prevalence of maxims elaborated by another race, and sprung out of a different social condition. It was the conflict of the Roman and Ecclesiastical laws with those of the Teutonic victors that produced that modified system of relations, under which, by the blessing of Providence, civilization has been maintained, the general well-being of mankind advanced, and human society firmly established throughout Europe, on a basis susceptible of progressive, perhaps illimitable improvement.

---

[1] Dönniges, Deut. Staatsr. p. 48 *seq.*

Useful as a counter-check to the somewhat disruptive system of the Germans, the Roman and Ecclesiastical laws have yet never been able to destroy the nationality, or abridge the freedom, of our races; while they have tended to give consistency and method to our own customs, and to reduce into form and harmony what, but for them, might have been liable to fall asunder from its own internal vigour. Like the centripetal and centrifugal forces, they have balanced one another, and held our social state together as one majestic and consistent whole.

The method of doing justice between man and man, which was the very foundation-stone of the Teutonic polity, was in direct opposition to the doctrines of Roman jurists and the practice of the church. Justice went out from among the people themselves, not from the king or the bishop. The people spoke both as to fact and law, the ancient customary law; nor did they at any time allow their relations as Christians to abrogate the older rights they had possessed as citizens, where the exercise of these was clearly compatible with the recognition of the former. In respect to their religion, they duly submitted to the ecclesiastical authority, made confession, performed penance, and hearkened to advice tendered by qualified functionaries; but they nevertheless still met in their folk- and shire-moots to hold plea, declare folk-right, and superintend its execution by their national officers. Not even to the clergy themselves did they accord an immunity from the universal duties

of freemen : and although they may have been disposed to acquiesce in the claim to be quit of personal military service, they never excused suit and
service to the popular courts. Only when the relation of a cleric to his superior was that of an
unfree man to his lord, did the state release him
from this duty, or rather did the state hold him
unworthy of this privilege.

The existence of such a body as the English
clergy could not possibly be ignored. As organized
agents of a system which professed to exercise
a right of rule over the most secret desires and
motives of men,—as students distinguished by their
knowledge, or remarkable for their piety,—as landlords, in the enjoyment of great wealth, and chiefs
of numerous dependents,—lastly as advisers and
ministers of the ruling class, or intermediaries in
the intercourse with foreign states,—they formed
a power whose claims to attention could not be
neglected. But their social position itself was that
which brought them continually in relation with
the other aggregates of freemen, and they were
therefore called upon to take their place with other
landowners, lords, or ministerials in the popular
councils.

With all their attachment to the customary law
and the national franchises, the Anglosaxons never
lost sight of the fact that Christianity had introduced new social relations : they were ready to
admit that there was now a godcund or *divine* as
well as woroldcund or *secular* right ; and in the exposition of the former they were willing to follow the

guidance of those who professed to make it their especial study. Moreover the system of Anglosaxon jurisprudence depended very much upon the trustworthy character of witnesses, and the ordination of the clergy was justly taken to have imposed upon them the obligation of a peculiar truthfulness. The testimony of members of their class became therefore a very important thing in the sight of the *moot-thanes* who might have disputed points to settle, or who, in mixed causes, might shrink from doing wrong to the venerable body by too strict an application of the principles by which themselves were bound. Lastly, as there was a merciful tendency among the people to have disputes settled by arbitration and on equitable grounds, rather than by the strict rules of law, the clergy, whose jurisdiction extended to the motives of Christians rather than the mere acts of citizens, were valuable intermediaries between contending parties. The dignity of the class—the *honor clericalis*—was cheerfully recognised, the wisdom and goodness of the body acknowledged, and the propriety of being to a great degree guided by the experience and enlightenment of their leaders, readily conceded. Accordingly the bishop became an inseparable assessor of the Frankish count and of the Anglosaxon ealdorman in their respective courts[1].

The duties of a bishop as the officer of a state, and contradistinguished from his merely ecclesias-

---

[1] See Leg. Eádg. ii. § 5. Cnut, ii. § 18.

tical functions, were to assist in the administration
of justice between man and man, to guard against
perjury, and to superintend the administration of
the ordeals; further to take care that no fraud was
committed by means of unjust measures, to which
end he was made the guardian of the standards,
and the judge of what work might be demanded
from the serf; above all, to watch over the maintenance of the peace, and the upholding of divine
as well as secular law[1]. The canons of the church
did indeed prohibit the presence of bishops on trials
which might involve the penalties of death or mutilation; and even the Constitutions of Clarendon,

[1] The 'Institutes of Ecclesiastical Polity' are very explicit upon
these points. They say:—" To a bishop belongs every direction, both
in divine and worldly things. He shall, in the first place, inform men
in orders, so that each of them may know what it properly behoves
him to do, and also what they have to enjoin to secular men. He shall
ever be [busied] about reconciliation and peace, as he best may. He
shall zealously appease strifes and effect peace, with those temporal
judges who love right. He shall in accusations direct the *lád*, so that
no man may wrong another, either in oath or ordeal. He shall not
consent to any injustice, or wrong measure, or false weight; but it is
fitting that every legal right (both 'burhriht' and 'landriht') go by
his counsel and with his witness: and let every burgmeasure, and every
balance for weighing be, by his direction and furthering, very exact;
lest any man should wrong another, and thereby altogether too greatly
sin . . . . . It behoves all Christian men to love righteousness, and shun
unrighteousness; and especially men in orders should ever exalt righteousness, and suppress unrighteousness: therefore should bishops,
together with temporal judges, so direct judgments, that, as far as in
them lies, they never permit any injustice to spring up there . . . . By
the confessor's direction, and by his own measure, it is justly fitting
that the thralls work for their lords over all the district in which he
shrives. And it is right that there be not one measuring-rod longer
than another, but all regulated by the confessor's measure; and let
every measure in his shrift-district, and every weight, be, by his direction, very rightly regulated: and if there be any dispute, let the bishop
arbitrate." Thorpe, ii. 312 *seq.*

the object of which was to place the clergy on their proper and ancient footing towards the other members of the church and state, recognised this exemption[1]: but there is little reason to suppose that it was regarded by the Anglosaxons; indeed the popular courts had no power to pass sentences of so deep a dye, until long after the custom of the bishop's presence therein had been established too firmly to be questioned.   It was otherwise among the Franks, and we may perhaps attribute this to the strong nationality of the Frankish clergy, which indisposed them to claim their canonical immunity.

Another exemption which the bishops properly possessed, seems also to have been often neglected in this country,—that namely of personal service in the field.   No doubt, all over Europe, as soon as the bishops became possessed of lands liable to the *hereban*, or military muster, they, like other lords, were compelled to place their armed tenants on foot, for the public service, when duly required: but their levies were mostly commanded by officers specially designated for that purpose and known under the names of *advocati, vicedomini,* or *vidames;* being in general nobles of power and dignity who assumed or accepted the exercise of the bishop's royalties, the management of his estates, the administration and execution of his justice, and a remu-

---

[1] " Archiepiscopi, episcopi et universae personae regni, qui de rege tenent in capite, habeant possessiones suas de rege sicut baroniam, et inde respondeant iusticiariis et ministris regis,et sequantur et faci nt omnes consuetudines regias ; et sicut caeteri barones, debent interesse iudiciis curiae regis quousque perveniatur ad diminutionem membrorum vel ad mortem." Rog. Wend. *anno* 1104. Coxe, ii. 301.

nerative share of his revenues and patronage. In
Saxon England, however, we do not meet with
these officers; and though it is probable that the
bishop's geréfa was bound to lead his contingent
under the command of the ealdorman, yet we have
ample evidence that the prelates themselves did not
hold their station to excuse them from taking part
in the just and lawful defence of their country and
religion against strange and pagan invaders[1]. Too
many fell in conflict to allow of our attributing
their presence on the field merely to their anxiety
lest the belligerents should be without the due
consolations of religion; and in other cases, upon
the alarm of hostile incursions, we find the levies
stated to have been led against the enemy by the
duke and bishop of the district.

Attention has been called in another chapter to
the fact that the bishops did not universally (or
indeed usually), make their residences in the principal cities[2]. A remarkable distinction thus arose
between themselves and the prelates of Gaul and
Germany. The latter, strong in the support of the
burgesses, and identified with the urban interests,
found means to consolidate a power which they
used without scruple against the king when it suited
their convenience, or which enabled them to extort from him the grant of offices that virtually
rendered them independent of his authority. This

---

[1] As late as 43 Edw. III. A.D. 1369, on an alarm of invasion, orders were
given to arm and array the clergy, as well as laity. Rym. Foed. vi. 631.

[2] The Normans adopted a different custom. Many of the cathedrals
were transferred from obscure sites to the cities which they now adorn,
by the first Norman bishops.

was generally effected through the bishop's obtaining the county, that is becoming the count, and thus exercising the palatine power in his city, as well as that which he might already possess *iure episcopii*, and as *defensor urbis* or patron of the municipality. This, rare indeed under Charlemagne, but not uncommon in the times which preceded and followed him, can at least not be proved to have taken place in England before the Conquest[1]. There is indeed one instance which might seem at first sight to contradict this assertion, but which upon closer investigation rather confirms it. We learn that certain thieves, having attempted a sacrilegious entry into the church of St. Eádmund, and being miraculously delivered into the hands of the authorities, were put to death by the orders of Ðeódred, then bishop of London and of Eastanglia[2]. This event took place after the conquest of the last-named province by Æðelstán, who about 930 drove the Danes from it or reduced them under his own power. At that time it appears uncertain whether the conquered kingdom had been duly arranged

---

[1] After the Conquest it did take place : Walcher bishop of Durham was made also count of the same in 1075, upon the capture of Earl Wæl-þeóf. Hist. Dunelm. Eccl. lviii. (lib. iii. cap. xxiii. p. 208). As late as the time of Richard the First, we find a successor of Walcher, Hugo de Pusac, purchasing the same county of the king, *anno* 1189. Ric. Divisiens. p. 8. One year later, Baldwin archbishop of Canterbury suspended Hugo, bishop of Coventry, because "contra dignitatem episcopalis ordinis, officium sibi vicecomitatus usurpaverat." Rog. Wend. an. 1190. Coxe, iii. 18.

[2] "Hic fecit suspendi latrones volentes infregisse aecclesiam Sancti Eadmundi, qui tamen erant miraculose impediti." Chron. de Passione S. Edmundi, cited by Wharton. Ep. et Dec. Lond. p. 29. See also Will. Malm. Gest. Pont. lib. ii.

and settled, or whether any ealdorman had been appointed to govern it. If not, we must imagine that Deódred, the only constituted authority on the spot, acted at his own discretion in a case of urgency, without absolutely possessing the legal power to do so; that the act was in short one of those examples of what in modern times we understand by the term Lynch-law, that law which men are obliged to administer for themselves in the absence of the regular machinery of government. But it is further observable that, according to the terms of the legend itself, these thieves were taken *in the manner*, and consequently liable to capital punishment without any trial at all[1]; this justice we may suppose Deódred to have executed, and to its summary character we may attribute the regrets he expressed on the subject at a later time. It is also possible to account for the act by supposing that even at this early period the bishop possessed his sacu and sócn in the demesne of St. Eádmund, and that he proceeded to execute his thieves by his right as lord of the sócn: but there is no clear proof that the immunity did exist before the time of Cnut, and I therefore incline to the second explanation as the most probable. But if Deódred did not act in pursuance of possessing the comitial power, we may safely say that there is no evidence

---

[1] William of Malmesbury seems to allude to this point, when he says of St. Eádmund: "Latrunculos, noctu sacram aedem expilare aggressos, invisis loris in ipsis conatibus irretivit; formoso admodum spectaculo, quod praeda praedones tenuit, ut nec coepto desistere, nec inchoata valerent perficere." Gest. Reg. i. 366, § 213.

whatever of any Saxon bishop having exercised it[1].
As assessor to the ealdorman, the bishop was especially charged to attend to the due levy of tithe
and other church imposts ; but this was clearly because he had a direct interest in the law that decreed their punctual payment, and was certain not
to connive at any neglect in its execution, which
the ealdorman out of favour or carelessness might
possibly have been disposed to do.

But a still higher authority was placed in the
hands of the bishop, derived in fact from the assumed pre-eminence of the ecclesiastical over the
secular power.   If the geréfa would not do justice,
and maintain the peace in the land, then the bishop
was especially commanded to enforce the fines
which the king and his witan had apportioned to
that officer's offence[2].   It was no doubt argued that
no geréfa would be found bold enough to incur the
danger of offering violent resistance to the sacred
person of the prelate ; and even the ealdorman, who

[1] By the law of Eádweard the Confessor, " cyricbryce " belonged to
the bishop.   " Si quis sanctae aecclesiae pacem fregerit, episcoporum
tum est iusticia." Leg. Eád. Conf. § vi. But this seems a different thing
altogether, and to be a violation of the "grið" only.

[2] " But if any of my reeves will not do this, and care less about it
than we have decreed, then let him pay my *oferhyrnes* [that is the fine
for *disobedience*], and I will find another, who will.   And let the bishop
exact the *oferhyrnes* of the reeve in whose district it may be." Leg.
Æðelst. i. § 26.   Thorpe, i. 212.   Again : "And let the judge that
giveth wrong judgment to another, pay to the king a *bót* of one hundred and twenty shillings ; unless he will venture to prove on oath that
he knew no better.   And let him forfeit his thaneship for ever, unless
he can redeem it from the king, as he may be willing to permit.   And
let the bishop of the shire exact the *bót* into the king's hand." Leg.
Eádg. ii. § 3. Thorpe, i. 266.

might have set the king at defiance, would tremble to encounter the substantial terrors of excommunication and a laborious penance.

The high station occupied by the bishop in the social hierarchy is proved by the amount of his wergyld and of the fines assigned to offences against his honour, his person, and his property. Although the bishop and the presbyter are in fact but of one order in the church, yet the state found it convenient to place the former on much the higher scale. In the "North-people's law" an archbishop is reckoned upon the same footing as an æðeling or prince of the blood, at fifteen thousand thrymsas, and a bishop upon the same footing as an ealdorman at eight thousand. The breach of a bishop's surety or protection, like the ealdorman's, rendered the offender liable to a fine of two pounds, which in the case of an archbishop rose to three[1]. He that drew weapon before a bishop or ealdorman was to be mulcted in one hundred shillings, before an archbishop, in one hundred and fifty[2]. Under Ini the violence done to a bishop's dwelling, and the seat of his jurisdiction, was to be compensated with one hundred and twenty shillings, while the ealdorman's was protected by a fine of only eighty: in this the episcopal dignity was placed upon a level with that of the king himself[3]. Similarly Wihtræd

---

[1] Leg. Ælfr. § 3. Cnut, ii. § 59. Thorpe, i. 62, 408. In this last passage, as in the North-people's law of wergyld, the archbishop's and æðeling's borh and mundbryce are reckoned alike at three pounds. So also Ll. Æðelr. vii. § 11. Thorpe, i. 330.

[2] Leg. Ælf. § 15. Æðelr. vii. § 12. Thorpe i. 70, 332.

[3] Leg. Ini, § 45. Thorpe, i. 130. This overrated estimate is cor-

had declared his mere word, without an oath, to be like the king's, incontrovertible.

The ecclesiastical functions of the bishops were here the same as elsewhere. To them belonged the ordination of priests and deacons, the hallowing of chrism, the ceremonies of confirmation, the consecration of churches and churchyards, nuns and monks; they had a right to regulate the lives and conversation of their clergy, to superintend the monastic foundations, and in general to watch that every detail of the ecclesiastical establishment was duly regarded and maintained. In their peculiar synods they could frame canons of discipline, to be enforced in the several dioceses. They were the receivers-general of all ecclesiastical revenue, which they distributed to the inferior clergy under their government, according to certain specified regulations; providing out of the common fund for the due maintenance of the priests, the buildings, and minor accessories required for decent celebration of the rites of religion.

But the most important of their functions was that which is technically called *iurisdictio fori interni*, their jurisdiction in matters of conscience, their dealing with the motives and feelings, rather than the acts of men. This—which practically they exercised through the several presbyters who were, for the general convenience, dispersed over

rected by Ælfred, who settles the sums thus: king, one hundred and twenty scill.; archbishop, ninety scill.; bishop and ealdorman, sixty scill. Leg. Ælf. § 40. Thorpe, i. 88.

[1] Leg. Wihtr. § 16. Thorpe, i. 40.

the face of the country,—was the true source of
their power, and measure of their social influence.
Positive law deals only with the actions of men,
and then only when they are perfected or completed : religion regulates the inward impulses from
which those actions spring, and its authority extends both before and beyond them : intention, not
act, is its proper province. But the secret intentions and motives of men are known perfectly to
God alone ; the man himself may, and often does
possess but an indistinct and fallacious notion of
his own impulses ; and as it is in these, rather than
in the acts which are their results, that the essence
of guilt lies, the Christian was taught to unbosom
himself to one of more experienced and disciplined
feelings ;—one whose profession was to console
the distracted sinner, and who, on genuine repentance, was empowered to announce the glad tidings
of reconciliation with God.   Confession of sins was
the mode pointed out by the founder of the church,
to obtain the blessings of almighty mercy ; but how
were the ignorant, the obstinate, or the despairing to know the right manner of such confession ?
How could they know in what form confession was
effectually to be made to God ?   How could they,
plunged in sin and foulness, dare to approach the
source of all purity and holiness ?   What hope
could the grovelling outcast have of being admitted to the throne of his glorious King, even for
the purpose of renouncing his state of rebellion
and apostasy ?   But the glorious King was a merciful sovereign, who had commissioned certain of his

servants, reconciled sinners themselves, to be intermediaries between his own majesty and the terror-
stricken offender : they had been sent forth armed
with full power to receive the submission which
the guilty feared to offer to Himself in person, furnished with instructions as to the exact mode in
which the satisfactory propitiation was to be made.
These commissioners were the especial body of the
clergy,—the successors and representatives of the
Levitical Priests under the Law,—the offerers of the
sacrifices,—to whom the spirit of God had been
exclusively communicated in the ceremony of their
ordination, and who thereby became possessors of
the divine authority, to bind and loose, to forgive
sins on earth and in the world to come. The
clergy therefore undertook to direct the suffering
and heart-broken outlaw to the throne of peace.
Again, as the merely human preacher of atonement possessed of himself no means of ascertaining the genuineness of repentance, a system of
penances was established which might serve as a
test of the penitent's earnestness : and too soon a
miserable error grew up that, by submitting to self-
inflicted punishments, the sinner might diminish
the weight of the penalties which he had earned in
a future state. But he might exceed or fall short
of the just measure, if not duly weighed and apportioned by those who were in possession of the divine will in that respect : men had even without
their own knowledge become holy and justified by
their works of self-abasement and humiliation and
charity : such men might exceed the necessary

limit of penance and mortification:—happily for the sinner and the saint, the priest had a code of instructions at hand by which the difficulties in all cases could be readily adjusted.

These codes of instructions, known by the names of Confessionalia, Poenitentialia, Modus imponendi Poenitentiam, and the like, were compiled by the bishops, to whom the *iurisdictio fori interni* was exclusively competent, as soon as the episcopal system became firmly settled. The presbyter exercised it only as the bishop's vicar, when it became inconvenient for the penitent to visit a distant cathedral or metropolis. The episcopal right was open to every bishop: each one might, if he dared, embody his own ideas on the subject in a code, which would derive its authority from conformity to the recognised customs of the church, the personal reputation of its author, and the general acceptance by his episcopal peers throughout the world. The differing circumstances of differing states of society required skilful adaptation of general rules; and therefore any bishop who felt in his conscience that he was qualified for the task, might bring the light of his wisdom to the consideration of this weighty matter, and make such regulations as to himself seemed good, for the management of his own diocese,—certain that, if the blessing of God rested upon his endeavours, his views would be widely circulated and adopted by his neighbours. There is perhaps no more melancholy evidence in existence of the vanity and worthlessness of human endeavours than the celebrated works which thus

arose in various parts of Europe; and nothing can
demonstrate more strikingly the folly and wicked-
ness of squaring and shaping the unlimited mercy
of God by the rule and measure of mere human
intelligence. With the contents of these Poenitentials we have of course not here to deal; but I am
bound to say that I know of no more fatal sources
of antichristian error, no more miserable records
of the debasement and degradation of human intellect, no more frightful proofs of the absence of genuine religion. It was the evil tendency of those
barbarous early ages not to be satisfied with the
simple promises of divine mercy, and faith was
clouded and confused by the crowd of incongruous
images which were raised between itself and its all-
glorious object. At one time terrified by the con-
sciousness of sin, at another deluded by the cheap
hope of ceremonial justification, the human race
eagerly rushed to multiply the means of salvation,
and franticly rejoiced in the establishment of a host
of mediators between themselves and their cruci-
fied Redeemer, between the frightened but uncon-
verted sinner, and his offended Lord and Maker.
The pure Word of God was not then, as it now is,
accessible to every reader; and those whose duty
it was to proclaim what the mass of men could not
obtain access to themselves, had erred into a devious labyrinth of traditions, through which the
weary wayfarer circled and circled in endless, ob-
jectless gyrations, at every turn more distant only
from the goal he pursued. Pure and good were
no doubt the objects sought by Cummian, and

Theodore and Ælfríc, and pious the spirit in which
they wrought; but the foundation of their house
was upon sand, and when the rains fell and the
tempests roared around it vanished in a moment
from before the sight of God and man, never to be
reconstructed, even until the closing of the ages.

The sources of revenue by which the bishops
supported their temporal power will be considered
in a subsequent chapter : it is enough that we find
them to have been amply endowed with fitting
means, in every part of Europe.   During the Anglosaxon period, poverty and self-denial were not
the characteristics of the class, however they may
have distinguished certain members of the body.
Nor will the philosophical enquirer see cause for
regret in this : far more will he rejoice in the establishment of any system which tends to draw closer
the bonds of intercourse between the clerical and
lay members of the church, which leads to the
identification of their worldly as well as their eternal interests, and unites them in one harmonious
work of praise and thanksgiving, one active service
of worship and charity and love, before the face of
Him in whom they are united as one holy priesthood.   It is the separation of the clergy from the
laity, as a class, to which the world owes so many
ages of misery and error ; and to the comparative
union of both orders in the church, we may perhaps attribute the general quiet which, in these
respects, characterized the Anglosaxon polity.   On
these points of separation I shall also have something to say hereafter ; but for the present one

more subject alone remains to be treated of in this chapter, the last but not least remarkable function of the episcopal authority and power. By far the most important point of the public ecclesiastical jurisdiction,—for the *iurisdictio fori interni* is quite another thing,—lay in the questions of marriage, which were especially reserved for the bishop's cognizance. The prohibitions which the clergy enforced were obviously unknown to the strict Teutonic law, which permitted considerable licence in these respects. From Tacitus we learn that a sort of polygamy was not unknown on the part of the princes ; it was probably looked upon as a useful mode of increasing the alliances of the tribe[1],— the only conceivable ground on which it could have been allowed by a race so strict in the observance of marriage. We do not know within what degrees the Germans permitted unions which the Roman clergy considered incestuous, but we do know that Gregory considered a relaxation of the strict rule necessary to the success of Augustine in Britain ; that he gave the missionary positive instructions upon the subject, and, when blamed by his episcopal brother of Messina for this concession, justified his course by the danger which he apprehended for his plan of conversion, if the prejudices of the Saxons on so vital a point were too hastily shocked[2].

[1] "Nam prope soli barbarorum singulis uxoribus contenti sunt, exceptis admodum paucis, qui non libidine, sed ob nobilitatem plurimis nuptiis ambiuntur.' Tac. Germ. xviii.

[2] See Felix's letter, Bed. Op. Min. ii. 239. He not only expresses his own surprise, but adds that other clergymen had been greatly disturbed by Gregory's departure from the rule of the church: "non modicum murmur super hac re nobiscum versatur." Gregory replies

From these directions of Gregory we learn not only that the marriage of first cousins was common, but —what is much more surprising—that the marriage with a father's widow was so likewise. Nor can we doubt this, when we not only find recorded cases of its occurrence, but when we have a Teutonic king distinctly affirming it to be the legal custom of his people : in the sixth century Ermengisl king of the Varni can say, " Let Radiger my son marry his step-mother, even as our national custom permits[1] ; " and therefore when we find Beda speaking of a similar marriage, and declaring Eádbald to have been " fornicatione pollutus tali qualem nec inter gentes auditam Apostolus testatur,

in some detail, and especially says : " Quod autem scripsi Augustino, Anglorum gentis episcopo, alumno videlicet, ut recordaris, tuo, de consanguinitatis coniunctione, ipsi et Anglorum genti, quae nuper ad fidem venerat, ne a bono quod coeperat metuendo austeriora recederet, specialiter et non generaliter caeteris me scripsisse cognoscas." Bed. Op. Min. ii. 242. The following are the directions referred to :—" Quinta interrogatio Augustini. Usque ad quotam generationem fideles debeant cum propinquis sibi coniugio copulari ? et novercis et cognatis si liceat copulari coniugio ? Respondit Gregorius. Quaedam terrena lex in Romana republica permittit ut, sive frater et soror, seu duorum fratrum germanorum, vel duarum sororum filius et filia misceantur ; sed experimento didicimus ex tali coniugio sobolem non posse succrescere, et Sacra Lex prohibet cognationis turpitudinem revelare. Unde necesse est ut iam tertia vel quarta generatio fidelium licenter sibi iungi debeat ; nam secunda, quam praediximus, a se omni modo debet abstinere. Cum noverca autem miscere grave est facinus, quia et in Lege scriptum est, ' Turpitudinem patris tui non revelabis ' ...... Quia vero sunt multi in Anglorum gente qui, dum adhuc in infidelitate essent, huic nefando coniugio dicuntur admixti, ad fidem venientes admonendi sunt ut se abstineant et grave hoc esse peccatum cognoscant." The correspondence with Felix apparently refers to further regulations on the subject which are no longer found in the copies of Gregory's answers to Augustine.

[1] 'Ραδίγερ δὲ ὁ παῖς ξυνοικιζέσθω τῇ μητρυιᾷ τὸ λοιπὸν τῇ αὑτοῦ, καθάπερ ὁ πάτριος ἡμῖν ἐφίησι νόμος. Procop. Bel. Got. iv. 20.

ita ut uxorem patris haberet[1]," or Asser on another such occasion saying that it was " contra Dei interdictum, et Christianorum dignitatem, nec non et contra omnium Paganorum consuetudinem," we can only suppose that they either did not know, or that they deemed it advisable not to recognise, the ancient heathen practice.

In both the cases referred to, the obvious scandal was put a stop to by the separation of the parties[2],— Eádbald being evidently led to this step by superstitious fears, rather than submitting to an episcopal authority exercised by Laurentius. It is certainly strange in the case of Æðelbald, if there really were a separation, that we hear nothing of the interference of the Church to produce so important an event.

---

[1] Hist. Eccl. ii. 5. The words of St. Paul, here referred to, are in 1 Cor. v. 1. Asser, Vit. Ælf. 858. The very words of Beda himself seem to prove that Eádbald's marriage was closely connected with heathendom,—perhaps was intended to be a public profession of it. He says that the king, being terrified by Laurentius's account of a miraculous vision he had had, " anathematizato omni idolatriae cultu, abdicato connubio non legitimo, suscepit fidem Christi, et baptizatus aecclesiae rebus quantum valuit, in omnibus consulere et favere curavit." Hist. Eccl. ii. 6. In fact the politics of that day seem generally to have consisted in the apostasy of a converted king's successor. The heathen priests could hardly be expected to yield quite without a struggle. The cases are curious enough to merit a detailed record. What the age of Æðelberht's second wife may have been is unknown to us; but there is some probability that Æðelwulf's marriage was never really consummated, that it was never a marriage at all. Judith can hardly have been more than twelve when Æðelwulf married her, and within two years he died.

[2] Eádbald's divorce is recorded, as we have seen, by Beda. Æðelbald's rests on much less sure authority,—that only of Matthew Westminster, and Rudborne, Annal. Winton. Judith, after her return to France, eloped with Baldwin of Flanders, to whom she bore Matilda, William the Conqueror's wife. See Warnkönig, Hist. Fland. i. 144.

We learn that by degrees the time arrived at which the clergy thought themselves strong enough to insist upon a stricter observance of the canonical prohibitions, and various instances are on record where their intervention is mentioned, to separate persons too nearly connected by blood. It is probable that many more of these are intended than we actually know; for unhappily the monkish writers are over-fond of using strong expressions both of praise and blame, and not rarely fling *pellex scortum* and *concubina* at the heads of women who were for all that, legally speaking, very honest wives. One celebrated case has obtained a world-wide reputation,—that of Eádwig, the details of whose unhappy fate will probably for ever remain a mystery. Political calculations, and unreconciled national jealousies were in all probability the main-springs of the events of his troublous life; but that which lends it all its romance—his separation from Ælfgyfu—was the act of a prelate determined upon upholding the ecclesiastical law of marriage. It is to be regretted that we do not know the exact degree of relationship between the royal victims. It may have been too close, in the eyes of the stricter clergy; yet we cannot close our eyes to the fact that it was long acquiesced in by the English nobles; nor, had Eádwig shown himself more pliant to the pretensions of Dúnstán, might we ever have heard of it at all. History, deprived of all its materials, will here fail to do even late justice to the sufferers; but it will not fail to stamp with its enduring brand the brutal conduct of their persecu-

tors[1]. However conscientious may have been the
intentions of archbishop Oda, it is to be lamented

[1] There cannot be the slightest doubt that Ælfgyfu was Eádwig's
wife, or that she was separated from him on the ground of too near
consanguinity. The charter, Cod. Dipl. No. 1201, which is in every
respect an authentic document, mentions her as "Ælfgyfu, ðæs cynges
wíf," the king's wife ; and this, in addition to herself, was witnessed by
her mother Æðelgyfu, by four bishops, and by three principal noblemen
of the court. If that charter be not genuine, there is not one genuine
in the whole Codex Diplomaticus, and I cannot see the shadow of a reason to question it, as Lingard has done. The reader will probably be
glad to see it, as it occurs in *two* manuscripts, the Cotton MSS. Claud.
B. vi. fol. 54. and C. ix. fol. 112, one copy being in the original Saxon,
the other a statement in Latin drawn up from it.

" Ðis is seó geræðnes ðe Byrht-
elm biscop and Æðelwold abbud
hæfdon ymbe hira landgehwerf:
ðæt is ðonne ðe se biscop gesealde
ða hída æt Cenintúne intó ðære
cyricean æt Abbendúne tó écan
yrfe ; and se abbud gesealde ðæt
seofontyne hýda æt Crydanbricge
ðán biscope tó écnesse, ge on lífe
ge æfter lífe ; and hí eác ealra
þinga gehwyrfdon ge on cwican
ceápe ge on óðrum, swá swá hí
betwihs him geræddon. And ðis
wæs Eádwiges leáf cyninges ; and
ðis syndon ða gewitnessa. Ælf-
gifu ðæs cininges wíf, and Æðelgyfu, ðæs cyninges wífes módur,
Ælfsige biscop, Osulf biscop,
Coenwald biscop, Byrhtnóð ealdorman, Ælfheáh cyninges discþegn, Eádríc his bródur."

" This is the agreement that bishop Byrhthelm and abbot Æðelwold made about their exchange
of lands: that is then, that the
bishop gave the hides at Kenning-
ton to the church at Abingdon
for an eternal inheritance ; and
the abbot gave the bishop the
seventeen hides at Crida's bridge,
for ever both during life and after
life: and they also exchanged every
thing upon the lands, both live
stock and other, as they agreed
between them. And this was by
leave of king Eádwig ; and these
are the witnesses : Ælfgyfu the
king's wife, and Æðelgyfu, the
king's wife's mother, bishop Ælfsige, bishop Oswulf, bishop Coenwald, Byrhtnoð the ealdorman,
Ælfheáh the king's dapifer, Eádríc
his brother."

The Latin abstract of this important document is as follows:—" Do-
minus autem abbas Æðelwoldus commutationem eiusdem terrae, id est
Cenintun, concedente eodem rege, egit apud Brihtelmum episcopum.
In cuius vicissitudine ipse episcopus accepit illam villam quae appellatur
Crydanbricge. Testes autem fuerunt huius commutationis Ælfgifa regis
uxor, et Æðelgifa mater eius, Ælfsige episcopus, Osulfus episcopus,
Kenwald episcopus, et multi alii." The date of this document is 956,

that a stain of barbarous cruelty attaches to his
memory, for the part he took in this transaction. If

in which year Eádwig came to the throne, and therefore certainly subsequent to the coronation, the celebrated scene of Dúnstán's insolence.
The prelates and nobles present were Ælfsige bishop of Winchester,
Oswulf bishop of Ramsbury, Cénwald bishop of Worcester, Byrhthelm
bishop of London, Æðelwald then abbot of Abingdon and afterwards
the celebrated bishop of Winchester—the Father of the Monks, as he
was called ; Byrhtnóð the ealdorman an equally decided patron of the
monastic order ; Ælfheáh no less a man than the dapifer regis, or seneschal of Eádwig's house. This then was not a thing done in a corner,
and the testimony is conclusive that Ælfgyfu was Eádwig's queen. It
is also beyond doubt that, in the year 958, Oda separated Eádwig from
his wife on the ground of their being too nearly related : one of the
MSS. of the Saxon Chronicle says clearly, "Her on ðissum geare Oda
arcebiscop tótwǽmde Eádwi cyning and Ælfgyfe, forðám ðe hí wǽron tó
gesybbe." Chron. Sax. an. 958. And Florence of Worcester, drawing
from an independent authority, but evidently confused by the slanderous
tales which had been spread of Eádwig, confirms the Chronicle, saying :—" Sanctus Odo Doruberniae archiepiscopus regem Westsaxonum
Eádwium et Ælfgivam, vel quia, ut fertur, propinqua illius extitit, vel
quia illam sub propria uxore adamavit, ab invicem separavit." Flor.
Wig. an. 958. William of Malmesbury speaks of her as " uxor, proxime
cognata " (Gest. Reg. § 147, i. 223), but soon after calls her *ganea* and
pellex in choice monkish style. Wendover and Paris are even more
insolent in their phraseology, but still there is the unlucky admission of
a marriage :—" Huic [sc. Eádwig] quaedam mulier inepta, licet natione
praecelsa [certainly very high birth indeed if Ælfgyfu was too near a relative of the king] cum adulta filia per nefandum familiaritatis lenocinium
adhaerebat, ut sese vel filiam suam sub coniugali titulo sociaret."
Wendov. i. 404. They go on to insinuate that there was an improper
familiarity between the king and both the women. With this I am
not at all concerned : Eádwig may have been a disorderly young prince,
as there have been other disorderly young princes,—as his much-
belauded brother Eádgár *was* in the highest degree. The ladies *may* have
been more than commonly depraved. But it may be observed that our
general experience is not in favour of a wife's permitting her husband
to be guilty of lascivious conduct towards another woman in her presence, or of a married daughter's conniving at her husband's irregularities with her own mother. Not a word have we of this disgusting in-
sinuation in the Chronicle, or Florence,—himself a monk,—or Æðelweard, or Huntingdon : and the two latter speak of Eádwig in terms
very far removed from those in which the adherents of Dúnstán's cause

he found it inevitable, after two years of wedded life further to humiliate his already humbled sovereign, by insisting upon the removal of his young consort, it was not necessary to disfigure her with hot searing-irons, or on her return from exile to put her to a cruel death. The asceticism of the savage churchman seems here to have been embittered by even less worthy considerations.

The history of mediæval Europe shows with what awful effect this tremendous power was wielded by unscrupulous popes and prelates, whenever it suited their purposes not to connive at marriages which, according to their teaching, were incestuous. But amidst the striking cases on record—the cases of kings and nobles—we look in vain for a true measure of the misery which these prohibitions must have entailed upon the humbler members of society, who possessed neither the influence to compel nor the wealth to purchase dispensations from an arbitrary and oppressive rule. The sense and feeling of mankind at once revolt against restrictions for which neither the law of God, nor the dictates of nature supply excuse, and which resting upon a

have chosen to characterize him:—" Quin successor eius Eáduuig in regnum, qui et, prae nimia etenim pulchritudine, Pancali sortitus est nomen a vulgo secundi. Tenuit namque quadriennio per regnum amandus." Æðelw. Chronic. iv. 8. " Rex autem praedictus Edwi non illaudabiliter regni infulam tenuit. Edwi rex anno regni sui quinto cum in principio regni eius decentissime floruerit, prospera et laetabunda exordia mors immatura perrupit." Hen. Hunt. lib. v. We must be excused for preferring this sort of record to the interested exaggerations of such biographers as Bridferð, whom the remainder of his work proves to have been either a very weak and credulous person or a very great rogue, or—as not unfrequently happens—perhaps both at once.

complicated calculation of affinity, were often the means of betraying the innocent and ignorant into a condition of endless wretchedness. But they were invaluable engines of extortion, and instruments of malice; they led to the intervention of the priest with the family, in the most intolerable form; they furnished weapons which could be used with almost irresistible effect against those whom nothing could reach but the tears perhaps and broken heart of a beloved companion. And therefore they were steadily upheld till the great day of retribution came, which involved so many traditions of superstition and error, so many engines of oppression and fraud, in one common and undistinguishing ruin: τὰ πρὶν δὲ πελώρια νῦν ἄϊστοι—things mighty indeed have perished away from the world; but thrice blessed was the day which left us free and unshackled to pursue the noblest and purest impulses of our human nature.

CHAPTER IX.

THE CLERGY AND MONKS.

THE almost total absence of documentary evidence leaves us in great doubt as to the condition of the church in England previous to the organization brought about by Theodore. It is nevertheless probable that it followed in all essential points the course which characterized other missionary establishments. The earliest missionaries were for the most part monks; but Augustine was accompanied by clerics also[1], and in every case the conversion of a district was rapidly followed by the establishment of a cathedral or a corresponding ecclesiastical foundation. These were at first central stations, from which the assembled clergy sallied forth to visit the neighbouring villages and towns, and preach the tidings of salvation: the necessities of daily provision, the attainment of greater security

---

[1] " Clerici extra sacros ordines constituti." Beda, H. E. i. 27. Gregory contemplated the marriage and separate dwelling of these persons. But for a long time it is improbable that any such arrangement could take place. Augustine separated his monks from the canons who had accompanied him (the presbyters he was to obtain in the neighbouring countries of Gaul: see Gregory's Epistles to Theodoric and Theodbert, and to Brunhild; Bed. Op. Min. ii. 234, 235), placing the latter in Christchurch, Canterbury. See Lingard, Ang. Sax. Church, i. 152, 153. But this sort of separation cannot have been always practicable. The Scottish missionaries were not all monks. Beda, H. E. iii. 3.

for their persons, the mutual aid and consolation
in the perils and difficulties of their task, all supplied motives in favour of a cœnobitical mode of
life: monks and clerics were confounded together
through the circumstances of the adventure in
which they shared; nay the very administration of
those rites by which the imagination of the heathen
Saxons was so strongly worked upon, could only
be conducted on a sufficiently imposing scale by an
assemblage of ecclesiastics. To this must be added
the protection to be derived from settling on one
spot, in the immediate neighbourhood of a royal
vill, and under the safeguard of the royal power:
for though the residences of kings were rarely in
cities, yet their proximity offered much more secure guarantees than the outlying villages and
clearings in the mark; even as the general tendencies of courtly life were likely to present fewer
points of opposition than the characteristic bigotry
of heathen, *i. e.* rural populations. This combination of circumstances probably led at an early period to that approximation between the modes of
life of monks and clerks, which at the close of the
eighth century Chrodogang succeeded in enforcing
in his archbishopric of Metz, but which had been
attempted four centuries earlier by Eusebius of
Vercelli[1]. Both the Roman and Scottish mission-

---

[1] Neander, Gesch. der Relig. u. Kirche, i. 322; ii. 553. Lingard,
Ang. Sax. Church, i. 150. Chrodogang's institution is thus described
by Paulus in his Gest. Episc. Mettens. "Hic clerum adunavit, et ad
instar coenobii intra claustrorum septa conversari fecit, normamque eis
instituit, qualiter in ecclesia militare deberent; quibus annonas vitae-
que subsidia sufficienter largitus est, ut perituris vacare negotiis non

aries followed the same plan, which indeed appears to be the natural one, and to have been generally adopted on all similar occasions, whether in ancient Germany, in Peru or in the most modern missions of Australia or New Zealand. In Beda's Ecclesiastical History, which in these respects no doubt was founded upon ancient and contemporary records, we frequently read of prelates leaving their monasteries (by which general name churches as well as collections of monks are designated) to preach the Gospel and administer the rite of baptism in distant villages[1]. But this system had also

indigentes, divinis solummodo officiis excubarent." Pertz, ii. 268. Chrodogang's rule is preserved in Labbé, Concil. vii. 1444. Harduin, Concil. iv. 1181. See Eichhorn, Deut. Staatsr. i. 760, § 179. It is in many respects similar to the rule of Benedict of Nursia, upon which it appears to have been modelled.

[1] " Quadam autem die dum parochiam suam circuiens, monita salutis omnibus ruribus, casis et viculis largiretur, nec non etiam nuper baptizatis ad accipiendam Spiritus sancti gratiam manum imponeret," etc. Beda, Vit. Cuthb. c. 29. This however is perhaps rather to be considered as an episcopal visitation. But there is abundant evidence that at first the custom was such as the text describes. It is said thus of Aidan, the Scottish bishop in Northumberland : " Erat in villa regia non longe ab urbe de qua praefati sumus [i. e. Bamborough]. In hac enim habens aecclesiam et cubiculum, saepius ibidem diverti ac manere, atque inde ad praedicandum circumquaque exire consueverat : quod ipsum et in aliis villis regis facere solebat, utpote nil propriae possessionis, excepta aecclesia sua et adiacentibus agellulis, habens." Beda, H. E. iii. 17. This was a small wooden church, and certainly never a cathedral. But the early custom of the Scottish church in Northumberland is further described by Beda : and one can only lament that it was not much longer maintained : for his own words show that he is contrasting it with the custom of his own times, nearly a century later ; he says : " Quantae autem parsimoniae, cuiusque continentiae fuerit ipse [i. e. Colman] cum praedecessoribus suis, testabatur etiam locus ille quem regebant, ubi abeuntibus eis, excepta aecclesia, paucissimae domus repertae sunt ; hoc est, illae solummodo, sine quibus conversatio civilis esse nullatenus poterat. Nil pecuniarum absque pecoribus ha-

inconveniences of no slight character; the distance
of the converts from the church, the necessity for
daily superintendence and continual exhortation
on the part of the preacher, the very danger and
fatigue of repeated journeys into rude, uncultivated
parts of the country, must have soon forced upon

bebant. Si quid enim pecuniae a divitibus accipiebant, mox pauperibus dabant. Nam neque ad susceptionem potentium saeculi, vel pecu-
nias colligi vel domus praevideri necesse fuit, qui nunquam ad aecclesiam nisi orationis tantum, et audiendi verbi Dei causa veniebant....
Tota enim fuit tunc solicitudo doctoribus illis Deo serviendi, non saeculo; tota cura cordis excolendi non ventris. Unde et in magna erat
veneratione tempore illo religionis habitus; ita ut ubicunque clericus
aliquis aut monachus adveniret, gaudentur ab omnibus tanquam Dei
famulus exciperetur: etiam si in itinere pergens inveniretur, adcurre-
bant, et flexa cervice vel manu signari, vel ore illius se benedici gaude-
bant; verbis quoque horum exhortatoriis diligenter auditum praebe-
bant. Set et diebus Dominicis ad aecclesiam, sive ad monasteria cer-
tatim, non reficiendi corporis, sed audiendi sermonis Dei gratia confluebant: et si quis sacerdotum in vicum forte deveniret, mox congregati
in unum vicani, verbum vitae ab illo expetere curabant. Nam neque alia
ipsis sacerdotibus aut clericis vicos adeundi, quam praedicandi, baptizandi, infirmos visitandi, et, ut breviter dicam, animas curandi causa
fuit: qui in tantum erant ab omni avaritiae peste castigati, ut nemo
territoria ac possessiones ad construenda monasteria, nisi a potentibus
saeculi coactus acciperet. Quae consuetudo per omnia aliquanto post
haec tempora in aecclesiis Nordanhymbrorum servata est." Bed. H. E.
iii. 26. Of Ceadda we learn that after his consecration as bishop of
York, he was accustomed, " oppida, rura, casas, vicos, castella, propter
evangelizandum, non equitando, sed apostolorum more pedibus ince-
dendo peragrare." Ibid. iii. 21. About the same period we learn from
Beda, that Cuthbert used to make circuits for the purpose of preach-
ing: " Erat quippe moris eo tempore populis Anglorum, ut veniente in
villam clerico vel presbytero, cuncti ad eius imperium verbum audituri
confluerent." Ibid. iv. 27. The words eo tempore also show that in
Beda's time this custom was no longer observed, which is naturally explained by the existence of parish-churches. The custom of itinerant
preachers in the west of England is also noted about the same period,
viz. 680. " Cum vero aliqui, sicut illis regionibus moris est, praesbyteri
sive clerici populares vel laicos praedicandi causa adiissent, et ad villam
domumque praefati patrisfamilias venissent," etc. Vit. Bonifac. Pertz,
ii. 334.

the clergy the necessity of providing other machinery than they as yet possessed. The multipli
cation of centres of instruction was the first and
greatest point to be ensured; whereby a more
constant intercourse between the neophyte and the
missionary might be attained. This had long been
secured in other countries by the appointment of
single presbyters to reside in single districts, under
the general direction of the bishop; or, where
circumstances required it, by the settlement of
several presbyters under an archipresbyter or archpriest, who was responsible for the conduct of his
companions. And as the district of the bishop
himself commonly went by the name of a diocese
or parish, both these terms were applied to denote
the smaller circuit within which the presbyter was
expected to exert himself for the propagation of the
faith, and the due performance of the established
rites, and to perform such functions as had been
entrusted to the ministers of the faithful, for the
better management of the ecclesiastical affairs of
the congregation. The custom of the neighbouring countries of Gaul offered sufficient evidence of
the practicability of such an arrangement, which
had long been in use in older established churches:
we may therefore readily suppose that so beneficial
a system would be adopted with all convenient
speed in England. As long as the possessions of
the clergy were confined to a small plot whereon
their church was built, and while they depended
for support upon the contributions in kind which
the rude piety of their new converts bestowed, the

bishops could naturally not proceed to plant these
clerical colonies of their own authority: though,
as soon as they became masters of vills and manors
and estates of their own, they probably adopted the
plan of sending single presbyters into them, partly
to discharge the clerical duties of their station,
partly to act as stewards, administrators or bailiffs
of the property, the proceeds of which were paid
over to the episcopal church, and laid out at the
discretion of the bishop [1]. But the zeal of the
people could here assist the benevolent objects of
the clergy. The inconvenience of having a distance
to traverse in order to attend the ministrations of
religion, the desire to aid in the meritorious work
of the conversion, the earnest hope to establish a
peculiar claim upon the favour of Heaven, nay
perhaps even the less worthy motives of vanity and
ambition, disposed the landowner to raise a church
upon his own estate for the use of himself and his
surrounding tenants or friends. From a very early
period this disposition was cultivated and encou-

[1] If a bishop found it convenient to build a church out of his own
diocese, the ecclesiastical authority remained to the bishop in whose
diocese it was built. " Si quis episcopus in alienae civitatis territorio
aecclesiam aedificare disponit, vel pro agri sui aut aecclesiastici utilitate, vel quacunque sui opportunitate, permissa licentia, quia prohiberi
hoc votum nefas est, non praesumat dedicationem, quae illi omnimodis
reservanda est in cuius territorio aecclesia assurgit; reservata aedifica-
tori episcopo hac gratia, ut quos desiderat clericos in re sua videre,
ipsos ordinet is cuius territorium est; vel si iam ordinati sunt, ipsos
habere acquiescat : et omnis aecclesiae ipsius gubernatio ad eum, in
cuius civitatis territorio aecclesia surrexit, pertinebit. Et si quid ipsi
aecclesiae fuerit ab episcopo conditore conlatum, is in cuius territorio
est, auferendi exinde aliquid non habeat potestatem. Hoc solum aedi-
ficatori episcopo credidimus reservandum." Concil. Arelat. iii. cap.
xxxvi. A.D. 452.

2 E 2

raged; and the bishops relinquished the patronage
of the church to the founder, reserving of course
to themselves the canonical subjection and consecration of the presbyter who was ordained to the
title. During the seventh century this had become
common in the Frankish empire, and Theodore followed, or introduced, the same rule in this country [1]. Whether under this influence or not, we find
churches to have so arisen during his government
of the English sees, whose sole archbishop he was.
Beda incidentally mentions the dedication by John
of Beverley of churches, for Puch and Addi, two
Northumbrian noblemen, and these were no doubt

[1] Elmham says of Theodore:—"Hic excitavit fidelium voluntatem, ut
in civitatibus et villis aecclesias fabricarentur, parochias distinguerent,
et assensus regios his procuravit, ut siqui sufficientes essent, super proprium fundum construere aecclesias, eorundem perpetuo patronatu
gauderent; si inter limites alterius alicuius dominii aecclesias facerent,
eiusdem fundi domini notarentur pro patronis." Such churches had
nevertheless at first not the full privileges of parish-churches. The
twenty-first canon of the Council of Agda decreed: "Si quis etiam extra
parochias, in quibus est legitimus ordinariusque conventus, oratorium
in agro habere voluerit, reliquis festivitatibus, ut ibi missas teneat,
propter fatigationem familiae, iusta ordinatione permittimus. Pascha
vero, Natale Domini, Epiphania, Ascensionem Domini, Pentecosten, et
Natalem sancti Johannis Baptistae, vel si qui maximi dies in festivitatibus habentur, non nisi in civitatibus, aut in parochiis teneant. Clerici
vero, si qui in festivitatibus quas supradiximus, in oratoriis, nisi iubente
aut permittente episcopo, missas facere aut tenere voluerint, a com-
munione pellantur."—Concil. Agathense, A.D. 506. cap. xxi. That
there were at this period parish-churches in Gaul, served by a single
presbyter, appears from other decisions usually attributed to this council, but really published by the Council of Albon, held eleven years
later. They are in fact not found in the three oldest MSS. of the Concilium Agathense. "Diacones vel presbyteri in parochia constituti de
rebus aecclesiae sibi creditis nihil audeant commutare, vendere vel do-
nare, quia res sacratae Deo esse noscuntur.... Quicquid parochiarum
presbyter de aecclesiastici iuris proprietate distraxerit, inane habeatur.
Presbyter, dum diocesim tenet, de his quae emerit ad aecclesiae nomen

private foundations [1]. We still possess various regulations of Theodore, and of nearly contemporary prelates, which refer to such separate churches, proving how very general they had become, and how strictly they required to be guarded against the avarice or other unworthy motives of the founders, and the simoniacal practices both of priest and layman. In the thirty-eighth chapter of his Capitula [2] we find the following directions:—"Any presbyter who shall have obtained a parish by means of a price, is absolutely to be deposed, seeing that he is known to hold it contrary to the discipline of ecclesiastical rule. And likewise, he who shall by means of money have expelled a presbyter lawfully ordained to a church, and so have obtained it entirely for himself; which vice, so widely diffused, is to be remedied with the utmost zeal. Also it is to be forbidden both to clerks and laics, that no one shall presume to give any church whatever to

scripturam faciat, aut ab eius quam tenuit aecclesiae ordinatione discedat." Concil. Epaonense. A.D. 517. As late as the time of Eádgár a regulation was made in England as to the payment of tithe by a landowner who happened to have a church with a churchyard upon his estate. "If there be any thane who has a church with a churchyard upon his bookland, let him give the third part of his tithe to his church. But if any one have a church that has no churchyard, let him give his priest what he will out of the nine parts,"—that is out of what remains after the payment of his tithe to the cathedral church. Eádg. i. § 2. Thorpe, i. 262. Probably there were many such churches in existence, which had descended together with the estates from the first founders, and whose owners could not agree with the ecclesiastical authorities as to their liabilities. The right of patronage was abused unfortunately at a very early period, both by clerics and laymen, as we learn abundantly from the decrees of the several provincial councils.

[1] Beda, Hist. Eccl. v. 4, 5.
[2] Thorpe, ii. 73. Kunstmann, Poenit. p. 121.

a presbyter, without the licence and consent of the bishop." These churches frequently were granted to abbeys or to the bishops themselves ; and in the latter case they were served by priests especially appointed thereunto from the cathedral [1]. At this early period when tithes were not demandable as matter of right, and when the founders of these churches were already betraying a tendency to speculate in church-building, by claiming for themselves the *altare* or produce of the voluntary oblations of the faithful, the bishops found it necessary to insist that every church should be endowed with a sufficient glebe or estate in land: the amount fixed was one hide, equivalent to the estate of a single family, which, properly managed, would support the presbyter and his attendant clerks. Archbishop Ecgberht rules [2]: " Ut unicuique aecclesiae vel una mansa integra absque alio servitio attribuatur, et presbyteri in eis constituti non de decimis neque de oblationibus fidelium nec de domibus, neque de atriis vel hortis iuxta aecclesiam positis, neque de praescripta mansa, aliquod servitium faciant, praeter aecclesiasticum : et si aliquod amplius habuerint, inde senioribus suis, secundum patriae morem, debitum servitium impendant." And this regulation. though probably already esta-

---

[1] As early as 587, I find a grant of a parish-church to the monastery of St. Peter at Lyons, by Gerart and his wife Gimbergia, on the ground of their daughter being professed there : " propterea cedimus et donamus nos vobis aliquid de rebus propriis iuris nostri . . . . . hoc est ecclesia de Darnas cum decimis et parochia." Bréquigny, Dipl. Chartar. i. 83. Bréquigny, Mabillon, and the editors of the Gallia Nova Christiana, all concur in recognising the genuineness of this charter.

[2] Excerpt. Ecgberhti, § 25. Thorpe, ii. 100.

blished by custom, obtained the force of law in the Frankish empire, by a constitution of Hludwich in 816 [1]. This glebe-land the bishop seems not to have been able to interfere with, so as to alienate it from the particular church, in favour of another, even when both churches were within his own subjection [2].

But although many churches may have arisen in this manner, a large proportion of which gradually found their way into the hands of bishops and abbots, and although these last may have erected churches, as the necessities of the case demanded, in the various districts over which they exercised rights of property, the greater number of parish-churches *(plebes, aecclesiae baptismales, tituli maiores)* had probably a very different origin. It

[1] " Volens etiam unamquamque aecclesiam habere proprios sumptus, ne per huiusmodi inopiam cultus negligerentur divini, inseruit praedicto edicto, ut super singulas aecclesias mansus tribueretur unus, cum pensatione legitima et servo et ancilla." Vita Hludovici Imp. Pertz, ii. 622. The tenth chapter of Hludwich's capitulary is drawn up in the same words as Ecgberht uses, with the sole exception of the Frankish *mansus* for the English *mansa*, and it is therefore probable that both drew from some common and early source; unless indeed we suppose that the Frankish clergy thought the English custom worthy of imitation. The proper name for this landed foundation is *dos aecclesiae*, or as it is called in the Langobardic law (lib. iii. tit. i. § 46), *mansus aecclesiasticus*. The result of this dotation is very evident in the next following chapter of the above-quoted capitulary, by which parish-churches are obviously intended. Cap. xi. " Statutum est ut, postquam hoc impletum fuerit, unaquaeque aecclesia suum Presbyterum habeat, ubi id fieri facultas providente episcopo permiserit."

[2] " Non licet abbati, neque episcopo, terram aecclesiae convertere ad aliam, quamvis ambae in potestate eius sint. Si mutare vult aecclesiae terram, cum consensu amborum sit. Si quis vult monasterium suum in alio loco ponere, cum concilio episcopi et fratrum suorum faciat, et dimittat in priorem locum presbyterum ad ministeria aecclesiae." Capit. Theodori. Thorpe, ii. 64.

had been shown that in all likelihood every Mark
had its religious establishment, its *fanum, delubrum,*
or *sacellum,* as the Latin authors call them, its
hearh, as the Anglosaxon no doubt designated
them [1]; and further, that the priest or priests
attached to these heathen churches had lands—
perhaps freewill offerings too—for their support.
It has also been shown that a well-grounded plan
of turning the *religio loci* to account was acted
upon by all the missionaries, and that wherever a
substantial building was found in existence, it was
taken possession of for the behoof of the new religion.   Under such circumstances it would seem
that nothing could be more natural than the establishment of a baptismal church in every independent mark that adopted Christianity, and that the
substitution of one creed for the other not only did
not require the abolition of the old machinery, but
would be much facilitated by retaining it.   It is in
this manner then that I understand the assertions
of Beda and others, that certain missionary prelates established churches *per loca,* such churches
being certainly not cathedrals [2] or abbey-churches.

[1] Besinga hearh, *fanum* Besingorum. Cod. Dipl. No. 994.

[2] For example, of the Scotch missionaries about the year 635, Beda
reports as follows : "Exin coepere plures per dies de Scottorum regione
venire Brittaniam, atque illis Anglorum provinciis quibus regnavit rex
Osuuald, magna devotione verbum fidei praedicare, et credentibus gratiam baptismi, quicumque sacerdotali erant gradu praediti, ministrare.
Construebantur ergo aecclesiae per loca, confluebant ad audiendum verbum populi gaudentes, donabantur munere regis possessiones, et territoria ad instituenda monasteria." Hist. Eccl. iii. 3.   Again in Essex,
between 650 and 660: "Qui, [i. e. Ced] accepto gradu episcopatus,
rediit ad provinciam, et maiori auctoritate caeptum opus explens, fecit per
loca aecclesias, presbyteros et diaconos ordinavit, qui se in verbo fidei et

There cannot be the least reason to doubt that
parish-churches were generally established in the
time of Beda, less than half a century after the
period to which most of the instances in the notes
refer [1] : and it is not very probable that they were
all owing to private liberality. In a similar manner probably arose the numerous parish-churches
which before the close of the eighth century were
founded, especially by the English missionaries,
on the continent of Europe [2]. Thus in the seventh

ministerio baptizandi adiuvarent, maxime in civitate quae lingua Saxonum Ythancaestir appellatur; sed et in illa quae Tilaburh cognominatur;
quorum prior locus est in ripa Pentae amnis, secundus in ripa Tamen-
sis ; in quibus collecto examine famulorum Christi, disciplinam vitae
regularis, in quantum rudes adhuc capere poterant, custodire docuit."
Hist. Eccl. iii. 22. About 690, Beda says of Cúðberht, " Plures per
regiones illas aecclesias, sed et monasteria nonnulla construxit." H. E.
iv. 28. And it is difficult to understand the passage about to be cited
of anything but heathen temples in the marks, which the zeal of the
bishop of Mercia, Gearoman, converted into Christian churches, that is
separate parish-churches. A pestilence raged in Essex : one of its kings,
Sigheri, apostatized together with all his part of the people, " and set
about restoring their deserted temples, and adoring images." To correct this error, Wulfheri of Mercia, the superior king, sent his bishop
Gearoman : " qui multa agens solertia...... longe lateque omnia per-
vagatus, et populum et regem praefatum ad viam iustitiae reduxit: adeo
ut relictis, sive destructis fanis arisque quas fecerant, aperirent aecclesias, ac nomen Christi, cui contradixerant, confiteri gauderent, magis
cum fide resurrectionis in illo mori, quam ,in perfidiae sordibus inter
idola vivere cupientes." Hist. Eccl. iii. 30. This was in 665.

[1] In his Poenitential he gives a general direction as to the penance
of the parish priest who loses his chrism. He says : " Qui autem in
plebe suo [var. suum] chrisma perdideret, et eam invenerit, xl dies vel
iii quadragesimas poeniteat." Bed. Poenit. xxiv. Kunstm. Poenit.
p. 165.

[2] " Cumque aecclesiarum esset non minima in Hassis et Thyringea
multitudo extructa, et singulis singuli providerentur custodes," etc.
Vit. Bonif. Pertz, ii. 346. " Praefato itaque regni eius tempore, servus
Dei Willehadus per Wigmodiam aecclesias coepit construere, ac presbyteros super eas ordinare, qui libere populis monita salutis, ac baptismi conferrent gratiam." Vit. Willehad. Pertz, ii. 381. " Aeccle-

century in England the ecclesiastical machinery consisted of episcopal churches served by a body of clerks or monks,—sometimes united under the same rule, and a sufficient number of whom had the necessary orders of priests, deacons and the like; probably also churches served by a number of presbyters under the guidance of an archipresbyter or archpriest [1], bearing some resemblance to our later collegiate foundations; and numerous parish-churches established on the sites of the ancient fanes in the marks, or erected by the liberality of kings, bishops and other landowners on

sias quoque destructas restauravit, probatasque personas qui populis monita salutis darent, singulis quibusque locis praeesse disposuit." Ibid. ii. 383. "Testes quoque aecclesiae quas per loca singula construxit, testes et famulantium Dei congregationes quas aliquibus coadunavit in locis." Vit. Liutgari, Pertz, ii. 409. "Itaque more solito, cum omni aviditate et sollicitudine rudibus Saxonum populis studebat in doctrina prodesse, erutisque ydolatriae spinis, verbum Dei diligenter per loca singula serere, aecclesias construere, et per eas singulos ordinare presbyteros, quos verbi Dei cooperatores sibi ipsi nutriverat." Ibid. ii. 411. He also founded a church of canons, "monasterium, sub regula canonica dominio famulantium," which afterwards became a cathedral. When Liutgar and his companions landed on the little island of Helgoland, they destroyed the heathen temples and built Christian churches. "Pervenientes autem ad eandem insulam, destruxerunt omnia eiusdem Fosetis fana quae illuc fuere constructa, et pro eis Christi fabricaverunt aecclesias." Pertz, ii. 410. In like manner Willibrord in Frisia established Christian churches on the sites of the heathen fanes. "Simul et reliquias beatorum apostolorum ac martyrum Christi ab eo sperans accipere, ut dum in gente cui praedicaret, destructis idolis aecclesias institueret, haberet in promptu reliquias sanctorum quas ibi introduceret; quibusque ibidem depositis, consequenter in eorum honorem quorum essent illae, singula quaeque loca dedicaret." Beda, H. E. v. 11. Again, "Plures per regiones illas aecclesias, sed et monasteria nonnulla construxit." Beda, H. E. v. 11. This was consonant with the wise advice of Pope Gregory to Augustine, already cited vol. i. p. 332, note 2.

[1] As late as the tenth century we read of an archipresbyter at the head of a church at Ely. Hist. Eliensis, Ang. Sac. i. 603.

their own manorial estates. The wealthy and
powerful had also their own private chaplains, who
performed the rites of religion in their oratories [1],
and who even at this early period probably bore
the name of handpreostas, by which in much later
times they were distinguished from the túnpreostas,
village or parochial priests [2].

As early as the fifth century the fourth general
council (Chalcedon, an. 451) had laid down the
rule that the ecclesiastical and political establishments should be assimilated as much as possible [3];
and as the central power was represented by the

[1] Æðelberht's queen Beorhte had a chaplain, bishop Liuthart, previous to the arrival of Augustine. Beda, H. E. i. 25. Paulinus was
Æðelburge's chaplain before the conversion of Northumberland. Ibid.
ii. 9. Oidilwald king of Deira maintained Caelin, a brother of bishop
Ced, in his family; "qui ipsi et familae ipsius, verbum et sacramenta
fidei, erat enim presbyter, ministrare solebat." Ibid. iii. 23. Lastly
we read of Wilfrið, that he was chaplain to Alchfrið of Northumberland, "desiderante rege ut vir tantae eruditionis et religionis sibi specialiter individuo comitatu sacerdos esset et doctor." Ibid. v. 19.

[2] The distinction is found in the Chron. Saxon. an. 870. The Saxon
handpreostas is translated in a Latin copy by *capellani clerici;* the
Saxon túnpreostas by *de villis suis presbyteri.*

[3] "Si qua civitas potestate imperiali novata est aut innovatur, civiles
dispositiones et publicas aecclesiasticarum quoque parochiarum ordines
subsequantur." Conc. Chalc. an. 451. This was an attempt to bring
the state generally into that condition which would have existed had
the church and the empire not been on terms of hostility when the
church first was founded. Had the heathen creed not stood in the way,
from the very first it is probable that the praefect of the city and the
mayor of the village would have been universally also the Episcopus
and Chorepiscopus of the community: but the χάρισμα κυβερνησέως
and χάρισμα διδασκαλίας would not then have united in the same hands.
The church assumed form and shape under pressure, and passed from
a molluscous into a vertebrated organization through its struggles to
resist persecution on the one hand and heresy on the other. When it
entered into its alliance with the state its outward constitution was
already completed. That alliance is not a metaphysical entity, but an
historical fact.

metropolitans and the bishops, so the subsidiary authorities had their corresponding functionaries in the parish priests, priests of collegiate churches and their dependents. We possess a curious parallel drawn by Walafrid Strabo in the earliest years of the ninth century, on this subject. In his book De Exordiis Rerum Aecclesiasticarum (cap. 31), he thus compares the civil and ecclesiastical polities : " Porro sicut comites quidam Missos suos praeponunt popularibus, qui minores causas determinent, ipsis maiora reservent, ita quidam episcopi chorepiscopos habent. Centenarii qui et centuriones et Vicarii, qui per pagos statuti sunt, Presbyteris Plebei, qui baptismales aecclesias tenent, et minoribus praesunt Presbyteris, conferri queunt. Decuriones et Decani, qui sub ipsis vicariis quaedam minora exercent, Presbyteris titulorum possunt comparari. Sub ipsis ministris centenariorum sunt adhuc minores qui Collectarii, Quaterniones, et Duumviri possunt appellari, qui colligunt populum, et ipso numero ostendunt se decanis esse minores. Sunt autem ista vocabula ab antiquitate mutuata," etc [1].

[1] Let us arrange these offices tabularly:—

Secular.	Ecclesiastical.
1. Comes.	1. Episcopus.
α. Missus.	α. Chorepiscopus. (The Archdeacon or the Rural Dean.)
2. Centenarius. Centurio, or Vicarius : qui per pagos constitutus est.	2. Presbyter Plebei qui baptismalem aecclesiam habet.
3. Decurio et Decanus.	3. Minor Presbyter tituli.
4. Collectarius. Quaternio. Duumvir.	

The count (in England Ealdorman) and bishop are on one line, and,

Both in spiritual and in temporal matters, the clergymen thus dispersed over the face of the country were accountable to the bishop, whose *vicars* they were taken to be, that is to say, in whose place (" quorum vice ") they performed their functions. The "presbyteri plebei" or parish priests had the administration of all the sacraments and rites, except those reserved to the bishop,—such for instance as confirmation, ordination, the consecration of churches, the chrism, and the like : these were denied them, but they could baptize, marry, bury, and administer the communion. And gradually, as matter of convenience, they were invested with the internal jurisdiction, as it was called, —the "iurisdictio fori interni,"—that is to say confession, penance and absolution, but solely as representatives and vicars of the bishop [1].

if we may anticipate a little for the sake of illustration, we may add the Eorl of Cnut's constitution on the one side, and the Metropolitan on the other. The Missus of the count and the chorepiscopus (in Strabo's time yet existing, though less important than his city brother) are on the second line ; nevertheless the Missus partakes of the comitial dignity, and the episcopal, though grudgingly, is still vouchsafed to the chorepiscopus. Next in rank is the Centenarius or president of the Hundred, the officer of the pagus : his equivalent is the priest in a church where baptism is performed, the peculiar distinctive of a parish-church. The Decurio or Decanus is on the same footing as the German Capellanus or Kaplan, who is indeed ordained to a title, but not with power to administer the sacraments. The Kaplan is in truth generally attached to the parish-church—a sort of curate,—and often succeeds to it. But how is it that the parallel can be carried no further ? Is it that the Deacon's ordination was not conclusive enough ? Or were Collectarii and Duumviri, beadles, tax-gatherers and bailiffs not dignified enough to compare with even acolytes and vergers?

[1] " De poenitentibus, ut a presbyteris non reconcilientur, nisi praecipiente episcopo.—Ex concilio Africano.—Ut poenitentibus, secundum differentiam peccatorum, episcopi arbitrio poenitentiae tempora decer-

It was this gradual extension of the powers of the presbyter that destroyed the distinction between the collegiate churches served by the archpriest and his clergy, and the church in which a single presbyter administered the daily rites of religion. The word *parochia* which at first had been properly confined to the former churches, became generally applied to the latter, when the difference between their spiritual privileges entirely vanished.

In the theory of the early church, the whole district subject to the rule of the bishop formed but one integral mass: the parochial clergy even in spirituals were but the bishop's ministers or vicars, and in temporals they were accountable to him for every gain which accrued to the church. This he was to distribute at his own discretion; it is true that there were canons of the church which in some degree regulated his conduct, and probably the presbyters of his cathedral, his witan or council, did not neglect to offer their advice on so interesting a subject. To him it belonged to assign the funds for the support of the parochial clergy, out of the

nantur, et ut presbyter, inconsulto episcopo, non reconciliet poenitentem, nisi absentia episcopi, necessitate cogente . . . . Item, Ex concilio Cartaginensi de eadem re. Aurelius episcopus dixit: 'Si quisquam in periculo fuerit constitutus, et se reconciliari divinis altaribus petierit, si episcopus absens fuerit, debet utique presbyter consulere episcopum, et sic periclitantem eius praecepto reconciliare : quam rem debemus salubri concilio roborare.' Ab universis episcopis dictum est : ' Placet quod sanctitas vestra necessaria nos instruere dignata est.' Romani reconciliant hominem intra absidem : Graeci nolunt. Reconciliatio penitentium in coena Domini tantum est ab episcopo, et consummata penitentia: si vero episcopo dificile sit, presbytero potest, necessitatis causa, praebere potestatem, ut impleat." Poen. Theodori. Thorpe, ii. 6. Aurelius of Carthage died in 430.

share which was commanded to be set apart for the
sustenance of the ministers of the altar : to him
also it belonged to apportion the share which was
directed to be applied to the repairs of the fabric of
the churches in his diocese ; and he also had the
immediate distribution of that portion which was
devoted to the charitable purposes of relieving the
poor and ransoming the enslaved,—a noble privilege, more valuable in rude days like those than in
our civilized age it could be, even had the sacrilegious hand of time not removed it from among
the jewels of the mitre.

Occasionally, no doubt, the parochial clergy,
though supported by their glebe-lands, had reason
to complain that the hospitality or charity of the
bishop, exceeding the bounds of the canonical division, left them but an insufficient remuneration for
their services : and more than one council found it
useful to impress upon the prelate the claims of his
less fortunate or deserving brethren [1] : but on the
whole there can be little question that piety on the
one hand and superstition on the other combined
to supply an ample fund for the support of the
clerical body ; and that what with free-will offerings, grants of lands, fines, rents, tithes, compulsory

[1] " Et ideo quia Carpentoracte convenientes huiusmodi ad nos querela
pervenit, quod ea quae a quibuscumque fidelibus parochiis conferuntur,
ita ab aliquibus episcopis praesumantur, ut aut parum, aut prope nihil,
aecclesiis quibus collata fuerint relinquatur ; ut si aecclesia civitatis eius
cui episcopus praeest, ita est idonea, ut Christo propitio nihil indigeat,
quidquid parochiis fuerit derelictum, clericis qui ipsis parochiis deserviunt, vel reparationibus aecclesiarum rationabiliter dispensetur," etc.
Concil. Carpentor. an. 527.

contributions, and the sums paid in commutation of penance, the clergy in England were at all times provided not only with the means of comfort, but even with wealth and splendour. The sources and nature of ecclesiastical income will form the subject of a separate chapter.

As a body the clergy in England were placed very high in the social scale: the valuable services which they rendered to their fellow-creatures,—their dignity as ministers and stewards of the mysteries of the faith,—lastly the ascetical course of life which many of them adopted, struck the imagination and secured the admiration of their rude contemporaries. At first too, they were honourably distinguished by the possession of arts and learning, which could be found in no other class; and although the most celebrated of their commentaries upon the Biblical books or the works of the Fathers, do not now excite in us any very great feelings of respect, they must have had a very different effect upon our simple progenitors. Whatever state of ignorance the body generally may have fallen into in the ninth and tenth centuries, the seventh and eighth had produced men famous in every part of Europe for the soundness and extent of their learning. To them England owed the more accurate calculations which enabled the divisions of times and seasons to be duly settled; the decency, nay even splendour, of the religious services were maintained by their skilful arrangement; painting, sculpture and architecture were made familiar through their efforts, and the best examples of these civilising arts were

furnished by their churches and monasteries : it is
probable that their lands in general supplied the
best specimens of cultivation, and that the leisure
of the cloister was often bestowed in acquiring the
art of healing, so valuable in a rude state of society,
liable to many ills which our more fortunate period
could, with ordinary care, escape [1]. Their manuscripts yet attract our attention by the exquisite
beauty of the execution ; they were often skilled in
music, and other pursuits which at once delight
and humanise us. To them alone could resort be
had for even the little instruction which the noble
and wealthy coveted : they were the only school-
masters [2] ; and those who yet preserve the affectionate regard which grows up between a generous
boy and him to whom he owed his earliest intellec-

---

[1] The extraordinary helplessness of early surgery is little appreciated
by us, nor are we duly grateful for the advance in that most noble study
which now secures to the lowest and poorest sufferer, alleviations once
inaccessible to the wealthiest and most powerful. An example in point
occurs to me in the case of Leopold, duke of Austria, the captor of
Coeur de Lion, in 1195. A fall from his horse produced a compound
fracture of the leg, which from the treatment it received soon mortified.
Amputation was necessary, and it was performed by the duke himself,
holding an axe to the limb, which his chamberlain struck with a beetle.
" Acciti mox medici apposuerunt quae expedire credebant; in crastino
vero pes ita denigratus apparuit, ut a medicis incidendus decerneretur;
et cum non inveniretur qui hoc faceret, accitus tandem cubicularius
eius, et ad hoc coactus, dum ipse dux dolabrum manu propria tibiae
apponeret, malleo vibrato, vix trina percussione pedem eius abscidit."
Walt. Heming. i. 210. Wendov. iii. 88. We feel no surprise that
death followed such treatment, even without the excommunication
under which the savage duke laboured.

[2] We do not sufficiently prize our own advantages, and the blessings
which the mercy of God has vouchsafed to us in this respect. But let
one fact be mentioned, which ought to arrest the attention of even the
least reflecting man. In the ninth century there was not a single copy

tual training, can judge with what force such motives acted in a state of society so different from our own. Moreover the intervention of the clergy in many most important affairs of life was almost incessant. Marriage—that most solemn of all the obligations which the man and the citizen can contract—was celebrated under their superintendence: without the instruments which they prepared no secure transfer of property could be made; and as arbitrators or advisers, they were resorted to for the settlement of disputed right, and the avoidance of dangerous litigation. Lastly, although during the Anglosaxon period we nowhere find them putting forward that shocking claim to consideration which afterwards became so common—the being makers of their Creator in the sacrament of the Eucharist,—we cannot doubt that their calling was supposed to confer a peculiar holiness upon them; or that the *hád*, the orders, they received, were taken to remove them from the class of common Christians into a higher and more sacred sphere.

Great privileges were accordingly given to them in a social point of view. They enjoyed a high wergyld, an increased mundbyrd, and a distinguished secular rank. The weofodþegn or servant of the altar who duly performed his important

of the Old and New Testaments to be found in the whole diocese of Lisieux. We learn this startling fact from a letter sent by Freculf, its bishop, to Hrabanus Maurus. "Ad haec vestrae charitatis vigilantia intendat, quoniam nulla nobis librorum copia suppeditat, etiamsi parvitas obtusi sensus nostri vigeret: dum in episcopio, nostrae parvitati commisso, nec ipsos Novi Veterisque Testamenti repperi libros, multo minus horum expositiones." Opera Hrabani. Ed. Colvener. ii. 1.

functions, was reckoned on the same footing as
the secular thane, worold þegn, who earned nobility
and wealth in the service of an earthly master.
The oaths of a priest or deacon were of more force
than those of a free man ; and it was rendered
easier for them to rebut accusations by the aid of
their clerical compurgators, than for the simple
ceorl or even þegn, and his gegyldan.

It was nevertheless a wise provision that their
privileges should not extend so far as to remove
them entirely from participation in the general
interests of their countrymen, or make them aliens
from the obligations which the Anglosaxon state
imposed upon all its members. Personal privileges they enjoyed, like other distinguished members of the body politic, as long as their conduct
individually was such as to merit them ; but they
were not cut off entirely from the common burthens
or the common advantages: and this will not un-
satisfactorily explain the immunity which England
long enjoyed, from struggles by which other European states—and in later periods even our own
—were convulsed to their foundations. In their
cathedrals and conventual churches, or scattered
through the parishes over all the surface of the
land, but sharing in the interests of all classes,
they acted as a body of mediators between the
strong and the weak, repressing the violent, con-
soling and upholding the sufferer, and offering even
to the despairing serf the hope of a future rest
from misery and subjection.

On the first establishment of conventual bodies

we have seen that a complete immunity had been granted from the secular services to which all other lands were liable [1]; but that the inconvenience of this course soon led to its abandonment. It is difficult to say whether this immunity was at any time extended to the hide, "mansus aecclesiasticus," or "dos aecclesiae" of the parish-church : it is on the contrary probable that it never was so extended ; for no hint of the sort occurs in our own annals or charters ; and it is well known that the church lands among the neighbouring Franks were subject, like those of the laity, to the burthens of the state [2]. From every hide which passed into clerical hands, the king could to the very last demand the *inevitable* dues, military service, repairs of roads and fortifications ; and though it is not likely that the parish priest was called upon to serve in person, it is also not likely that he was excused the payment of his quota toward the arming and support of a substitute in the field [3].

Nor did the legislation of the Teutonic nations contemplate the withdrawal of the clergy from the authority of the secular tribunals. The sin of the

---

[1] Vol. i. 302.   [2] Eichhorn, § 114. vol. i. 506.

[3] Exemption from *munera personalia* however was early claimed. "Presbyteros, diaconos, etc.....etiam personalium munerum expertes esse volumus." L. 6. C. de Episc. et Cleric. i. 3. Hence the king had an interest in forbidding the ordination of a free man without his consent. See the formulary in Marculfus, i. 19. See also the fourth and eighth canons of the Council of Orleans, A.D. 511. and Eichhorn, i. 484, 485. §§ 94, 96. From these we see that through ordination the king might lose his rights over the freeman and the master over his serf. Of the last case there cannot be the slightest doubt in England, and I should imagine little of the first.

clergyman might indeed be punished in the proper manner by his ecclesiastical superior : penance and censure might be inflicted by the bishop upon his delinquent brother ; but the crime of the citizen was reserved for the cognizance of the state[1].

This had been the custom of the Franks, even while they permitted the clergy, who belonged to the class of Roman provincials, to be judged by the Roman law[2] : it was for centuries the practice

[1] The great argument of the clergy in later times,—in the twelfth century particularly, when all over Europe the attempt was made to exempt them from secular jurisdiction,—"that no one ought to be punished twice for the same offence," had apparently not yet been thought of. The penances of the church, by which the sinner was to be reconciled to God, were still held quite distinct from the sufferings by which he expiated his violation of the law. Theodore alleviates, but does not remit, the penance of those whose guilt has bent their heads to human slavery. Theod. Poen. xvi. § 3. See this argument stated in the quarrel between Henry II. and Becket : "In contrarium sentiebat archiepiscopus, ut quos exauctorent episcopi a manu laicali postmodum non punirentur, quia bis in idipsum puniri viderentur." Rog. Wendov. an. 1164. vol. ii. 304. But this was a two-edged argument, as its upholders soon found, when the laity on the same grounds claimed exemption from secular punishment for offences committed upon the persons of the clergy ; justly urging, upon the premises, that they were excommunicated for their acts, and ought not to be subject to a second infliction. Accordingly in 1176, we find Richard archbishop of Canterbury attempting to explain away what Becket had so vigorously advanced : "Nec dicatur quod aliquis bis puniatur propter hoc in idipsum, nec enim iteratum est, quod ab uno incipitur et ab altero consummatur," etc. See his letter to the bishops in An. Trivet. 1176. p. 82 *seq.* We shall readily admit that the laity ought not to have been let loose upon the clergy ; but upon the same grounds we shall claim the subjection of the clergy to the secular tribunals for all secular offences.

[2] Concil. Autisiodor. an. 578. can. 43. Concil. Matiscon. an. 581. can. 7. "Quodsi quicunque iudex......clericum absque causa criminali, id est homicidio, furto aut maleficio, hoc [scil. iniuriam] facere fortasse praesumpserit, quamdiu episcopo loci illius visum fuerit, ab aecclesiae liminibus arceatur."

in England, and would probably so have remained had the error of the Conqueror in separating the civil and ecclesiastical jurisdictions not prepared the way for the troublous times of the Henries and Edwards. In the case of manslaughter, Ælfred commands that the priest shall be secularised before he is delivered for punishment to the ordinary tribunals[1]: ÆÐelred[2] and Cnut[3] decree that he is to be secularised, to become an outlaw and abjure the realm, and do such penance as the Pope shall prescribe; and they extend this penalty to other grievous offences besides homicide. Eádweard the elder enacts that if a man in orders steal, fight, perjure himself or be unchaste, he shall be subject to the same penalties as the laity under the same circumstances would be, and to his canonical penance besides[4]. But the plainest evidence that the clergy, even including the most dignified of their body, were held to answer before the ordinary courts, is supplied by the many provisions in the laws as to the mode of conducting their trials[5]. It could not indeed be otherwise in a country where every offence was to be tried by the people themselves.

---

[1] " If a priest kill another man, let all that he had acquired at home be given up, and let the bishop deprive him of his orders : then let him be given up from the minster, unless the lord will compound for the wergeld." Ælf. § 21.

[2] Leg. ÆÐelr. ix. § 26.   Thorpe, i. 346.

[3] Leg. Cnut, ii. § 41.   Thorpe, i. 400.

[4] Eád. GuÐ. § 3. Thorpe, i. 168. Yet immediately afterwards Eádweard says: " If a man in orders fordo himself with capital crime, let him be seized and held to the bishop's doom." Ibid. § 4.

[5] See Leg. Wihtr. § 18, 19.   ÆÐelr. ix. § 19–24, 27.   Cnut, i. § 5; ii. § 41.

But the most effectual mode of separating the clergy from the other members of the church yet remains to be considered. He that is permitted to contract marriage, to enjoy the inestimable blessings of a home, to connect himself with a family, and give the state dear pledges of his allegiance, can never cease to be a citizen of that polity in which his lot is cast. He can be no alien, no machine to be put in motion by foreign force. Accordingly, although the celibacy of the clergy is a mere point of discipline (and could therefore be dispensed with at once were it desired[1]), it has always been pertinaciously insisted upon by those whose interest it was to destroy the national feeling of the clergy in every country, and render them subservient to one centralising power. It is fitting that we enquire how far this was attempted in England, and how far the attempt succeeded.

The perilous position of the early Christians, and especially of the clergy, rendered it at least matter of prudence that they should not contract the obligation of family bonds which must prove a serious

---

[1] Whether it will ever be possible to surmount the difficulties which environ this subject, may be doubted ; but it cannot escape any one who has enjoyed the intimacy of the more enlightened Roman Catholics, whether cleric or laic, that a strong feeling exists in favour of a change. In Bohemia and other Slavonic countries, yet in communion with Rome, the celibacy of the clergy has ever been a stumbling-block and stone of offence, and has done more than anything else to keep alive old Hussite traditions. A few years ago so much danger was felt to lurk in the question, that the Vienna censorship thought fit to suppress portions of Palaczy's History, which favoured the national views. Nor has Germany, at almost any period, lacked thinkers who have vigorously protested against a practice which they assert to have no foundation in Holy Writ, and look upon as disastrous to the State.

hindrance to the performance of their duties.   It
is therefore easily conceivable that marriage should
in the first centuries have been discouraged among
the members of this particular class.   There was
also a tendency among the eastern Christians to engraft upon the doctrines of the faith, those peculiar
metaphysical notions which seem always to have
characterized the oriental modes of thought.   The
antagonism of spirit and matter, the degraded—
nay even diabolical[1]—nature of the latter, and the
duty of emancipating the spiritual portion of our
being from its trammels, were quite as prominent
doctrines of some Christian communities, as of the
Brahman or Buddhist.   The holiness of the priest
would, it was thought, be contaminated by his
union with a wife; and thus from a combination
of circumstances which in themselves had no necessary connexion, an opinion came to prevail that
a state of celibacy was the proper one for the ministers of the sacraments.   It was at first recommended, and then commanded, that those who wished
to devote themselves to the especial service of the
church, should not contract the bond of marriage.
Even the married citizen who accepted orders was
admonished to separate himself from the society of
his wife : and both were taught that a life of continence for the future would be an acceptable offering in the sight of God.   It seems unnecessary to

---

[1] Some sects believed the δημιουργός to have been the devil himself;
and as the Saviour is declared to have made the world, identified Jesus
with Satan !   Others entirely denied his human nature, on the ground
that the incarnation was a materialising of spirit.   The ascetic practices
of the Eastern church had a similar origin.

dilate upon the fallacy of these views, or to point out the gross and degrading materialism on which they are ultimately based. The historian, while he laments, must to the best of his power record the aberrations of human intelligence, under his inevitable conditions of place and time.

It is uncertain at what period this restriction was first attempted to be enforced in the Western Church, but there are early councils which notice the existence of a strong feeling on the subject[1]. In the year 376 a Gallic synod excommunicated those who should refuse the ministrations of a priest on the ground of his marriage[2]. But this can only prove that at the time there were married priests, whether living in continence or not, and that certain persons were scandalized at them. I cannot admit, as some authors have done, that the Council intended to make such marriages legal ; on the contrary, it seems to me that the intention of the canon is merely to assert the validity of the sacraments, however unworthy might be the person by whom they were administered[3].

[1] "Placuit etiam ut si diacones aut presbyteri coniugati ad torum uxorum suorum redire voluerint," etc. Concil. Agathense, an. 506. Can. 9.

[2] "Si quis secernat se a presbytero qui uxorem duxit, tanquam non oporteat, illo liturgiam peragente, de oblatione percipere, anathema sit." Concil. Gangrense, an. 376. Can. 4. This provision was retained by Burkhart of Worms in his collection of canons made in the eleventh century. See Dönniges, Deut. Staatsr. p. 507. Schmidt, Gesch. der Deutschen, IV Band, lib. 4. cap. 13.

[3] This was at least the feeling in the eleventh century. Wendover speaks in the following terms of the Council of Rome, celebrated by Gregory the Seventh in 1074:—"Iste papa in synodo generali simoniacos excommunicavit, uxoratos sacerdotes a divino removit officio, et

But restrictions which wound the natural feelings
of men are vain: popes and councils may decree,
but they cannot enforce obedience, and it seems to
me that on this particular subject they never entirely succeeded in carrying out their views. All
they did was to convert a holy and a blessed connexion into one of much lower character, and to
throw the doors wide open to immorality and
scandal. The efforts of Boniface in Germany were
particularly directed to this point [1], and his biogra-

laicis missas eorum audire interdixit, novo exemplo et, ut multis visum
est, inconsiderato iudicio, contra sanctorum patrum sententiam, qui
scripserunt, quod sacramenta quae in aecclesia fiunt, baptisma, chrisma,
corpus Christi et sanguis, Spiritu invisibiliter cooperante, eorundem
sacramentorum effectum [habeant], seu per bonos, seu per malos intra
Dei aecclesiam dispensentur; tamen quia Spiritus Sanctus mystice illa
vivificat, nec bonorum meritis amplificantur, nec peccatis malorum
attenuantur. Ex qua re tam grave oritur scandalum, ut nullius hae-
resis tempore sancta aecclesia graviori sit schismate discissa, his pro
iustitia, illis contra iustitiam agentibus; porro paucis continentiam ob-
servantibus, aliquibus eam causa lucri ac iactantiae simulantibus,
multis incontinentiam periurio multipliciori adulterio cumulantibus:
ad haec, opportunitate laicis insurgentibus contra sacros ordines, et se
ab omni aecclesiastica subiectione excutientibus, laici sacra mysteria
temerant et de his disputant, infantes baptizant, sordido aurium
humore pro sacro chrismate utentes et oleo, in extremo vitae viaticum
Dominicum et usitatum aecclesiae obsequium sepulturae a presbyteris
uxoratis accipere parvipendunt; decimas etiam presbyteris debitas
igne cremant, corpus Domini a presbyteris uxoratis consecratum
pedibus saepe conculcant, sanguinem Domini voluntarie frequenter in
terram effundunt." Wend. ii. 13. See the Acts of this Council in
Hardouin, vi. col. 1521 *seq.* In the following year, 1075, the abbot of
Pontoise was insulted and beaten in a council held at Paris, for
defending this decree of Gregory.

[1] Boniface appears to have been quite as earnest in the eighth as
Dunstan was in the tenth century. We are told of him in Thuringia,
that in accordance with the instructions of the Apostolical Pontiff,
" senatores plebis totiusque populi principes verbis spiritalibus affa-
tus est; eosque ad veram agnitionis viam et intelligentiae lucem pro-
vocavit, quam olim ante maxima siquidem ex parte pravis seducti

pher tells us on more than one occasion of his success in destroying the influence of married priests.
But it may be questioned whether the same result
attended the efforts of the Roman missionaries in
England. It seems to me, on the contrary, that we
have an almost unbroken chain of evidence to show
that, in spite of the exhortations of the bishops,

doctoribus perdiderunt; sed et sacerdotes ac presbiteros, quorum alii
religioso Dei se omnipotentis cultu incoluerunt, alii quidem fornicaria
contaminati pollutione castimoniae continentiam, quam sacris servientes altaribus servare debuerunt, amiserant, sermonibus evangelicis,
quantum potuit, a malitiae pravitate ad canonicae constitutionis rectitudinem correxit, ammonuit, atque instruxit." Pertz, ii. 341. " Quoniam cessante religiosorum ducum dominatu, cessavit etiam in eis Christianitatis et religionis intentio, et falsi seducentes populum introducti
sunt fratres, qui sub nomine religionis maximam haereticae pravitatis
introduxerunt sectam. Ex quibus est Torhtwine et Berhthere, Eanberhct
et Hunræd, fornicatores et adulteri, quos iuxta apostolum Dominus iudi-
cavit Deus." Pertz, ii. 344. These seem all to have been Anglosaxons.
  " Et recedens, non solum invitatus Baguariorum ab Odilone duce,
sed et spontaneus, visitavit incolas; mansitque apud eos diebus multis,
praedicans et evangelizans verbum Dei ; veraeque fidei ac religionis
sacramenta renovavit, et destructores aecclesiarum populique perver-
sores abigebat. Quorum alii pridem falso se episcopatus gradu prae-
tulerunt, alii etiam presbyteratus se officio deputabant, alii haec atque
alia innumerabilia fingentes, magna ex parte populum seduxerunt. Sed
quia sanctus vir iam Deo ab infantia deditus, iniuriam Domini sui non
ferens, supradictum ducem cunctumque vulgus ab iniusta haereticae
falsitatis secta et fornicaria sacerdotum deceptione coercuit; et provinciam Baguariorum, Odilone duce consentiente, in quattuor divisit
parochias, quattuorque his praesidere fecit episcopos, quos ordinatione scilicet facta, in episcopatus gradum sublevant." Pertz, ii. 346.
  " Domino Deo opitulante, ac suggerente sancto Bonifatio archiepiscopo, religionis christianae confirmatum est testamentum, et orthodox-
orum patrum synodalia sunt in Francis correcta instituta, cunctaque.
canonum auctoritate emendata atque expiata, et tam laicorum iniusta
concubinarum copula partim, exhortante sancto viro separata est, quam
etiam clericorum nefanda cum uxoribus coniunctio seiuncta ac segre-
gata." Pertz, ii. 346. The anonymous author of the life of Boniface
tells of a bishop Gerold, who held the see of Mayence : he had a son
who succeeded him in the bishopric. Pertz, ii. 354.

and the legislation of the witan, those at least of
the clergy who were not bound to cœnobitical
order, did contract marriage, and openly rear the
families which were its issue. From Eddius we
learn that Wilfriŏ, bishop of York, one of the
staunchest supporters of Romish views, had a son[1];
he does not indeed say that this son was born in
wedlock, nor does any author directly mention
Wilfriŏ's marriage : but we may adopt this view of
the matter, as the less scandalous of two alterna-
tives, and as rendered probable by the absence of
all accusations which might have been brought
against the bishop on this score by any one of his
numerous enemies. In a charter of emancipation
we find among the witnesses, Ælfsige the priest
and his son[2]: by another document a lady grants
a church hereditarily to Wulfmær the priest and
his offspring, as long as he shall have any in
orders[3], where a succession of married clergymen
is obviously contemplated. Again we read of Godwine at Worŏig bishop Ælfsige's son[4], and of the
son of Oswald a presbyter[5]. Under Eádweard the
Confessor we are told of Robert the deacon and his

---

[1] " Sanctus Pontifex noster de exilio cum filio suo proprio rediens,"
etc. Vit. Wilfr. cap. 57. [2] Cod. Dipl. No. 1352.

[3] " Wulfmær preóst and his bearnteám." Cod. Dipl. No. 946.

[4] " Godwine æt Worŏige, Ælfsiges bisceopes sunu." Chron. Sax.
an. 1001. This however was not confined to England : we hear of
more than one Frankish bishop having children : for example, " An-
chisus dux egregius, filius Arnulfi, episcopi Mettensis." Ann. Xantens.
an. 647. Pertz, ii. 219. See also Paul. Gest. Ep. Mettens. Pertz, ii.
264. [See also T. F. Klitsche, " Geschichte des Cölibats," etc. Augsb.
1830 ; J. A. Zaccaria. Storia Polemica del Sagro celibato, Roma, 1774 ;
and Suppl. to Engl. Cyclop., Arts and Sciences, *art.* Celibacy.]

[5] " Filius Oswaldi presbyteri." Hist. Rams., cap. xlv.

son-in-law Richard Fitzscrob[1], and of Gódríc a son
of the king's chaplain Gódman[2].

It may no doubt be argued that in some of these
instances the children may have been the issue of
marriages contracted before the father entered into
orders; but it is obvious that this was not the case
with all of them, nor is there any proof that any
were so. On the other hand we have evidence of
married priests which it would be difficult to reject.
Florence speaks of the newly born son of a certain
presbytera, or priest's wife[3]: I have already cited
a passage from Simeon of Durham which distinctly
mentions a married presbyter[4], about the year
1045: and the History of Ely records the wife and
family of an archipresbyter in that town[5]. Lastly
we are told over and over again that one principal
cause for the removal of the canons or prebendaries from the cathedrals and collegiate churches by
Æðelwold and Oswald was the contravention of
their rule by marriage.

The frequent allusion to this subject by the kings
in various enactments, serve to show very clearly
that the clergy would not submit to the restraint

---

[1] " Robertum diaconem et generum eius, Ricardum filium Scrob....
quos plus caeteris rex diligebat." Flor. Wig. an. 1052.

[2] " Godricum regis capellani Godmanni filium, abbatem constituit."
Flor. Wig. an. 1053.

[3] Flor. Wig. an. 1035. It is right to add that some MSS. of Florence
read *presbyteri*, not *presbyterae*.

[4] See vol. i. 145. "At ille qui ipsa nocte cum uxore dormierat," etc.
Sim. Dun. Eccl. Dun. cap. xlv.

[5] " Mox ingens pestis arripuit domum illius sacerdotis; quae conju-
gem eius ac liberos eius cita morte percussit, totamque progeniem funditus extirpavit." Hist. Eliens. Anglia Sacra, i. 603.

attempted to be enforced upon them. But we have
a still more conclusive evidence in the words of an
episcopal charge delivered by archbishop Ælfric.
He says, " Beloved, we cannot now compel you by
force to observe chastity, but we admonish you to
observe it, as the ministers of Christ ought, and as
did those holy men whom we have already mentioned, and who spent all their lives in chastity [1]."
It is thus very clear that the clergy paid little regard to such admonishments, unsupported by secular penalties.   In this, as perhaps in some other
cases, the good sense and sound feeling of the nation struggled successfully against the authority of
the Papal See.   In fact, though spirituality were the
pretext, a most abominable slavery to materialism
lies at the root of all the grounds on which the
Roman prelates founded the justification of their
course.   That they had ulterior objects in view
may easily be surmised, though these may have
been but dimly described and hesitatingly confessed,
until Gregory the Seventh boldly and openly
avowed them.   Had the Roman church ventured
to argue that the clergy ought to be separated entirely from the nation and the state, nay from
humanity itself, for certain definite purposes and
ends, it would at least have deserved the praise of
candour; and much might have been alleged in favour of this view while the clergy were still strictly
missionaries exposed to the perils and uncertainties
of a daily struggle.   But, in an absurd idolatry of

---

[1] Thorpe, ii. 376.

CH. IX.] THE CLERGY AND MONKS. 447

what was miscalled chastity, to proscribe the noblest condition and some of the highest functions
of man, was to set up a rule essentially false, and
literally hold out a premium to immorality; and so
the more reflecting even of the clergy themselves
admitted[1]. Whatever may have been the desire of
the prelates, we may be certain that not only in
England, but generally throughout the North of
Europe, the clergy did enter into quasi-marriages;
and as late as the thirteenth century, the priests in
Norway replied to Gregory the Ninth by setting
up the fact of uninterrupted custom[2].

[1] In 1102 archbishop Anselm excommunicated married priests, *sacerdotes concubinarios;* Wendover, who records this act, expresses a
doubt about its prudence. " Hoc autem bonum quibusdam visum est,
et quibusdam periculosum, ne, dum munditias viribus maiores expe-
terent, in immunditias labarentur." Wend. ii. 171. The results at this
day in Ireland are well known, and the case is very similar in the
Roman Catholic part of Hungary. See Paget, Hungary and Tran-
sylvania, i. 114. Shortly before the Reformation, the inconveniences
arising from this state of things were felt to be so intolerable, yet the
danger to society from a strict enforcement of the rule so great, that
in some parts of Europe the bishop licensed their priests to take concubines, at a settled tariff, and further raised a sum upon each child
born. Erasmus relates that one bishop had admitted to him the issuing
of no less than twelve thousand such licenses in one year. In his diocese
the tax was probably light, the peasants sturdy, and the female population more than ordinarily chaste. It was not unusual for the English
kings to compel the priests to redeem their *focariae* or concubines,
which amounts to much the same thing. This occurred in the years
1129 and 1208. See Wendover, ii. 210; iii. 223.

[2] Gregory writes thus upon the subject to Sigurdr, archbishop of
Nidaros : " Sicut ex parte tua fuit propositum coram nobis tam in dio-
cesi quam in provincia Nidrosensi abusus detestandae consuetudinis in-
olevit, quod videlicet sacerdotes inibi existentes matrimonia contrahunt,
et utuntur tanquam laici sic contractis. Et licet tu iuxta officii tui
debitum id curaveris artius inhibere, multi tamen praetendentes excu-
sationes frivolas in peccatis, scilicet quod felicis recordationis Hadrianus
papa praedecessor noster, tunc episcopus Albanensis, dum in partibus

In addition to the clergy who either in their conventual or parochial churches administered the rites of religion to their flocks, very considerable monastic establishments existed from an early period in England. It is true that not every church which our historians call *monasterium* was really a monastic foundation, but many of them undoubtedly were so; and it is likely that they supplied no small number of presbyters and bishops to the service of the church. The rule of St. Benedict was well established throughout the West long before Augustine set foot in Britain; and although monks are not necessarily clergymen, it is probable that many of the body in this country took holy orders. Like the clergy the monks were subject to the control of the bishop, and the abbots received consecration from the diocesan. Till a late period in fact, there is little reason to suppose that any English monastery succeeded in obtaining exemption from episcopal visitation: though on the other hand it is probable that monasteries founded by powerful and wealthy laymen did contrive practically to establish a considerable independence. This is the more conceivable, because we cannot doubt that a great difference did from the first exist be-

illis legationis officio fungeretur, hoc fieri permisisset, quanquam super hoc nullum ipsius documentum ostendant, perire potius eligunt quam parere, longam super hoc nichilominus consuetudinem allegando. Cum igitur diuturnitas temporis peccatum non minuat sed augmentet, mandamus quatenus, si ita est, abusum huiusmodi studeas extirpare, et in rebelles, si qui fuerint, censuram aecclesiasticam exercere. Datum Viterbii, xvii Kal. Junii, anno undecimo." This is A.D. 1237. Diplom. Norweg. No. 19, vol. i. pag. 15.

tween the rules adopted by various congregations of monks, or imposed upon them by their patrons and founders, until the time when greater familiarity with Benedict's regulations, and the customs of celebrated houses, produced a more general conformity.

One of the most disputed questions in Anglosaxon history is that touching the revival of monkery by Dúnstán and his partizans. Its supposed connexion with the tragical story of Eádwig, and the dismemberment of England by Eádgár, have lent it some of the attractions of romance; and by the monastic chroniclers in general, it has very naturally been looked upon as the greatest point in the progressive record of our institutions. Connected as it is with some of the most violent prejudices of our nature, political, professional and personal, it has not only obtained a large share of attention from ecclesiastical historians of all ages, but has been discussed with great eagerness, not to say acrimony, by those who differed in opinion as to the wisdom and justice of the revival itself. Yet it does not appear to me to have been brought to the degree of clearness which we should have expected from the skill and learning of those who have undertaken its elucidation. Neither the share which Dúnstán took in the great revolution, nor the extent to which Æðelwold and Oswald succeeded in their plans, are yet satisfactorily settled; and great obscurity still hangs both over the manner and the effect of the change.

Few things in history, when carefully investi-

gated, do really prove to have been done in a hurry.
Sudden revolutions are much less common than we
are apt to suppose, and fewer links than we imagine are wanting in the great chain of causes and
effects.   Could we place ourselves above the exaggerations of partizans, who hold it a point of honour
to prove certain events to be indiscriminately right
or indiscriminately wrong, we should probably find
that the course of human affairs had been one
steady and very gradual progression ; the reputation of individual men would perhaps be shorn of
part of its lustre ; and though we should lose some
of the satisfaction of hero-worship, we might more
readily admit the constant action of a superintending providence, operating without caprice through
very common and every-day channels.   But it
would have been too much to expect an impartial
account of the events which led to the reformation
of the Benedictine order in England ; like Luther
in the fifteenth, Dúnstán must be made the principal figure in the picture of the tenth century :
throughout all great social struggles the protagonist
stalks before us in gigantic stature,—glorious as
an archangel, or terrible and hideous as Satan.

The writers who arose shortly after the triumph
of the Reformation have revelled in this fruitful
theme.   The abuses of monachism,—not entirely
forgotten at the beginning of the seventeenth century,—its undeniable faults, and the mischief it
entails upon society,—judged with the exaggeration
which unhappily seems inseparable from religious
polemics, produced in every part of Europe a suc-

cession of violent and headlong attacks upon the institution and its patrons, which we can now more readily understand than excuse.   But just as little can the calm, impartial judgment of the historian ratify the indiscriminate praise which was lavished by the Roman Catholics upon all whom the zeal of Protestants condemned, the misrepresentations of fact by which they attempted to fortify their opinions, or the eager credulty which they showed when any tale, however preposterous, appeared to support their particular objects.   In later times the controversy has been renewed with greater decency of language, but not less zeal.   The champion of protestantism is the Rev. Mr. Soames : Dr. Lingard takes up the gauntlet on behalf of his church.   It is no intention of mine to balance their conflicting views as to the character and intentions of Dúnstán and his two celebrated coadjutors ; these have been too deeply tinged by the ground-colour that lies beneath the outlines.   But I propose to examine the facts upon which both parties seem agreed, though each may represent them variously in accordance with a favourite theory.

It admits of no doubt whatever that monachism, and monachism under the rule of St. Benedict, had been established at an early period in this country[1] ;

---

[1] Mr. Soames (Anglosax. Church, p. 179, third edit.) says that Dúnstán's monastery at Glastonbury was the first establishment of the kind ever known in England, and Dúnstán the first of English Benedictine abbots. Nothing can possibly be more inexact than this assertion. Biscop's foundation at Wearmouth was a Benedictine one. In an address to his monks, he himself is represented to say :—" Ideo multum cavetote, fratres, semper, ne secundum genus unquam, ne deforis aliunde vobis Patrem quaeratis ; sed iuxta quod Regula magni quondam abbatis

but it is equally certain that the strict rule had very generally ceased to be maintained at the time

Benedicti, iuxta quod privilegii nostri continent decreta, in conventu vestrae congregationis communi consilio perquiratis, qui secundum vitae meritum et sapientiae doctrinam aptior ad tale ministerium perficiendum digniorque probetur; et quemcunque omnes unanimae charitatis inquisitione optimum cognoscentes eligeretis, hunc vobis, accito episcopo, rogetis abbatem consueta benedictione formari." Beda, Vit. Bened. § 12. (Opera Minora, ii. 151.) The same author tells us of abbot Céolfrið:—" Multa diu secum mente versans, utilius decrevit, dato Fratribus praecepto, ut iuxta sui statuta privilegii, iuxtaque Regulam sancti abbatis Benedicti, de suis sibi ipsi Patrem, qui aptior esset, eligerent, etc." Vit. Bened. § 16. (Op. Min. ii. 156.) The author of the anonymous life of St. Cúðberht, which is earlier than that of Beda, says of Cúðberht at Lindisfarne:—" Vivens ibi quoque secundum sanctam Scripturam, contemplativam vitam in actuali agens, et nobis regularem vitam primus componens constituit, quam usque hodie cum Regula Benedicti observamus." Anon. Cúðb. § 25. (Bed. Op. Min. ii. 271.) At a still later period, viz. the close of the seventh century, we learn that the monastery of Hnutscilling or Nursling in Hampshire was a Benedictine one, and St. Boniface a Benedictine monk. His contemporary biographer Willibald says:—" Maxime suo sub regulari videlicet disciplina abbati, monachica subditus obedientia praebebat, ut labore manuum cottidiano et disciplinali officiorum amministratione incessanter secundum praefinitam beati Patris Benedicti rectae constitutionis formam insisteret," etc.   Vit. Bonif. Pertz, ii. 336. One can hardly imagine how Mr. Soames should suffer himself to be misled by the exaggerations of Dúnstán's monkish biographers: they are of a piece with their whole story. That the rule had become very much relaxed even in the Benedictine abbeys of this country is not to be doubted: the same thing took place on the continent. Many had perished in the Danish invasions; many had passed insensibly into the hands of secular canons: and it is not at all improbable that in the middle of the tenth century there was not a genuine Benedictine society left in England. But this will certainly not justify the assertions of Bridferð or Adelard, that Dúnstán was the first of English Benedictine monks or abbots. " Et hoc praedicto modo saluberrimam sancti Benedicti sequens institutionem, primus abbas Anglicae nationis enituit," (Bridferð. MS. Cott. Cleop. B. xii. fol. 72.)—" Monachorum ibi scholam primo primus instituere coepit,"—(Adel. in Angl. Sacra, ii. 101 note) are at the least grave mistakes: one desires to believe that they are not something worse; but they warn us to be extremely cautious how we admit the authority of their writers as to any facts they may please to record.

when Dúnstán undertook its restoration. Many
of the conventual churches had never been connected with monks at all; while among the various
abbeys which the piety or avarice of individuals had
founded, there were probably numerous instances
where no rule had ever prevailed, but the caprice
of the founders, who *iure dominii* imposed such regulations as their vanity suggested, or their industry
gleaned from the established orders of Columba,
Benedict, and other credited authorities [1]. The

[1] On this point Beda speaks most explicitly: "Sunt loca innumera,
ut novimus omnes, in monasteriorum ascripto vocabulum, sed nihil
prorsus monasticae conversationis habentia." Ep. Ecgb. § 10. "Quod
enim turpe est dicere, tot sub nomine monasteriorum loca hi, qui mona-
chicae vitae prorsus sunt expertes, in suam ditionem acceperunt, sicut
ipse melius nosti," etc. Ibid. § 11. "At alii graviore adhuc flagitio,
quum sint ipsi laici et nullius vitae regularis vel usu exerciti, vel
amore praediti, data regibus pecunia, emunt sibi sub praetextu monasteriorum construendorum territoria, in quibus suae liberius vacent libidini, et haec insuper in ius sibi haereditarium edictis regalibus faciunt
ascribi, ipsas quoque litteras privilegiorum suorum, quasi veraciter Deo
dignas, pontificum, abbatum et potestatum seculi, obtinent subscrip-
tione confirmari. Sicque usurpatis sibi agellulis sive vicis, liberi exinde
a divino simul et humano servitio, suis tantum inibi desideriis laici
monachis imperantes deserviunt; immo non monachos ibi congregant,
sed quoscunque ob culpam inobedientiae veris expulsos monasteriis
alicubi forte oberrantes invenerint, aut evocare monasteriis ipsi value-
rint; vel certe quos ipsi de suis satellitibus ad suscipiendam tonsuram,
promissa sibi obedientia monachica, invitare quiverint. Horum distor-
tis cohortibus suas, quas instruxere, cellas implent, multumque informi
atque inaudito spectaculo, idem ipsi viri modo coniugis ac liberorum
procreandorum curam gerunt, modo exsurgentes de cubilibus, quid
intra septa onasteriorum geri debeat sedula intentione pertractant.
....Sic per annos circiter triginta, hoc est ex quo Aldfrid rex humanis
rebus ablatus est, provincia nostra vesano illo errore dementata est, ut
nullus pene exinde praefectorum extiterit, qui non huiusmodi sibi monasterium in diebus suae praefecturae comparaverit, suamque simul
coniugem pari reatu nocivi mercatus astrinxerit; ac praevalente pessi-
ma consuetudine, ministri quoque regis ac famuli idem facere satege-
rint. Atque ita ordine perverso innumeri sunt inventi, qui se abbates

chapters, whatever their origin, had in process of time slid into that easy and serene state of secular canons, which we can still contemplate in the venerable precincts of cathedral closes. The celibacy of the clergy had not been maintained : and even in the collegiate churches the presbyter and prebendaries had permitted themselves to take wives, which could never have been contemplated even by those who would have looked with indulgence upon that connexion on the part of parish priests. Moreover in many places, wealthy ease, power, a dignified and somewhat irresponsible position had produced their natural effect upon the canons, some of whom were connected with the best families of the state ; so that, in spite of all the deductions which must be made for exaggeration on the part of the monkish writers, we cannot deny that many instances of profligacy and worldly-minded-

pariter et praefectos, sive ministros, aut famulos regis appellant ; qui, etsi aliquid vitae monasterialis ediscere laici, non experiendo sed audiendo, potuerint, a persona tamen illa ac professione, quae hanc docere debeat, sunt funditus exsortes ; et quidem tales repente, ut nosti, tonsuram pro suo libitu accipiunt, suo examine de laicis non monachi sed abbates efficiuntur." Ibid. § 12, 13. (Bed. Op. Min. ii. 216, 218 *seq.*) On these and other grounds Beda earnestly impresses upon Ecgberht the duty of founding the twelve bishoprics contemplated by Gregory in the province of York, in order to multiply the means of ecclesiastical supervision. But if this was the condition of the Northumbrian monasteries in the year 734, the period of Northumbria's greatest literary eminence, what may we conclude to have been the condition of similar establishments in less instructed parts of England, especially after a century of cruel wars had relaxed all the bonds of civilized society ? We may not greatly admire monachism, or believe it useful to a state ; but we can hardly blame those, who, finding the institution in existence, desire to make the men who are attached to it worthy and not unworthy members of their profession.

ness did very probably disgrace the clerical profession. It would be strange indeed if what has taken place in every other age and country should have been unexampled only among the Anglosaxons of the ninth and tenth centuries, or that their monks and clergy should have enjoyed a monopoly of purity, holiness and devotion to duty [1].

As we have seen already, it was only towards the end of the eighth century that Chrodogang introduced a cœnobitical mode of life in the cathedral of his archdiocese. Long before this time the great majority of our churches had been founded; and among them some may possibly from the first have been served by clergymen resident in their own detached houses, and who merely met at stated hours to perform their duties in the choir, living at other times apart upon their præbenda or allowances from the general fund. But some of the cathedrals had been founded in connexion with abbeys; and it is probable that a majority of these great establishments were provided with some Rule of life, and demanded a cœnobitical though not strictly monastic habit. This is too frequently alluded to by the prelates of the seventh century, not to be admitted. But whatever may have been the

---

[1] In the often-cited letter to Ecgberht, Beda gives but a bad character to some among the prelates of his time. He says : " Quod non ita loquor, quasi te aliter facere sciam, sed quia de quibusdam episcopis fama vulgatum est, quod ipsi ita Christo serviant, ut nullos secum alicuius religionis aut continentiae viros habeant ; sed potius illos qui risui, iocis, fabulis, commessationibus, et ebrietatibus, caeterisque vitae remissioris illecebris subigantur, et qui magis quotidie ventrem dapibus quam mentem sacrificiis coelestibus pascant." § 4 (Op Min. ii. 209, 210).

details in different establishments, we may be certain that residence, temperance, soberness, chastity, and a strict attendance upon the divine services were required by the Rule of every society. Unfortunately these are restrictions and duties which experience proves to have been sometimes neglected; nor can we find any great improbability in the assertion of the Saxon Chronicle, that the canons of Winchester would hold no rule at all [1]; or in the accusations brought against them in the Annals of Winchester [2], and in Wulfstán's Life of Æðelwold [3], of violating every one of their obligations. I do not see any reason to doubt the justice of the charge made against some of their body by the last-named author, of having deserted the wives they had taken, and living in open and scandalous disregard of morality as well as canonical restraint. Wulfstán very likely made the most of his facts, but it is to be remembered that he was an eyewitness; and it is improbable that he should have been indebted exclusively to his invention for charges so boldly made, so capable of being readily brought to the test, and containing in truth nothing

[1] "Dráf út ða clerca of ða biscopríce, forðan ðæt hí noldon nán Regul healdan." Chron. Sax. an. 963.

[2] "Clerici illi, nominetenus Canonici, frequentationem chori, labores vigiliarum, et ministerium altaris vicariis suis utcumque sustentatis relinquentes, et ab aecclesiae conspectu plerumque absentes septennio, quidquid de praebendis percipiebant, locis et modis sibi placitis absumebant. Nuda fuit aecclesia intus et extra." An. Wint. p. 289.

[3] "Erant Canonici nefandis scelerum moribus implicati, elatione et insolentia, atque luxuria praeventi, adeo ut nonnulli eorum dedignarentur missas suo ordine celebrare, repudiantes uxores quas illicite duxerant, et alias accipientes, gulae et ebrietati iugiter dediti." Vit. Æðelw. p. 614.

repugnant to our experience of human nature. The
canons of Winchester, many of whom were highly
connected, wealthy beyond those of most other
foundations, and established in the immediate vicinity of the royal court, may possibly have been
more than ordinarily neglectful of their duties [1];
and they do appear in fact to have been treated in
a much more summary way than the prebendaries
of other cathedrals; yet perhaps not with strict
justice, unless it can be shown that Winchester was
ever a monastic establishment, which, previous to
Æðelwold, I do not remember it to have been.
Lingard who would have gratefully accepted any
evidence against the canons in the other cathedrals,
confines himself to Winchester; yet it strikes one
as some confirmation of the general charge, even
against their brethren at Worcester, that among
the signatures to their charters so few are those of
deacons and presbyters, till long after Oswald's
appointment to the see. This, although the silence
of their adversaries allows us to acquit them of the
irregularities laid to the charge of the canons at
Winchester, may lead us to infer that they were

---

[1] The description of a secular clerk given by the anonymous author
of the Gesta Abbatum Fontanellensium, written in the ninth century,
was probably not exaggerated. He says of Wido, a relative of Charles
Martel, " Erat de saecularibus clericis, gladioque quem semispatium
vocant semper accinctus, sagoque pro cappa utebatur, parumque aecclesiasticae disciplinae imperiis parebat. Nam copiam canum multiplicem
semper habebat, cum qua venationi quotidie insistebat, sagittatorque
praecipuus in arcubus ligneis ad aves feriendas erat, hisque operibus
magis quam aecclesiasticae disciplinae studiis se exercebat.' It does
not surprise us to learn that this prelate was also " ignarus litterarum."
Pertz, i. 284, 285.

not scrupulously diligent in fulfilling the duties of
their calling.

We cannot feel the least surprise that Dúnstán
desired to reform the state of the church. The
peculiar circumstances of his early years, even the
severe mental struggles which preceded and explain
his adoption of the monastic career, were eminently
calculated to train him for a *Reviver ;* and Revival
was the fashion of his day. Arnold earl of Flanders [1] had lent himself with the utmost zeal to the
reform of the Benedictine abbeys in his territory,
and they were the models selected for imitation, or
as schools of instruction, by other lands, especially
England so closely connected with Flanders by
commerce and the alliances of the reigning houses [2].

---

[1] Arnold died in 964, but his reforms began twenty years earlier.
However, between the years 912 and 942, Berno, and his still more
celebrated successor Odo, abbots of Cluny, had introduced a reform of
the Benedictine rule in a great number of monasteries. Flodoardus
calls Odo : "Dominus Odo, venerabilis abbas, multorum restaurator
monasteriorum, sanctaeque Regulae reparator." See Pagi. Baron. ad
an. 942. This example was not lost upon Dúnstán.

[2] "Baudouin le chauve, IIe comte de Flandre, s'empara, en 900, des
deux abbayes de St. Vaast et St. Bertin.... Dès l'année 944, Arnould-
le-vieux, rentré en possession de St. Vaast, entreprit la réforme de ces
abbayes, par les soins de St. Gérard de Brognes, qu'il nomma abbé de
St. Bertin. Il le chargea ensuite (probablement vers 950) de celle
des abbayes de St. Pierre et de St. Bavon à Gand, qu'il avait égale-
ment sous son pouvoir : Womare en fut nommé abbé. Ces reformes,
sans doute d'après la règle de Cluny, créé en 910 [read 912 not 910],
s'étendirent d'après la chronique de St. Bertin (Thes. Anecd. iii. 552,
553), à dix-huit abbayes de l'ordre de Saint Benoit (Chron. de Jean de
Thielrode, édit. de M. Vanlokeren, p. 127). Les moines qui refusèrent
de s'y soumettre, furent expulsés de leurs monastères : quelques-uns
émigrèrent en Angleterre ou ailleurs." Warnkönig, Hist. Fland. ii.
338 *seq.* In 956 Dúnstán flying from England, found hospitality and
rest in one of these reformed houses, that of Blandinium or St. Peter,
at Ghent.

Yet with it all, Dúnstán does not appear to have taken a very prominent part in the proceedings of the friends of monachism,—certainly not the prominent part taken by Oswald or Æðelwold, the last of whom merited the title of the "Father of Monks," by the attention he paid to their interests. In the archbishop's own cathedral at Canterbury, the canons were left in undisturbed possession of their property and dignity, nor were monks introduced there by archbishop Ælfríc till some years after Dúnstán's death. And even this measure, although supported by papal authority [1], was not final : it was only in the time of Lanfranc that the monks obtained secure possession of Christchurch. Dúnstán very probably continued throughout his life to be a favourer of the Order, and merited its gratitude by giving it valuable countenance and substantial protection against violence. But he was assuredly not himself a violent disturber, casting all things divine and human into confusion for the sake of a system of monkery. His recorded conduct shows nothing of the kind. I believe his monkish and very vulgar-minded panegyrists to have done his character and memory great wrong in this respect ; and that they have measured the distinguished statesman by the narrow gauge of their own intelligence and desire. Troublous no doubt were his commencements; and in the days of his misery, while his mind yet tossed

---

[1] Chron. Sax. an. 995. Probably it never had been monastic from the very time of Augustine : and the setting up a claim on the part of the monks, derived from Augustine himself, was totally inadmissible.

and struggled among the awful abysses of an un-
fathomed sea in the fierce conflicts of his ascetic
retirement, where the broken heart sought rest
and found it not, he may have given credence himself to what he considered supernatural visitations
vouchsafed, and powers committed, to him. But
when time had somewhat healed his wounds, when
the first difficulties of his political life were sur-
mounted, and he ruled England,—nominally as the
minister of Eádgár, really as the leader of a very
powerful party among the aristocracy,—there can
be little doubt that the spirit of compromise, which
always has been the secret of our public life, produced its necessary effect upon himself. Dúnstán
was neither Richelieu nor Mazarin, but the servant
of a king who wielded very limited powers; he had
first attained his throne through a revolt, the pretext for which was his brother's bad government,
and its justification,—the consequent right of the
people to depose him. Whatever may have been
the archbishop's private leaning, he appears to
have conducted himself with great discretion, and
to have very skilfully maintained the peace between the two embittered factions; he perhaps
encouraged Eádgár to manifest his partiality for
monachism by the construction or reform of abbeys;
he probably supported Oswald and Æðelwold by
his advice, and by preventing them from being
illegally interfered with in the course of their lawful actions; but as prime minister of England, he
maintained the peace as well for one as for the
other, and there is no evidence that any measure

of violence or spoliation took place by his conni-
vance or consent. Neither the nation, nor the
noble families whose scions found a comfortable
provision and sufficient support in the prebends,
would have looked calmly upon the .unprovoked
destruction of rights sanctioned by prescription.
But there is indeed no reason to believe that violent measures were resorted to in any of the establishments, to bring about the changes desired.
Even in Winchester, where more compulsion seems
to have been used than anywhere else, the evicted
canons were provided with pensions. I strongly
suspect that in fact they did retain during their
lives the prebends which could not legally be taken
from them, though they might be expelled from
the cathedral service and the collegiate buildings;
and that this is what the monkish writers veil
under the report that pensions were assigned
them.

Dr. Lingard has very justly observed that Oswald, with all his zeal, made no change whatever
in his cathedral of York, which archdiocese he at
one time held together with Worcester; and that,
generally speaking, the new monasteries were either
reared upon perfectly new ground, or on ancient
foundations then entirely reduced to ruins [1]. With
regard to Worcester, he says:—"Of Oswald we

---

[1] Hist. and Ant. Ang. Church, ii. 290, 294. This was certainly the
case with several of Æðelwold's monasteries ; and I regret to think that
many of the Saxon charters which pretend to the greatest antiquity
were forged on occasion of this revival, to enlarge the basis of the
restored foundations.

are told that he introduced monks in the place
of clergymen into seven churches within his bishopric; but there is reason to believe that some
of the seven were new foundations, and that in
some of the others the change was effected with
the full consent of the canons themselves. In his
cathedral he succeeded by the following artifice.
Having erected in its vicinity a new church to the
honour of the Virgin Mary, he entrusted it to the
care of a community of monks, and frequented it
himself for the solemn celebration of mass. The
presence of the bishop attracted that of the people; the ancient clergy saw their church gradually
abandoned; and after some delay, Wensine, their
dean, a man advanced in years and of unblemished
character, took the monastic habit, and was advanced three years later to the office of prior. The
influence of his example and the honour of his
promotion, held out a strong temptation to his
brethren; till at last the number of canons was so
diminished by repeated desertions, that the most
wealthy of the churches of Mercia became without
dispute or violence, by the very act of its old possessors, a monastery of Benedictine monks [1]. In
what manner Oswald proceeded with the other
churches we are ignorant; but in 971 he became
archbishop of York, and though he held that high
dignity during twenty years, we do not read that
he introduced a single colony of monks or changed

[1] Eadmer, Vit. Oswald, p. 202. Ang. Sac. i. 542. Hist. Rames.
p. 400.

the constitution of a single clerical establishment, within the diocese.   The reason is unknown."

It might not unfairly be suggested either that the rights of the canons were too well established to be shaken, or that experience had changed his own mind as to the necessity of the alteration. High station, active engagement with the details of business, increasing age, and a natural mutual respect which grows with better acquaintance, may have convinced Oswald that his youthful zeal had a little outrun discretion, and that the canons in his province and diocese were not so utterly devoid of claims to consideration as he once had imagined in his reforming fervour.   But the reader of Anglo-saxon history will not fail to have observed that the measured and in general fair tone of Dr. Lingard differs very widely from that of early monkish chroniclers, and that he himself attributes to Oswald a much less active interference than is asserted by many protestant historians.   That he is right I do not for a moment doubt; for not only are the accounts of Oswald's biographers inconsistent with one another, and improbable, but we have very strong evidence that the eviction of the canons from Worcester was not completed in Oswald's lifetime. We possess no fewer than seventy-eight charters granted by his chapter, and these comprise several signed in 990 and 991, the years immediately preceding that in which he died [1]: these charters are signed in part by presbyters

---

[1] Cod. Dipl. Nos. 674–678.

and deacons, in part by clerics, and there is but one signature of a monk [1], though there are at least six *clerici* who subscribe. Although from an examination of the charters I entertain no doubt that several, if not all, the presbyters and deacons were monks, still it is clear that a number of the canons still retained their influence over the property of the chapter till within a few months of Oswald's decease. This prelate came to his see in 960, and according to many accounts immediately replaced the canons of Worcester by monks: all agree that he lost no time about it, and Florence [2], himself a monk of that place, fixes his triumph in the year 969. Consistently with this we have a grant of that year [3], in which Wynsige the monk, and all the monks at Worcester are named: we have a similar statement [4] in another document of 974: and in subsequent charters monks are named. A good example occurs in a grant of the year 977, to which are appended the names of eight monks [5]: but coupled with these are also the names of sixteen clerics, exclusive of a presbyter and deacon of old standing, whom the chapter had probably caused to be ordained long

---

[1] In Nos. 675, 678. In the other charters where this Leófwine occurs, he is even called *clericus*, unless it were another person of the same name.

[2] An. 969. " S. Oswaldus, sui voti compos effectus, clericos Wigorniensis aecclesiae monachilem habitum suscipere renuentes de monasterio expulit; consentientes vero, hoc anno, ipso teste monachizavit, eisque Ramesiensium coenobitam Wynsinum, magnae religionis virum, loco decani praefecit."

[3] Cod. Dipl. No. 553.   [4] Ibid. No. 586.

[5] Ibid. No. 615.

before, to do the service for them.   All at once the
addition *monachus* to seven of these eight names
vanishes, and is replaced by *presbyter* or *diaconus*.
Henceforth the number of *clerici* gradually diminishes, but, as we have seen, is not entirely gone
in 991, the year before Oswald's death.   I do not
believe that the bishop had any power to expel the
canons, and that he was compelled to let them
remain where they were until they died : but he
perhaps could prevent any but monks from being
received in their places, and it is to be presumed
that he could refuse to admit any but monks to
priests' and deacons' orders.   This, we may gather
from the charters, was the plan he pursued ; and
when we consider the dignity and power possessed
by the Anglosaxon priesthood, we shall confess that
it was one which threw every advantage into the
scale of monachism.

Had we similar means of enquiry, it is very probable that we should come to the same conclusion
with regard to other establishments from which
the canons are said to have been forcibly driven.
However enough seems to have been said, to
prove that we must be very careful how we trust to
the random assertions of partizans either on one
side or the other.   Let us be ready to condemn
ecclesiastical tyranny and arrogance, wherever it is
proved to have disgraced the clerical profession;
but let us not forget that it is our duty to judge
charitably.   In the case which we have now considered, I think we shall be disposed to acquit

some men, whose names fill a conspicuous place in Saxon history, of the violence and folly which their own over-zealous partizans have laid to their charge, and which have been used in modern times to embitter the separation unfortunately existing between two great bodies of Christians.

CHAPTER X.

THE INCOME OF THE CLERGY.

THE means provided for the support of the clergy were various at various periods, consisting sometimes merely of voluntary donations on the part of the people, sometimes of grants of lands, or settled endowments, and sometimes of fixed charges upon persons and property, recognized by the state and levied under its authority: and after the secure establishment of a Christian church in Britain, it is probable that all these several sources of income were combined to supply its ministers with a decent maintenance, if not even an easy competence. The grant of lands whereon to erect a church or a monastery was generally calculated also to furnish arable and pasture for the support of its inmates: for the earliest clergy were in fact cœnobites, and lived in common, even if they were not monks, and subject to the Benedictine or some other Rule. It is not at all probable that the heathen priesthood should have been without an adequate provision, whether in land or the free oblations of the people, and very likely that their Christian successors profited by the custom. As the piety or superstition of the masses increased the landed possessions of the clergy, these not only could depend upon the

2 H 2

produce of their estates, but upon the rents in kind, in money or in service, which they received from tenants or poor dependents. And from early periods, either custom or positive law had established a right to claim certain contributions at fixed periods of the year, or on particular occasions; such were tithes of fruits of the earth, and young of cattle; cyricsceat or first-fruits of seed, light-money, plough-alms, and sáwlsceat or mortuary fees. The numberless grants of lands recorded in the Codex Diplomaticus in favour of the clergy, dispense with the necessity of entering at any length upon this head; but some more detailed examination of the other church-dues is desirable, inasmuch as they have been in some degree misunderstood by several writers who have heretofore treated of them. In truth, it was comparatively difficult to deal with these subjects, till the publication of all the Anglo-saxon laws and a very large body of the charters so greatly increased the number of data upon which alone sound conclusions could be formed.

The subject of tithe is surrounded with difficulty, not only from the obscurity which belongs to its history, but still more from the nature of the discussions to which it has given rise. That from periods so early as to transcend historical record the clergy should have been permitted universally to claim a tenth of all increase, does indeed seem so startling a proposition, that we are little surprised at its having met with angry opposition. It does not seem consonant to the general experience of man that in all nations precisely the same mode

should be adopted of supporting any class of men;
nor is it natural or easy to believe that a missionary
body, in constant danger of finding all their efforts
vain, should prevail at once to establish so serious
a claim against the income of their converts.

Still there are various circumstances which tend
to explain this process and show how a general
consent upon this subject did gradually prevail.
From the first moment when the clergy appear as
a separate class from the whole body of the faithful, they appear as a body formed upon the plan
and guided by the maxims of the Jewish hierarchy.
While the church was literally performing the command of the Saviour,—when those who had anything, sold all they had and gave it to the poor,
through the hands of the Apostles,—there was no
particular necessity to define very closely the functions or the remuneration of the ministers; these
gave their services as others did their wealth, as an
acceptable sacrifice to the Giver of all good things.
But when the number of the congregations increased, when compromises were made, and more
complicated duties were imposed upon the ministers
of the church, it was only reasonable that some arrangement should be made for their support, and
some rule imposed for their direction.   It was not
too much to require that they should devote their
whole time and talents to the service of the congregation, and that these in turn should relieve
them from the necessity of daily labour for subsistence.   When the duty of teaching, as well as
visiting the sick, distributing the alms of the faith-

ful, and providing for the due celebration of the religious rites, principally devolved upon them, it would have been as impolitic as unjust to have condemned them to uncertainty or anxiety as to their daily bread. At a very early period the voluntary oblations of the faithful were duly apportioned, and a part devoted to the support of the clergy. But no one, I imagine, will consider this to be a perfectly satisfactory mode of providing for the ministers of the church: its inconveniences are daily manifested in our own time, and would now probably not be submitted to at all, had opposition not lent a dignity to the principle, and did the case present any but the actual alternative. It nevertheless seems that for nearly four hundred years this was the only mode of providing not only for the maintenance of the clergy, but for the acts of charity which the Christian congregations considered their especial duty[1]; although perhaps here and there

[1] " Till toward the end of the first four hundred [years] no payment of them [*i. e.* tithes] can be proved to have been in use. Some *opinion* is of their being due, and *constitutions* also, but such as are of no credit. For the first, 'tis best declared by showing the course of the church-maintenance in that time. So liberal in the beginning of Christianity was the devotion of the believers, that their bounty to the evangelical priesthood far exceeded what the tenth could have been. For if you look to the first of the Apostles' times, then the unity of heart among them about Jerusalem, was such that all was in common and none wanted, ' and as many as were possessors of lands or houses, sold them and brought the price of the things that were sold, and laid it down at the Apostles' feet, and it was distributed unto every man, according as he had need [a].' And the whole church, both lay and clergy, then lived in common as the monks did afterward about the end of the first four hundred years as St. Chrysostome notes [b]; οὕτως, says he, οἱ ἐν τοῖς

[a] Acts iv. 34.   [b] Hom. 11. in Acta.

the wealthier or more pious communicants might
have charged their estates with settled payments at

μοναστηρίοις ζῶσι νῦν ὥσπερ τότε οἱ πιστοὶ, that is, 'So they live now in
monasteries as then the believers lived.' But this kind of having all
things in common scarce at all continued. For we see not long after
in the church of Antiochia (where Christianity was first of all by that
name professed) every one of the disciples had a special ability or estate
of his own[a]. So in Galatia and in Corinth where St. Paul ordained
that weekly offerings for the Saints should be given by every man as he
had thrived in his estate[b]. By example of these, the course of monthly
offerings succeeded in the next ages. These monthly offerings given
by devout and able Christians, the bishops or officers appointed in the
church received[c]; and carefully and charitably disposed them on
Christian worship, the maintenance of the clergy, feeding, clothing,
and burying their poor brethren, widows, orphans, persons tyrannically
condemned to the mines, to prison, or punished by deportation into
isles. They were called *Stipes* (which is a word borrowed from the
use of the heathens in their collections made for their temples and
deities), neither were they exacted by canon or otherwise, but arbi-
trarily given; as by testimony of most learned Tertullian[d], that lived
about CC years after Christ, is apparent: 'Neque pretio (are his
words) ulla res Dei constat. Etiam si quod arcae genus est, non de
oneraria summa quasi redemptae religionis congregatur, modicam unusquisque Stipem, menstruâ die, vel cum velit, et si modo velit, et si
modo possit, apponit. Nam nemo compellitur, sed sponte confert.
Haec quasi deposita pietatis sunt.' And then he shewes the employment of them in those charitable uses. Some authority is[e], that about
this time lands began also to be given to the church. If they were
so, out of the profits of them, and this kind of offerings, was made
a treasure; and out of that, which was increased so monthly, was
a monthly pay given to the priests and ministers of the Gospel
(as a salarie for their service), and that either by the hand or care
of the bishop, or of some elders appointed as Oeconomi or War-
dens. These monthly pays they called Mensurnae divisiones, as you
may see in St. Cyprian[f], who wrote, being bishop of Carthage, about

---

[a] Acts xi. 29.
[b] 1 Cor. xvi. 2.   Ockam, in Oper. xc dierum, cap. 107.
[c] Synod. Gangr. can. lxvi.   [d] Apologetic. cap. 39, 42.
[e] Urban. i. in Epist. c. 12, q. 1, c. 16, i. Sed et vide Euseb. Eccles.
Hist. lib. 9. cap. 9.   Edict. Maximin. et lib. 10. cap. 5.   Edict. Constant. et in lib. 2. de vita Constantini, cap. 39.
[f] Cyprian, Epist. 27, 34 : et vide Epist. 36, editione Pammeliana.

fixed times; or the liberality of individuals might
have presented estates to the church of particular

the year CCL, and, speaking familiarly of this use, calls the brethren
that cast in their monthly offerings, *fratres sportulantes*, understanding the offerings under the word Sportulae, which at first in
Rome denoted a kind of running banquets distributed at great men's
houses to such as visited for salutation, which being ofttimes also given
in money, the word came at length to signify both those salaries, wages
or fees which either judges[a] or ministers of courts of justice received
as due to their places, as also to denote the oblations given to make a
treasure for the salaries and maintenance of the ministers of the church
in this primitive age, and to this purpose was it also used in later
times[b]. But because that passage of St. Cyprian, where he uses this
phrase, well shows also the course of the maintenance of the church in
his time, take it here transcribed: but first know the drift of his Epistle
to be a reprehension of Geminius Faustinus a priest his being troubled
with the care of a wardship, whereas such as take that dignity upon
them, should, he says, be free from all secular troubles like the Levites,
who were provided for in tithes. ' Ut qui (as he writes[c]) operationibus
divinis insistebant, in nulla re avocarentur, nec cogitare aut agere
saecularia cogerentur.' And then he adds : ' Quae nunc ratio et forma
in Clero tenetur, ut qui in ecclesia Domini ad ordinationem clericalem
promoventur, nullo modo ab administratione divina avocentur, sed in
honore sportulantium fratrum, tanquam Decimas ex fructibus accipientes, ab Altari et Sacrificiis non recedant, et die ac nocte coelestibus
rebus et spiritualibus serviant;' which plainly agrees with that course
of monthly pay, made out of the oblations brought into the Treasury
which kind of means he compares to that of the Levites, as being proportionable. But hence also 'tis manifest, that no payment of tithes
was in St. Cyprian's time in use, although some, too rashly, from this
very place would infer so much, those words *tanquam Decimas accipientes* (which continues the comparing of ministers of the Gospel with
the Levites) plainly exclude them. And elsewhere also the same Father,
finding fault with a coldness of devotion that then possest many, in
regard of what was in use in the Apostles' times, and seeing that the
Oblations given were less than usually before, expresses[d] their neglect

---

[a] Papinian. de Decurion. L 6. § 1. et C. *tit.* de Sportulis. Et vid.
Glossar. Græc. iuris in Σπόρτουλα.

[b] Concil. Chalced. A.D. 451. in libell. Samuelis et al. contra Iban. et
videsis tom. 3. Concil. fol. 231. cap. 31. Edit. Binii penultima.

[c] Epist. 266. ed. Pammel.   [d] De Unitate Ecclesiae, § 23.

districts; or some imperfect system of funding might have been adopted by the managers to equalise the otherwise irregular income of various years.

The growing habit of looking upon the clergy as the successors and representatives of the Levites under the Old Law, may very likely have given the impulse to that claim which they set up to the payment of tithes by the laity. But it is also probable that in course of time tithes had actually been given to them among other oblations, and had so helped to strengthen the application of the Levitical Law by an apparent legal prescription. There is not the least reason to doubt that payments of a tenth had been in very common use before the introduction of Christianity, and among people who have a decimal system of notation, a tenth is not an unlikely portion to be claimed as a royalty, a recognitory service, or a rent. The emperors had royalties of a tenth in mines: the landlords very frequently reserved a tenth in lands which they put out on usufructuary tenure. These rents and royalties, like other property, had been granted to the church. Again the piety of the laity had occasionally remitted the tenths due upon

to the church with, ' ac nunc de patrimonio nec Decimas damus :' whence, as you may gather, that no usual payment was of them, so withall observe in his expression, that the liberality formerly used had been such, that, in respect thereof, Tenths were but a small part : understand it as if he had said, ' but now we give not so much as any part worth speaking of.' Neither for aught appears in old monuments of credit, till near the end of this first four hundred years, was any payment to the Church of any tenth part, as a Tenth, at all in use." Selden on Tithes, cap. iv. p. 35 *seq.*

the lands in the holding of the clergy, which was in fact equivalent to a grant of the tithe[1]. And lastly tithe being paid on some estates to the clergy as landlords, there was a useful analogy, and colourable claim of right: and thus sufficient authority was found in custom itself to corroborate pretensions set up on grounds which could not be very satisfactorily or safely demurred to, in the fourth and fifth centuries.

But there is not the slightest proof that tithe of increase was demanded as of right even in the fifth century, in all the churches; although a growing tendency in that direction may be detected in the African and the Western establishments. Nor does any general council exist containing any regulation on the subject[2], till far later periods. But in 567 the clergy at the synod of Tours for the first time positively called upon the faithful to pay tithes[3], and eighteen years later at the Council of Macon,

[1] One of the clearest examples that occur to me at present is from a capitulary of the Merwingian Chlotachari in 560. " Agraria, pascuaria, vel decimas porcorum, aecclesiae, pro fidei nostrae devotione, concedimus, ita ut actor aut decimator in rebus aecclesiae nullus accedat: aecclesiae vel clericis nullam requirant agentes publici functionem qui avi vel genitoris aut germani nostri immunitatem meruerunt." Pertz, iii. 3. This is clearly a remission of tithe due to the king from lands held by the clergy, and bears some resemblance to Æðelwulf's celebrated release.

[2] The earliest is the Council of Lateran, held by Calixtus II. in 1123. The Council of Lateran, A.D. 1179, commanded that those who at the peril of their souls retained property in tithes, should not, under any pretence, transfer it to lay hands. But no general Council assumes the payment of tithes to be due of common right to the parochial Rector, before the Council of Lateran held by Innocent III. in 1215.

[3] Epist. Episc. Prov. Turon. ad plebem Missa; Labbe. v. 868. Eichhorn, §186. vol. i. 779 seq.

the command was enforced, as a return to a just and goodly custom which had fallen into desuetude, but which had the sanction of " the divine law, specially taking care of the interests of priests and ministers of churches." The daringly false assertions by which this usurpation was attempted to be justified are recorded in the annexed note, if indeed the acts of this council are genuine [1] : I have only to add that they were subscribed by forty-six bishops, and the representatives of twenty more,—

[1] Conc. Matiscon. 585. can. 5. " Omnes igitur reliquas fidei causas, quas temporis longitudine cognovimus deterioratas fuisse, oportet nos ad statum pristinum revocare, ne nobis simus adversarii, dum ea quae cognoscimus ad nostri ordinis qualitatem pertinere, aut non corrigimus, aut, quod nefas est, silentio praeterimus. Leges itaque divinae, consulentes sacerdotibus ac ministris aecclesiarum, pro haereditatis portione omni populo praeceperunt decimas fructuum suorum locis sacris praestare, ut nullo labore impediti, horis legitimis spiritualibus possent vacare ministeriis. Quas leges Christianorum congeries longis temporibus custodivit intemeratas ; nunc autem paulatim praevaricatores legum poene Christiani omnes ostenduntur, dum ea quae divinitus sancita sunt, adimplere negligunt. Unde statuimus et decernimus, ut mos antiquus a fidelibus reparetur, et decimas aecclesiasticis famulantibus caeremoniis populus omnis inferat, quas sacerdotes aut in pauperum usum, aut in captivorum redemptionem praerogantes, su's orationibus pacem populo et salutem impetrent. Si quis autem contumax nostris statutis saluberrimis fuerit, a membris aecclesiae omni tempore separetur." It must be confessed that Selden has thrown very great doubts upon the authenticity of this canon of the Council of Macon, and that it is of very questionable authority. See his History of Tithes, cap. 5. p. 65. It is hardly consistent with what Agobard of Lyons, who shortly after was bishop of the see itself in which Macon lies, declares: "Iam vero de donandis rebus et ordinandis aecclesiis nihil unquam in Synodis constitutum est, nihil a sanctis patribus publice praedicatum. Nulla enim compulit necessitas, fervente ubique religiosa devotione, et amore illustrandi aecclesias ultro aestuante," etc. Agob. Lugdun. de Dispensatione, etc. p. 276. (Ed. Masson. Parisiis.) But as Eichhorn, who has deeply investigated this subject, appears to differ here from Selden, I have cited this Council on his responsibility, and with the more readiness, that it rather opposes than confirms my own opinion.

making a total of sixty-six prelates, a number quite sufficient in the year 585 to gain currency for any fabrication however impudent. The clergy however still thundered in vain; nor was it till 779 that they succeeded in getting legislative and state authority for their claim through the political interests of the Frankish princes. The Capitulary of that year enacts that every one shall give tithes, and that these shall be distributed by the direction of the bishop[1].

Ten years after the council of Macon had thus boldly announced its views with regard to tithe, Augustine set out for England.

The question as to the origin of tithes in England, as to its date, and the authority on which the impost rested, has been much discussed, but not altogether satisfactorily. Nevertheless when divested of the extraneous difficulties with which polemical zeal, and selfish class-interests have overwhelmed it, it does not seem incapable of a reasonable solution. It is well known that the earliest legislative enactment on the subject in the Anglo-saxon laws is that of Æðelstán, bearing date in the first quarter of the tenth century; and that nearly every subsequent king recognized the right of the clergy to tithe, and made regulations either for the levying or the distribution of it[2]. But although this is the case, I entertain no doubt whatever that the payment of tithe was become very general in England at an earlier period. It is recognised in

---

[1] " De decimis, ut unusquisque decimam donet, atque per iussionem pontificis dispensentur." Capit. 779, cap. 7. Pertz, iii.

[2] See Appendix to this volume.

the articles of the treaty of peace between Eádweard the elder and Guð́orm, in A.D. 900 or 901,
in such a way as to assume its being a well-known
and established due to the Church[1], even though
no legislative enactment on the subject can be
shown in the Codes of Ælfred, Ini or the Kentish
kings[2]. The well-known tradition of Æð́elwulf's
granting tithe, throughout at least his kingdom of
Wessex, carries it back still half a century. But
even this falls short of the antiquity which we must
assume for the custom, if we believe in the genuineness of the ancient Poenitentials and Confessionals. In the eighth century Theodore deter-
mines, in a work especially intended for the instruction of the clergy, "Tributum aecclesiae sit,
sicut est consuetudo provinciae, id est, ne tantum
pauperes in decimis, aut in aliquibus rebus vim
patiantur. Decimas non est legitimum dare, nisi
pauperibus et peregrinis[3]."

---

[1] "If any one withhold tithes, let him pay lahslít among the Danes,
wíte among the English." Eád. Guð́. § 6. Thorpe, i. 170.

[2] Brompton says that Offa granted it, as far as Mercia was concerned,
p. 772. Certainly, in general, Brompton's authority is not very great;
but I think that in this case he has probability on his side, if we re-
strict the grant to Offa's demesne lands, or to a release of a tenth of
the dues payable to the king on Folcland. A general enactment, comprising the whole kingdom, would scarcely have been omitted in any
subsequent collection of laws. The law of Offa is indeed lost, but some
of its provisions probably survive in the legislation of later kings. See
Ælfr. Proem. Thorpe, i. 58. The absence of all mention of tithe by
Ælfred is not conclusive: he takes just as little notice of cyricsceat,
leohtsceat, sáwlsceat, and other payments which were unquestionably
claimed by the church. Eádweard's treaty with Guð́orm, though it
does not define the parties from whom tithe was demandable, treats
subtraction of it as an offence punishable at law.

[3] Capitula et Fragm. Theod. Thorpe, ii. 65.

The Excerptions of Archbishop Ecgberht[1] contain a prohibition against subtracting tithes from churches of old foundation, on pretence of giving them to new oratories. And further, the following exhortation respecting this payment[2]: " In lege Domini scriptum est: ' Decimas et primitias non tardabis offerre.' Et in Levitico : ' Omnes decimae terrae, sive de frugibus, sive de pomis arborum, Domini sunt ; boves, et oves, et caprae, quae sub pastoris virga transeunt, quicquid decimum venerit, sanctificabitur Domino.' Non eligetur nec bonum nec malum, nec alterum commutabitur. Augustinus dicit: Decimae igitur tributae sunt aecclesiarum et egentium animarum. O homo, inde Dominus decimas expetit, unde vivis. De militia, de negotio, de artificio redde decimas ; non enim eget Dominus noster, non proemia postulat, sed honorem." The same ancient authority thus also impresses upon priests the duty of collecting and distributing the tithe[3]:—" Ut unusquisque sacerdos cunctos sibi pertinentes erudiat, ut sciant qualiter decimas totius facultatis aecclesiis divinis debite offerant. Ut ipsi sacerdotes a populis suscipiant decimas, et nomina eorum quicumque dederint scripta habeant, et secundum auctoritatem canonicam coram [Deum] timentibus dividant; et ad ornamentum aecclesiae primam eligant partem ; secundam autem, ad usum pauperum atque peregrinorum, per eorum manus misericorditer cum

---

[1] Excerpt. Ecgberhti, No. 24. Thorpe, ii. 100.
[2] Excerpt. Ecgberhti, Nos. 101, 102. Thorpe, ii. 111, 112.
[3] Excerpt. Ecgberhti, Nos. 4, 5. Thorpe, ii. 98.

omni humilitate dispensent; tertiam vero sibimet-
ipsis sacerdotes reservent[1]."

When we consider the growing tendency in the
clergy to make payment of tithe compulsory, the
repeated exhortations of provincial synods to that

[1] The custom of the Romish church, as is well known, divided every
oblation, or gain that accrued to the church from the contributions of
the faithful, into four parts,—one for the bishop, one for the poor, one
for the clergy, and one for the repairs of the fabric. Othlon, who wrote
the Life of St. Boniface in the twelfth century, thus appeals to the universal custom of the church : " Quando quidem iuxta sanctorum canonum decreta decimas in quatuor portiones dividentes, unam, sibi [i. e.
the bishops], alteram clericis, tertiam pauperibus, quartam restaurandis
aecclesiis tradiderunt ? Numquid avaritiae suae tantummodo consulentes, in distributione decimarum obliti sunt pauperum, restaurationis-
que aecclesiarum, sicut modo, pro dolor ! cernimus agi ? Canones enim
sancti, ex quorum auctoritate exiguntur decimae, non solum decimas
dari, sed etiam inter varios aecclesiae usus distribui ; ut in urbibus qui-
buslibet et vicis Xenodochia habeantur, ubi pauperes et peregrini alan-
tur. Sed tam sanctum et tam necessarium praeceptum in pluribus
locis non solum minime curatur, sed etiam poene ignoratur. Nam solummodo illud legitur, quod epicopis decimae sint tribuendae; quid
vero exinde agendum sit, vel si quidquam aliud curandum sit circa monasteria, tam a clericis—miserabile dictu—quam a laicis destructa, ci-
traque iudicia religionis Christianae subversa, oblivioni seu ignorantiae
commendatur." Pertz, ii. 358. In the commencement of the seventh
century, Gregory, in his rules for the government of the newly-planted
English church, directed Augustine to make not four but three portions, inasmuch as he being a monk could have no separate share of
his own. He says : " Mos autem sedis apostolicae est ordinatis episcopis praecepta tradere, ut in omni stipendio, quod accedit, quatuor
debeant fieri portiones : una videlicet episcopo et familiae propter hos-
pitalitatem atque susceptionem, alia clero, tertia pauperibus, quarta
aecclesiis reparandis. Sed quia tua fraternitas monasterii regulis eru-
dita, seorsum fieri non debet a clericis suis in aecclesia Anglorum quae,
auctore Deo, nuper adhuc ad fidem adducta est, hanc debet conversa-
tionem instituere, quae initio nascentis aecclesiae fuit patribus nostris ;
in quibus nullus eorum ex his, quae possidebant, aliquid suum esse dicebat, sed erant eis omnia communia." Beda, H. E. i. 27. The original canon is in Gratian. Caus. 12. q. ii. c. 30. Ed. Pithæi. fol. Paris
1687, i. 240. Hence the directions of the Anglosaxon prelates, and
the regulation of Æðelred, as to a threefold division.

effect, and the universal ignorance of the people, we shall have little difficulty in acknowledging that the English prelates laid a good foundation for the custom of tithing, long before they succeeded in obtaining any legal right from the State. In the course of three centuries which preceded Eád-weard's reign they had ample time and opportunity to threaten or cajole a simple-minded race into the belief that they had a right to impose the levitical obligations upon them : in the seventh century Boniface testifies to the payment of tithe in England, nearly a century before the state enacted it in Germany : about the same period Cædwealha of Wessex, though yet nominally a pagan, tithed his spoils taken in war ; and I have little doubt that at least prædial tithe was almost universally levied long before the Witena gemót made it a legal charge, though I cannot concur with Phillips in believing that it was so decreed by Offa, or confirmed by Æðelwulf [1], for the whole kingdoms of Mercia and Wessex.

We will now return to Æðelwulf's so-called grant, in which many of our lawyers and historians have been content to see the legal origin of tithing in this country [2]; but which I must confess appears to me to have nothing to do with tithing whatever, in the legal sense of the word. The reports of the later chroniclers need not be taken into account ;

---

[1] Angelsäch. Recht. p. 251. He appeals only to Brompton, whose authority is by no means conclusive.

[2] This is Selden's view, and Hume's, and has been generally followed.

we may confine ourselves to the early and trustworthy sources, whose assertions we are quite as
likely to make proper use of as the compilers of
the fourteenth century.

Under date of the year 855, the Saxon Chronicle
says. "This same year, Æðelwulf booked the
tenth part of his land throughout his realm, for
God's glory and his own salvation." Asser, who
was no question well acquainted with the traditions of Æðelwulf's house, varies the statement:
"Eodem anno Æðhelwulfus praefatus venerabilis
rex decimam totius regni sui partem ab omni regali servitio et tributo liberavit, in sempiternoque
graphio in cruce Christi, pro redemptione animae
suae et antecessorum suorum, uni et trino Deo
immolavit[1]." In this he is followed verbatim by
Florence of Worcester. Æðelweard, a direct descendant of Æðelwulf, thus records the grant[2]:
"In eodem anno decumavit Aðulf rex de omni
possessione sua in partem Domini, et in universo
regimine principatus sui sic constituit."

Simeon has:—"Quo tempore rex Ethelwulfus
rex decimavit totum regni sui imperium, pro redemptione animae suae et antecessorum suorum."

Huntingdon:—"Æðelwulfus decimo nono anno
regni sui totam terram suam ad opus aecclesiarum
decumavit, propter amorem Dei et redemptionem
sui."

Roger of Wendover and Matthew Paris, upon
the authority of Æðelwulf's charter of 854, say:—

---

[1] *In anno* 855.   [2] Chronic. lib. iii.

" Eodem anno rex magnificus Athelwulfus decimam regni sui partem Deo et Beatae Mariae et omnibus sanctis contulit, liberam ab omnibus servitiis saecularibus exactionibus et tributis." And again in 857, speaking of Æðelwulf's will :—" Pro utilitate animae suae et salute, per omne regnum suum semper in decem hidis vel mansionibus pauperem unum indigenam, vel peregrinum cibo, potu et operimento, successoribus suis usque in finem saeculi post se pascere praecepit, ita tamen ut si terra illa pecoribus abundaret et ab hominibus coleretur."

Malmesbury, who calls the charter of 854 "scriptum libertatis aecclesiarum quod toti concessit Angliae," thus describes its effect :—" Ethelwulfus..... decimam omnium hidarum infra regnum suum Christi famulis concessit, liberam ab omnibus functionibus, absolutam ab omnibus inquietudinibus." And in 857, with reference to Æðelwulf's will :— " Semperque ad finem saeculi in omni suae haereditatis decima hida pauperem vestiri et cibari praecepit."

These passages obviously relate to two several transactions, one which took place in the year 854, before Æðelwulf's visit to Rome, the second in the year 857, after his return to England : and the Codex Diplomaticus contains a series of documents referring to them [1]. A portion of these fall under the description of Malmesbury, viz. that of " scriptum libertatis aecclesiarum . " and as he cites one

[1] Cod. Dipl. Nos. 270, 271, 275, 276, 1048, 1050, 1051, 1052, 1053 1054, 1057

of them himself by that title, it is certain that these are what he intends. Now this document, after the usual proem, recites that Æðelwulf with the consent of his witan, not only gave the tenth part of the lands throughout his realm to holy churches, but granted to his ministers, appointed throughout the same, to have in perpetual freedom, so that his donation might remain for ever free from all royal and secular burthens: in consideration of which the bishops agreed to a special service weekly for the king and his nobles[1], every Saturday.

Another class, and probably the most genuine, comprises the numbers 275 and 1048; in these documents, which are also grants of immunity to the clergy and to laics, the granting words are as follows:—"Quamobrem ego Æðelwulfus rex Occidentalium Saxonum cum consilio episcoporum et principum meorum, consilium salubre atque uniforme remedium affirmavi; ut aliquam portionem terrarum haereditariam, antea possidentibus gradibus omnibus,—sive famulis et famulabus Dei Deo

---

[1] The actual words are these :—" Ut decimam partem terrarum per regnum nostrum, non solum sanctis aecclesiis darem verumetiam et ministris nostris in eodem constitutis, in perpetuam libertatem habere concessimus, ita ut talis donatio fixa incommutabilisque permaneat ab omni regali servitio et omnium saecularium absoluta servitute." These are the expressions of Nos. 270, 271, 1050, 1054; which are respectively dated at Wilton on the 22nd of April, 854, and convey grants of separate lands to the thane Wigferð, to Malmesbury church, to Glastonbury, and to the thane Hunsige, as appears by the statements in the body of the charters, as well as by the endorsements, which are to this effect:— No. 270. " Ista est libertas quam Æðelwulf rex suo ministro Wiferðe in perpetuam haereditatem habere concessit, unum cassatum in loco qui dicitur Heregearding hiwisc :" *Endorsed,* " Ðis seondan æꝫ landes béc ðe Æðelwulf cyning Wiferðe his þegne salde."

2 I 2

servientibus, sive laicis,—semper decimam mansio-
nem, ubi minimum sit, tum decimam partem,—in
libertatem perpetuam perdonare diiudicavi; ut sit
tuta et munita ab omnibus saecularibus servitutibus,
fiscis regalibus, tributis maioribus et minoribus, sive
taxationibus quae nos dicimus Wíteræden; sitque
libera omnium rerum, pro remissione animarum et
peccatorum nostrorum, Deo soli ad serviendum,
sine expeditione, et pontis instructione et arcis
munitione, ut eo diligentius pro nobis ad Deum
preces sine cessatione fundant, quo eorum servi-
tutem saecularem in aliqua parte levigamus." In
consideration of this alleviation the grateful clergy
were to perform on the Wednesday in every week
the same services as the first class of documents
stipulates for the Saturday. It is to be observed
that the two documents of this particular class,
though the authority for them is of the lowest description, and the dates are altogether suspicious,
seem to be of a much more genuine character as
to the grant itself than the first class: there is a
certain satisfactory accuracy about the definition of
Wíteræden which is in so far suggestive of an authentic original; and when we translate the very
bad Latin " sine expeditione," etc. by the genuine
" bútan fyrdfare," etc., we shall have the following
reasonable account to give of the proceedings.
Æðelwulf, being humbled and terrified by the dis-
tresses of wars and the ravages of barbarous and
pagan invaders, devised as a useful remedy thus; he
determined to liberate from all those various exactions and services which went by the general name

of wíteræden, the tenth part of the estates which,
though hereditary tenure had grown up in them,
were still subject to the ancient burthens of folcland, whether they were in the hands of laics or
clergy ; that where the estate amounted to ten
hides, one was to be free ; where it was a very
small quantity, at all events a tenth was to be so
enfranchised : and as the greater part of this land
either was in the hands of the clergy, or was very
likely ultimately to come there, he granted this
charitable act of enfranchisement that on these
estates the holders might be the better able to devote themselves to the service of God, all other
service being discharged, except indeed the inevitable three.   This seems best to accord with
Asser's assertion that the king sacrificed to God
the services which arose to himself over a tenth
part of all his realm.   Now it is to be observed
that this could not apply to booklands which
already possessed an exemption, but only to folcland, whether become hereditary or not ; nor could
regnum possibly mean territory, but royal rights,
for Æðelwulf had no *territory* except his private
estates ; nor could the " trinoda necessitas " be
called a " regale servitium et tributum."   These
were the dues demandable by the king from folcland, and could only be discharged by consent of
the Wítan.   The expression of Simeon appears
also to be susceptible of no other translation :
when he says the king tithed " totum regni sui
imperium," I can see no territorial division in
his words, but only that the king relinquished a

tenth part of those imperial rights which he had as
king.

A third class of documents however yet remains
to be considered.   In these a clear division of lands
is intended and is recorded.   The first of these in
point of time are the Nos. 1051 and 1052, which
bear the suspicious dates of Easter in the year 854,
the first indiction, and the palace at Wilton: that
is, with the exception of the indiction, the dates of
the first class of documents.   These two charters
declare that Æðelwulf being determined by the advice of St. Swithin to tithe the lands of all the
realm that God had given him[1], increased the estate
which queen Friðogyð had granted to the church
at Winchester, in Taunton, by a certain amount
of hides in various places.   These are followed by
another of the same year, but with the proper indiction, viz. the second, declaring that on the same
occasion he gave other lands to Winchester[2] ; and
in the succeeding year 855, we find him giving an
estate in Kent to Dun a minister or thane, " pro
decimatione agrorum, quam Deo donante, caeteris
ministris meis facere decrevi."   I do not very much
insist upon giving one sense rather than another

[1] " Totius regni mihi a Deo collati decimans rura." Nos. 1051, 1052.
[2] " Quando decimam partem terrarum per omne regnum meum
sanctis aecclesiis dare decrevi," etc. No. 1053. The Saxon version,
whether it were the original or only a translation, gives us the true
sense of this assertion : it runs thus :—" ðá ðá he teoðode gynd eall
his cynerice, ðone teoðan dǽl ealra his landa, mid his witena geþeahte,
into hálgum stowum,"—'when throughout all his realm, he tithed
the tenth of all *his lands* into holy places, by the counsel of his witan.'
There was nothing to prevent Æðelwulf from giving a tenth or a half
of all his *own* lands to whom he pleased.

to this "*pro* decimatione," and am ready to admit
that it may mean, ' in respect of the general tithing
of lands which I intend to make to yourself as well
as the rest of my thanes,' or that it may be read,
' in place of that tithing of lands which I intend to
make to the rest of my thanes, I give you such
and such a particular estate.' We must not be very
fastidious with Æðelwulf's Latin, especially as
there is much reason to believe that in this case it
is a mere translation of what would have been far
more intelligible and trustworthy Saxon.

Trustworthy, however, I can hardly term the last
document I have to notice[1], Saxon though it be:
this appears to be one of a very suspicious series
of instruments, prepared for the purpose of corrobo-
rating some ancient claim on the part of Winchester, to have its hundred hides at Chilcombe
rated at *one* hide only. It bears marks of forgery in
every line, and seems to have been made up out of
some history of Æðelwulf's sojourn in Rome, but
still is worth citing as evidence of the tradition respecting tithe :—" In the name of him who writeth
in the book of life in heaven those who in this life
please him well, I Aðulf the king in this writ
notify concerning the franchise of Chilcombe, which
Kynegils the king, who first of all the kings in
Wessex became a Christian, granted to his baptismal father Saint Birinus ; and which since then
all the kings who have succeeded one another in
Wessex have enfranchised and advanced, although

---

[1] Cod. Dipl. No. 1057.

it never was reduced to writing until the time of myself, who am the ninth king. Also I notify that I established this franchise before Saint Peter in Rome, and the holy Pope Leo, even so as it was settled between me and all my people, ere I went to Rome, that is, that all the land comprised in this franchise shall for ever be acquitted for one hide; because God's possessions should ever be more free than any worldly possession: and also my son Ælfred, who went with me and was there consecrated king, pledged himself to the Pope, both to further this franchise himself, and to urge his children to the same, if God should grant him any. I also, before the same Pope, tithed all the landed possessions which I had in England, to God, into holy places for myself and for all my people: and in Rome with the assistance and by the leave of the Pope, I wrought a minster for the honour of God and to the worship of Saint Mary, his holy mother, and placed therein a company of English, who ever both by night and day shall serve God, for our people: and when I returned home I told all the people what I had done in Rome. And they very earnestly thanked both God and me for this, and all this pleased them well, and they said that with their good will it should be so for ever. Now I implore, through the holy Trinity and Saint Peter, and all the halidome that I visited in Rome, both for myself and my people, that never either king or prince, bishop or ealdorman, thane or reeve diminish what hath been established with such witness: doubtless he that doth so will anger God and Saint

Peter, and all the saints that repose in the churches at Rome, and miserably earn for himself the punishments of hell.   Moreover, the aforesaid holy Pope Leo laid God's curse and Saint Peter's, and all the Saints' and his own, on him that ever violates this; and also all this people both ordained and laic did the like when I returned home and announced this to them."

If these data then be correct, Æðelwulf did three distinct things at different times : he first released from all payments, except the inevitable three, a tenth part of the folclands or unenfranchised lands, whether in the tenancy of the church or of his thanes.   In this tenth part of the lands so burthened in his favour he annihilated the royal rights, regnum or imperium; and as the lands receiving this privilege were secured by charter, the Chronicle can justly say that the king *booked* them to the honour of God.   A second thing he did, inasmuch as he gave a tenth part of his own private estates of bookland to various thanes or clerical establishments.   And lastly, upon every ten hides of his own land he commanded that one poor man, whether native born or stranger, that is, whether of Wessex or some other kingdom, should be maintained in food and clothing.   It is unnecessary to waste words in showing how utterly different all this really is from any grant of tithe, and how entirely unfounded is the opinion that Æðelwulf made the first legal enactment in behalf of tithe in this country.   All that it proves is, that Æðelwulf made a handsome endowment for the clergy, and that a tenth part or a tenth person seemed to him to mark the proper proportion between what he kept and what he gave up. It renders it probable that the claim to tithe had already become familiar, since Æðelwulf divided his land by ten; but it also shows that even the Levitical tithe itself was misrepresented, if he believed this donation of his to bear any resemblance to it. We may suppose the squire in a country parish to have let the parson a house, and subsequently excused him a tenth of the rent. This might be a very charitable act, and might be done from very pure religious motives; but it would scarcely be called tithe in the proper ecclesiastical sense of that word. This is precisely what Æðelwulf did in Wessex.

In addition to leohtsceat, or money paid to supply lights, sulhælmysse or plough-alms, and sáwl-sceat, a present made to the church where a testator desired to rest, in consideration of religious services to be performed for the good of his soul, there was a due commonly known under the name of cyric-sceat. It is not clear what was the nature of this impost, and its amount is uncertain, as well as the persons who were liable to its payment. But in all probability it was at first a recognitory rent paid to the particular churches from estates leased by them; not so much in the nature of a fair equivalent for the use of such lands, but as a token of beneficiary tenure, in the spirit of the following words:— "Solventes inde censum per singulos annos missis rectorum praedicti ·monasterii, iv denarios in festivitate sancti Remigii Confessoris, ne

videamur eas ex proprio, sed iure beneficiario pos-
sidere[1]." It is therefore not unusual to find this
impost particularly mentioned in church-leases,
under the names of cyricsceat, census aecclesiasticus, cyriclád, aecclesiae munus, and similar terms.
The true character of the payment appears from
two very clear examples which I shall quote at
length. " That in truth may say the thane Ælfsige Hunláfing in respect to his obtaining this land
free from every burthen, to himself and his heirs,
except burhbót, bridge-work, and military service,
remembering to his *landlord*, cyricsceat, sáwlsceat
and his tithes[2]." This landlord was a bishop, in
all probability, but he is not named.

In the year 902, Denewulf bishop of Winchester
leased fifteen hides of land to Beornwulf and his
heirs, reserving a rent of forty-five shillings yearly.
" And every year let him assist in the bót of the
church[3] which that land belongeth to, in the same
proportion as the other folk do, each by the measure of his land ; and let him justly pay his cyricsceat, and perform his military service and bridge

[1] Schannat. Tradit. Fuldens. No. 452. So also in the Worcester
Domesday, Hemm. 500, 501. " De eodem manerio tenet Hugo de
Grentesmaisnil dimidiam hidam ad Lapeuuerte, et Baldewinus de eo ;
et fuit et est de soca episcopi. De hac terra per singulos annos red-
duntur viii denarii ad ecclesiam de Wirecestre, pro *circette* et recog-
nitione terre."

[2] Cod. Dipl. No. 433.

[3] Hardly the repairs of the church, which were thus to be attended
to yearly ; although in religious as in secular tenures, there can be no
doubt that the tenant was liable to be called upon to assist in the repairs of the lord's buildings. The distinction between " ðæt óðer folc,"
that is the other tenants, and " eal folc," that is everybody throughout
the realm, is clear.

and fortress work, as they do throughout all the folk[1]."

Between the years 879 and 909, the same bishop gave forty hides to Ælfred, for his life. Upon these he reserved a rent of three pounds, cyricsceats, cyricsceat-work, and the services of Ælfred's men when required at the bishop's hunting and reaping[2]. In like manner Oswald reserved, in all the grants he made out of the church property at Worcester, the church rights, that is to say, cyricsceat, toll, tax and pannage, and also the services of the tenants at his hunting[3]. Lastly between the years 871 and 877, bishop Ealhfrið granting eight hides for three lives to duke Cúðred, reserved bridge-work, military service, eight cyricsceats, the mass-priest's rights and soulsceats[4].

This cyricsceat then appears to have been origi-nally a recognitory service due to the lord from the tenant on church-lands. But it is very clear that in process of time a new character was assumed for it, and it was claimed of all men alike, as a due to the clergy. Here, again, the Levitical legislation was taken to be applicable to the Chris-tian ministry. The Jews had been commanded to give first-fruits[5], as well as tithes; and if tithes belonged to the clergy by virtue of God's com-mandment, so did first-fruits also. These appear

---

[1] " And eác ælce geare fultumien tó ðære cyrican bote ðe ðet land tó hyrð be ðém dæle ðe ðet óðer folc dó ælc be his landes meðe and ða cyricsceáttes mid rihte ágyfe and fyrde and brycge and festergeweorc hewe swá mon ofer eall folc dó." Cod. Dipl. No. 1079.

[2] Cod. Dipl. No. 1086.   [3] See vol. i. p. 518. App. E.
[4] Cod. Dipl. No. 1062.   [5] Deut. xviii. 4.

also to have been called cyricsceat, and after a time became an established charge upon the land of the freeman as well as the unfree. The earliest legislation which we can discover, bearing unquestionably upon this point, is that of Eádmund toward the middle of the tenth century[1];. he strictly commands payment of tithe, cyricsceat, and almsfee, and declares that he who will not do it shall be excommunicated. By the time of Eádgár however the matter seems to have been quite settled, and cyricsceat is directed to be paid from the hearth of every freeman to the old minster,—most likely to prevent a course similar to the arbitrary consecration of tithes. And this remained a fixed charge upon the land till the time of the Conquest, when it ceased to be generally paid, as we may judge from the expressions of Fleta and other jurists[2]; it

---

[1] Leg. Eádm. i. § 2. Thorpe, i. 244. The earlier notices are Leg. Ini, § 4, 61. Æðelst. i. Thorpe, i. 104, 140, 196. But these are not at all conclusive, and would be equally applicable to the case of the liability to this impost being confined to the tenants of the church. Ini's law only regulates the time at which the impost is to be paid, and the particular estate from which it is due. Æðelstán confines himself to commanding that his officers shall see the cyricsceat paid at the proper times and to the proper places.

[2] "Churchesed certam mensuram bladi tritici signat, quam quilibet olim sanctae Ecclesiae die sancti Martini, tempore tam Britonum quam Anglorum, contribuerunt. Plures tamen magnates post Normannorum adventum in Angliam, illam contributionem secundum veterem legem Moysi, nomine Primitiarum dabant; prout in brevi regis Knuti ad summum Pontificem transmisso continetur, in quibus illam contributionem appellant Churchsed, quasi *semen ecclesiae.*" Fleta, i. 47, § 28. "Chichesed, al. chircheomer, al. chircheambre :—un certein de blé batu ke checun home devoit au tens de Bretuns e de engleis a le eglise le iur seint Martin mes pus le venue de Normans si le priserent a lur vs plusur seinourages, e le donerunt solum la veile lei Moysi, et no-

had passed in some cases into the hands of secular lords, with lands alienated by the clergy, or taken from them. But in the time of Cnut it was still paid as *primitiae seminum*, and it is not probable that his successors altered his arrangements in this respect.

The liberality of the Anglosaxons was by no means confined to the grants of land which they conferred upon the several churches, although it is impossible to deny that these were most extravagant[1]. At the same time it is to be borne in mind that the clergy were always certain to command a more than adequate supply of free and unfree labour ; and that, if their landed possessions thus increased their wealth to an extraordinary degree, they also were the greatest contributors to

mine primiciarum sicum lem troue en le lettres cnikt ke il envea a rome, e est dit chirchesed quasi semen ecclesiae." MS. Soc. Ant. lx fol. 228, b. This writ of Cnut to the Pope is not known to me, but we have a letter addressed by him to his Witan from Rome, to which Fleta probably alludes. "Nunc igitur praecipio et obtestor omnes meos episcopos et regni praepositos, per fidem quam Deo et mihi debetis, quatenus faciatis, ut antequam ego Angliam veniam, omnia debita, quae Deo secundum legem antiquam debemus, sint soluta, scilicet eleemosynae pro aratris, et decimae animalium ipsius anni procreatorum, et denarii quos Romae ad sanctum Petrum debemus, sive ex urbibus sive ex villis, et mediante Augusto decimae frugum, et in festivitate sancti Martini *primitiae seminum* ad ecclesiam sub cuius parochia quisque est, quae Anglice *Circesceat* nominantur." Flor. Wigorn. ad. an. 1031.

[1] The estate of Chilcombe alone, belonging to Winchester, is reckoned at one hundred hides, or at least three thousand acres, which they succeeded in getting rated to the public burthens at one hide only. Cod. Dipl. No. 642. But the whole of their estates in Hampshire appear from the same document to have comprised no less than five hundred and seventy-eight hides, which at my very low estimate of the hide amount to *seventeen thousand, three hundred and forty acres,*— a very pretty provision for one Chapter. The amount of lands and chattels devised by various prelates almost exceeds belief.

the general well-being through the superior excel-
lence of their cultivation.   But the piety or the
fears of the laity did not stop short at gifts of land
and serfs : jewels, cups, rings, crosses and caskets,
money, tapestry, and vestments, annual foundations
of bread, wine, beer, honey, and flesh, sometimes
to enormous amounts, were devised by the will
of wealthy and penitent sinners : houses and curti-
lages, tolls and markets, forests, harbours, fisheries,
mines, commons of pasture and mast, flocks and
herds of swine, horses and oxen, testified to the
liberality of ealdormen and kings.   Nor was the
opportunity of investing their surplus profitably
always wanting : more than one mortgage is recorded, on terms sufficiently favourable to the
mortgagors ; and loans on excellent security, show
that if the nobles knew where to find capitalists
in their need, the capitalist also knew very well
how to turn his facilities to good account.   The
necessity of providing out of these large funds for
the proper maintenance of the churches and the
due celebration of religious rites, can hardly be
looked upon as a great hardship ; and although the
demands of charity and the duties of hospitality,
may have seemed a heavy charge to the avaricious
or the selfish, we cannot but conclude, that no
class of the community occupied so dignified or so
easy a position as the Anglosaxon clergy.   The
State, fully aware of the value of their services,
was not niggardly in rewarding them.   There was
a ready acquiescence on the part of the laity in
the claims of the clergy to respect and trust ; and,

while these continued to maintain a decent conformity to the duties of their calling, we find a perfectly harmonious co-operation of all classes in the
church. Nor, amongst all the writings which the
clergy—the only writers—have left us, do we find
any of those complaints and grievances, which are
apt to be made prominent enough when the members of that powerful body believe their pretensions
to be treated with less than due consideration. The
devoted partizan of Rome might choose to declare
the English church subject to such bondage as no
other suffered ; but, except from quarrels of their
own, the clergy never were exposed here to those
inconveniences which are unavoidable, upon any
attempt on their part to separate themselves from
their fellow-members in the Christian communion.

CHAPTER XI.

THE POOR.

THERE is hardly a question connected with the march of civilization more difficult to answer satisfactorily than this : What is to be done with the Poor ?

In our own day, when subdivision of labour has been carried to an unheard of extent, when property follows the natural law of accumulation in masses, and society numbers the proletarian as an inevitable unit among its constituents, the question presents itself in a threatening and dangerous form, with difficulty surrounding it on every side, and anarchy scowling in the background, hardly to be appeased or vanquished. But such circumstances as those we live under are rare, and almost unexampled in history: even the later and depraved days of Roman civilization offer but a very insufficient pattern of a similar condition [1]. Above all it would

---

[1] The Roman poor-law was, consequently upon the Roman imperial institutions, of a strange, exceptional and most dangerous character. The rulers literally fed the people : *panem et circenses,* food and amusements ; these were the relief which the wealthy and powerful supplied, and if ever these were sparingly distributed, convulsions and revolution were inevitable. The Λειτουργίαι, public dinners, and other doles of a compulsory nature assisted the poorer among the Athenians. (I have not cancelled this note, which was written long before the events of February 1848 and their consequences had added another pregnant example to the store of history.)

be difficult to find any parallel for them in countries where land is abundant, and the accumulation
of property slow : there may be pauperism in New
York, but scarcely in the valley of the Mississippi.
The cultivator may live hardly, poorly ; but he can
live, and as increasing numbers gather round him
and form a market for his superfluous produce, he
will gradually become easy, and at length wealthy.
It is however questionable whether population will
really increase very fast in an agricultural community where a sufficient provision is made for every
family, and where there is an unlimited fund, and
power of almost indefinite extension. On the contrary, it seems natural under these circumstances
that the proportion between the consumers and the
means of living should long continue to be an advantageous one, and no pressure will be felt as long
as no effort is made to give a false direction to the
energies of any portion of the community.

But this cannot possibly be the case in a system
which limits the amount of the estate or hýd.
Here a period must unavoidably arise where population advances too rapidly for subsistence, unless
a manufacturing effort on an extensive scale is
made, and made with perfect freedom from all re-
straints, but those which prudence and well-regu-
lated views of self-interest impose. If want of rapid
internal communication deprive the farmer of a
market, and compel him to limit his produce to
the requirements of his own family, there cannot
be a doubt not only that he will be compelled to
remain in a stationary and not very easy position,

but that a difficulty will arise as to the disposal of a redundant population. Many plans have been devised to meet this difficulty; a favourite one has been at all times, to endeavour to find means of limiting population itself, instead of destroying all restrictions upon occupation. The profoundest thinkers of Greece, considering that a pauper population is inconsistent with the idea of state, have positively recommended violent means to prevent its increase [1] : infanticide and exposition thus figure among the means by which Plato and Aristotle consider that full and perfect citizenship is to be maintained. I have already touched upon some of the means by which our forefathers attempted this regulation: emigration was as popular a nostrum with them as with us: service in the comitatus, even servitude on the land, were looked to as an outlet, and slavery probably served to keep up something of a balance: moreover it is likely that a large proportion of the population were entirely prevented from contracting marriage : of this last

---

[1] Περὶ δὲ ἀποθέσεως καὶ τροφῆς τῶν γιγνομένων ἔστω νόμος μηδὲν πεπηρωμένον τρέφειν, διὰ δὲ πλῆθος τέκνων, ἐὰν ἡ τάξις τῶν ἐθῶν κωλύῃ, μηδὲν ἀποτίθεσθαι τῶν γιγνομένων· ὥρισται γὰρ δὴ τῆς τεκνοποιίας τὸ πλῆθος. Arist. Polit. vii. c. 14. See also Plato, Leg. bk. 5. Ed. Bekk. p. 739, 740, etc. Ed. Stalbaum, vol. vi. p. 131, etc. The tendency of Aristotle's ideas on the subject may be gathered from his notion that the Cretans encouraged παιδεραστία, in order to check population. I am informed upon good authority, that in the Breisgau, and especially the See-Kreis of Baden, the younger children, or any supposed surplus, are permitted to die, of want of food, in order that the property (Bauerngut), amounting sometimes to 100 morgen or 66 acres of land, may remain undivided. It is also certain that in other parts of Europe, a woman who bears more than a certain settled number of children is looked upon with contempt.

2 K 2

number the various orders of the clergy, and the monks must have made an important item. It is even probable that the somewhat severe restrictions imposed upon conjugal intercourse may have had their rise in an erroneous view that population might thus be limited or regulated [1]. But still, all these means must have furnished a very inadequate relief: even the worn-out labourer, especially if unfree, must have become superfluous, and if he was of little use to his owner, there was little chance of his finding a purchaser. What provision was made for him ?

The condition of a serf or an outlaw from poverty is an abnormal one, but only so in a Christian community. In fact it seems to me that the State neither contemplates the existence of the poor, nor cares for it : the poor man's right to live is derived from the moral and Christian, not from the public law : so little true is the general assertion that the poor man has a right to be maintained upon the land on which he was born. The State exists for its members, the full, free and independent citizens, self-supported on the land ; and except as self-supported on the land it knows no citizens at all. Any one but the holder of a free hýd must either fly to the forest or take service, or steal and become a þeóv. How the pagan Saxons contemplated this fact it is impossible to say, but at the period when

---

[1] The Pœnitentials recommend abstinence every Wednesday, Friday and Sunday throughout the year : on all great fasts, high feasts and festivals : during all penances, general or special : seven months before and after parturition.

we first meet with them in history, two disturbing
causes were in operation; first the gradual loosen-
ing of the principle of the mark-settlement, and the
consequent accumulation of landed estates in few
hands; secondly the operation of Christianity.

This taught the equality of men in the eye of
God, who had made all men brothers in the mystery
of Christ's passion. And from this also it followed
that those who had been bought with that precious
sacrifice were not to be cast away. The sin of
suffering a child to die unbaptized was severely
animadverted upon. The crime of infanticide could
only be expiated by years of hard and wearisome
penance; but the penance unhappily bears witness
to the principle,—a principle universally pagan,
and not given up, even to this day, by nations and
classes which would repudiate with indignation the
reproach of paganism, though thoroughly imbued
with pagan habits. In the seventh century we read
of the existence of poor, and we read also of the
duty of assisting them. But as the State had in
fact nothing to do with them, and no machinery of
its own to provide for them, and as the clergy were
ex officio their advocates and protectors, the State
did what under the circumstances was the best
thing to do, it recognized the duty which the clergy
had imposed upon themselves of supporting the
poor. It went further,—it compelled the freeman
to supply the clergy with the means of doing it.

In the last years of the sixth century, Gregory
the Great informed Augustine that it was the custom of the Roman church to cause a fourth part of

all that accrued to the altar from the oblations of
the faithful to be given to the poor; and this was
beyond a doubt the legitimate substitute for the old
mode of distribution which the Apostles and their
successors had adopted while the church lurked in
corners and in catacombs, and its communicants
stole a fearful and mysterious pleasure in its ministrations under the jealous eyes of imperial paganism. As soon however as the accidental oblations
were to a great degree replaced by settled payments
(whether arising out of land or not[1]), and these
were directed to be applied in definite proportions,
we may venture to say that the State had a poor-
law, and that the clergy were the relieving officers.
The spirit of Gregory's injunction is that a part of
all that accrues shall be given to the poor; and
this applies with equal force to tithes, churchshots,
bóts or fines, eleemosynary grants, and casual oblations. In this spirit, it will be seen, the Anglosaxon clergy acted, and we may believe that no
inconsiderable fund was provided for distribution.
The liability of the tithe is the first point upon
which I shall produce evidence. The first secular
notice of this is contained in the following law of
Æðelred, an. 1014:—"And concerning tithe, the

---

[1] "To shipmen it is commanded, like as it also is to husbandmen,
that they should give unto God the tenth part of all the increase upon
their stock, and moreover give alms from the nine parts that are their
own. And so is it commanded to every man that from the same craft
wherewith he provides for his body's need, he provide for that of his
soul also, which is better than the body." Ecc. Institutes. Thorpe, ii.
432. "O homo, inde Dominus decimas expetit, unde vivis. De
militia, de negotio, de artificio redde decimas." St. Augustine, cited
by Ecgb. Excerp. 102. Thorpe, ii. 112.

king and his *witan* have chosen and said, as right
it is, that the third part of the tithe which belongs
to the church, shall go to the reparation of the
church, and a second part to the servants of God,
and the third to God's poor and needy men in
thraldom[1]."

But if positive public enactment be rare, it is
not so with ecclesiastical law, and the recommendations of the rulers of the Anglosaxon church. The
Poenitentials, Confessionals, and other works compiled by these prelates for the guidance and instruction of the clergy abound in passages wherein
the obligation of providing for the poor out of
the tithe is either assumed or positively asserted.
In the 'Capitula et Fragmenta' of Theodore, dating
in the seventh century, it is written, "It is not
lawful to give tithes save unto the poor and pilgrims[2]," which can hardly mean anything but a
prohibition to the clergy, to make friends among
the laity by giving them presents out of the tithe ;
but which shows what were the lawful or legitimate
uses of tithe. Again he says[3],—"If any one ad-

[1] Æðelred, ix. § 6. Thorpe, i. 342. This passage of Augustine is
referred to in the collection commonly attributed to Ed. Conf. And a
detailed enumeration is given of tithe : thus, the tenth sheaf of corn ;
from a herd of mares, the tenth foal ; where there are only one or two
mares, a penny per foal. Similarly of cows, the tenth calf or an *obolus*
per calf. The tenth cheese, or the tenth day's milk. The tenth lamb,
fleece, measure of butter, and pig. Of bees according to the yearly
yield : from groves and meadows, mills and waters, parks, stews,
fisheries, brushwood, orchards ; the produce of all business, and indeed
of everything the Lord has given, the tenth part shall be rendered.
Thorpe, i. 445.

[2] Cap. et Fragm. Theod. Thorpe, ii. 65.

[3] Ibid. Thorpe, ii. 80. These xenodochia were hospitals or almshouses.

ministers the xenodochia of the poor, or has received the tithes of the people, and has converted any portion thereof to his own uses," etc.

In the Excerptions of archbishop Ecgberht we find the following canon:—" The priests are to take tithes of the people, and to make a written list of the names of the givers, and according to the authority of the canons, they are to divide them, in the presence of men that fear God. The first part they are to take for the adornment of the church; but the second they are in all humility, mercifully to distribute with their own hands, for the use of the poor and strangers; the third part however the priests may reserve for themselves [1]."

In the Confessional of the same prelate we find the following exhortation, to be addressed by the priest to the penitent:—" Be thou gentle and charitable to the poor, zealous in almsgiving, in attendance at church, and in the giving of tithe to God's church and the poor [2]."

In the canons enacted under Eádgár, but which are at least founded upon an ancient work of Cummianus, there is this entry:—" We enjoin that the priests so distribute the people's alms, that they do both give pleasure to God, and accustom the people to alms [3];" to which however there is an addition which can scarcely well be understood of anything but tithe: " and it is right that one part be delivered to the priests, a second part for the need of the church, and a third part for the poor."

---

[1] Excerp. Ecgb. Thorpe, ii. 98.
[2] Confes. Ecgb. Thorpe, ii. 132. [3] Thorpe, ii. 256.

The Canons of Ælfríc have the same entry, and the same mode of distribution as those of Ecgberht: " The holy fathers have also appointed that men shall pay their tithes into God's church. And let the priest go thither, and divide them into three: one part for the repair of the church; the second for the poor; the third for God's servants who attend to the church [1]."

Thus according to the view of the Anglosaxon church, ratified by the express enactment of the witan, a third of the tithe was the absolute pro perty of the poor. But other means were found to increase this fund: not only was the duty of almsgiving strenuously enforced, but even the fasts and penances recommended or imposed by the clergy were made subservient to the same charitable purpose. The canons enacted under Eádgár provide [2], that " when a man fasts, then let the dishes that would have been eaten be all distributed to God's poor." And again the Ecclesiastical Institutes declare [3]: " It is daily needful for every man that he give his alms to poor men; but yet when we fast, then ought we to give greater alms than on other days; because the meat and the drink, which we should then use if we did not fast, we ought to distribute to the poor."

So in certain cases where circumstances rendered the strict performance of penance difficult or impossible, a kind of tariff seems to have been devised, the application of which was left to the

---

[1] Thorpe, ii. 352.   [2] Ibid. ii. 286.   [3] Ibid. ii. 437.

discretion of the confessor. The proceeds of this commutation were for the benefit of the poor. Thus Theodore teaches [1] :—" But let him that through infirmity cannot fast, give alms to the poor according to his means; that is, for every day a penny or two or three . . . . For a year let him give thirty shillings in alms; the second year, twenty; the third, fifteen."

Again[2] :—" He that knows not the psalms and cannot fast, must give twenty-two shillings in alms for the poor, as commutation for a year's fasting on bread and water; and let him fast every Friday on bread and water, and three forties; that is, forty days before Easter, forty before the festival of St. John the Baptist, and forty before Christmas-day. And in these three forties let him estimate the value or possible value of whatsoever is prepared for his use, in food, in drink or whatever it may be, and let him distribute the half of that value in alms to the poor," etc.

When we consider the almost innumerable cases in which penance must have been submitted to by conscientious believers, and the frequent hindrances which public or private business and illness must have thrown in the way of strict performance, we may conclude that no slight addition accrued from this source to the fund at the disposal of the church for the benefit of the poor. Even the follies and vices of men were made to contribute their quota

---

[1] Poenit. Thorpe, ii. 61: see also ii. 83. Tit. de incestis.
[2] Thorpe, ii. 68. See also pp. 67, 69, 70, 134, 222.

in a more direct form. Ecgberht requires that a
portion of the spoil gained in war shall be applied
to charitable purposes[1]; and he estimates the
amount at no less than a third of the whole booty.
Again, it is positively enacted by Æðelred and his
witan that a portion of the fines paid by offenders
to the church should be applied in a similar manner: they say[2], that such money " belongs lawfully, by the direction of the bishops, to the buying
of prayers, to the behoof of the poor, to the reparation of churches, to the instruction, clothing and
feeding of those who minister to God, for books,
bells and vestments, but never for idle pomp of
this world."

More questionable is a command inculcated by
archbishop Ecgberht, that the over-wealthy should
punish themselves for their folly by large contributions to the poor[3]: " Let him that collecteth
immoderate wealth, for his want of wisdom, give
the third part to the poor."

Upon the bishops and clergy was especially imposed the duty of attending to this branch of
Christian charity, which they were commanded to
exemplify in their own persons: thus the bishops
are admonished to feed and clothe the poor[4], the
clerk who possessed a superfluity was to be excom-

---

[1] Poenit. Ecgb. Thorpe, ii. 232.
[2] Æðelr. vi. § 51.   Thorpe, i. 328.   [3] Thorpe, ii. 232.
[4] Archbishop Ecgberht, from the Canons of the Council of Orleans :
" Episcopus pauperibus et infirmis, qui debilitate faciente non possunt
suis manibus laborare, victum et vestimentum, in quantum possibilitas
fuerit, largiatur." Thorpe, ii. 105.

municated if he did not distribute it to the poor[1],
nay the clergy were admonished to learn and practise handicrafts, not only in order to keep themselves out of mischief and avoid the temptations of
idleness, but that they might earn funds wherewith
to relieve the necessities of their brethren[2]. Those
who are acquainted with the MSS. and other remains of Anglosaxon art are well-aware how great
eminence was attained by some of these clerical
workmen, and how valuable their skill may have
been in the eyes of the wealthy and liberal[3].

Another source of relief remains to be noticed:
I mean the eleemosynary foundations. It is of
course well known that every church and monastery comprised among its necessary buildings a
xenodochium, hospitium or similar establishment,
a kind of hospital for the reception and refection of
the poor, the houseless and the wayfarer. But I
allude more particularly to the foundations which
the piety of the clergy or laics established without
the walls of the churches or monasteries. Æðelstán commanded the royal reeves throughout his
realm to feed and clothe one poor man each: the
allowance was to be, from every two farms, an
amber of meal, a shank of bacon, or a ram worth
fourpence, monthly, and clothing for the whole
year. The reeves here intended must have been
the bailiffs (villici, praepositi, túngeréfan) of the

[1] Theod. Poen. xxv. § 6.   [2] Ecc. Inst. Thorpe, ii. 404.

[3] We know that Benedict Biscop received as much as eight hides of
land for one volume of geographical treatises, illustrated and illumi-
nated. Bed. Op. Min. 155.

royal vills; and, if they could not find a poor man in their vill, they were to seek him in another[1]. In the churches which were especially favoured with the patronage of the wealthy and powerful, it was usual for the anniversary of the patron to be celebrated with religious services, a feast to the brotherhood and a distribution of food to the poor, which was occasionally a very liberal one. In the year 832 we learn incidentally what were the charitable foundations of archbishop Wulfred. He commanded twenty-six poor men to be daily fed on different manors, he gave each of them yearly twenty-six pence to purchase clothing, and further ordered that on his anniversary twelve hundred poor men should receive each a loaf of bread and a cheese, or bacon and one penny[2].

Oswulf, who was duke of East Kent at the commencement of the ninth century, left lands to Canterbury charging the canons with doles upon his anniversary: twenty ploughlands or about twelve hundred acres at Stanstead were to supply the canons and the poor on that day with one hundred and twenty wheaten loaves, thirty of pure wheat, one fat ox, four sheep, two flitches, five geese, ten hens, ten pounds of cheese (or if it happened to be a fastday, a weigh of cheese, fish, butter and eggs *ad libitum*), thirty measures of good Welsh ale, and a tub of honey or two of wine. From the lands of the brotherhood were to issue one hundred and twenty *sufl* loaves, apparently a kind of cake; while

---

[1] Thorpe, i. 196.   [2] Cod. Dipl. No. 230.

his lands at Bourn were to supply a thousand loaves of bread and a thousand *sufls*[1]. Towards the end of the tenth century Wulfwaru devised her lands to various relatives, and charged them with the support of twenty poor men[2]. About the same period Æ∂elstán the æ∂eling gave lands to Ely on condition that they fed one hundred poor men on his anniversary, at the expense of his heirs.

From what has preceded it may fairly be argued that at all times there was a very sufficient fund for the relief of the poor, seeing that tithe, penance, fine, voluntary contribution, and compulsory assessment all combined to furnish their quota. It now remains to enquire into the method. of its distribution.

The gains of the altar, whether in tithes, oblations, or other forms, were strictly payable over to the metropolitan or cathedral church of the district. The division of the fund was thus committed to the consulting body of the clergy, and their executive or head ; and the several shares were thus distributed under the supervision and by the authority of the bishop and his canons in each diocese. Private alms may have remained occasionally at the disposal of the priest in a small parish, but the recognized public alms which were the property of the poor, and held in trust for them by the clergy,

---

[1] Cod. Dipl. No. 226. I think these súfls must be *subflata,* raised or leavened bread. The contrast afforded by the heavy black rye bread of Westphalia—technically Pumpernickel—will serve to explain the term. In the east of England still a kind of cakes are called *Souls,* probably Sufls.

[2] Cod. Dipl. No. 694.

were necessarily managed by the principal body, the clergy of the cathedral. To the vicinity of the cathedral flocked the maimed, the halt, the blind, the destitute and friendless, to be fed and clothed and tended for the love of God. In that vicinity they enjoyed shelter, defence, private aid and public alms; and as in some few cases the cathedral church was surrounded by a flourishing city, they could hope for the chances which always accompany a close manufacturing or retailing population. In this way the largest proportion of the poor must have been collected near the chief church of the diocese, on whose lands they found an easy settlement, in whose xenodochia, hospitals and almshouses they met with a refuge, to whom they gave their services, such as they were, and from whom they received in turn the support which secular lords were unable or unwilling to give: for the cathedral church being generally a very considerable landowner, had the power of employing much more labour than the majority of secular landlords in any given district.

But it must not be imagined that the poor could obtain no relief save at the cathedral: every parish-church had its share of the public fund, as well as private alms, devoted to this purpose; and to the necessary buildings of every parish-church, however small, a xenodochium belonged. When now we consider the great number of churches that existed all over England in the tenth century, a number which most likely exceeded that now in being, and consequently bore a most dispropor-

tionate ratio to the then population of the country,
—when we further consider that the poor were comparatively few (so that a provision was absolutely
made for the case where a pauper could not be
found in a royal village), we shall have no difficulty
in concluding that relief was supplied in a very
ample degree to the needy.

It does not necessarily follow, although in itself
very probable, that the claim to relief was a territorial one, that is that the man was to have relief
where he was born, lived or had gained a settlement
by labour. As some landowners, particularly in
later times, especially honoured certain churches
with the grant of tithes consecrated to them, it is
possible that some paupers may have followed the
convenient precedent, and argued that whither the
fund went, thither might the recipients go also.
And inasmuch as in many cases they would appear
under the guise of poor pilgrims, we can readily
understand the immense resort to particular shrines
at particular periods, without overrating the devotion or the superstition of the multitude. But all
this might have led to very serious consequences,
had the facilities *really* been so great. In point of
fact there were no facilities at all except for such
as were from age or infirmity incapable of doing
any valuable service. For among the Saxons the
law of settlement applied inexorably to all classes:
no man had a legal existence unless he could be
shown to belong to some association connected
with a certain locality, or to be in the hand, protection and surety of a landed lord. Even a

man of the rank nearest the princes or ealdorman
could not leave his land without having fulfilled
certain conditions; and the illegal migration of a
dependent man from one shire or one estate to
another was punished in the severest manner, in
the persons of all concerned. He was called a
Flýma or fugitive, and the receiving or harbouring him was a grave offence, punishable with a
heavy fine, to be raised for the benefit of the king's
officers in the shire the fugitive deserted, as well as
that wherein he was received [1]. Even if the vigi-
lance of the sheriffs and ealdorman in two shires
could be lulled, it was difficult to disarm the selfishness of a landlord or an owner who thought
the runaway's services of any value, or his price
worth securing. A year and a day must elapse ere
the right abated from the "lord in pursuit," for so
was the lord called over all Europe in the idioms
of the several tongues [2]; and hence it cannot have
been a very easy matter for any man to take advantage of the poor-law, while it remained any one's
advantage to keep him from falling into the state
of pauperism: in other words, no man whose labour
still possessed any value would be so cast upon the
world as to have no refuge but what the church in
Christian charity provided. And this was the real
and trustworthy test of destitution. If a man was
so helpless, friendless and useless that he could
find no place in one of the mutual associations, or

---

[1] Ælfr. § 33. "Be boldgetæle."
[2] In Germany the Nachfolgende, Nachjagende Herr. See Fleta i.
cap. 7. § 7, 8.

in a lord's family, it is clear that he must become
an outlaw as far as the State is concerned[1]: he
must fly to the woods, turn serf or steal, or else
commend himself as a pauper to the benefits of
clerical superintendence: but it is perfectly obvious
that none but the hopelessly infirm or aged could
ever be placed under such difficulty, in a country
situated like England at any period of the Saxon
rule, and hence pauper relief was in practice strictly
confined to those for whom it was justly intended.
The Saxon poor-law then appears simple enough,
and well might it be so : they had not tried many
unsuccessful and ridiculous experiments in œco-
nomics, suffered themselves to be misled by very
many mischievous crochets, nor on the whole did
they find it necessary to make so expensive a
protest against bad commercial legislation as our
poor-law has proved to us.   But it is not quite the
simple thing it seems, and requires two elements
for its efficient working, which are not to be found
at every period, namely a powerful, conscientious
clergy, and a system of property founded exclusively upon the possession of land, and guarded by

---

[1] The lordless man, of whom no right could be got, i. e. who being
in no sort of association, could neither support himself nor offer any
guarantee to society, was to be got into one by his family. If they
either could not or would not produce him at the folcmót and find a
lord for him, he became an outlaw, and any one might slay him. Leg.
Æðelstán. Thorpe, i. 200.   The same prince decided that if any land-
less man, who followed a lord in some other shire, should revisit his
family, they might receive him on condition of being answerable for
his offences. Thorpe, i. 204. But this seems to me to be the case
merely of a temporary visit, made of course with the knowledge and
permission of his lord.

a compulsory distribution of all citizens into certain fixed and settled associations.

I have already called attention to the fact that it was usual, if not necessary, on emancipating a serf, to provide for his subsistence. It is however not improbable that, though such emancipated serfs remained for the most part upon the land, and in the protection of their former lord, they found some assistance from the poor fund, either directly from the church, or indirectly through the private alms of the lord.

To resume all the facts of the case:—the State did not contemplate the existence or provide for the support of any poor : it demanded that every man should either be answerable for himself in a mutual bond of association with his neighbours; or that he should place himself under the protection of a lord, if he had no means of his own, and thus have some one to answer for him. If unfree, the State of course held him to be the chattel of his owner, who was only responsible to God for his treatment of him. He therefore who had no means and could find no one to take charge of him was an outlaw, that is, had no civil rights of any kind.

But Christianity taught that there was something even above the State, which the State itself was bound to recognize. It accordingly impressed upon all communicants the moral and religious duty of assisting those of their brethren whom the strict law condemned to misery; and the clergy presented their organization as a very efficient machinery for the proper distribution of alms. The voluntary

2 L 2

oblations became in time replaced by settled payments; but the law did not alter the disposition
which the clergy had adopted; it only recognized
and sanctioned it; first by making the various
church payments compulsory upon all classes; and
secondly by enacting that the mode of distribution
long prevalent should be the legal one, in a secular
as well as an ecclesiastical obligation. And thus
by slow degrees, as the State itself became Chris-
tianized, the moral duty became a legal one; and
the merciful intervention of religion was allowed to
supply what could not be found in the strict rule
of law.

It is unnecessary here to enquire how the power
of the clergy to assist the poor was gradually diminished, by the arbitrary consecration or total subtraction of tithe, and other ecclesiastical payments;
or how the burthen of supporting the poor, having
become a religious as well as a civil duty, was
shifted from one fund to another. It is enough to
have shown how the difficulty was attempted to be
met during the continuance of the Anglosaxon institutions. Under the present circumstances of
almost every European state, it is admitted that no
man is to perish for want of means, while means
anywhere exist to feed him: and but two questions can be admitted, namely:—Who is really in
want? and,—How is he to be fed at the least possible
amount of loss to others? This is as far as the
State will go. Religion, properly considered, im-
poses very different duties, and very different tests:
but public morality alone ought to teach that

where the State has interfered on one side, it must pay the penalty on the other; and that where it has positively prescribed the directions in which men shall seek their subsistence, it is bound to indemnify those whom these restrictions have tended to impoverish. Every Poor Law is a protest against some wrong done: and in proportion to the wrong is the energy of the protest itself. Do not interfere with industry, and it will be very safe to leave poverty to take care of itself. It is quite possible to conceive a state of things in which crime and poverty shall be really convertible ideas, but of this the history of the world as yet has given us no example.

APPENDIX.

APPENDIX A.

THE DOOMS OF THE CITY OF LONDON.

(Æðelstán V. Thorpe, i. 228, sq.)

" THIS is the ordinance which the bishops and the reeves belonging to London have ordained, and with weds confirmed, among our ' frith gegildas,' as well corlish as ceorlish, in addition to the dooms which were fixed at Greatanlea and at Exeter and at Thunresfeld.

" *This then is first.*

" 1. That no thief be spared over XII pence, and no person over XII years, whom we learn according to folkright that he is guilty, and can make no denial; that we slay him, and take all that he has; and first take the ' ceapgild ' from the property; and after that let the surplus be divided into II : one part to the wife, if she be innocent, and were not privy to the crime ; and the other into II ; let the king take half, half the fellowship. If it be bócland or bishop's land, then has the landlord the half part in common with the fellowship.

" 2. And he who secretly harbours a thief, and is privy to the crime and to the guilt, to him let the like be done.

" 3. And he who stands with a thief, and fights with him, let him be slain with the thief.

" 4. And he who oft before has been convicted openly of theft, and shall go to the ordeal, and is there found guilty ; that he be slain, unless the kindred or the lord be willing to release him by his ' wer,' and by the full ' ceap-gild,' and also have him in 'borh,' that he thenceforth desist from every kind of evil. If after that he again steal, then let his kinsmen give him up to the reeve to whom it may appertain, in such custody as they before took him out of from the ordeal, and let him be slain in retribution of the theft. But if any one defend him, and will take him, although he was convicted at the ordeal, so that he might not be slain; that he should be liable in his life, unless he should flee to the king, and he should give him his life ; all as it was before ordained at Greatanlea, and at Exeter, and at Thunresfeld.

" 5. And whoever will avenge a thief, and commits an assault, or makes an attack on the highway; let him be liable in cxx shillings to the king. But if he slay any one in his revenge, let him be liable in his life, and in all that he has, unless the king is willing to be merciful to him.

" Second.

" That we have ordained : that each of us should contribute iv pence for our common use within xii months, and pay for the property which should be taken after we had contributed the money ; and that all should have the search in common ; and that every man should contribute his shilling who had property to the value of xxx pence, except the poor widow who has no ' for-wyrhta' nor any land.

" Third.

" That we count always ten men together, and the chief should direct the nine in each of those duties which we have all ordained : and [count] afterwards their ' hyndens' together, and one ' hyn-den-man ' who shall admonish the x for our common benefit ; and let these xi hold the money of the ' hynden,' and decide what they shall disburse when aught is to pay, and what they shall receive, if money should arise to us, at our common suit; and let them also know that every contribution be forthcoming which we have all ordained for our common benefit, after the rate of xxx pence or one ox; so that all be fulfilled which we have ordained in our ordinances, and which stands in our agreement.

" Fourth.

" That every man of them who has heard the orders should be

aidful to others, as well in tracing as in pursuit, so long as the track is known; and after the track has failed him, that one man be found where there is a large population, as well as from one tithing where a less population is, either to ride or to go (unless there be need of more) thither where most need is, and as they all have ordained.

"*Fifth.*

"That no search be abandoned, either to the north of the march or to the south, before every man who has a horse has ridden one riding; and that he who has not a horse, work for the lord who rides or goes for him, until he come home; unless right shall have been previously obtained.

"*Sixth.*

"1. Respecting our 'ceapgild': a horse at half a pound, if it be so good; and if it be inferior, let it be paid for by the worth of its appearance, and by that which the man values it at who owns it, unless he have evidence that it be as good as he says, and then let [us] have the surplus which we there require.

"2. An ox at a mancus, and a cow at xx, and a swine at x, and a sheep at a shilling.

"3. And we have ordained respecting our 'theowmen' whom men might have; if anyone should steal him, that he should be paid for with half a pound; but if we should raise the 'gild,' that it should be increased above that, by the worth of his appearance, and that we should have for ourselves the surplus that we then should require. But if he should have stolen himself away, that he should be led to the stoning, as it was formerly ordained; and that every man who had a man, should contribute either a penny or a halfpenny, according to the number of the fellowship, so that we might be able to raise the worth. But if he should make his escape, that he should be paid for by the worth of his appearance, and we all should make search for him. If we then should be able to come at him, that the same should be done to him that would be done to a Wylisc thief, or that he be hanged.

"4. And let the 'ceapgild' always advance from xxx pence to

half a pound, after we make search ; further, if we raise the 'ceap-gild' to the full 'angilde'; and let the search still continue, as was before ordained, though it be less.

" Seventh.

" That we have ordained : let do the deed whoever may that shall avenge the injuries of us all, that we should be all so in one friendship as in one foeship, whichever it then may be ; and that he who should kill a thief before other men, that he be xii pence the better for the deed, and for the enterprize, from our common money. And he who should own the property for which we pay let him not forsake the search, on peril of our 'oferhyrnes,' and the notice therewith, until we come to payment : and then also we would reward him for his labour, out of our common money, according to the worth of the journey, lest the giving notice should be neglected.

" Eighth.

" 1. That we gather to us once in every month, if we can and have leisure, the 'hynden men' and those who direct the tithings, as well with 'bytt-fylling,' as else it may concern us, and know what of our agreement has been executed ; and let these xii men have their refection together, and feed themselves according as they may deem themselves worthy, and deal the remains of the meat for the love of God.

" 2. And if it then should happen that any kin be so strong and so great, within land or without, whether 'xii hynde' or 'twy hynde,' that they refuse us right, and stand up in defence of a thief ; that we all of us ride thereto with the reeve within whose 'manung' it may be.

" 3. And also send on both sides to the reeves, and desire from them aid of so many men as may seem to us adequate for so great a suit, that there may be the more fear in those culpable men for our assemblage, and that we all ride thereto, and avenge our wrong, and slay the thief, and those who fight and stand with him, unless they be willing to depart from him.

" 4. And if any one trace a track from one shire to another, let the men who there are next take to it, and pursue the track till it be made known to the reeve; let him then with his 'manung' take to it, and pursue the track out of his shire, if he can; but if he cannot, let him pay the 'angylde' of the property, and let both reeveships have the full suit in common, be it wherever it may, as well to the north of the march as to the south, always from one shire to another; so that every reeve may assist another, for the common 'frith' of us all, by the king's 'oferhyrnes.'

"5. And also that everyone shall help another, as it is ordained and by 'weds' confirmed; and such man as shall neglect this beyond the march, let him be liable in xxx pence, or an ox, if he aught of this neglect which stands in our writings, and we with our 'weds' have confirmed.

"6. And we have also ordained respecting every man who has given his 'wed' in our gildships, if he should die, that each gild-brother shall give a 'gesufel' loaf for his soul, and sing a fifty, or get it sung within xxx days.

"7. And we also command our 'hiremen' that each man shall know when he has his cattle, or when he has not, on his neighbour's witness, and that he point out to us the track, if he cannot find it within three days; for we believe that many heedless men reck not how their cattle go, for over-confidence in the 'frith.'

"8. Then we command that within iii days he make it known to his neighbours, if he will ask for the 'ceap-gild'; and let the search nevertheless go on as it was before ordained, for we will not pay for any unguarded property, unless it be stolen. Many men speak fraudulent speech. If he cannot point out to us the track, let him show on oath with iii of his neighbours that it has been stolen within iii days, and after that let him ask for his 'ceap-gild.'

"9. And let it not be denied nor concealed, if our lord or any of our reeves should suggest to us any addition to our 'frith-gilds' that we will joyfully accept the same, as it becomes us all, and may be advantageous to us. But let us trust in God, and our kingly lord, if we fulfil all things thus, that the affairs of all folk will be better with respect to theft than they before were. If, however, we slacken in the 'frith' and the 'wed' which we have given, and the king has commanded of us, then may we expect, or well know, that these thieves will prevail yet more than they did before. But let us keep our 'weds' and the 'frith' as is pleasing to our lord; it greatly behoves us that we devise that which he wills; and if he order and instruct us more, we shall be humbly ready.

" Ninth.

"That we have ordained: respecting those thieves whom one cannot immediately discover to be guilty, and one afterwards learns that they are guilty and liable; that the lord or the kinsmen should release him in the same manner as those men are released who are found guilty at the ordeal.

" Tenth.

" That all the 'witan' gave their 'weds' altogether to the arch-bishop at Thunresfeld, when Ælfeah Stybb and Brihtnoth Odda's son came to meet the 'gemot' by the king' command; that each reeve should take the 'wed' in his own shire: that they would all hold the 'frith' as king Æthelstan and his 'witan' had counselled it, first at Greatanlea, and again at Exeter, and afterwards at Feversham, and a fourth time at Thunresfeld, before the arch-bishop and all the bishops, and his 'witan' whom the king him-self named, who were thereat: that those dooms should be ob-served which were fixed at this 'gemot,' except those which were there before done away with; which was, Sunday marketing, and that with full and true witness any one might buy out of port.

" Eleventh.

" That Æthelstan commands his bishops and his 'ealdormen' and all his reeves over all my realm, that ye so hold the 'frith' as I and my 'witan' have ordained; and if any of you neglect it, and will not obey me, and will not take the 'wed' of his 'hire-men,' and he allow of secret compositions, and will not attend to these regulations as I have commanded, and it stands in our writs; then be the reeve without his 'folgoth,' and without my friendship, and pay me cxx shilling; and each of my thanes who has land, and will not keep the regulations as I have commanded, [let him pay] half that.

" *Twelfth.*

" 1. That the king now again has ordained to his ' witan' at Witlanburh, and has commanded it to be made known to the archbishop by bishop Theodred, that it seemed to him too cruel that so young a man should be killed, and besides for so little, as he has learned has somewhere been done. He then said, that it seemed to him, and to those who counselled with him, that no younger person should be slain than xv years, except he should make resistance or flee, and would not·surrender himself; that then he should be slain, as well for more as for less, whichever it might be. But if he be willing to surrender himself, let him be put into prison, as it was ordained at Greatanlea, and by the same let him be redeemed.

" 2. Or if he come not into prison, and they have none, that they take him in ' borh' by his full ' wer,' that he will evermore desist from every kind of evil. If the kindred will not take him out, nor enter into ' borh' for him, then let him swear as the bishop may instruct him, that he will desist from every kind of evil, and stand in servitude by his ' wer.' But if he after that again steal, let him be slain or hanged, as was before done to the elder ones.

" 3. And the king has also ordained, that no one should be slain for less property than xii pence worth, unless he will flee or defend himself; and that then no one should hesitate, though it were for less. If we it thus hold, then trust I in God that our ' frith '. will be better than it has before been."

The following Flemish Charters of Liberties seemed to me fitting to be recorded here. They are taken from the ' Piéces justificatives ' of Warnkönig's History of Flanders, vol. ii.

I. *Première Charte ou* Keure *de la ville de St. Omer, accordée par Guillaume de Normandie, comte de Flandre, et confirmée par Louis-le-Gros, roi de France.* 14 *Avril* 1127.

" Ego Guillelmus Dei gratia Flandrensium Comes petitioni Burgensium Sancti Audomari contraïre nolens, pro eo maxime quia meam de Consulatu Flandriæ petitionem libenti animo receperunt, et quia honestius et fidelius cæteris Flandrensibus erga me semper se habuerunt, lagas seu consuetudines subscriptas perpetuo eis iure concedo, et ratas manere præcipio.

" § 1. Primo quidem ut erga unumquemque hominem, pacem eis faciam et eos sicut homines meos sine malo ingenio manuteneam et defendam ; rectumque iudicium scabinorum erga unumquemque hominem, et erga me ipsum eis fieri concedam ; ipsisque scabinis libertatem, qualem melius habent scabini terræ meæ constituam.

" § 2. Si quis Burgensium Sancti Audomari alicui pecuniam suam crediderit, et ille cui credita est, coram legitimis hominibus et in villa sua hereditariis sponte concesserit, quod si die constituta pecuniam non persolverit, ipse vel bona eius, donec omnia reddat, retineantur : si persolvere noluerit, aut si negaverit hanc conventionem, et testimonio duorum Scabinorum, vel duorum iuratorum inde convictus fuerit, donec debitum solvat, retineatur.

" § 3. Si quis de iure christianitatis ab aliquo interpellatus fuerit, de villa Sancti Audomari alias pro iustitia exequenda, non exeat : sed in eadem villa coram episcopo vel eius Archidiacono, vel suo presbytero, quod iustum est clericorum, scabinorumque iudicio exequatur : nec respondeat alicui, nisi tribus de causis ; videlicet de infractura ecclesiæ, vel atrii, de lesione clerici, de oppressione et violatione feminæ : quod si de aliis causis querimonia facta fuerit coram iudicibus et præposito meo hoc finiatur. Sic enim coram K. Comite et episcopo Johanne statutum fuit.

" § 4. Libertatem vero, quam antecessorum meorum temporibus habuerunt eis concedo. Scilicet quod nunquam de terra sua in expeditionem proficiscentur, excepto si hostilis exercitus terram Flandriæ invaserit ; tunc me et terram meam defendere debebunt.

" § 5. Omnes qui Gildam eorum habent, et ad illam pertinent,

et infra cingulam villæ suæ manent, liberos omnes a teloneo facio,
ad portum Dichesmudæ et Graveningis; et per totam terram
Flandriæ, eos liberos a Sewerp facio. Apud Batpalmas teloneum,
quale donant Atrebatenses, eis constituo.

" § 6. Quisquis eorum ad terram imperatoris pro negotiatione
sua perexerit, a nemine meorum hansam persolvere cogatur.

" § 7. Si contigerit mihi aliquo tempore præter terram Flandriæ aliam conquirere, aut si concordia pacis inter me et avuncu-
lum meum H. regem Angliæ facta fuerit, in conquisita terra
illa aut in toto regno Anglorum eos liberos ab omni teloneo et ab
omni consuetudine in concordia illa recipi faciam.

" § 8. In omni mercato Flandriæ si quis clamorem adversus
eos suscitaverit iudicium scabinorum de omni clamore sine duello
subeant; ab duello vero ulterius liberi sint.

" § 9. Omnes qui infra murum sancti Audomari habitant et
deinceps sunt habitaturi, liberos a Cavagio hoc est a capitali censu,
et de advocationibus constituo.

" § 10. Pecuniam eorum quæ post mortem Comitis K. eis ablata
est, et quæ propter fidelitatem quam erga me habent adhuc eis
detinetur, aut infra annum reddi faciam, aut iudicio scabinorum
institiam eis fieri concedam.

" § 11. Præterea rogaverunt regem Franciæ et Raulphum de
Parona, ut ubicumque in terram illorum venerint, liberi sint ab
omni teloneo, et traverso et passagio; quod et concedi volo.

" § 12. Communionem autem suam sicut eam iuraverunt per-
manere præcipio, et a nemine dissolvi permitto, et omne rectum
rectamque iustitiam sicut melius stat in terra mea, scilicet in Flan-
dria, eis concedo.

" § 13. Et sicut meliores et liberiores Burgenses Flandriæ ab
omni consuetudine liberos deinceps esse volo; nullum scoth, nullam taliam, nullam pecuniæ suæ petitionem ab eis require.

" § 14. Monetam meam in Sancto Audomaro unde per annum
xxx libras habebam et quidquid in ea habere debeo, ad restau-
rationem damnorum suorum et gildæ suæ sustentamentum constituo. Ipsi vero Burgenses monetam per totam vitam meam stabi-
lem et bonam, unde villa sua melioretur, stabiliant.

" § 15. Custodes qui singulis noctibus per annum vigilantes castellum Sancti Audomari custodiunt, et qui præter feodum suum et præbendam sibi antiquitus constitutam in avena et caseis et in pellibus arietum, iniuste et violenter ab unaquaque domo in eadem villa, scilicet ad Sanctum Audomarum sanctumque Bertinum in natali domini panem unum et denarium unum aut duos denarios exigere solent, aut pro hiis pauperum vadimonia tollebant, nihil omnino deinceps præter feodum suum et præbendam suam exigere audeant.

" § 16. Quisquis ad Niuverledam venerit, undecumque venerit, licentiam habeat veniendi ad Sanctum Audomarum cum rebus suis in quacunque navi voluerit.

" § 17. Si cum Boloniensium comite S. concordiam habuero, in illa reconciliatione eos a Teloneo et Seuwerp apud Witsant et per totam terram eius liberos esse faciam.

" § 18. Pasturam adiacentem villæ Sancti Audomari in nemori, quod dicitur Lo, et in paludibus et in pratis et in bruera et in Hongrecoltra, usibus eorum, exceptâ terrâ Lazarorum, concedo, sicut fuit tempore Roberti Comitis Barbati.

" § 19. Mansiones quoque, quæ sunt in ministerio Advocati Sancti Bertini, illas videlicet quæ inhabitantur, ab omni consuetudine liberas esse volo: dabuntque singulæ denarios xii in festo Sancti Michaelis, et de brotban denarios xii et de byrban denarios xii. Vacuæ autem nihil dabunt.

" § 20. Si quis extraneus aliquem Burgensium Sancti Audomari agressus fuerit, et ei contumeliam vel iniuriam irrogaverit vel violenter ei sua abstulerit, et cum hac iniuria manus eius evaserit, postmodum vocatus a castellano vel uxore eius seu ab eius dapifero, infra triduum ad satisfactionem venire contempserit aut neglexerit ; ipsi communiter iniuriam fratris sui in eo vindicabunt, in qua vindicta si domus diruta vel combusta fuerit, aut si quispiam vulneratus vel occisus fuerit, nullum corporis aut rerum suarum periculum, qui vindictam perpetravit, incurrat, nec offensam meam super hoc sentiat vel pertimescat ; si vero, qui iniuriam intulit presentialiter tentus fuerit, secundum leges et consuetudines villæ presentialiter iudicabitur et secundum quantitatem

facti punietur; scilicet oculum pro oculo, dentem pro dente, caput
pro capite reddet.

" § 21. De morte Eustachii de Stenford quicunque aliquem
Burgensium Sancti Audomari perturbaverit et molestaverit, reus
proditionis et mortis K. Comitis habeatur; quoniam pro fidelitate
mea factum est, quidquid de eo factum est; et sicut iuravi et fidem
dedi, sic eos erga parentes eius reconciliare et pacificare volo.

" § 25. Hanc igitur Communionem tenendam, has supradictas
consuetudines et conventiones esse observandas fide promiserunt
et sacramento confirmaverunt: Ludovicus rex Francorum, Guillelmus comes Flandriæ, Raulphus de Parona, Hugo Candavena,
Hosto Castellanus, et Guillelmus frater eius, Robertus de Bethuna,
et Guillelmus filius eius, Anselmus de Hesdinio, Stephanus Comes
Boloniensis, Manasses Comes Gisnensis, Galterus de Lillers,
Balduinus Gandavensis, Hiuvannus frater eius, Rogerus Castellanus Insulensis, et Robertus filius eius, Razo de Gavera, Daniel
de Tenremot, Helias de Sensen, Henricus de Brocborc, Eustachius
advocatus, et Arnulphus filius eius, Castellanus Gandavensis, Gervasius Petrus dapifer, Stephanus de Seningaham. Confirmatum
est hoc privilegium et a Comite Guillelmo et prædictis Baronibus
istis fide et sacramento sancitum, et collaudatum anno dominicæ
Incarnationis MCXXVII, xviii Kl. Maii, feria Vª die festo Sancti
Tiburtii et Valeriani."

II. *Additions et changemens faits à la* Keure *précédente par le
Comte Thierri d'Alsace. 22 Août* 1128.

" § 1. Monetam quam Burgenses Sancti Audomari habuerant,
Comiti liberam reddiderunt eo quod eos benignius tractaret, et
lagas suas eis libentius ratas teneret: et insuper ut ceteri Flandrenses eidem sua incrementa celerius redderent.

" § 2. Teloneum vero suum ab eodem in perpetuo censu receperunt, quotannis C solidos dando.

" § 3. Si quis etiam eorum mortuo aliquo consanguineo suo,
portionem aliquam possessionis illius sibi obvenire credens et in
comitatu Flandriæ manens, cum eo, qui possessionem illam tenebit,
vel partiri infra annum neglexerit, vel eum super hoc per iudices et

scabinos minime convenerit; qui per annum integrum sine legitima calumnia tenuerit, quiete deinceps teneat, et nulli super hoc respondeat. Si autem heres in comitatu Flandriæ non fuerit, infra annum, quo redierit, cum possessore agat supradicto modo : alioquin qui tenebit sine ulla inquietatione teneat. Si autem herede aliquandiu peregre commorante, et cum redierit portionem suam requirente, possidens se cum eo partitum esse dixerit, si ille per quinque Scabinos probare falsum esse poterit, hereditas quæ eum attingit ei reddetur : alioquin possidens per quatuor legitimos viros se ei portionem suam dedisse probabit ; et ita quietus erit. Quod si heres infra annos discretionis fuerit, pater vel mater, si supervixerint, vel qui eum manutenebit, portionem quæ illum attinget scabinis et aliis legitimis viris infra annum obitus illius ostendat, et si eis visum fuerit quod ille fideliter servare debeat, ei comittatur. Sin autem iudicio et providentia illorum ita disponatur, ne heres damnum alioquod patiatur ; et cum ad annos discretionis venerit, et opportunum fuerit, hereditate sua integre et sine aliqua diminutione investiatur.

" § 4. Item si quis alicui filium suum, vel filiam in matrimonio coniunxerit, et filius ille, vel filia sine prole obierint, ad patrem et matrem eorum si supervixerint, si autem mortui fuerint ad alios filios eorum, vel filios filiorum redeat hereditas quæ pertinebat ad filium vel filiam, quos aliis matrimonio copulaverant ; et viventibus patre vel matre eorum hereditas illa cum supradictis personis tantum dividatur : mortuis autem illis propinquiores consanguinei illam, prout iustum est, sortiantur.

" Hanc igitur communionem tenendam, et supradictas institutiones et conventiones esse observandas fide promiserunt et sacramento confirmaverunt Theodoricus, Comes Flandriæ, Willelmus Castellanus Sancti Audomari, Willelmus de Lo, Iwannus de Gandavo, Danihel de Tenramunda, Raso de Gavera, Gislebertus de Bergis, Henricus de Broburc, Castellanus de Gandavo, Gervasius de Brugis.—Præfati Barones insuper iuraverunt, quod si Comes Burgenses Sancti Audomari extra consuetudines suas eiicere et sine iudicio Scabinorum tractare vellet, se a comite discessuros et cum eis remansuros, donec comes eis suas consuetudines integre restitueret et iudicium Scabinorum eos subire permitteret. Actum anno dominicæ Incarnationis MCXXVIII in octavis assumptionis Beatæ Mariæ."

III. *Charte de donation du fonds de la Gild-halle de St. Omer aux Bourgeois de cette ville.* 1151.

" Ego Theodoricus Dei patientia Flandrensium Comes, consensu uxoris meæ Sibillæ, concedente ita quoque Philippo filio meo, terram in qua Ghildhalla apud sanctum Audomarum in foro sita est, cum scopis et adpenditiis suis tam ligneis quam lapideis, burgensibus eiusdem villæ hereditario iure possidendam, et ad omnem mercaturam tam in appenditiis, quam in Ghildhalla exercendam tradidi : hanc quoque libertatem eis concessi, ut si quis in eam venerit, undecunque reus fuerit, in ipsa domo iudici in eum manum non mittere licebit; ille autem sub cuius custodia Ghildhalla tenetur, admonitus a iudice reum extra limen Ghildhallæ conducens nisi fideiussione se defenderit, in præsentia duorum scabinorum vel plurium eum iudici tradet: iudex vero eum in potestate sua habens secundum quantitatem facti cum eo aget. Illud quoque addidimus, quod alienus negotiator nusquam, nisi in prædicta domo aut in appendiciis eius, vel in pleno foro merces suas vendendas exponat aut vendat. Solis autem burgensibus in foro, in Ghildhalla, seu magis velint, is propria domo sua, vendere liceat.

" Quoniam autem humana omnia ex rerum et temporum varietate senescunt, sigilli mei auctoritate et subscriptorum testimonio hoc corroboravi. Walterus Castellanus sancti Audomari, Arnoldus Comes de Gisnes, Gerardus Præpositus, Arnulphus de Arde, Henricus Castellanus de Brübborg, Elenardus de Sinningehem, Hugo de Ravensberghe, Baldevinus de Bailgul, Michael Iunior, Christianus de Aria, Guido Castellanus de Bergis, Rogerus de Wavrin, Helinus filius eius."

IV. *Keure de Bruges.* Vers 1190.

" Hæc est lex et consuetudo quam Brugenses tenere debent a comite Philippo instituta. Si quis alicui vulnus fecerit infra pontem sanctæ Mariæ, infra Botrebeika, infra usque ad domum Galteri

Calvi, infra usque ad domum Lanikini carpentarii, supra terram Balduini de Prat, infra fossatum veteris molendini, et illud veritate scabinorum cognoscatur de quacunque re factum sit, ad domum in qua ille manet, qui vulnus imposuit, per scabinos et per iustitiam comitis submoneatur. Qui submonitus, si scabinis se præsentet, veritate inquisita de illo qui vulnus fecerit per sexaginta libras forefactum emendet, et si scabini sciunt quod vulnus non fecerit, liber et in pace remanebit. Si die quâ submonebitur se non præsentaverit, remanebat in forefacto sexaginta librarum, et si scabini voluerint domum eius prosternere, poterunt et in respectum ponere, sed ex toto condonare non possunt nisi voluntate Comitis.

"2. Si verò quis aliquem in domo suâ assiluerit, unde clamor factus sit, scabini et iustitia domum ibunt inspicere : et si scabini poterunt videre, assultum esse apparentem, illo de quo clamor factus est submoneri debet ; qui si scabinis se præsentaverit et illum intellexerint assultum fecisse, LX libras amittet. Si vero cognoverint illum assultum non fecisse, liber et in pace recedat. Si autem ad diem submonitionis venire noluerit, domo ejus prostrata LX librarum reus erit. Quod si alii assultui interfuerint, de quibus clamor factus non sit, si comes super hoc veritatem scabinorum requisierit, scabini veritatem inquirere debent, et quotquot veritate scabinorum de assultu tenebuntur, unusquisque eorum LX librarum reus erit, ac si de eo clamor factus sit. Si vero scabini nullum assultum agnoscere potuerunt ab ipsis super hoc veritas est inquirenda.

"3. Qui cum armis molutis infra præfinitos terminos aliquem fugaverit, si veritate scabinorum convincatur forisfacto librarum LX tenebitur : si aliquis assiliatur, quidquid ipse faciat in defendendo corpus suum nullo tenebitur forisfacto.

"4. Qui aliquem bannitum occiderit in hoc nullum facit forisfactum.

'5. Quicumque testimonio scabinorum convictus fuerit de rapina, LX lib. de forisfacto dabit et dampnum rapinæ restituet.

"6. Qualemcunque concordiam bannitus faciat comiti, remanebit tamen bannitus, donec viris Brugensibus ad opus castri LX solidos dederit.

" 7. Qui bannitum de forefacto LX libr. hospitio susceperit, veritate scabinorum convictus LX libras amittet.

" 8. Qui aliquem fuste vel baculo percusserit, convictus a scabinis in forisfacto x lib. incidit de quibus comes habebit v lib. Castellanus xx sol. ille qui percussus est LX sol. et ad opus castri xx sol.

" 9. Qui pugno vel palma aliquem percusserit seu per capillos acceperit inde per scabinos convictus LX sol. dabit unde xxx solidi comitis erunt, percussi xv sol. castallani x sol. ad opus castri v sol. Qui aliquem per capillos ad terram traxerit sive per lutum trahendo pedibus conculcaverit, x lib. comiti dabit, maletractato xv solidos, Castellano x sol. et ad castrum v solidos.

" 10. Qui vero alicui convitia dixerit, si testimonio duorum scabinorum convincatur, illi cui convicia dixerit v solidos dabit, Iusticiæ xii denarios.

" 11. Qui duobus scabinis aut pluribus inducias pacis, quæ treuiæ dicuntur, de quâlibet discordiâ dare noluerit, illud emendabit per LX lib.

" 12. Si dissensiones aut discordiæ aut guerræ aut aliquod aliud malum inter probos viros oppidi exoriatur, unde ad aures scabinorum clamor perveniat, salvo iure comitis, scabini illud componere et pacificare poterunt. Qui verò compositionem vel pacem quam super hoc scabini consolidaverint, sequi noluerit, forisfactum LX lib. incurret.

" 13. Qui ea dedixerit quæ scabini in iudicio vel testimonio affirmaverint, LX lib. amittet, et unicuique scabinorum qui ab eo dedictus erit x libras dabit.

" 14. Quicumque per vim fœminam violaverit, si de eo veritate scabinorum convincatur, eâdem pœnâ dampnabitur, quantâ a prædecessoribus comitibus, tales malefactores dampnari solent in Flandriâ.

" 15. Quicumque per malum in scabinos manum suam immiserit, si scabini illud testificentur, LX libras dabit.

" 16. Præterea sciant omnes, quod vir de oppido Brugensi, cuiuscumque forisfacti se reum fecerit, non amplius quam LX libr. amittere poterit, nisi legitime per scabinos convictus fuerit de raptu, ut dictum est, vel de latrocinio, vel de falsitate, vel nisi hominem occiderit. Qui verò occiderit hominem, caput pro capite dabit, et omnia sua in potestate comitis erunt absque omni contradictione, si de homicidio veritate scabinorum teneatur.

" 17. Nemo infra præfinitos terminos manens infra muros castri gladium ferat, nisi sit mercator vel alius qui gratiâ negocii sui per castrum transeat. Si verò castrum intraverit causâ inibi morandi, gladium extra in suburbio dimittat. Quod si non fecerit, LX solidos et gladium amittet. Iusticiis vero comitis et ministris earum, quia pacem castri observare debent, nocte et die infra castrum arma ferre licebit. Viris etiam Brugensibus gladium portare et reportare licebit, dummodo castro exeant festinanter. Si quis autem eorum moras faciendo, vel per castrum vagando, gladium portaverit, LX solid. et gladium amittet.

" 18. Si scabini gratiâ emendationis villæ assensu iustitiæ comitis bannum in pane et vino et cæteris mercibus constituerint, medietas eorum quæ ex banno provenient, comitis erit, et altera medietas castellani et oppidi.

" 19. Si mercator sive alius homo extraneus ante scabinos iustitiæ causâ venerit, si illi, de quibus conqueritur presentes sint vel inveniri possint infra tertium diem vel saltem infra octavum, plenariam ei scabini iustitiam faciant iuxta legem castri.

" 20. Nemini in foro comitis stallos locare licebit, quod si locaverit et veritate scabinorum super hoc convictus fuerit, LX solidos comiti dabit.

" 21. Si aliquis de infracturis castri coram scabinis falsum testimonium portaverit si scabini illud cognoverint LX libras amittet.

" 22. Quando aliquis scabinus decedet, alius ei substituetur electione Comitis non aliter.

" 23. Si scabinus testimonio scabinorum parium suorum de falsitate convictus fuerit, ipse et omnia sua in potestate Comitis erunt.

" 24. Si Scabini a Comite vel a ministro Comitis submoniti, falsum super aliqua re iudicium fecerint, veritate scabinorum Atrebatensium, sive aliorum qui eandem legem tenent, comes eos convincere poterit ; et si convicti fuerint, ipsi et omnia sua in potestate comitis erunt. Quoties verò super huiusmodi falsitate submoniti fuerint, nullatenus contradicere poterunt, quin diem sibi a Comite praefixum teneant, ubicumque Comes voluerit in Flandriâ.

" 25. De omnibus verò aliis causis ad Comitem pertinentibus, Brugis in castello vel ante castellum placita tenebunt in praesentia Comitis vel illius quem loco suo ad iustitiam tenendam instituerit. Instituto autem ad eius submonitionem de omnibus tanquam Comiti respondebunt, quamdiù in hoc servitio comitis erit.

Ad hoc nec scabini nec Brugenses aliquid addere, mutare, vel corrigere poterunt, nisi per consilium Comitis vel illius quem loco suo ad iustitiam tenendam instituerit.

V. *Ordonnance du comte Philippe d'Alsace, sur les attributs des Baillis en Flandre.* Vers 1178.

" Hæc sunt puncta, quæ per universam terram suam Comes observari præcepit.

" § 1. Primo qui hominem occiderit, caput pro capite dabit.

" § 2. Item baillivus Comitis poterit arrestare hominem qui forefecit sine Scabinis donec ante Scabinos veniat, et per consilium eorum plegium accipiat de forisfacto.

" § 3. Item si baillivus volens hominem arrestare, non potuerit et auxilium vocaverit, qui primus fuerit, et baillivum non adiuverit in forisfacto erit, sicut Scabini considerabunt ; nisi forte ostendere quis potuerit per Scabinos quod ille qui arrestandus erat, inimicus eius sit de mortali faidâ ; et tunc sine forisfacto erit licet baillivum non adiuverit ad capiendum suum inimicum.

" § 4. Item baillivus Comitis erit cum Scabinis, qui eligent probos viros villæ ad faciendas tallias et Assisas, sed cum talliabunt Scabini vel Iudicia facient, vel inquisitiones veritatis, vel protractiones, non intererit baillivus : aliis autem consiliis quæ ad utilitatem villæ pertinebunt, baillivus intererit cum Scabinis, scriptum autem talliæ et assisæ reddent Scabini baillivo, si postulaverit.

" § 5. Item baillivus accipiet forisfactum adiudicatum Comiti per Scabinos, ubicumque illud invenerit extra ecclesiam et ubicumque accipi debet per Scab nos.

" § 6. Item qui bannitum de pecuniâ receptaverit eâdem lege de pecuniâ tenebitur quâ bannitus; et si fuerit capite bannitus qui receptatus est, tunc receptans tenebitur de forisfacto LX lib. Quod si vir domi non fuerit, et ejus uxor bannitum receptaverit, rediensque vir, tertiâ manu proborum virorum iurare potuerit: quod bannitum in domam suam receptum esse nescierit; sine forisfacto remanebit: si autem absentiâ mariti, uxori prohibitum fuerit per Scabinos, ne bannitum receptet, de cætero non poterit eum sine forisfacto receptare.

" § 7. Item de quindenâ in quindenam, habet comes, vel bâillivus ex eius parte, veritatem si voluerit.

" § 8. Item domus diruenda Judicio Scabinorum, post quindenam a scabinis indultam, quandocunque Comes præceperit, aut baillivus eius, diruetur a Communia villæ, campana pulsata per Scabinos: et qui ad diruendam domum illam non venerit, in forisfacto erit, sicut Scabini considerabunt, nisi talem excusationem habuerit, quæ Scabinis sufficiens videatur.

" § 9. Item pater non poterit forisfacere domum vel rem filiorum, quæ eis ex parte matris contingit; nec filii poterunt forisfacere rem vel domum patris, quæ ex parte patris venit.

" § 10. Item si homo per Scabinos domum suam sine scampo invadiaverit, eam forisfacere non poterit, nisi salvo catallo eius, qui domum illam vadet in vadio.

" § 11. Item fugitivus de aliquâ villâ pro debito, si in aliâ villâ inventus fuerit, arrestabitur, et ad villam, de quâ fugerat, reducetur, et iudicium Scabinorum illius villæ subire cogetur.

" § 12. Item si quis vulneratus fuerit, et videatur Scabinis' quod non sit vulneratus ad mortem, et postea de illo vulnere mortuus fuerit, Scabini non erunt in forisfacto contra Comitem, qui minorem plegiaturam acceperunt de eo qui eum vulneravit, quam si mortaliter fuisset vulneratus."

The following charters of the French communes are taken from M. Thierry's Lettres sur l'Histoire de France.

I. *Charte de Beauvais.*—"Tous les hommes domiciliés dans l'enceinte du mur de ville et dans les faubourgs, de quelque seigneur que relève le terrain où ils habitent, prêteront serment à la commune. Dans toute l'étendue de la ville, chacun prêtera secours aux autres, loyalement et selon son pouvoir.

" Treize pairs seront élus par la commune, entre lesquels, d'après le vote des autres pairs et de tous ceux qui auront juré la commune, un ou deux seront créés majeurs.

" Le majeur et les pairs jureront de ne favoriser personne de la commune pour cause d'amitié, de ne léser personne pour cause d'inimitié, et de donner en toute chose, selon leur pouvoir, une décision équitable. Tous les autres jureront d'obéir et de prêter main forte aux décisions du majeur et des pairs [1].

" Quiconque aura forfait envers un homme qui aura juré cette commune, le majeur et les pairs, si plainte leur en est faite, feront justice du corps et des biens du coupable.

" Si le coupable se réfugie dans quelque château fort, le majeur et les pairs de la commune parleront sur cela au seigneur du château ou à celui qui sera en son lieu ; et si, à leur avis, satisfaction leur est faite de l'ennemi de la commune, ce sera assez ; mais si le seigneur refuse satisfaction, ils se feront justice à eux-mêmes sur ses hommes.

" Si quelque marchand étranger vient à Beauvais pour le marché, et que quelqu'un lui fasse tort ou injure dans les limites de la banlieue ; si plainte en est faite au majeur et aux pairs, et que le marchand puisse trouver son malfaiteur dans la ville, la majeur et les pairs en feront justice, à moins que le marchand ne soit un des ennemis de la commune.

" Nul homme de la commune ne devra prêter ni créancer son argent aux ennemis de la commune tant qu'il y aura guerre avec eux, car s'il le fait il sera parjure ; et si quelqu'un est convaincu de leur avoir prêté ou créancé quoique ce soit, justice sera faite de lui, selon que le majeur et les pairs en décideront.

[1] Ann. de Noyon, t. ii. p. 805.
Turbulenta conjuratio facta communionis (epistolæ Ivonis Carnotensis episcopi, apud script. rer. franc., t. xv. p. 105).
Cum primùm communia acquisita fuit, omnes Viromandiæ pares, et omnes clerici, salvo ordine suo, omnesque milites, salvâ fidelitate comitis, firmiter tenendam juraverunt. (Recueil des ordonnances des rois de France, t. xi, p. 270.)

" S'il arrive que le corps des bourgeois marche hors de la ville contre ses ennemis, nul le parlamentera avec eux si ce n'est avec licence du majeur et des pairs.

" Si quelqu'un de la commune a confié son argent à quelqu'un de la ville, et que celui auquel l'argent aura été confié se réfugie dans quelque château fort, le seigneur du château, en ayant reçu plainte, ou rendra l'argent ou chassera le débiteur de son château ; et s'il ne fait ni l'une ni l'autre de ces choses, justice sera faite sur les hommes de ce château.

" Si quelqu'un enlève de l'argent à un homme de la commune et se réfugie dans quelque château fort, justice sera faite sur lui si on peut le recontrer, ou sur les hommes et les biens du seigneur du château, à moins que l'argent ne soit rendu.

" S'il arrive que quelqu'un de la commune ait acheté quelque héritage et l'ait tenu pendant l'an et jour, et si quelqu'un vient ensuite réclamer et demander le rachat, il ne lui sera point fait de réponse, mais l'acheteur demeurera en paix.

" Pour aucune cause la présente charte ne sera portée hors de la ville."

II. *Charter of the Commune of Laon.*—" Nul ne pourra se saisir d'aucun homme, soit libre, soit serf, sans le ministère de la justice.

" Si quelqu'un a, de quelque manière que ce soit, fait tort à un autre, soit clerc, soit chevalier, soit marchand indigène ou étranger, et que celui qui a fait le tort soit de la ville, il sera sommé de se présenter en justice par-devant le majeur et les jurés, pour se justifier ou faire amende ; mais s'il se refuse à faire réparation, il sera exclu de la ville avec tous ceux de sa famille. Si les propriétés du délinquant en terres ou en vignes sont situées hors du territoire de la ville, le majeur et les jurés réclameront justice contre lui, de la part du seigneur dans le ressort duquel ses biens seront situés ; mais si l'on n'obtient pas justice de ce seigneur, les jurés pourront faire dévaster les propriétés du coupable. Si le coupable n'est pas de la ville, l'affaire sera portée devant la cour de l'évêque, et si, dans le délai de cinq jours, la forfaiture n'est pas reparée, le majeur et les jurés en tireront selon leur pouvoir.

" En matière capitale, la plainte doit d'abord être portée devant le seigneur justicier dans le ressort duquel aura été pris le coupable, ou devant son bailli s'il est absent ; et si le plaignant ne peut obtenir justice ni de l'un ni de l'autre, il s'adressera aux jurés.

" Les censitaires ne paieront à leur seigneur d'autre cens que celui qu'ils le doivent par tête. S'ils ne le paient pas au temps marqué, ils seront punis selon la loi qui les régit, mais n'accorderont rien en sus à leur seigneur que de leur propre volonté.

" Les hommes de la commune pourront prendre pour femmes les filles des vassaux ou des serfs de quelque seigneur que ce soit, à l'exception des seigneuries et des églises qui font partie de cet commune. Dans les familles de ces dernières ils ne pourront prendre des épouses sans le consentement du seigneur.

" Aucun étranger censitaire des églises ou des chevaliers de la ville ne sera compris dans la commune que du consentement de son seigneur.

" Quiconque sera reçu dans cet commune, bâtira une maison dans le délai d'un an, ou achetera des vignes, ou apportera dans la ville assez d'effets mobiliers pour que justice puisse être faite, s'il y a quelque plainte contre lui. Les main-mortes sont entièrement abolies. Les tailles seront réparties de manière que tout homme devant taille paie seulement quatre deniers à chaque terme et rien de plus, à moins qu'il n'ait une terre devant taille, à laquelle il tienne assez pour consentir à payer la taille."

III. *Charter of the Commune of Amiens.*—" Chacun gardera fidélité à son juré et lui prêtera secours et conseil en tout ce qui est juste.

" Si quelqu'un viole sciemment les constitutions de la commune et qu'il en soit convaincu, la commune, si elle le peut, démolira sa maison et ne lui permettra point d'habiter dans ses limites jusqu'à ce qu'il ait donné satisfaction.

" Quiconque aura sciemment reçu dans sa maison un ennemi de la commune et aura communiqué avec lui, soit en vendant et achetant, soit en buvant et mangeant, soit en lui prêtant un secours quelconque, ou lui aura donné aide et conseil contre le commune, sera coupable de lèse-commune, et, à moins qu'il ne donne promptement satisfaction en justice, la commune, si elle le peut, démolira sa maison.

" Quiconque aura tenu devant témcin des propos injurieux pour la commune, si la commune en est informée, et que l'inculpé refuse de répondre en justice, la commune, si elle le peut, démolira sa maison et ne lui permettra pas d'habiter dans ses limites jusqu'à ce qu'il ait donné satisfaction.

" Si quelqu'un attaque de paroles injurieuses le majeur dans l'exercice de sa juridiction, sa maison sera démolie, ou il paiera rançon pour sa maison en la miséricorde des juges.

" Que nul n'ait la hardiesse de vexer au passage, dans la banlieue de la cité, les personnes domiciliées dans la commune, ou les marchands qui viennent à la ville pour y vendre leurs denrées. Si quelqu'un ose le faire, il sera réputé violateur de la commune et justice sera faite sur sa personne ou sur ses biens.

" Si un membre de la commune enlève quelque chose à l'un de ses jurés, il sera sommé par le maire et les échevins de comparaître en présence de la commune, et fera réparation suivant l'arrêt des échevins.

" Si le vol a été commis par quelqu'un qui ne soit pas de la commune, et que cet homme ait refusé de comparaître en justice dans les limites de la banlieue, la commune, après l'avoir notifié aux gens du château où le coupable a son domicile, le saisira, si elle le peut, lui ou quelque chose qui lui appartienne, et le retiendra jusqu'à ce qu'il ait fait réparation.

" Quiconque aura blessé avec armes un de ses jurés, à moins qu'il ne se justifie par témoins et par le serment, perdra le poing ou paiera neuf livres, six pour les fortifications de la ville et de la commune, et trois pour la rançon de son poing ; mais s'il est incapable de payer, il abandonnera son poing à la miséricorde de la commune.

" Si un homme, qui n'est pas de la commune, frappe ou blesse quelqu'un de la commune, et refuse de comparaître en jugement, la commune, si elle le peut, démolira sa maison ; et si elle parvient à le saisir, justice sera faite de lui par-devant le majeur et les échevins.

" Quiconque aura donné à l'un de ses jurés les noms de serf, récréant, traître ou fripon, paiera vingt sous d'amende.

" Si quelque membre de la commune a sciemment acheté ou vendu quelque article provenant de pillage, il le perdra et sera tenu de le restituer aux dépouillés, à moins qu'eux-mêmes ou leurs seigneurs n'aient forfait en quelque chose contre la commune.

" Dans les limites de la commune, on n'admettra aucun champion gagé au combat contre l'un de ses membres.

" En toute espèce de cause, l'accusateur, l'accusé et les témoins s'expliquéront, s'ils le veulent, par avocat.

" Tous ces articles, ainsi que les ordonnances du majeur et de la commune, n'ont force de loi que de juré à juré : il n'y a pas égalité en justice entre le juré et le non-juré."

IV. *Charter of the Commune of Soissons.*—" Tous les hommes habitant dans l'enciente des murs de la ville de Soissons et en dehors dans le faubourg, sur quelque seigneurie qu'ils demeurent, jureront la commune : si quelqu'un s'y refuse, ceux qui l'auront jurée feront justice de sa maison et de son argent.

" Dans les limites de la commune, tous les hommes s'aideront mutuellement, selon leur pouvoir, et ne souffriront en nulle manière que qui que ce soit enlève quelque chose ou fasse payer des tailles à l'un d'entre eux.

" Quand la cloche sonnera pour assembler la commune, si quelqu'un ne se rend pas à l'assemblée, il payera douze deniers d'amende.

" Si quelqu'un de la commune a forfait en quelque chose, et refuse de donner satisfaction devant les jurés, les hommes de la commune en feront justice.

" Les membres de cette commune prendront pour épouses les femmes qu'ils voudront, après en avoir demandé la permission aux seigneurs dont ils relèvent ; mais, si les seigneurs s'y refusaient, et que, sans l'aveu du sien, quelqu'un prît un femme relevant d'une autre seigneurie, l'amende qu'il paierait dans ce cas, sur la plainte de son seigneur, serait de cinq sols seulement.

" Si un étranger apporte son pain ou son vin dans la ville pour les y mettre en sûreté, et qu'ensuite un différend survienne entre son seigneur et les hommes de cette commune, il aura quinze jours pour vendre son pain et son vin dans la ville et emporter l'argent, à moins qu'il n'ait forfait ou ne soit complice de quelque forfaiture.

" Si l'évêque de Soissons amène par mégarde dans la ville un homme qui ait forfait envers un membre de cette commune, après qu'on lui aura remontré que c'est l'un des ennemis de la commune, il pourra l'emmener cette fois ; mais ne le ramènera en aucune manière, si ce n'est avec l'aveu de ceux qui ont charge de maintenir la commune.

"Toute forfaiture, hormis l'infraction de commune et la vieille haine, sera punie d'une amende de cinq sous."

It would be easy to add other examples of these early covenants between the towns and their seigneurs : but enough seems to have been said, to illustrate the line of argument adopted in the text. There is no single point in all mediæval history of more importance than the manner in which the towns assumed their municipal form ; and none in which the gradual progress of the popular liberties can be more securely traced. But all these compromises imply a long apprenticeship to freedom before the "master's" dignity was attained : and great is the debt of gratitude we owe to those whose sufferings and labour have enabled us to understand and to record their struggles.

APPENDIX B.

TITHE.

THE importance of this subject requires a full statement of details : the following are all the passages in the Anglosaxon law which have reference to this impost.

"I Æðelstán the king, with the counsel of Wulfhelm, archbishop, and of my other bishops, make known to the reeves in each town, and beseech you, in God's name, and by all his saints, and also by my friendship, that ye first of my own goods render the tithes both of live stock and of the year's increase, even as they may most justly be either measured or counted or weighed out ; and let the bishops then do the like from their own property, and my ealdormen and reeves the same. And I will, that the bishop and the reeves command it to all who are bound to obey them, so that it be done at the right term. Let us bear in mind how Jacob the Patriarch spoke : ' Decimas et hostias pacificas offeram tibi ; ' and how Moses spake in God's law : ' Decimas et primitias non tardabis offerre Domino.' It is for us to reflect how awfully it is declared in the books : if we will not render the tithes to God, that he will take from us the nine parts when we least expect ; and, moreover, we have the sin in addition thereto." Æðelst. i. Thorpe, i. 195.

There is a varying copy of this circular, or whatever it is, coinciding as to the matter, but differing widely in the words. Thorpe, i. 195. The nature of the sanction is obvious : it is the old, unjustifiable application of the Jewish practice, which fraud or ignorance had made generally current in Europe. The tithe mentioned by Æðelstán is the prædial tithe, or that of increase of the fruits of the earth, and increase of the young of cattle.

The next passage is in the law of Eádmund, about 940. He says: "Tithe we enjoin to every Christian man on his christendom, and church-shot, and Rome-fee and plough-alms. And if any one will not do it, be he excommunicate." Thorpe, i. 244.

"Let every tithe be paid to the old minster to which the district belongs; and let it be so paid both from a thane's *inland* and from *geneátland*, as the plough traverses it. But if there be any thane who on his bookland has a church, at which there is a burial-place, let him give the third part of his own tithe to his church. If any one have a church at which there is not a burial-place, then of the nine parts let him give his priest what he will...... And let tithe of every young be paid by Pentecost, and of the fruits of the earth by the equinox......and if any one will not pay the tithe, as we have ordained, let the king's reeve go thereto, and the bishop's, and the mass-priest of the minster, and take by force a tenth part for the minster whereunto it is due; and let them assign to him the ninth part; and let the eight parts be divided into two, and let the landlord seize half, the bishop half, be it a king's man or a thane's." Eádg. i. § 1, 2, 3. Thorpe, i. 262. Cnut, i. § 8. 11. Thorpe, i. 366.

"This writing manifests how Eádgár the king was deliberating what might be a remedy for the pestilence which greatly afflicted and decreased his people, far and wide throughout his realm. And first of all it seemed to him and his Witan that such a misfortune had been merited by sin, and by contempt of God's commandments, and most of all by the diminution of that *need-gafol* (necessary tax or rent or recognitory service) which men ought to render to God in their tithes. He looked upon and considered the divine usage in the same light as the human. If a geneát neglect his lord's *gafol*, and do not pay it at the appointed time, it may be expected, if the lord be merciful, that he will grant forgiveness of the neglect, and accept the *gafol* without inflicting a further penalty. But if the lord, by his messengers, frequently remind him of his *gafol*, and he be obdurate and devise to resist payment, it is to be expected that the lord's anger will so greatly increase, that he will grant his debtor neither life nor goods. Thus is it to be expected that our Lord will do, through the audacity with which the people have resisted the frequent admonition of their teachers, respecting the *need-gafol* of our Lord, namely our tithes and church-shots. Now I and the archbishop command that ye anger not God, nor earn either sudden death in this world, nor a future and eternal death in hell, by any diminution of God's rights; but that rich and poor alike, who have any tilth, joyfully and ungrudgingly yield his tithes to God, according to the ordinance of the witan at Andover, which they have now confirmed with their pledges at Wihtbordesstán. And I command my reeves, on pain of losing my friendship and all they own, to punish all that will not make this payment, or by any remissness break the pledge of my witan, as the aforesaid ordinance directs: and of such punishment let there be no remission, if he be so wretched as either to diminish what is God's to his own soul's perdition, or in the insolence of his mood to account them of less importance than what he reckoneth as his own: for that is much more his own which lasteth to all eternity, if he would do it without grudging and with perfect gladness. Now it is my will that these divine rights stand alike all over my realm, and that the servants of God who receive the moneys which we give to God, live a pure life: that so, through their purity, they may intercede for us with God; and that I and my thanes direct our priests to that which the shepherds of our soul's teach us, that is, our bishops, whom we ought never to disobey in any of those things which they declare to us in God's behalf; so that through the obedience with which we obey them for God's sake, we may merit that eternal life for which they fit us by their doctrine and the example of their good works." Eádgár, Suppl. Thorpe, i. 270 *seq.* Such are the views of Eádgár under the influence of Dúnstán, Æðelwold and Oswald.

"And let God's dues be willingly paid every year; that is, plough-alms fifteen days after Easter, the tithe of young by Pentecost, and of the fruits of the earth by Allhallows' Mass, and Rome-fee by St. Peter's mass, and lightshot thrice a year." Æðelr. v. § 11; vi. § 17; ix. § 9. Cnut, i. § 8.

"Et ut detur de omni caruca denarius vel denarium valens, et omnis qui familiam habet, efficiat ut omnis hirmannus suus det unum denarium; quod si non habeat, det dominus eius pro eo. Et omnino Thaynus decimet totum quicquid habet." Æðelr. viii. § 1. Thorpe, i. 336.

"Et praecipimus, ut omnis homo, super dilectionem Dei et omnium sanctorum, det Cyricsceattum et rectam decimam suam, sicut in diebus antecessorum nostrorum stetit, quando melius stetit; hoc est, sicut aratrum peragrabit decimam acram. Et omnis consuetudo reddatur super amicitiam Dei ad matrem nostram aecclesiam cui adiacet. Et nemo auferat Deo quod ad Deum pertinet, et praedecessores nostri concesserunt." Æðelr. viii. § 4. Thorpe, i. 338.

"And with respect to tithe, the king and his witan have chosen and decreed, as right it is, that one third part of the tithe which belongs to the church, go to the reparation of the church, and a second part to God's servants there; the third part to God's poor and needy men in thraldom." Æðelr. ix. § 6. Thorpe, i. 342.

"And be it known to every Christian man that he pay to the Lord his tithe justly, ever as the plough traverses the tenth field, on peril of God's mercy, and of the full penalty, which king Eádgár decreed; that is; If any one will not justly pay the tithe, then let the king's reeve go, and the mass-priest of the minster or the landlord, and the bishop's reeve, and take by force the tenth part for the minster to which it is due, and assign to him the ninth part: and let the remaining eight parts be divided into two; and let the landlord seize half, and the bishop half, be it a king's man or a thane's." Æðelr. ix. § 7, 8. Thorpe, i. 342. Cnut, i. § 8. Thorpe, i. 366. Leg. Hen. I. xi. § 2. Thorpe, i. 520.

"De omni annona decima garba sanctae aecclesiae reddenda est. Si quis gregem equarum habuerit, pullum decimum reddat; qui unam solam vel duas, de singulis pullis singulos denarios. Qui vaccas plures habuerit, vitulum decimum; qui unam vel duas, de singulis obolos singulos. Et si de eis caseum fecerit, caseum decimum, vel lac decima die. Agnum decimum, vellus decimum, caseum decimum, butirum decimum, porcellum decimum. De apibus, secundum quod sibi per annum inde profecerit. Quin-etiam de boscis et pratis, aquis, molendinis, parcis, vivariis, piscariis, virgultis, ortis, negotiationibus, et de omnibus similiter rebus quas dederit Dominus, decima reddenda est ; et qui eam detinuerit, per iusticiam sanctae aecclesiae et regis, si necesse fuerit, ad redditionem cogatur. Haec praedicavit sanctus Augustinus, et haec concessa sunt a rege, et confirmata a baronibus et populis : sed postea, instigante diabolo, ea plures detinuerunt, et sacerdotes qui divites erant non multum curiosi erant ad perquirendas eas, quia in multis locis sunt modo iiii vel iii aecclesiae, ubi tunc temporis non erat nisi una ; et sic inceperunt minui." Eádw. Conf. § vii. viii.

Such are all the passages in the Anglosaxon Laws, directing the levy and distribution of the tithe.

APPENDIX C.

TOWNS.

THE strict meaning of *burh*, appears to be *fortified place* or *stronghold*. It can therefore be applied to a single house or castle, as well as to a town. There is a softer form *byrig*, which in the sense of a town can hardly be distinguished from *burh*, but which, as far as I know, is never used to denote a single house or castle. Rome and Florence, and in general all large towns, are called Burh or Byrig. This is the widest term.

Port strictly means an enclosed place, for sale and purchase, a market: for " Portus est conclusus locus, quo importantur merces, et inde exportantur. Est et statio conclusa et munita." (Thorpe, i. p. 158.)

Wic is originally *vicus*, a vill or village. It is strictly used to denote the country-houses of communities, kings or bishops.

Ceaster seems universally derived from *castrum*, and denotes a place where there has been a Roman station. Now every one of these conditions may concur in one single place, and we accordingly find much looseness in the use of the terms: thus,

London is called Lundenwíc[1], Hhoðh. § 16. Chron. 604: but Lundenburh or Lundenbyrig, Chron. 457, 872, 886, 896, 910, 994, 1009, 1013, 1016, 1052. And it was also a port, for we find its geréfa, a port-geréfa. Again York, sometimes Eoferwíc, sometimes Eoferwíc-ceaster (Chron. 971) is also said to be a burh, Chron. 1066. Dovor is called a burh, Chron. 1048; but a port, Chron. 1052. So again Hereford, in Chron. 1055, 1056, is called a port, but in Chron. 1055 also a burh. Nor do the Latin chroni-

---

" Forum rerum venalium Lundenwíc." Vit. Bonif. Pertz, Mon. ii. 338.

clers help us out of the difficulty; on the contrary, they continually use the words *oppidum, civitas, urbs* and even *arx* to denote the same place.

The Saxon Chronicle mentions the undernamed cities :—

Ægeles byrig, now Aylesbury in Bucks. Chron. Sax. 571, 921.

Acemannes ceaster or Baðan byrig, often called also Æt baðum or Æt hátum baðum, the Aquae Solis of the Romans and now Bath in Somerset. This town in the year 577 was taken from the British. The Chronicle calls it Baðanceaster: see also Chron. 973.

Ambresbyrig, now Amesbury, Wilts. Chron. 995.

Andredesceaster. Anderida, sacked by Ælli. Chron. 495. Most probably near the site of the present Pevensey: see a very satisfactory paper by Mr. Hussey, Archæol. Journal, No. 15, Sept. 1847.

Baddanbyrig, now Badbury, Dorset. Chron. 901.

Badecanwyl, now Bakewell, Derby, fortified by Eádweard. Chron. 923. Florence says he built and garrisoned a town there: " urbem construxit, et in illa milites robustos posuit." an. 921.

Banesingtún, now Bensington, Oxf. Chron. 571, 777.

Bebbanburh, now Bamborough in Northumberland. This place, we are told, was first surrounded with a hedge, and afterwards with a wall. Chron. 642, 926, 993. Florence calls it " urbs regia Bebbanbirig." an. 926.

Bedanford, now Bedford. There was a burh here which Eádweard took in 919: he then built a second burh upon the other side of the Ouse. Chron. 919. Florence calls it " urbem." an. 916.

Beranbyrig. Chron. 556.

Bremesbyrig. At this place Æðelflǽd built a burh. Chron. 910. Florence says " urbem." an. 911: perhaps Bromsgrove in Worcestershire, the Æt Bremesgráfum of the Cod. Dipl. Nos. 183, 186.

Brunanburh, Brunanbyrig, and sometimes Brunanfeld: the site of this place is unknown, but here Æðelstán and Eádmund defeated the Scots. Chron. 937.

Brycgnorð, Bridgenorth, Salop. Here Æðelflǽd built a burh. Chron. 912: " arcem munitam." Flor. an. 913.

Bucingahám, now Buckingham. Here Eádweard built two burhs, one on each side of the Ouse. Chron. 918. Florence calls them "munitiones." an. 915.

Cantwarabyrig, the city of Canterbury. Dorobernia, ciuitas Doruuernensis, the metropolis of Æðelberht's kingdom in 597. Beda, H. E. lib. i. c. 25. In the year 1011 Canterbury was sufficiently fortified to hold out for twenty days against the Danish army which had overrun all the eastern and midland counties, and was then only entered by treachery. Flor. Wig. an. 1011. I have already noticed both king's reeves and port-reeves, the ingang burhware and cnihta gyld of Canterbury. There can be little doubt that king, archbishop, abbot and corporation had all separate jurisdictions and rights in Canterbury : see Chron. 633, 655, 995, 1009, 1011.

Cirenceaster, now Cirencester in Gloucestershire, the ancient Durocornovum. Chron. 577, 628.

Cissanceaster, now Chichester, the Roman Regnum. Chron. 895.

Cledemúða. Here Eádweard built a burh. Chron. 921.

Colnceaster, now Colchester in Essex, the first Roman Colonia, destroyed by Boadicea. In 921 Colchester was sacked by Eádweard's forces, and taken from the Danes, some of whom escaped over the *wall*. In the same year Eádweard repaired and fortified it. Chron. 921. "murum illius redintegravit, virosque in ea bellicosos cum stipendio posuit." Flor. 918.

Coludesburh, Coldingham. Chron. 679.

Cyppanham, Chippenham, Wilts. Chron. 878.

Cyricbyrig, a city built by Æðelflæd. Flor. 916. Cherbury.

Deóraby, Derby, one of the Five Burgs taken by Æðelflæd from the Danes. Chron. 917, 941. A city with gates. Flor. 918. "civitas." Flor. 942.

Dofera, Dover in Kent. Chron. 1048, 1052. There was a fortified castle on the cliff, which in 1051 was seized by the people of Eustace, count of Boulogne, against the town. Flor. Wig. 1051.

Dorceceaster, Dorchester, Oxon. Chron. 954, 971. For some time a bishop's see, first for Wessex, which was afterwards removed to Winchester: afterwards for Leicester.

Dorceceaster, Dornwaraceaster, Dorchester, Dorset. Chron. 635, 636, 639.

Eádesbyrig, a place where Æðelflǽd built a burh. Chron. 914. Florence says a town. an. 915. Eddisbury, Cheshire?

Eligbyrig, Ely in Cambridgeshire. Chron. 1036.

Egonesham, now Eynesham, Oxon. Chron. 571.

Eoforwíc, Eoforwíc ceaster, now York; Kair Ebrauc, Eboracum; the seat of an archbishop, a bishop, and again an archbishop. It seems to have been always a considerable and important town. In the tenth century it was one of the seven confederated burgs, which Æðelflǽd reduced. The strength however which we should be inclined to look for in a city, which once boasted the name of *altera Roma*, is hardly consistent with Asser's account of it. Describing the place in the year 867, he says: "Praedictus Paganorum exercitus .... ad Eboracum ciuitatem migravit, quae in aquilonari ripa Humbrensis fluminis[1] sita est." After stating that Ælla and Osberht, the pretenders to the Northumbrian crown, became reconciled in presence of the common danger, he continues: "Osbyrht et Ælla, adunatis viribus, congregatoque exercitu Eboracum oppidum adeunt, quibus advenientibus Pagani confestim fugam arripiunt, et intra urbis moenia se defendere procurant: quorum fugam et pavorem Christiani cernentes, etiam intra urbis moenia persequi, et murum frangere instituunt: quod et fecerunt, non enim tunc adhuc illa civitas firmos et stabilitos muros illis temporibus habebat. Cumque Christiani murum, ut proposuerant, fregissent, etc.[2]" We may infer from Asser himself that the Saxon mode of fortification was not strong: speaking of a place in Devonshire, called Cynuit (which he describes as *arx*), he says: "Cum Pagani arcem imparatam atque omnino immunitam, nisi quod moenia nostro more erecta solummodo haberet,

---

[1] He clearly considers the northern branch of the Humber, which we now call the Ouse, to be the continuation of the river.

[2] Vit. Ælfr. an. 867.

cernerent, non enim effringere moliebantur, quia et ille locus situ terrarum tutissimus est ab omni parte, nisi ab orientali, sicut nos ipsi vidimus, obsidere eam coeperunt[1]." York however continued to be an important town. It was retaken by Æðelflǽd who subdued the Danes there; and again by Eádred in 950. At this time it appears to have been principally ruled by its archbishop Wulfstán. For York, see Chron. 971, 1066, etc.

Exanceaster, now Exeter, the Isca Damnoniorum or Uxella, of the Romans. Chron. 876, 894, 1003. As the Saxon arms advanced westward, Exeter became for a time the frontier town and market between the British and the men of Wessex: in the beginning of the tenth century there appears to have been a mixed population. But at that period[2] Æðelstán expelled the British inhabitants, and fortified the town: he drove the Cornwealhas over the Tamar, and made that their boundary, as he had the Wye for the Bretwealas. William of Malmesbury tells us: "Illos (i. e. Cornewalenses) impigre adorsus, ab Excestra, quam ad id temporis aequo cum Anglis iure inhabitarunt, cedere compulit: terminum provinciae suae citra Tambram fluvium constituens, sicut aquilonalibus Britannis amnem Waiam limitem posuerat. Urbem igitur illam, quam contaminatae gentis repurgio defaecaverat, turribus munivit, muro ex quadratis lapidibus cinxit[3]. Et licet solum illud, ieiunum et squalidum, vix steriles avenas, et plerumque folliculum inanem sine grano producat, tamen pro civitatis magnificentia, et incolarum opulentia, tum etiam convenarum frequentia, omne ibi adeo abundat mercimonium, ut nihil frustra desideres quod humano usui conducibile existimes[4]." Thus situated, about ten miles from the sea, Exanceaster could not fail to become an important commercial station; the Exa being navigable for ships of considerable burthen, till in 1284, Hugh Courtenay interrupted the traffic by building a

[1] Vit. Ælfr. an. 878. [2] Probably in 926.

[3] The author of the Gesta Stephani, a contemporary of Malmesbury, declares that the city was "vetustissimo Cæsarum opere murata:" and that its castle was "muro inexpugnabili obseptum, turribus Cæsarianis incisili calce confectis firmatum," p. 21.

[4] Will. Malm. Gest. Reg. lib. ii. § 134 (Hardy's Ed. vol. i. p. 214); see also Gest. Pontif. lib. ii. § 95 (Hamilton's Ed. p. 201).

weir and quay at Topsham. It is probable that Æðelstán placed his own geréfa in the city. But in the year 1003, queen Emme Ælfgyfu seems to have been its lady; for it is recorded that through the treachery of a Frenchman Hugo, whom she had made her reeve there, the Danes under Svein sacked and destroyed the city, taking great plunder [1]. It was afterwards restored by Cnut; but appears to have been still attached to the queens of England, for after the conquest we find it holding out against William, under Gýð, the mother of Harald.

Exanmúða, now Exmouth. Chron. 1001.

Genisburuh, now Gainsborough. Chron. 1013, 1014.

Glæstingaburh or Glæstingabyrig, now Glastonbury, Som. Urbs Glastoniae, Chron. 688, 943.

Gleawanceaster, now Gloucester; Kair glou, and the Roman Glevum. Urbs Gloverniae, Glocestriae. A fortified city of Mercia. Chron. 577, 918.

Hæstingas, now Hastings in Kent. A fortification, and probably at one time the town of a tribe so called. Chron. 1066. It was reduced by Offa, and probably ruined in the Danish wars of Ælfred and Æðelred.

Hagustaldes hám or Hagstealdeshám, now Hexham in Northumbria: the ancient seat of a bishopric. Chron. 685.

Hamtún, now Southampton. Chron. 837.

Hamtún, now Northampton, *quod vide.*

Heanbyrig, now Hanbury in Worcest. Chron. 675.

Heortford, now Hertford. Chron. 913. *urbs.* Flor. 913.

Hereford, now Hereford. Chron. 918, 1055, 1066.

Hrofesceaster, Durocobrevis, Hrofesbreta, now Rochester; a bishop's see for West Kent, probably once the capital of the West Kentish kingdom: a strong fortress. Chron. 604, 616, 633, 644. Asser. 884.

Huntena tún, now Huntingdon. Originally, as its name implies, a town or enclosed dwelling of hunters; but in process of time a city. Chron. 921. *civitas.* Flor. 918.

Judanbyrig, perhaps Jedburgh. Chron. 952.

[1] Chron. Sax. 1003.

Legaceaster, Kairlegeon, now Chester, a Roman city. Chron. 607; deserted, Chron. 894; restored, Chron. 907. Flor. 908.

Legraceaster, now Leicester. Chron. 918, 941, 943. *civitas*. Flor. 942.

Lindicoln, the ancient Lindum, now Lincoln, the capital city of the Lindissi; a bishop's see: then one of the five or seven burhs. Chron. 941. *civitas*. Flor. 942.

Lundenbyrig, Lundenwíc, Londinium, now London. The principal city of the Cantii; then of the Trinobantes; Kair Lunden, Troynovant. Locally in Essex, but usually subject to Mercian sovereignty. Towards the time of the conquest more frequently the residence of the Saxon kings, and scene of their witena gemóts. A strongly fortified city with a fortified bridge over the Thames connecting it with Southwark, apparently its Tête de pont. Chron. 457, 604, 872, 886, 896, 910, 994, 1009, 1013, 1016, 1052.

Lygeanbyrig, now Leighton buzzard. Chron. 571.

Maidulfi urbs, Meldumesbyrig, now Malmesbury in Wilts. Flor. 940.

Mameceaster, now Manchester: " urbem restaurarent, et in ea fortes milites collocarent." Flor. 920.

Mealdun, now Maldon in Essex. Chron. 920, 921. *urbs*; rebuilt and garrisoned by Eádweard. Flor. 917.

Medeshámstede: afterwards Burh, and from its wealth Gyldenburh: now Peterborough. Chron. 913.

Merantún, now Merton in Oxfordshire. Chron. 755.

Middeltún, Middleton in Essex, a fortress built by Hæsten the Dane. Chron. 893.

Norðhamtún, more frequently Hámtún only, now Northampton: a town or "Port," burnt by the Danes under Svein. Chron. 1010.

Norðwíc, now Norwich, a burh, burned by Svein. Chron. 1004.

Oxnaford, Oxford: a burh in Mercia, taken into his own hands by Eádweard on the death of Æðelflǽd. The burh was burnt by Svein. Chron. 1009.

Possentesbyrig. Chron. 661. ? Pontesbury, co. Salop.

Rædingas, now Reading: a royal vill, but, as many or all probably were, fortified. Asser. 871.

Runcofa, now Runcorn, *urbs*, Flor. Wig. 916.

Sandwíc, now Sandwich, a royal vill, and harbour, whose tolls belonged to Canterbury. Chron. 851.

Searoburh, now Salisbury, the ancient Kairkaradek. Chron. 552.

Scœrgeat, now Scargate, built by Æðelflæd. Chron. 912; *arx munita*, Flor. Wig. 913.

Sceaftesbyrig, Shaftsbury, the seat of a nunnery founded by Ælfred. Chron. 980, 982.

Sceobyrig, now Shoebury in Essex; a fort was built there in 894 by the Danes. Chron. 894.

Seletún, perhaps Silton in Yorkshire. Chron. 780.

Snotingahám, now Nottingham: the British Tinguobauc, or *urbs speluncarum*. Asser. 868; Chron. 868, 922, 923, 941. There were two towns here, one on each side the river. Flor. Wig. 919, 921; *civitas*, Flor. Wig. 942.

Soccabyrig, probably Sockburn in Durham. Chron. 780.

Stæfford, now Stafford, a vill of the Mercian kings, fortified by Æðelflæd. Chron. 913; *arx*, Flor. Wig. 914.

Stamford in Lincolnshire. Chron. 922, 941; *arx* and *civitas*, Flor. Wig. 919, 942.

Sumertún, now Somerton in Oxfordshire, taken by Æðelbald of Mercia from Wessex. Chron. 733.

Súðbyrig, now Sudbury in Suffolk. Chron. 797.

Swanawíc, probably Swanwick, Hants. Chron. 877.

Temesford, Tempsford in Bedfordshire, a Danish fortress and town. Chron. 921.

Tofeceaster, Towchester in Northampton. Chron. 921; *civitas*, Flor. Wig. 918; walled with stone, Flor. ibid.

Tomaworðig, now Tamworth in Staffordshire; a favourite residence of the Mercian kings. Chron. 913, 922; fortified by Æðelflæd; *urbs*, Flor. Wig. 914.

Wæringawíc, now Warwick. Chron. 914; *urbs*, Flor. Wig. 915.

Weardbyrig, now Warborough, Oxford; *urbs*, Flor. Wig. 916.

Wigingamere, probably in Hertfordshire. Chron. 951; *urbs*, Flor. Wig. 918; *civitas*, ibid.

Wigornaceaster, Worcester, a fortified city.   Chron. 922, 1041.

Wihtgarabyrig, now Carisbrook.   Chron. 530, 544.

Wiltún, Wilton in Wiltshire.   Chron. 1008.

Wintanceaster, Winchester, the capital of Wessex, a fortified city.   Chron. 643, 648.

Withám, now Witham in Essex; a city and fortress.   Chron. 913; Flor. Wig. 914.

Ðelweal, Thelwall in Cheshire, a fortress and garrison town. Chron. 923; Flor. Wig. 920.

Ðetford, now Thetford in Norfolk; a fortress and city.   Chron. 952, 1004.

It is not to be imagined that this list nearly exhausts the number of fortresses, towns and cities extant in the Saxon times.   It is only given as a specimen, and as an illustration of the averments in the text.   The reader who wishes to pursue the subject, will find the most abundant materials in the Index Locorum appended to Vol. VI. of the " Codex Diplomaticus Aevi Saxonici; " and to this I must refer him for any ampler information.

APPENDIX D.

CYRICSCEAT.

I do not think it necessary to repeat here the arguments which I have used elsewhere[1], to show that Cyricsceat has nothing whatever to do with our modern church-rates, or that these arose from papal usurpation very long after the Norman Conquest. I can indeed only express my surprise that any churchman should still be found willing to continue a system which exposes the dignity and peace of the church to be disturbed by any schismatic who may see in agitation a cheap step to popularity. But as the question has been put in that light, it may be convenient for the sake of reference to collect the principal passages in the laws and charters which refer to the impost. They are the following:—

" Be cyricsceattum. Cyricsceattas sẏn ágifene be Seint Martines mæssan. Gif hwá ðæt ne gelǽste, sẏ he scyldig LX scill. and be twelffealdum ágyfe ðone cyricsceat." Ine, § 4; Thorpe, i. 104.

" Be cyricsceattum. Cyricsceat mon sceal ágifan tó ðæm healme and to ðæm heorðe ðe se man on bið tó middum wintra." Ine, § 61; Thorpe, i. 140.

" And ic wille eác ðæt míne geréfan gedón ðæt man ágyfe ða cyricsceattas and ða sáwlsceattas tó ðám stowum, ðe hit mid rihte tó gebyrige." Æthelst. i.; Thorpe, i. 196.

" Be teoðungum and cyricsceattum. Teoðunge we bebeódað ǽlcum cristenum men be his cristendóme, and cyricsceat, and ælmesfeoh. Gif hit hwá dón nylle, sẏ he amansumod." Eádm. i. § 2; Thorpe, i. 244.

" Be cyricsceat. Gif hwá ðonne þegna sẏ, ðe on his bóclande cyrican hæbbe, ðe legerstowe on sẏ, gesylle he ðonne þriddan dǽl his ágenre teoðunge intó his cyrican, Gif hwá cyrican hæbbe,

[1] A Few Historical Remarks upon the supposed Antiquity of Church-rates. Ridgway, 1836.

ðe legerstow on ne sꝺ, ðonne dó he of ðǽm nygan dǽlum his preost ðæt ðæt he wille. And gá ylc cyricsceat intó ðæm ealdan mynster be ǽlcum frigan (h)eorðe." Eádgár, i. § 1, 2; Thorpe, i. 262.

" Neádgafol úres drihtnes, ðæt sýn úre te oðunga and cyric-sceattas." Eádgár, Supp. § 1; Thorpe, i. 270.

"And cyricsceat tó Martinus mæssan." Æðelr. vi. § 18; Thorpe, i. 320.

" And cyricsceat gelǽste man be Martinus mæssan, and seðe ðæt ne gelǽste, forgilde hine mid twelffealdan, and ðám cyninge cxx scill." Æðelr. ix. § 11; Thorpe, i. 342.

" Et præcipimus, ut omnis homo super dilectionem dei et omnium sanctorum det cyricsceattum et rectam decimam suam, sicut in diebus antecessorum nostrorum stetit, quando melius stetit; hoc est, sicut aratrum peragrabit decimam acram." Æðelr. viii. § 4; Thorpe, i. 338.

" De ciricsceatto dicit vicecomitatus quod episcopus, de omni terra quæ ad ecclesiam suam pertinet, debet habere, in die festivitatis sancti Martini, unam summam annonæ, qualis melior crescit in ipsa terra, de unaquaque hida libera et villana; et si dies ille fractus fuerit, ille qui retinuerit reddet ipsam summam, et undecies persolvat; et ipse episcopus accipiat inde forisfacturam qualem ipse debet habere de terra sua. De ciricsceatto de Perscora dicit vicecomitatus quod illa ecclesia de Perscora debet habere ipsum ciricsceattum de omnibus ccc hidis, scilicet de unaquaque hida ubi francus homo manet, unam summam annonæ, et si plures habet hidas, sint liberæ; et si dies fractus fuerit, in festivitate sancti Martini, ipse qui retinuerit det ipsam summam et undecies persolvat, abbati de Perscora; et reddat forisfacturam abbati de Westminstre quia sua terra est." Cart. Heming. i. 49, 50. " De ciricsceate. Dicit vicecomitatus quod de unaquaque hida terræ, libera vel villana, quæ ad ecclesiam de Wirecestre pertinet, debet episcopus habere, in die festo sancti Martini unam summam annonæ, de meliori quæ ibidem crescit; quod si dies ille non reddita annona transierit, qui retinuit annonam reddat, undecies persolvet, et insuper forisfacturam episcopus accipiet, qualem et sua terra habere debet." Ibid. 1, 308.

The only instance that I can find of this impost being noticed in the Ecclesiastical Laws, or Recommendations of the Bishops and Clergy, is in the Canons attributed to Eádgár:—

" And we enjoin, that the priests remind the people of what they ought to do to God for dues, in tithes and in other things; first plough-alms, xv days after Easter; and tithe of young, by Pentecost; and of fruits of the earth, by All Saints; and Rómfeoh (Peter-pence) by St. Peter's Mass; and Cyricsceat by Martinmass[1]."

" Nunc igitur praecipio et obtestor omnes meos episcopos et regni præpositos, per fidem quam Deo et mihi debetis, quatenus faciatis, ut antequam ego Angliam veniam, omnia debita, quae Deo secundum legem antiquam debemus, sint soluta, scilicet eleemosynae pro aratris, et decimae animalium ipsius anni procreatorum, et denarii quos Romæ ad sanctum Petrum debemus, sive ex urbibus sive ex villis, et mediante Augusto decimae frugum, et in festivitate sancti Martini *primitiae seminum* ad ecclesiam sub cuius parochia quisque est, quae Anglice ·*Circesceat* nominantur[2]."

Oswald's grants often contain this clause: " Sit autem terra ista libera omni regi nisi aecclesiastici censi." See Codex Dipl. Nos. 494, 498, 515, 540, 552, 558, 649, 680, 681, 682. But sometimes the amount is more closely defined: thus in No. 498, two bushels of wheat. In No. 511 we have this strong expression: " Free from all *worldly service* (weoruldcund þeówet), except three things, one is cyricsceat, and that he (work) with all his might, twice in the year, once at mowing, once at reaping." And in No. 625 he repeats this, making the land granted free, " ab omni *mundialium* servitute tributorum, exceptis sanctae Dei aecclesiae necessitatibus atque utilitatibus." Again, " Et semper possessor terrae illius reddat tributum aecclesiasticum, quod ciricsceat dicitur, tó Pirigtúne; et omni anno unus ager inde aretur tó Pirigtúne, et iterum metatur."—Cod. Dipl. No. 661. " Sit autem hoc praedictum rus liberum ab omni *mundiali* servitio, ... excepta sanctae Dei basilicae suppeditatione ac ministratione."—Ibid. No. 666.

[1] Thorpe, ii. 256.   [2] Epist. Cnut. Flor. Wig. an. 1031.

The customs of Dyddanham[1] impose upon the gebúr the duty of finding the cyricsceat to the lord's barn, but whether because the lord was an ecclesiastic does not clearly appear.

The important provisions of Denewulf's and Ealhfrið's charters have been sufficiently illustrated in the text.

After the conquest, Chirset or Chircettum, as it is called, was very irregularly levied : it appears to have been granted occasionally by the lords to the church, but no longer to have been a general impost : and nothing is more common than to find it considered as a set-off against other forms of rent-paying, on lay as well as ecclesiastical land. If the tenant gave *work*, he usually paid no chircet : if he paid chircet, his amount of labour-rent was diminished : a strong evidence, if any more were wanted, that cyricsceat has nothing whatever to do with church-rate.

[1] Now Tidenham in Gloucestershire, near the point where the Wye falls into the Severn, nearly 2° 36' west longitude from Greenwich.

THE END.

Printed by Taylor and Francis, Red Lion Court, Fleet Street.